THE SOCIAL GROUPS
BEHIND THE PENTATEUCH

ANCIENT ISRAEL AND ITS LITERATURE

Thomas C. Römer, General Editor

Editorial Board:
Susan Ackerman
Thomas B. Dozeman
Alphonso Groenewald
Shuichi Hasegawa
Annette Schellenberg
Naomi A. Steinberg

Number 44

THE SOCIAL GROUPS BEHIND THE PENTATEUCH

Edited by
Jaeyoung Jeon

SBL PRESS

Atlanta

Copyright © 2021 by SBL Press

All rights reserved. No part of this work may be reproduced or transmitted in any form or by any means, electronic or mechanical, including photocopying and recording, or by means of any information storage or retrieval system, except as may be expressly permitted by the 1976 Copyright Act or in writing from the publisher. Requests for permission should be addressed in writing to the Rights and Permissions Office, SBL Press, 825 Houston Mill Road, Atlanta, GA 30329 USA.

Library of Congress Control Number: 2021952655

Contents

Acknowledgments vii
Abbreviations ix

Methodological Considerations

Introduction: The State of Pentateuchal Research
    Jaeyoung Jeon 3

Textual, Historical, Sociological, and Ideological Cornerstones
    of the Formation of the Pentateuch
    Konrad Schmid 29

Contributions from Lay Scribal Circles in Yehud

The Relationship between Moses and Aaron and the Question
    of the Composition of the Pentateuch
    Thomas Römer 55

The Elders Redaction (ER) in the Pentateuch:
    Scribal Contributions of an Elders Group in the
    Formation of the Pentateuch
    Jaeyoung Jeon 73

J's Problem with the East: Observations on the So-Called
    Yahwistic Texts in Genesis 1–25
    Jürg Hutzli 99

Contributions from Priestly Scribal Circles in Yehud

Formulae That Equate the גר and the Israelite: Literary Activity in the
    Priestly Writings
    Itamar Kislev 123

From Sources to Redaction: Identifying the Authors
of Numbers 16
Thomas B. Dozeman and Jaeyoung Jeon 163

In Between Sources, Fragments, and Redactions:
Numbers 16–17 as a Test Case for Reconstructing
the Literary History of the Pentateuch
Katharina Pyschny 203

The Formation of the Wilderness Narratives in the
Book of Numbers
Ndikho Mtshiselwa 237

Perspectives of the Diaspora and Samaritan Communities

Transjordan in the Book of Numbers
Olivier Artus 273

What Is the Contribution of the Samaritans to the Pentateuch?
Innocent Himbaza 289

Shechem and Bethel in the Patriarchal Narratives:
A Samaritan Rereading of Gen 12:1–9* and 35:2–4?
Dany Noquet 313

Ancient Sources Index 335
Modern Authors Index 342
Subject Index 344

Acknowledgments

This volume consists mainly of the papers presented at the conference "Who Wrote the Pentateuch?" held at the university of Lausanne in October 2016, organized by Thomas Römer and Jaeyoung Jeon. The conference was programmed within the framework of the project "Composition and Redaction of the Wilderness Narrative in Their Pentateuchal and Hexateuchal Context," which was enabled by the generous financial support by the Swiss National Science Foundation (SNSF). In addition, the support from L'institut romand des sciences bibliques (IRSB) at the Université de Lausanne was indispensible for the successful organization of the conference. I appreciate the members of IRSB, who were very cooperative during its preparation.

The goal of the conference was to move beyond the diachronic presentations of successive literary layers in the Pentateuch and to investigate the social groups, contexts, and scribal circles that contributed to its formation. The papers presented and revised for this volume, as well as some invited papers, share this direction. To be sure, the grouping and dating of the pentateuchal texts are still much disputed, without a consensus being reached. Diverse theories and hypotheses are suggested by competing formation models of the Pentateuch. There is seen, at the same time, a recent increase in interest in the sociohistorical contexts of the pentateuchal texts. This volume endeavors to respond to these interests.

I would like to express gratitude first and foremost to Professor Römer for inviting me to this project and for his valuable advice and help editing this volume. I also appreciate the authors, who patiently cooperated in the lengthy process of the publication of the volume. For her initial copyediting of the volume, I am grateful to Dr. Angela Roskop. I appreciate also Bob Buller and Nicole Tilford at SBL Press, who accelerated the publication especially at the last stage. There was a lengthy delay in the publication process due to the complicated situation created by the worldwide pandemic. Again, I would like to express my gratitude to the authors, who showed great patience during this period.

The ten essays included in this volume may not provide the final answers to the question of the social groups behind the formation of the Pentateuch. Nevertheless, I hope that the volume will stimulate broader and deeper studies on this significant issue.

Jaeyoung Jeon
Lausanne, December 2021

Abbreviations

AASOR	Annual of the American Schools of Oriental Research
AB	Anchor Bible
ABS	Archaeology and Biblical Studies
AcT	*Acta Theologica*
A.J.	Josephus, *Antiquitates judaicae*
AIL	Ancient Israel and Its Literature
AnBib	Analecta Biblica
ANEM	Ancient Near East Monographs
AOAT	Alter Orient und Altes Testament
4QGen	4QGenesis
AS	Assyriological Studies
ATANT	Abhandlungen zur Theologie des Alten und Neuen Testaments
ATD	Das Alte Testament Deutsch
AYBRL	Anchor Yale Bible Reference Library
BBB	Bonner biblische Beiträge
BDB	Brown, Francis, S. R. Driver, and Charles A. Briggs. *A Hebrew and English Lexicon of the Old Testament.* Oxford: Clarendon, 1907.
BEATAJ	Beiträge zur Erforschung des Alten Testaments und des antiken Judentum
BETL	Bibliotheca Ephemeridum Theologicarum Lovaniensium
BHT	Beiträge zur historischen Theologie
Bib	*Biblica*
BibInt	Biblical Interpretation
B.J.	Josephus, *Bellum judaicum*
BJS	Brown Judaic Studies
BK	*Bibel und Kirche*
BKAT	Biblischer Kommentar, Altes Testament

BN	*Biblische Notizen*
BWANT	Beiträge zur Wissenschaft vom Alten und Neuen Testament
BZ	*Biblische Zeitschrift*
BZABR	Beihefte zur Zeitschrift für altorientalische und biblische Rechtsgeschichte
BZAW	Beihefte zur Zeitschrift für die alttestamentliche Wissenschaft
C.Ap.	Josephus, *Contra Apionem*
CAT	Commentaire de l'Ancien Testament
CBET	Contributions to Biblical Exegesis and Theology
CBQ	*Catholic Biblical Quarterly*
CHANE	Culture and History of the Ancient Near East
ConBNT	Coniectanea Neotestamentica
ConBOT	Coniectanea Biblica: Old Testament Series
DB	Darius, Bisitun
DBAT	Dielheimer Blätter zum Alten Testament und seiner Rezeption in der Alten Kirche
DJD	Discoveries in the Judaean Desert
DMOA	Documenta et Monumenta Orientis Antiqui
DNa	Darius, Naqsh-i Rustam
DSD	*Dead Sea Discoveries*
Ebib	Etudes bibliques
EBR	*Encyclopedia of the Bible and Its Reception*
EvT	*Evangelische Theologie*
FAT	Forschungen zum Alten Testament
FB	Forschung zur Bibel
FRLANT	Forschungen zur Religion und Literatur des Alten und Neuen Testaments
GAT	Grundrisse zum Alten Testament
HALOT	Koehler, Ludwig, Walter Baumgartner, and Johann J. Stamm. *The Hebrew and Aramaic Lexicon of the Old Testament.* Translated and edited under the supervision of Mervyn E. J. Richardson. 4 vols. Leiden: Brill, 1994–1999.
HAT	Handbuch zum Alten Testament
HBAI	*Hebrew Bible and Ancient Israel*
HBS	Herders Biblische Studien
HCOT	Historical Commentary on the Old Testament
HKAT	Handkommentar zum Alten Testament

HS	*Hebrew Studies*
HThKAT	Herders Theologischer Kommentar zum Alten Testament
HUCA	*Hebrew Union College Annual*
ICC	International Critical Commentary
IEJ	*Israel Exploration Journal*
JAJ	*Journal of Ancient Judaism*
JAJSup	Journal of Ancient Judaism Supplements
JCS	*Journal of Cuneiform Studies*
JHS	*Journal of Hellenic Studies*
JNES	*Journal of Near Eastern Studies*
JSJ	*Journal for the Study of Judaism in the Persian, Hellenistic, and Roman Periods*
JBL	*Journal of Biblical Literature*
JBS	Jerusalem Biblical Studies
JSNL	*Journal of Northwest Semitic Languages*
JSOT	*Journal for the Study of the Old Testament*
JSOTSup	Journal for the Study of the Old Testament Supplement Series
JSS	*Journal of Semitic Studies*
KHC	Kurzer Hand-Commentar zum Alten Testament
LAI	Library of Ancient Israel
LD	Lectio Divina
LHBOTS	The Library of Hebrew Bible/Old Testament Studies
LSTS	The Library of Second Temple Studies
LXX	Septuagint
m.	Mishnah
MdB	Monde de la Bible
MT	Masoretic Text
Mur.	Murabbaʻat
NEA	*Near Eastern Archaeology*
NEAEHL	Stern, Ephraim, ed. *The New Encyclopedia of Archaeological Excavations in the Holy Land*. 4 vols. Jerusalem: Israel Exploration Society & Carta; New York: Simon & Schuster, 1993.
NICOT	New International Commentary on the Old Testament
OBO	Orbis Biblicus et Orientalis
OBS	Österreichische biblische Studien

OEANE	Meyers, Eric M., ed. *The Oxford Encyclopedia of Archaeology in the Near East.* 5 vols. New York: Oxford University Press, 1997.
OLA	Orientalia Lovaniensia Analecta
OLZ	*Orientalistische Literaturzeitung*
OTE	*Old Testament Essays*
OTL	Old Testament Library
OtSt	Oudtestamentische Studiën
P.Rylands	Rylands Papyrus
PAAJR	*Proceedings of the American Academy of Jewish Research*
Qad	Qadmoniot
RB	*Revue biblique*
RBS	Resources for Biblical Study
RGRW	Religions in the Graeco-Roman World
RTL	*Revue th.ologique de Louvain*
Sanh.	Sanhedrin
SBAB	Stuttgarter biblische Aufsatzbände
SBLDS	Society of Biblical Literature Dissertation Series
SBLMS	Society of Biblical Literature Monograph Series
SBLSP	Society of Biblical Literature Seminar Papers
SBLStBL	Society of Biblical Literature Studies in Biblical Literature
SBS	Stuttgarter Bibelstudien
SCS	Septuagint and Cognate Studies
Sem	*Semitica*
SJ	Studia Judaica
SJLA	Studies in Judaism in Late Antiquity
SR	*Studies in Religion*
SymS	Symposium Series
T. Levi	Testament of Levi
TA	*Tel Aviv*
TAD	Porten, Bezalel, and Ada Yardeni. *Textbook of Aramaic Documents from Ancient Egypt.* 4 vols. Jerusalem: Hebrew University Press, 1986–1999.
Tanh.	Tanhuma
TDOT	Botterweck, G. Johannes, and Helmer Ringgren, eds. Theological Dictionary of the Old Testament. Translated by John T. Willis et al. 15 vols. Grand Rapids: Eerdmans, 1974–2006.

THAT	Jenni, Ernst, ed. *Theologisches Handwörterbuch zum Alten Testament*. Assisted by Claus Westermann. 2 vols. Munich: Kaiser; Zürich: Theologischer Verlag, 1971–1976.
ThT	*Theologisch tijdschrift*
Transeu	*Transeuphratène*
TRE	*Theologische Realenzyklopädie*. Edited by Gerhard Krause and Gerhard Müller. Berlin: de Gruyter, 1977–.
TRu	*Theologische Rundschau*
TSAJ	Texte und Studien zum antiken Judentum
TZ	*Theologische Zeitschrift*
VT	*Vetus Testamentum*
VTSup	Supplements to Vetus Testamentum
WBC	Word Biblical Commentary
WD	Dušek, Jan. *Les manuscrits araméens du Wadi Daliyeh et la Samarie vers 450–332 av. J.-C.* CHANE 30. Leiden: Brill, 2007.
WMANT	Wissenschaftliche Monographien zum Alten und Neuen Testament
WO	*Die Welt des Orients*
WUNT	Wissenschaftliche Untersuchungen zum Neuen Testament
XPh	Xerxes, Daiva Inscription at Persepolis
ZABR	*Zeitschrift für altorientalische und biblische Rechtgeschichte*
ZAW	*Zeitschrift für die alttestamentliche Wissenschaft*
ZBK	Zürcher Bibelkommentare
ZDPV	*Zeitschrift des deutschen Pal.stina-Vereins*
ZKT	*Zeitschrift für katholische Theologie*
ZTK	*Zeitschrift für Theologie und Kirche*

Methodological Considerations

Introduction: The State of Pentateuchal Research

Jaeyoung Jeon

During the last several decades, scholars in pentateuchal studies have endeavored to suggest new compositional models that would replace the classical Documentary Hypothesis. Such efforts, however, have produced more divergence than convergence, leaving many scholars with a rather pessimistic outlook regarding the possibility of a new consensus in the near future. A good example of such a state of the art is the recently published volume, *The Formation of the Pentateuch: Bridging the Academic Cultures of Europe, Israel, and North America*.[1] As the title of the volume indicates, it collects different views and models of the formation of the Pentateuch from Europe, Israel, and North America, producing a huge volume without reaching any consensus.

In spite of the diversity in current pentateuchal scholarship, there are some trends that may drive scholarship forward. Those trends are detected differently in studies of non-Priestly (or non-priestly), hereafter non-P/p, and priestly (P) texts.[2] For the former, rejection of the classical hypothesis of a J (Jahwist) document has prompted a major shift. The pioneering works published in the 1970s by Hans Heinrich Schmid and John Van Seters dated the J (or JE: the Jehowist) text to the exilic period.[3] Rolf Rend-

---

1. Jan C. Gertz et al., eds., *The Formation of the Pentateuch: Bridging the Academic Cultures of Europe, Israel, and North America*, FAT 111 (Tübingen: Mohr Siebeck, 2016).

2. I agree with the recent tendency to limit P (P^g) in the Sinai pericope. I am using "Priestly" or the siglum "P" with capital letter for the P^g text from Genesis through the Sinai periocope (most likely Lev 16), while the texts with priestly flavor in the post-Sinai narratives so far regarded as parts of P are marked simply as "priestly" or "p" (lowercase).

3. Hans H. Schmid, *Der sogenannte Jahwist: Beobachtungen und Fragen zur Pentateuchforschung* (Zurich: TVZ, 1976); and John Van Seters, *Abraham in History and Tradition* (New Haven: Yale University Press, 1975).

torff, in particular, even denied the existence of such a literary source.[4] The exilic dating of the non-P/p text has made a considerable impact, at least on European scholarship, especially in terms of its literary relationship with Deuteronomistic literature. According to the classical Documentary Hypothesis, J or JE predates D/Dtr which depends on it; the late dating of the former understands the literary influence to work in reverse and makes prophetic texts such as Isaiah, Jeremiah, and Ezekiel possible literary sources used by the non-P/p texts. Van Seters's late J model assumes that J has been influenced by D/Dtr and prophetic literature, while Erhard Blum develops Rendtorff's notion that D/Dtr redacted the patriarchal narrative and suggests that there is a D/Dtr composition (KD) of the entire Pentateuch.[5] The relatively simple, two-strata models of Van Seters (late J and a P redaction) and, in particular, Blum (KD and KP) have gained some support in North America. David M. Carr and Thomas B. Dozeman, for instance, have advanced similar models of Deuteronomistic composition followed by Priestly composition.[6] There is renewed interest in classical

---

4. Rolf Rendtorff, *Das überlieferungsgeschichtliche Problem des Pentateuch*, BZAW 147 (Berlin: de Gruyter, 1977), argued, like Van Seters, that P is a redactional layer rather than a separate document.

5. For Van Seters, see e.g., John Van Seters, *Prologue to History: The Yahwist as Historian in Genesis* (Zurich: TVZ, 1992); and Van Seters, *The Life of Moses: The Yahwist as Historian in Exodus–Numbers* (Louisville: Westminster John Knox, 1994). Christoph Levin, *Der Jahwist*, FRLANT 157 (Göttingen: Vandenhoeck & Ruprecht, 1993), suggests a late but pre-P J redaction, yet he finds the J text mostly in Genesis, with significantly less in Exodus and Numbers. Reinhard G. Kratz, *The Composition of the Narrative Books of the Old Testament* (London: T&T Clark, 2005), 248–94, understands J as limited to Genesis. For Blum, see Erhard Blum, *Die Komposition der Vätergeschichte*, WMANT 57 (Neukirchen-Vluyn: Neukirchener Verlag, 1984); and Blum, *Studien zur Komposition des Pentateuch*, BZAW 189 (Berlin: de Gruyter, 1990). But Blum has modified his view, denying the existence of KD in Genesis and understanding that KD begins only in Exod 3. The composition that encompasses the whole Pentateuch is the P-composition (KP); see Blum, "Die Literarische Verbindung von Erzvätern und Exodus: Ein Gespräch mit neueren Forschungshypothesen," in *Abschied vom Jahwisten: Die Komposition des Hexateuch in der jüngsten Diskussion*, ed. Jan C. Gertz, Konrad Schmid, and Markus Witte, BZAW 315 (Berlin: de Gruyter, 2002), 119–56, as well as Martin Rose, *Deuteronomist und Jahwist: Untersuchungen zu den berührungspunkten beider Literaturwerke*, ATANT 67 (Zurich: TVZ, 1981).

6. See, e.g., David M. Carr, *Reading the Fractures of Genesis: Historical and Literary Approaches* (Louisville: Westminster John Knox, 1996); and Thomas B. Dozeman, *The Pentateuch: Introducing the Torah*, Introducing Israel's Scriptures (Minneapolis: Fortress, 2017). Carr later proposes a "Lay Source" that is more or less equivalent to

source criticism in North America and to some extent in Israel, advocated in the "Neo-Documentarian" view, an extreme four-source (JEDP) theory assuming only one relatively mechanical compiler.⁷

In Europe, however, the newer models have been developed in more complicated ways, which cannot be exhaustively described here. In most cases, different types of models, such as fragments, sources, supplements, or compositions, are combined and applied to different stages in the formation process.⁸ For instance, the quite complicated models of Reinhard Kratz and, in a different way, Erich Zenger combine those different models throughout the formation history of the Pentateuch.⁹ Nevertheless, the

---

the D-composition; see Carr, *An Introduction to the Old Testament: Sacred Texts and Imperial Contexts of the Hebrew Bible* (Malden, MA: Wiley-Blackwell, 2010).

7. See, e.g., Menahem Haran, *The Biblical Collection: Its Consolidation to the End of the Second Temple Times and Changes of Form to the Middle Ages* [Hebrew], 2 vols. (Jerusalem: Magnes, 2004); Baruch J. Schwartz, "Israel's Holiness: The Torah Traditions," in *Purity and Holiness: The Heritage of Leviticus*, ed. Marcel Poorthuis and Joshua Schwartz, Jewish and Christian Perspectives Series 2 (Leiden: Brill, 2000), 47–59; and Joel Baden, *J, E, and the Redaction of the Pentateuch*, FAT 68 (Tübingen: Mohr Siebeck, 2009). It is, however, notable that several recently published dissertations in the United States follow more complicated European models; see, e.g., Roy E. Garton, *Mirages in the Desert: The Tradition-Historical Developments of the Story of Massah-Meribah* (Berlin: de Gruyter, 2017); Stephen Germany, *The Exodus-Conquest Narrative: The Composition of the Non-Priestly Narratives in Exodus–Joshua*, FAT 115 (Tübingen: Mohr Siebeck, 2017); and Matthew C. Genung, *The Composition of Genesis 37: Incoherence and Meaning in the Exposition of the Joseph Story*, FAT 2/95 (Tübingen: Mohr Siebeck, 2017).

8. For an elaborate categorization of the different models, see Erich Zenger and Christian Frevel, eds., *Einleitung in das Alte Testament*, Kohlhammer Studienbücher Theologie 1.1 (Stuttgart: Kohlhammer, 2012), 67–228; and Cristophe Nihan and Thomas Römer, "Le débat actuel sur la formation du Pentateuque," in *Introduction à l'Ancien Testament*, ed. Thomas Römer, Jean-Daniel Macchi, and Christophe Nihan, 2nd ed., MdB 49 (Geneva: Labor et Fides, 2009), 158–84. For a methodological analysis, see Jaeyoung Jeon, *The Call of Moses and the Exodus Story: A Redactional-Critical Study in Exodus 3–4 and 5–13*, FAT 2/60 (Tübingen: Mohr Siebeck, 2013), 7–64.

9. For Kratz, see Kratz, *Composition of the Narrative Books*, esp. 248–99 suggests that smaller pieces of stories were collected to gradually form Genesis (JG) and Exodus–Joshua (EG or GH), which developed separately until the exilic period, when they were connected and further developed by P and RPJE. The complicated so-called Münster Model proposed by Zenger and Frevel, *Einleitung in das Alte Testament*, 123–35, assumes two major stages of formation for the pre-P texts: a "Jerusalemite historical work (J)" from around 700 BCE and an "exilic historical work" that is more or less equivalent to JED.

major change especially in recent European pentateuchal scholarship is a growing acceptance of a literary separation between the patriarchal and exodus–wilderness stories in pre-P stage, namely, that the two stories were literarily connected only by P and thus that most of the non-P texts presupposing the literary connection are to be dated as post-P. This notion is compatible neither with the hypotheses of a literary source such as J (early or late) nor with the idea of overarching pre-P redaction encompassing Genesis–Numbers. Among those who advance and advocate this view are scholars such as Albert de Pury, Thomas Römer, Eckart Otto, Konrad Schmid, Jan Christian Gertz, and Erhard Blum.[10]

The separation between the patriarchal and exodus narratives in the pre-P stage has allowed new interpretive possibilities for identifying the non-P/p texts in Exodus and Numbers. The new possibilities have resulted in attributing an increasing number of those texts to different layers of post-P redaction made during the Persian period. Gertz and Ranier Albertz, for instance, assign much of the non-P text in the first half of the book of Exodus to multiple layers of post-P redactions.[11] Similarly, Otto and Reinhard Achenbach attribute a significant amount of the text in Exodus–Numbers to the two stages of post-P redaction, the Hexateuchal

---

10. See, e.g., Eckart Otto, "Die nachpriesterschriftliche Pentateuchredaktion," in *Studies in the Book of Exodus: Redaction, Reception, Interpretation*, ed. Marc Vervenne, BETL 126 (Leuven: Leuven University Press, 1996), 61–111; Albert de Pury, "Pg as the Absolute Beginning," in *Les dernières rédactions du Pentateuque, de l'Hexateuque et de l'Ennéateuque*, ed. Thomas Römer and Konrad Schmid, BETL 203 (Leuven: Peeters, 2007), 99–128; Konrad Schmid, *Genesis and the Moses Story: Israel's Dual Origins in the Hebrew Bible*, trans. James D. Nogalski, Siphrut 3 (Winona Lake, IN: Eisenbrauns, 2010); and Schmid, "Genesis and Exodus as Two Formerly Independent Traditions of Origins of Ancient Israel," *Bib* 93 (2012): 187–208. See also the discussions by Blum and Gertz in Jan C. Gertz, Konrad Schmid, and Markus Witte, eds., *Abschied vom Jahwisten: Die Komposition des Hexateuch in der jüngsten Diskussion*, BZAW 215 (Berlin: de Gruyter, 2002), where Blum corrects his view of the overarching KD and denies the existence of KD in Genesis. See also Thomas B. Dozeman and Konrad Schmid, eds., *A Farewell to the Yahwist: The Composition of the Pentateuch in Recent European Interpretation*, SymS 34 (Atlanta: Society of Biblical Literature, 2006). Kratz, *Composition of the Narrative Books*, 248–94 argues for a pre-Priestly connection yet still supports their separate development until the sixth century BCE.

11. Jan C. Gertz, *Tradition und Redaktion in der Exoduserzählung: Untersuchungen zur Endredaktion des Pentateuch*, FRLANT 186 (Göttingen: Vandenhoeck & Ruprecht, 2000); and Rainer Albertz, *Exodus*, 2 vols., ZBK 2 (Zurich: TVZ, 2012–2015).

Redaction (HexRed) followed by the Pentateuchal Redaction (PentRed).[12] In Otto's redactional analysis, non-P/p texts and those with priestly flavor are mixed up in HexRed and PentRed, for these layers were, according to Otto, influenced also by both P and D. Achenbach modifies Otto's layer division to assign the non-P/p texts mainly to HexRed and the texts with priestly flavor mainly to PentRed and later Theocratic Revision (ThB). The recent tendency in studies of non-P/p texts is therefore marked by several features: (1) reduced interest in early oral transmission and increased emphasis on later redactional process, (2) differentiation of an important number of literary layers, and (3) and post-P dating of most of those layers, especially to the Persian period.[13]

1. Priestly Scribal Works

In spite of the radical changes in recent pentateuchal studies, P has often been regarded as the only hypothetical source that remains valid. Nevertheless, recent developments in pentateuchal studies, especially in Europe, include a redefinition of the classical notion of P, particularly concerning its end. With some exceptions, an increasing number of critics find P's original ending in the Sinai pericope.[14] Initiated by Thomas Pola, critics find its end in different chapters in Exodus and Leviticus.[15] Otto, most radically, understands P to extend only up to Exod 29.[16] Pola, Kratz, and others find its conclusion in

---

12. Eckart Otto, *Das Deuteronomium im Pentateuch und Hexateuch: Studien zur Literaturgeschichte von Pentateuch und Hexateuch im Lichte des Deuteronomiumrahmens*, FAT 30 (Tübingen: Mohr Siebeck, 2000); and Reinhard Achenbach, *Die Vollendung der Tora: Studien zur Redaktionsgeschichte des Numeribuches im Kontext von Hexateuch und Pentateuch*, BZABR 3 (Wiesbaden: Harrassowitz, 2003).

13. On the first feature, see, however, the reconstruction of a pre-P exodus story in Rainer Albertz, "Der Beginn der vorpriesterlichen Exoduskomposition (K^{EX})," *TZ* 67 (2011): 223–62; and, for the patriarchal narratives, Israel Finkelstein and Thomas Römer, "Comments on the Historical Background of the Abraham Narrative: Between 'Realia' and 'Exegetica,'" *HBAI* 3 (2014): 3–23; and Finkelstein and Römer, "Comments on the Historical Background of the Jacob Narrative in Genesis," *ZAW* 126 (2014): 317–38.

14. For the exceptions, see, e.g., Blum, *Studien zur Komposition des Pentateuch*; Christian Frevel, *Mit Blick auf das Land die Schöpfung erinnern: Zum Ende der Priestergrundschrift*, HBS 23 (Freiburg im Breisgau: Herder, 2000).

15. Thomas Pola, *Die ursprüngliche Priesterschrift: Beobachtungen zur Literarkritik und Traditionsgeschichte von Pg*, WMANT 70 (Neukirchen-Vluyn: Neukirchener Verlag, 1995), 213–98.

16. Eckart Otto, "Forschungen zur Priesterschrift," *TRu* 62 (1997): 24–28.

Exod 40.[17] Zenger finds the end of P in Lev 9.[18] And Matthias Köckert, Christophe Nihan, and Römer consider Lev 16 to be the conclusion of P.[19]

To be sure, P has never been understood simply as a single-layer document. Julius Wellhausen and Abraham Kuenen already assumed multiple priestly layers within the Hexateuch, such as P^g/P^s and $P^1/P^2/P^3$, which led to further divisions within the so-called P texts.[20] The extent of P has also been gradually shortened. Martin Noth's separation of the Deuteronomistic History from the Tetrateuch (Genesis–Numbers) and his understanding of Deuteronomy as the joint between DtrH and the Pentateuch defined the end of Deuteronomy as the extent of P.[21] Lothar Perlitt then denied the existence of P in Deuteronomy, confining the end of P to Num 27.[22] The recent tendency to understand the Sinai pericope as the

---

17. Pola, *Die ursprüngliche Priesterschrift*, 213–98; Kratz, *Composition of the Narrative Books*, 225–47; A. Graeme Auld, "Leviticus at the Heart of the Pentateuch?," in *Reading Leviticus: A Conversation with Mary Douglas*, ed. John F. A. Sawyer, JSOTSup 227 (Sheffield: Sheffield Academic, 1996), 40–51; Auld, "Leviticus: After Exodus before Numbers," in *The Book of Leviticus: Composition and Reception*, ed. Rolf Rendtorff and Robert A. Kugler, VTSup 93 (Leiden: Brill, 2003), 41–54.

18. Zenger and Frevel, *Einleitung in das Alte Testament*, 183–209; and Erich Zenger, "Priesterschrift," *TRE* 27 (1997): 435–46, esp. 438–39.

19. Matthias Köckert, "Leben in Gottes Gegenwart: Zum Verstädnis des Gesetzes in der priesterschriftlichen Literatur," *Jahrbuch Biblische Theologie* 4 (1989): 29–61, esp., 56–58; Christoph Nihan, *From Priestly Torah to Pentateuch: A Study in the Composition of the Book of Leviticus*, FAT 2/25 (Tübingen: Mohr Siebeck, 2007), 340–94; Thomas Römer, "Der Pentateuch," in *Die Entstehung des Alten Testaments*, ed. Walter Dietrich et al., Theologische Wissenschaft 1 (Stuttgart: Kohlhammer, 2014), 90–93.

20. Julius Wellhausen, *Die Composition des Hexateuchs und der historischen Bücher des Alten Testaments*, 3rd ed. (Berlin: Reimer, 1899); and Abraham Kuenen, *An Historico-critical Inquiry into the Origin and Composition of the Hexateuch (Pentateuch and Book of Joshua)*, trans. Philip H. Wiksteed (London: Macmillan, 1886).

21. Martin Noth, *Überlieferungsgeschichtliche Studien* (Halle: Niemeyer, 1943), 191–201 assigns Deut 34:1*, 7–9 to P, arguing that this fragmentary passage was taken from its original place in Num 27 and placed in its current position by the Pentateuch redactor in favor of P. Yet some critics still support the idea that P ends in Joshua; see, e.g., Ernst A. Knauf, "Die Priesterschrift und die Geschichten der Deuteronomisten," in *The Future of the Deuteronomistic History*, ed. Thomas Römer, BETL 147 (Leuven: Peeters, 2000), 101–18; and Norbert Lohfink, "Die Priesterschrift und die Geschichte," in *Studien zum Pentateuch*, ed. Norbert Lohfink, SBAB 4 (Stuttgart: Katholisches Bibelwerk, 1988), 213–53.

22. Lothar Perlitt, "Priesterschrift im Deuteronomoum?," *ZAW* 100 (1988): 65–88, who is followed by Jean-Louis Ska, "Le récit sacerdotal: Une 'histoire sans

end of P is therefore in line with the gradual shortening of the extent of P throughout the history of modern pentateuchal scholarship.²³

The theories of P's end in the Sinai pericope have provoked discussions focused on redefining the post-Sinai narratives especially in Numbers. The thesis of a short P categorizes Genesis–Leviticus (or Exodus) as a large literary unit formulated in its current form mainly by P, thus creating a literary gap between the Priestly edition of Genesis–Leviticus (Exodus) and the Dtr edition of Deuteronomy (and Joshua). Otto and Achenbach attempt to fill this gap with their model of a post-Priestly HexRed that connects the two parts and a PentRed that separates the Pentateuch from the Hexateuch. Achenbach assigns especially the texts with priestly flavor in Numbers either to PentRed or the even later ThB. The latter is, for Achenbach, the last redactional phase by late priestly scribal groups during the mid-/late Persian period.²⁴ Römer proposes a bridge model in which the post-Sinai narratives in Numbers, both priestly and nonpriestly, were produced as a literary bridge between Genesis–Leviticus and Deuteronomy.²⁵ For Römer, many of the texts in Numbers were produced in post-P and post-Dtr stages, based on both the Priestly and Deuteronomistic texts. Albertz combines different formational models based on Römer's view of Numbers.²⁶ A marked effect of the short P model in current scholarship is that the model puts P at a relatively early stage in the formation of the Pentateuch and thus attributes an increasing number of texts to post-P layers.²⁷

This brief survey reveals that there are several noticeable features in the recent development of pentateuchal study for both non-P/p and

---

fin'?," in *The Books of Leviticus and Numbers*, ed. Thomas Römer, BETL 215 (Leuven: Peeters, 2008), 631–53.

23. For a detailed discussion and a summary of scholarship, see Jaeyoung Jeon, "The Promise of the Land and the Extent of P," *ZAW* 130 (2018): 513–28.

24. Achenbach, *Die Vollendung der Tora*.

25. See, e.g., Walter Dietrich et al., eds. *Die Entstehung des Alten Testaments*, Theologische Wissenschaft: Sammelwerk für Studium und Beruf 1 (Stuttgart: Kohlhammer, 2014), 135–49.

26. See, e.g., Rainer Albertz, "Das Buch Numeri jenseits der Quellentheorie: Eine Redaktionsgeschichte von Num 20–24," *ZAW* 123 (2011): 171–83, 336–47; Albertz, "A Pentateuchal Redaction in the Book of Numbers?," *ZAW* 125 (2013): 220–33.

27. For this trend, see the recent discussions in Federico Giuntoli and Konrad Schmid, eds., *The Post-Priestly Pentateuch: New Perspectives on Its Redactional Development and Theological Profiles*, FAT 101 (Tübingen: Mohr Siebeck, 2015).

P/p portions. (1) Critics detect more literary layers. (2) Literary units are more segmented. And (3) an increasing amount of text is assigned to post-P layers and dated to late periods, the Persian period in particular. The current state of research on the literary stratigraphy of the Pentateuch thus necessitates serious investigation of the historical contexts of those late-dated texts, especially in the complex sociohistorical situation of the Persian period.

2. New Sociohistorical Contexts for the Formation of the Pentateuch

Investigation of the sociohistorical contexts is further necessitated by the significant influence of pentateuchal studies on biblical studies in general. Earlier generations could systematically explain the historical contexts of the pentateuchal sources within the frame of the classical Documentary Hypothesis: J is from Judah in general or, according to Gerhard von Rad, from the Jerusalem court during the so-called Solomonic enlightenment of the late tenth century BCE.[28] E is from northern Israel around ther ninth–eighth centuries BCE. The Jehowist (JE redaction) fits in Jerusalem after the fall of the Northern Kingdom in the eighth–seventh centuries BCE. D may be from the Northern Kingdom but was reformulated in the Jerusalem court during the Josianic reform in the seventh century BCE. P was written by a priestly scribe in the exilic period. And the redaction of the Pentateuch, the final combination of these sources, took place in the Persian period. This historical scheme could locate the formulation and combination of sources at the major historical junctures, providing a useful interpretive framework covering over five hundred years of Israel's known history. This large frame included discussions of the different traditions in the Northern and Southern Kingdoms and different generations and groups of scribes in the courts and temples of Jerusalem and Samaria, as well as their exilic/postexilic tradents. A history of the Pentateuch was therefore a history of religion of Israel and Judah, which enabled classical source criticism to function as a basic framework for biblical scholarship for about a century.

But the recent developments in pentateuchal criticism outlined above make this classical identification and dating of the texts no longer tenable.

---

28. Gerhard von Rad, *The Problem of the Hexateuch and Other Essays*, trans. E. W. Trueman Dicken (New York: McGraw-Hill, 1966).

The newly identified texts, authors, and redactors are concentrated in the exilic and Persian periods, a relatively short time span of less than three centuries. To be sure, traces of old traditions from the monarchic and even premonarchic periods still may be found in the texts. It is, however, broadly accepted that old traditions, either oral or written, were repeatedly reinterpreted, reformulated, and re-created in later periods. The existence of old traditions behind the texts is one thing, but the production of the current form of texts is another.

Since Max Weber's seminal social study *Das antike Judentum* (1921), the Persian period has been understood mainly in terms of social and religious factions among diverse socioreligious classes and parties.[29] The notion that these groups were in competing positions has served as a useful frame for understanding the diverse voices in the Bible, the Pentateuch in particular, as scribal contributions that reflect the varying interests of the groups. Otto Plöger, for instance, developed a model of two major scribal traditions in the Second Temple period: priestly and eschatological.[30] This model has been further developed by Odil Hannes Steck and Frank Crüsemann.[31] In North America, Paul D. Hanson and Morton Smith have advanced theories of conflict among different religiopolitical parties and groups such as priests, prophets, and lay leaders.[32] Albertz, in his two-volume work *Religionsgeschichte Israels in alttestamentlischer Zeit* (1992), presented a comprehensive reconstruction of a history of Israelite reli-

---

29. Max Weber, *Das antike Judentum*, vol. 3 of *Gesammelte Aufsätze zur Religionssoziologie* (Tübingen: Mohr Siebeck, 1921). For a thorough survey of Weber's influence in Old Testament study, see Andrew D. H. Mayes, *The Old Testament in Sociological Perspective* (London: Marshall Pickering, 1989), 36–77; and Eckart Otto, *Max Webers Studien des antiken Judentums: Historische Grundlegung einer Theorie der Moderne* (Tübingen: Mohr Siebeck, 2011).

30. Otto Plöger, *Theokratie und Eschatologie*, WMANT 2 (Neukirchen: Neukirchner Verlag, 1959).

31. Odil H. Steck, "Das Problem theologischer Strömungen in nachexilischer Zeit," *EvT* 28 (1969): 182–200; Frank Crüsemann, "Israel in der Perserzeit: Eine Skizze in Auseinandersetzung mit Max Weber," in *Max Webers Sicht des antiken Christentums: Interpretation und Kritik*, ed. Wolfgang Schluchter (Frankfurt am Main: Suhrkamp, 1985), 205–32; and Crüsemann, *Die Tora: Theologie und Sozialgeschichte des Alttestamentlichen Gesetzes* (Munich: Kaiser, 1992).

32. Paul D. Hanson, *The Dawn of Apocalyptic: The Historical and Sociological Roots of Jewish Apocalyptic Eschatology*, rev. ed. (Philadelphia: Fortress, 1983); and Morton Smith, *Palestinian Parties and Politics That Shaped the Old Testament*, 2nd ed. (London: SCM, 1987).

gion and biblical text based on conflicts and dialogues among competing groups and their scribes.[33] Most of these studies are based on the classical Documentary Hypothesis, while Albertz built his view on Blum's model of KD and KP, which consequently led him to assume a rivalry between the lay (KD) and priestly (KP) groups.[34]

Recent developments in the study of the Pentateuch have nevertheless revealed that the formation of the Pentateuch was a much more complicated process. At the same time, recent sociohistorical studies of the Persian period suggest that the fabric of the social, religious, and political conflicts among different classes and groups was far more intricate than what has been previously assumed.[35] The focus of study is no longer confined to Yehud but has been extended to other Judahite communities in the diaspora, including Elephantine, as well as the Samaritan community. Such developments in both pentateuchal study and sociohistorical study of the Persian period set a proper academic context for setting the diverse voices in the different layers of Pentateuch as we now understand them within the complex social, religious, and political conflicts and debates of the day.

3. The Purpose and Contents of This Volume

Against this backdrop, this volume aims to identify some groups of texts, scribal circles behind the texts, and their social, political, and theological interests. Firstly, renewed attention is paid to the lay leadership and its

---

33. For English translation, see Rainer Albertz, *A History of Israelite Religion in the Old Testament Period*, 2 vols. (London: SCM, 1994).

34. Albertz, *History of Israelite Religion*, 2:464–92.

35. See, e.g., Joel Weinberg, *The Citizen-Temple Community*, JSOTSup 15 (Sheffield: JSOT Press, 1992); Charles E. Carter, *The Emergence of Yehud in the Persian Period: A Social and Demographic Study*, JSOTSup 294 (Sheffield: Sheffield Academic, 1999); Philip R. Davies, *Scribes and Schools: The Canonization of Hebrew Scriptures*, LAI (Louisville: Westminster John Knox, 1998); Norman K. Gottwald, *The Politics of Ancient Israel* (Louisville: Westminster John Knox, 2001); Gabriele Boccaccini, *Roots of Rabbinic Judaism: An Intellectual History, From Ezekiel to Daniel* (Grand Rapids: Eerdmans, 2001); Jon L. Berquist, *Judaism in Persia's Shadow: A Social and Historical Approach* (Minneapolis: Fortress, 1995); Erhard S. Gerstenberger, *Israel in der Perserzeit: 5. und 4. Jahrhundert v. Chr.* (Stuttgart: Kohlhammer, 2005); Richard A. Horsley, *Scribes, Visionaries, and the Politics of Second Temple Judea* (Louisville: Westminster John Knox, 2007); and Benedikt Hensel, *Juda und Samaria: Zum Verhältnis zweier nach-exilischer Jahwismen*, FAT 110 (Tübingen: Mohr Siebeck, 2017).

scribal contribution to the Pentateuch. The essays by Römer and Jaeyoung Jeon, respectively, focus on the group of elders and their literary contributions, which deviate from the much-discussed connection between lay leadership and the Dtr scribal circle. Jürg Hutzli investigates redactional works by nonpriestly scribes in Jerusalem during the Persian period and their theological characteristics.

The religiopolitical agenda behind the late priestly texts is also investigated. Dozeman and Jeon investigate the Zadokite priests' power struggle against the lay leadership and Levitical groups reflected in Num 16. Katharina Pyschny provides a different redaction-critical and sociohistorical analysis of Num 16 (17), one that often contradicts the contribution of Dozeman and Jeon. Olivier Artus deals with the priestly attempt to enhance their religious and political rule over the diaspora community reflected especially in Num 32. Ndikho Mtshiselwa applies the notion of power struggle to the formation of the major chapters of the book of Numbers. Itamar Kislev traces the change of the attitude toward the stranger (גר) in late priestly redactional activity.

The impact of the Samaritan community on the formation of the Pentateuch is explored by Innocent Himbaza and Dany Noquet, respectively. They argue that northern traditions such as the Jacob cycle and some chapters in Deuteronomy, as well as texts that emphasize or legitimate northern sanctuaries such as Bethel and Shechem, can be reinterpreted in connection with the Samaritan community rather than with the early context of the Northern Kingdom.

The major theses of the eleven essays included in this volume can be summarized with further details as follows. We start with Schmid's introductory essay, "Textual, Historical, Sociological, and Ideological Cornerstones of the Formation of the Pentateuch." Schmid first affirms the validity of our discussion of the formation of the Pentateuch by proving that the Masoretic Text (MT) is reliable with minor exceptions considering the textual evidence from Qumran and the Septuagint (LXX). Schmid then sets a basic guideline for our discussion by framing a *terminus a quo* and *terminus ad quem* for the composition of the Pentateuch. He sets the ninth–eighth centuries BCE as the *terminus a quo* based on the development of Israel and Judah as states, as well as their literacy. Indeed, we observe a significant increase in the number of written texts, with higher quality, in this period. Notably, Schmid admits that Tell Deir Allah and Kuntillet Ajrud were school sites of a sort. For the *terminus ad quem* he suggests the mid-second century BCE based on several observations: (1)

the Pentateuch was translated into Greek (LXX) in that period; (2) the fall of Persia is not alluded to in the Pentateuch, which implies a pre-Hellenistic date; and (3) the so-called small apocalypse in Num 24:14–24, one of the latest passages in the Pentateuch, mentions the victory of the ships of the Kittim over Ashur and Eber, alluding to the battles between Alexander and the Persians.

Schmid further narrows the time frame for the composition of the Pentateuch based on cultural influences from the neighbors in the text. Firstly, he mentions that the book of Deuteronomy was influenced by Assyrian treaty rhetoric, agreeing that at least the core part of Deuteronomy originated in the late Neo-Assyrian period in an anti-Assyrian milieu of scribes. At the other end of the Pentateuch, the table of nations in Gen 10 (mainly P) promulgates the idea that God intended humanity to live in different nations, with different lands and different languages. Schmid argues that Gen 10 is probably a Persian-period text reflecting this basic conviction of Persian imperial ideology, which is also attested, for example, in the Behistun inscription. As such, Schmid actually suggests that the major parts of the Pentateuch were composed between the late Neo-Assyrian and Persian periods. He concludes, however, that the Pentateuch grew over centuries as a complex of different voices that establish its overall beauty and richness.

In his contribution, "The Relationship between Moses and Aaron and the Question of the Composition of the Pentateuch," Thomas Römer delves into the question of the different scribal groups behind some texts that hold different views on the relationship between Moses and Aaron. He first reviews the context of the promulgation of Torah in the Persian period and argues that different groups such as lay leaders, priests, and Levites were involved in its formation. Römer then focuses on those groups' scribal debates concerning the figures of Moses and Aaron. For the priestly group, he focuses on the late priestly texts such as Exod 6:14–26 and Num 18:1–24. The former is a genealogy focused on Aaron's family, yet nothing is said about Moses's offspring. Especially in Exod 6:26, *Aaron*, ahead of Moses, appears as the privileged interlocutor commanded by YHWH to lead the Israelites out of Egypt, contrary to the majority of the texts in Exodus. Interestingly, this has been immediately corrected in the following verse in MT, where Moses is again put in the first position. So it seems that later redactors wanted to emphasize that Moses stands over Aaron. A similar phenomenon occurs in Num 18:1–24, which is, with Lev 10:8, the only text in the Torah where YHWH speaks only to Aaron. In this speech, YHWH grants to Aaron and his sons a perpetual income and taxes from the sacrifices to be offered by the Israelites. Interestingly, a passage was added at the end of the chapter (vv. 25–32) in which YHWH speaks no longer to Aaron but to Moses. Both Exod 6 and Num 18 seem to reflect a struggle between Aaron (and the group behind him) and Moses (and the group behind him).

The last two texts also affirm the superiority of Aaron and his offspring over the other Levites. The genealogy in Exod 6 shows interest in the Korahites, who appear in conflict with Moses and Aaron in Num 16–17; Num 18:1–24 clearly postulates the superiority of Aaron and his sons over the other Levites, who are said to be "assistants" and cannot approach the utensils of the sanctuary or the altar (v. 3). Verses 25–32 in Num 18 also stipulate the superiority of the Aaronides over the Levites, here by claiming that the Levites should receive a tithe from the Israelites but that they should also give a tithe from their income to Aaron and his sons.

Römer finds attempts by the Levites to challenge the superiority of Aaron and his offspring. In Exod 32, for instance, Aaron is presented as the creator of the golden calf and the inventor of grave idolatry in the wilderness. The negative image of Aaron is contrasted with the appearance of the Levites, who are presented as the only group that was on the side of YHWH and Moses. Römer assumes that Exod 32 was at least revised by the same Levitical scribal group that is criticized in Num 16.

Römer argues that the scribal response to the priestly scribal work can be found in the texts that emphasize Moses's superiority over Aaron. In Exod 4:13–17, for instance, Aaron is downgraded as Moses's spokesperson. Similarly, Moses's special status and superiority over Aaron and Miriam are emphasized in Num 12, and, for Römer, the chapter counters other priestly texts like Num 18. Römer then concludes that the Pentateuch appears in this regard not only as a compromise but also as the record of scribal conflicts that were never totally resolved.

Hutzli endeavors to identify a nonpriestly, late redactional layer in his essay, "J's Problem with the East: Observations on the So-Called Yahwistic Texts in Genesis 1–25." As the title of the essay indicates, Hutzli makes the concept of "east" (קדם) the major criterion for distinguishing different J layers. For instance, while the location of Eden is in the East according to the older J (Gen 2:8), later editorial passages put the primeval couple and Cain east of Eden (Gen 3:24; 4:16) and consequently locate Eden in the West. Hutzli argues, following Gertz, that this contradictory location of Eden in the late layer was inspired by the theology of the Jerusalem temple, making Eden compatible with Jerusalem.

Hutzli finds a continuation of this late non-P redactional layer in the stories of the Tower of Babel (Gen 11:1–9, esp. v. 2) and Abraham sending his sons (esp. Gen 25:6), where the East appears with negative connotations. He claims that especially the motif of the name (or fame, שם) in the former (Gen 11:4) indicates vanity of reputation by human effort, in a sharp contrast with the divine promise of fame (שם) for Abraham in the following chapter (Gen 12:2).

The image of the East is positive in various biblical texts: the location of Eden (Gen 2:8), the birthplace of great nations (the table of nations in Gen 10*), and the cradle of wisdom (e.g., Num 23:7; 1 Kgs 5:10). Hutzli argues that the late non-P (J) redactional layer reacts against this positive notion of the East and describes it as the place for sinners, transgressors, and people ruled by vain ambitions. Such a devaluation of the East (in particular Babylon) on behalf of Jerusalem is, according to Hutzli, the literary contribution of a lay circle within the Jerusalem elite during the Persian period.

The essay by Jeon, "The Elders Redaction (ER) in the Pentateuch: Scribal Contributions of an Elders Group in the Formation of the Pentateuch," endeavors to detect the scribal contribution from a lay leadership group in the Yahwistic community of Yehud in the Persian period. This study suggests that a series of texts in Exodus–Numbers–Deuteronomy is marked by its particular notion of the prophetic Tent of Meeting, which is distinguished from the priestly Tabernacle. Those texts elevate the status of the seventy elders but diminish prophetic and priestly authorities. The group of texts may be designated as the "Elders Redaction" (ER), which has two phases: the first (ER^1) consists of Exod 33:7–11a; Num 11:16–17, 24b–25, 30; 12:1*, 2, 4–8, 9*, 10a, 11b; and Deut 34:10–12, while the second (ER^2) consists of Exod 17:8–16; 33:11b; 24:13*–14; 32:17–18; Num 11:26–29; and Deut 31:14–15, 23. ER^1 focuses on the special status of Moses and the lay leaders who share his spirit, while ER^2 elevates especially the status of Joshua as head of the lay leadership.

Against the models that regard those passages as parts of larger source or compositional layer such as the Elohist (E), the Deuteronomistic composition (KD), or the PentRed, the essay argues that ER is a separate literary work already presupposing an idea of a Pentateuch. In pentateuchal stratigraphy, the two phases of ER are found in post-P and post-Dtr layers. ER was most likely produced by a scribal circle belonging to or advocating the interests of the lay leadership of the Yahwistic community of Yehud in the Persian period. The lay leadership in the exilic and

Persian periods has often been connected to the Deuteronomistic scribal circle. This essay, however, suggests that there was a lay leadership group in the Persian period that did not necessarily belong to the Deuteronomistic circle.

The essay also reveals that ER has a dynamic literary relationship, often polemical, with the different layers of priestly scribal work. This aspect strongly implies that the Pentateuch has been formulated, especially in its last phases, through scribal debates between different social and religious groups as means of pursuing hegemony in the political structure of the Yahwistic community of Yehud.

Mtshiselwa's essay, "The Formation of the Wilderness Narratives in the Book of Numbers," provides an overview of the pentateuchal discussion especially concerning the different scribal groups that contributed to the formation of the book of Numbers. Summarizing a broad-range discussion of the date of the scribal activities in Numbers, Mtshiselwa concludes that texts in Numbers were produced after P^g and H (Holiness Code) in the middle of the fifth century BCE and later. He then identifies the three groups that contributed to the Pentateuch in general and Numbers in particular as the Zadokite priests, the Levitical priests, and the Samaritans and Transjordanians. To the Zadokite scribes he assigns the legitimation of the office of Eleazar in the narrative of Aaron's death (Num 20:22–29; Deut 10:6–7; 11:2) as well as the covenant of eternal priesthood for Phinehas at Baal Peor (Num 25:6–15). He also argues that the so-called priestly layers of the Korah story (Num 16–17) are a Zadokite response to Num 12. Mtshiselwa assumes that the contributions of the Levitical priests include some passages in Deuteronomy, such as the judicial authority of the Levitical priests (Deut 17:9; 21:5) and their preserving and teaching the Torah (Deut 17:18). The increased influence of the Levitical priests is reflected in the Zadokite redaction of Korah (Num 16).

Mtshiselwa finds contributions or reflections of the positions of the Samaritans and the Judahites in Transjordan. For him, the characters of Caleb and Joshua in Num 13–14 symbolize Samaritan and Judean Judaism, respectively; the list of the tribes in Num 13:4–15 recalls Deut 27:12–13, and the two passages presuppose the worship of YHWH in Samaritan circles. Also, Deut 27:5–10 (as well as Josh 8:30–35) envisions Mount Ebal as the place of worship, which is attributed to the Samaritans, while Num 32, together with Josh 22, deals with the structural organization of Judaism in the diaspora and legitimizes the YHWH cults and the communities in Transjordan.

Kislev delves into the issue of the legal status of the stranger (גר) in his article, "Formulae That Equate the גר and the Israelite: Literary Activity in the Priestly Writings." Providing a detailed redaction critical analysis of the seventeen occurrences of what he calls the "equating formulae" in the priestly parts of the Pentateuch and two cases in Ezekiel, Kislev concludes that those formulae or the passages including them are all late additions. He argues that the occurrences in Exod 12:48–49; Lev 16:29; Num 19:10; Num 35:15; and Josh 20:9 are definitive cases that prove the editorial nature of the formulae, although the other cases in Lev 17; Num 15:22–31; Exod 12:19; and Num 15:14–16 can also be seen as additions. Kislev also suggests that two occurrences in Ezekiel (14:7; 47:23) are additions made under the influence of similar formulae in the Pentateuch.

Kislev finds the context of these editorial activities in Yehud in the Persian period and the burning question of identity at that time. He argues that these additions sought to completely equalize the גרים and the Israelites, mainly in terms of their legal rights and obligations, as opposed to the separatist tendency found in Ezra–Nehemiah. Kislev also argues that the equation formula is generally found in priestly texts and not in the basic stratum of the priestly legislation (Lev 1–16), which implies that P was an independent source rather than a redactional layer.

Dozeman and Jeon delve into compositional and sociohistorical issues related to the Korah rebellion story (Num 16). Their coauthored essay, titled "From Sources to Redaction: Identifying the Authors of Numbers 16," consists of two main parts. In the first part, the history of the scholarship of the chapter is reviewed by comparing the classical source-critical interpretation of George Buchanan Gray and the more recent redaction-critical study by Achenbach. The comparison reveals that, while Gray found the JE source (Dathan and Abiram, ninth–seventh centuries BCE), P^g (Korah and the 250 lay leaders, ca. 500 BCE), and P^s (Korah and the Levites, 500–250 BCE), Achenbach's model defines the authors as HexRed (Dathan and Abiram, early fifth century BCE), PentRed (the 250 lay leaders, late fifth century BCE), and ThB (Korah and the Levites, fourth century BCE). The result shows that, although there is not much difference between them in the division of the layers or sources, the identification of the authors and dating diverge significantly.

The second part of the essay focuses on the sociohistorical profile of the two later layers (the 250 chieftains layer and the Korah-Levites layer). It is argued that the two layers represent two historical stages of power struggle among rival groups in the temple of Jerusalem. In the earlier,

250 chieftains layer, a (Zadokite) priestly scribe endeavors to polemicize the custom of lay incense offering in the temple and to limit the influence of the lay leaders in temple politics. The layer of Korah and the Levites reflects a later stage when the Levites grew stronger and were able to challenge the priesthood. The two redactional phases aim equally to protect or promote the exclusive priestly prerogative in temple ritual by monopolizing the incense offering. Notably, the incense rite in the temple emerged as a symbol of priesthood throughout the Hellenistic and Roman periods. The significance of the incense offering as a symbol of priesthood is also found in Chronicles, particularly in the account of King Uzziah's leprosy (2 Chr 26:16–21).

Pyschny presents a different view on the formation and sociohistorical contexts of Num 16–17. Her "In Between Sources, Fragments, and Redactions: Numbers 16–17 as a Test Case for Reconstructing the Literary History of the Pentateuch" challenges the dominant view on several points. Concerning the formation of the chapters, Pyschny argues that the 250-men stratum constitutes the first stage and the Dathan-Abiram stratum the last. According to Pyschny, the first stratum is a post-P independent fragment written by the priestly (scribal) circles at the Jerusalem temple in the beginning or the middle of the fifth century BCE. The priests wrote this stratum in order to enforce their leadership claims against lay elites as well as to increase their own economic power.

The first stage is followed by the Korah-Levites redaction, according to Psychny. She argues that the Korah traditions stemmed from Chronicles and found their way into the Pentateuch from there in order to incorporate or strengthen Levitical leadership in the Torah. The purpose of the redaction is thus not to devalue the Levites with respect to the Aaronides but to highlight their cultic importance vis-à-vis the Aaronide priests. The stratum was added in the middle or the late fifth century BCE by one of the priestly (scribal) circles in Jerusalem that sought to legitimize an inclusive cultic order. The complementary interrelationship between (Aaronide) priests and Levites is again supported by another post-P addition of Num 17:16–28, where Aaron represents the whole tribe of Levi.

The last stage is, for Pyschny, the incorporation of the Dathan and Abiram episode. Focusing on the mention of מנחה (Num 16:15), Pyschny argues that the Reubenites regularly make offerings, and the rejection of their offerings is a very strong plea against presenting offerings outside the land and away from the central sanctuary. Dathan and Abiram could represent, according to her, groups outside of Yehud (and Samaria) who deny the priestly authority of those officiating at the temples in Jerusalem or Gerizim.

Artus focuses on the sociohistorical profile of the last part of Numbers, especially Num 32, in his article "Transjordan in the Book of Numbers." After a brief review of recent compositional models for the book of Numbers, Artus undertakes a comparison between Deut 1–3 and the relevant texts in Numbers. He concludes that, while the conquest account of Sihon and Og in Num 21 has no theological evaluation, for it is older tradition than Deut 2:24–3:3, the account of the settlement in Transjordan in Num 32 (cf. Deut 2:12b–22) is highly theological, a sign of lateness.

Artus claims that Num 32 should be understood in the context of Num 26–36, for there are not only special linguistic features that construct these chapters as a compositional unit but also thematic connections between Num 1–25 and 26–36; the latter should therefore be read in connection with the former. He observes that Num 11–25 is marked by two categories of sin: sins of military disobedience (chs. 13–14) and sins involving challenge to religious authority (chs. 16–17). Read in this context, the settlement account in Num 32 is not only about a military issue but also about the religiopolitical problem. According to Artus, this account thus reflects a challenge to the authority of the high priest and the hierocratic organization of the community of Yehud.

In the context of the Persian period, the two-and-a-half tribes in the account symbolize the Judahites in diaspora as well as the Judahite settlement in Moab as a historical reality. He concludes that Num 32, which is critical of the Transjordan tribes, should be read as a polemic against diaspora Judahites or the Judahite settlement in Moab because of their challenge to the hierocratic order of Yehud.

Himbaza provides an overview of the discussion of how role of the leaders of the Samaritan community is relevant to the promulgation of the Pentateuch in "What Is the Contribution of the Samaritans to the Pentateuch?" Modifying Benedikt Hensel's view, Himbaza argues that the schism between Jerusalem and Gerizim began only in the second century BCE, when both Jews and Samaritans rejected each other. He claims that the project of writing the Pentateuch may have begun before the tensions between the two Yawhistic community appeared, and probably the Persian authorities of both the provinces of Yehud and Samaria may have been behind the compromise. Jews and Samaritans may have read the same Pentateuch, according to Himbaza, until the second century BCE, in which a literary schism concerning the place of worship occurred. Yet it is not the Samaritans who were responsible for the harmonizations in the Samaritan Pentateuch, as the Dead Sea Scrolls exhibit. The Samaritans may have chosen the harmonized text in order to use a perfect Torah without textual and literary discrepancies.

Himbaza generally assigns the texts from Genesis to Joshua that positively refer to the region of Shechem, including the story of Joseph (Gen 37–50) and some passages in Deuteronomy (e.g., Deut 11 and 27), to the literary contribution from the Samaritan community during the fifth century BCE. He then deals with the issue of the separation between the Pentateuch and the Hexateuch. In the current form of the Hexateuch, the major place of worship would be Ebal and Gerizim. If the book of Joshua is separated from the Pentateuch and read as an independent unit followed by the Prophets, Shechem becomes one of many other places of worship. The Prophets may conclude, then, that Jerusalem is the ultimate chosen place because, from the book of Judges onward, Shechem is negatively portrayed as a place of division, apostasy, and crime (Judg 9; 1 Kgs 12; Jer 41:4–7; Hos 6–9). For Himbaza, the rejection of the Hexateuch reflects the end of a peaceful period and the beginning of difficult relationships among YHWH worshipers. Especially in the Former Prophets, he argues, the Northern Kingdom is portrayed negatively on the whole because the Samaritans were already rejected and therefore did not participate in the (final) redaction of the Prophets and the Writings.

In his essay, "Shechem and Bethel in the Patriarchal Narratives: A Samaritan Rereading of Gen 12:1–9* and Gen 35:2–4?," Noquet focuses on the appearance of Shechem and Bethel as significant cultic places in the Abraham (Gen 12:1–9) and Jacob (Gen 35:2–4) narratives. Genesis 12:1–9* introduces Shechem as the first station in Canaan in Abraham's journey as well as the first place to worship YHWH. According to Noquet, the passage legitimizes Shechem as the oldest center of YHWH worship in Israel. Following the tendency in recent pentateuchal discussion, Noquet assigns the divine speech of YHWH (Gen 12:1–4a) and the references to Shechem and Bethel (vv. 6–9) to a post-P and post-D final stage of pentateuchal redaction. He observes that there is no mention of the Judean territory in the divine speech to Abraham and that his itinerary from Haran to Shechem has no connection to a return from the Judean exile; he argues that the late redaction of those verses is a literary contribution from the Samaritan community of the fifth century BCE. Therefore, Gen 12:1–9* is a Samaritan reformulation of the Abraham tradition originally belonging to the south of Hebron. Through this reformulation, for Noquet, Abraham, the "figure of the Babylonian deportee," becomes the patriarch who legitimizes the Yahwistic orthodoxy of the Samaritan community in the Persian period.

Genesis 12:6–9 mentions (near) Bethel as another place for Abraham's altar together with Shechem, and the close topographic and religious connection between the two sites is found again in the account of Jacob's return to Bethel and Shechem in Gen 35:2–4. Following Blum, Noquet assigns the verses to the most recent redactional stage in Gen 35 and also defines this redaction equally as a literary contribution from the Samaritan community at the end of the fifth century BCE. Contrary to the view that Gen 35:2–4 contains a polemic against Shechem, Noquet claims that the passage describes Shechem positively as the place where iconoclastic worship of YHWH originated, and that it reflects the strength of the Samaritan community around its sanctuary on Mount Gerizim.

The essays collected in this volume deal with a broad range of pentateuchal texts from Genesis to Deuteronomy, yet most find their contexts in the Persian period. As we have seen, the social, religious, and political complexity confronted by the Yahwistic communities in Yehud, Samaria, and other diaspora communities is capable of explaining the diverse voices reflected in the Pentateuch and the fabric of their intertextual relationships.

To be sure, this volume is not designed to provide a comprehensive answer to the bold question of who wrote the Torah. It is impossible to investigate in this small volume the complexity of the pentateuchal texts and their sociohistorical contexts in an exhaustive way. The volume may nevertheless contribute to a renewed discussion of the shift of the focus of the pentateuchal study from the literary stratification of different layers to social, economic, religious, and political agendas behind the texts and the scribes who produced them.

Bibliography

Achenbach, Reinhard. *Die Vollendung der Tora: Studien zur Redaktionsgeschichte des Numeribuches im Kontext von Hexateuch und Pentateuch*. BZABR 3. Wiesbaden: Harrassowitz, 2003.

Albertz, Rainer. "Das Buch Numeri jenseits der Quellentheorie: Eine Redaktionsgeschichte von Num 20–24." *ZAW* 123 (2011): 171–83, 336–47.

———. "Der Beginn der vorpriesterlichen Exoduskomposition (K^{EX})." *TZ* 67 (2011): 223–62.

———. *Exodus*. 2 vols. ZBK 2. Zurich: TVZ, 2012–2015.
———. *A History of Israelite Religion in the Old Testament Period*. 2 vols. London: SCM, 1994.
———. "A Pentateuchal Redaction in the Book of Numbers?" *ZAW* 125 (2013): 220–33.
Auld, A. Graeme. "Leviticus: After Exodus and before Numbers" Pages 41–54 in *The Book of Leviticus: Composition and Reception*. Edited by Rolf Rendtorff and Robert A. Kugler. VTSup 93. Leiden: Brill, 2003.
———. "Leviticus at the Heart of the Pentateuch?" Pages 40–51 in *Reading Leviticus: A Conversation with Mary Douglas*. Edited by John F. A. Sawyer. JSOTSup 227. Sheffield: Sheffield Academic, 1996.
Baden, Joel. *J, E, and the Redaction of the Pentateuch*. FAT 68. Tübingen: Mohr Siebeck, 2009.
Berquist, Jon L. *Judaism in Persia's Shadow: A Social and Historical Approach*. Minneapolis: Fortress, 1995.
Blum, Erhard. *Die Komposition der Vätergeschichte*. WMANT 57. Neukirchen-Vluyn: Neukirchener Verlag, 1984.
———. "Die Literarische Verbindung von Erzvätern und Exodus: Ein Gespräch mit neueren Forschungshypothesen." Pages 119–56 in *Abschied vom Jahwisten: Die Komposition des Hexateuch in der jüngsten Diskussion*. Edited by Jan C. Gertz, Konrad Schmid, and Markus Witte. BZAW 315. Berlin: de Gruyter, 2002.
———. *Studien zur Komposition des Pentateuch*. BZAW 189. Berlin: de Gruyter, 1990.
Boccaccini, Gabriele. *Roots of Rabbinic Judaism: An Intellectual History, From Ezekiel to Daniel*. Grand Rapids: Eerdmans, 2001.
Carr, David M. *An Introduction to the Old Testament: Sacred Texts and Imperial Contexts of the Hebrew Bible*. Malden, MA: Wiley-Blackwell, 2010.
———. *Reading the Fractures of Genesis: Historical and Literary Approaches*. Louisville: Westminster John Knox, 1996.
Carter, Charles E. *The Emergence of Yehud in the Persian Period: A Social and Demographic Study*. JSOTSup 294. Sheffield: Sheffield Academic, 1999.
Crüsemann, Frank. *Die Tora: Theologie und Sozialgeschichte des alttestamentlichen Gesetzes*. Munich: Kaiser, 1992.
———. "Israel in der Perserzeit: Eine Skizze in Auseinandersetzung mit Max Weber." Pages 205–32 in *Max Webers Sicht des antiken Chris-*

tentums: Interpretation und Kritik. Edited by Wolfgang Schluchter. Frankfurt am Main: Suhrkamp, 1985.

Davies, Philip R. *Scribes and Schools: The Canonization of Hebrew Scriptures*. LAI. Louisville: Westminster John Knox, 1998.

Dietrich, Walter, Hans-Peter Mathys, Thomas Römer, and Rudolf Smend, eds. *Die Entstehung des Alten Testaments*. Theologische Wissenschaft: Sammelwerk für Studium und Beruf 1. Stuttgart: Kohlhammer, 2014.

Dozeman, Thomas B. *The Pentateuch: Introducing the Torah*. Introducing Israel's Scriptures. Minneapolis: Fortress, 2017.

Dozeman, Thomas B., and Konrad Schmid, eds. *A Farewell to the Yahwist: The Composition of the Pentateuch in Recent European Interpretation*. SymS 34. Atlanta: Society of Biblical Literature, 2006.

Finkelstein, Israel, and Thomas Römer. "Comments on the Historical Background of the Abraham Narrative: Between 'Realia' and 'Exegetica.'" *HBAI* 3 (2014): 3–23.

———. "Comments on the Historical Background of the Jacob Narrative in Genesis." *ZAW* 126 (2014): 317–38.

Frevel, Christian. *Mit Blick auf das Land die Schöpfung erinnern: Zum Ende der Priestergrundschrift*. HBS 23. Freiburg im Breisgau: Herder, 2000.

Garton, Roy E. *Mirages in the Desert: The Tradition-Historical Developments of the Story of Massah-Meribah*. Berlin: de Gruyter, 2017.

Genung, Matthew C. *The Composition of Genesis 37: Incoherence and Meaning in the Exposition of the Joseph Story*. FAT 2/95. Tübingen: Mohr Siebeck, 2017.

Germany, Stephen. *The Exodus-Conquest Narrative: The Composition of the Non-Priestly Narratives in Exodus–Joshua*. FAT 115. Tübingen: Mohr Siebeck, 2017.

Gerstenberger, Erhard S. *Israel in der Perserzeit: 5. und 4. Jahrhundert v. Chr.* Stuttgart: Kohlhammer, 2005.

Gertz, Jan C. *Tradition und Redaktion in der Exoduserzählung: Untersuchungen zur Endredaktion des Pentateuch*. FRLANT 186. Göttingen: Vandenhoeck & Ruprecht, 2000.

Gertz, Jan C., Bernard M. Levinson, Dalit Rom-Shiloni, and Konrad Schmid, eds. *The Formation of the Pentateuch: Bridging the Academic Cultures of Europe, Israel, and North America*. FAT 111. Tübingen: Mohr Siebeck, 2016.

Gertz, Jan C., Konrad Schmid, and Markus Witte, eds. *Abschied vom Jahwisten: Die Komposition des Hexateuch in der jüngsten Diskussion*. BZAW 215. Berlin: de Gruyter, 2002.

Giuntoli, Federico, and Konrad Schmid, eds. *The Post-Priestly Pentateuch: New Perspectives on Its Redactional Development and Theological Profiles*. FAT 101. Tübingen: Mohr Siebeck, 2015.

Gottwald, Norman K. *The Politics of Ancient Israel*. Louisville: Westminster John Knox, 2001.

Hanson, Paul D. *The Dawn of Apocalyptic: The Historical and Sociological Roots of Jewish Apocalyptic Eschatology*. Rev. ed. Philadelphia: Fortress, 1983.

Haran, Menahem. *The Biblical Collection: Its Consolidation to the End of the Second Temple Times and Changes of Form to the Middle Ages* [Hebrew]. 2 vols. Jerusalem: Magnes, 2004.

Hensel, Benedikt. *Juda und Samaria: Zum Verhältnis zweier nach-exilischer Jahwismen*. FAT 110. Tübingen: Mohr Siebeck, 2017.

Horsley, Richard A. *Scribes, Visionaries, and the Politics of Second Temple Judea*. Louisville: Westminster John Knox, 2007.

Jeon, Jaeyoung. *The Call of Moses and the Exodus Story: A Redactional-Critical Study in Exodus 3–4 and 5–13*. FAT 2/60. Tübingen: Mohr Siebeck, 2013.

———. "The Promise of the Land and the Extent of P." *ZAW* 130 (2018): 513–28.

Knauf, Ernst A. "Die Priesterschrift und die Geschichten der Deuteronomisten." Pages 101–18 in *The Future of the Deuteronomistic History*. Edited by Thomas Römer. BETL 147. Leuven: Peeters, 2000.

Kratz, Reinhard G. *The Composition of the Narrative Books of the Old Testament*. London: T&T Clark, 2005.

Köckert, Matthias. "Leben in Gottes Gegenwart: Zum Verstädnis des Gesetzes in der priesterschriftlichen Literatur." *Jahrbuch Biblische Theologie* 4 (1989): 29–61.

Kuenen, Abraham. *An Historico-critical Inquiry into the Origin and Composition of the Hexateuch (Pentateuch and Book of Joshua)*. Translated by Philip H. Wiksteed. London: Macmillan, 1886.

Levin, Christoph. *Der Jahwist*. FRLANT 157. Göttingen: Vandenhoeck & Ruprecht, 1993.

Lohfink, Norbert. "Die Priesterschrift und die Geschichte." Pages 213–53 in *Studien zum Pentateuch*. Edited by Norbert Lohfink. SBAB 4. Stuttgart: Katholisches Bibelwerk, 1988.

Mayes, Andrew D. H. *The Old Testament in Sociological Perspective*. London: Marshall Pickering, 1989.

Nihan, Christoph. *From Priestly Torah to Pentateuch: A Study in the Composition of the Book of Leviticus.* FAT 2/25. Tübingen: Mohr Siebeck, 2007.

Nihan, Cristophe, and Thomas Römer. "Le débat actuel sur la formation du Pentateuque." Pages 158–84 in *Introduction à l'Ancien Testament.* Edited by Thomas Römer, Jean-Daniel Macchi, and Christophe Nihan. 2nd ed. MdB 49. Geneva: Labor et Fides, 2009.

Noth, Martin. *Überlieferungsgeschichtliche Studien.* Halle: Niemeyer, 1943.

Otto, Eckart. *Das Deuteronomium im Pentateuch und Hexateuch: Studien zur Literaturgeschichte von Pentateuch und Hexateuch im Lichte des Deuteronomiumrahmens.* FAT 30. Tübingen: Mohr Siebeck, 2000.

———. "Forschungen zur Priesterschrift." *TRu* 62 (1997): 1–50.

———. *Max Webers Studien des antiken Judentums: Historische Grundlegung einer Theorie der Moderne.* Tübingen: Mohr Siebeck, 2011.

———. "Die nachpriesterschriftliche Pentateuchredaktion." Pages 61–111 in *Studies in the Book of Exodus: Redaction, Reception, Interpretation.* Edited by Marc Vervenne. BETL 126. Leuven: Leuven University Press, 1996.

Perlitt, Lothar. "Priesterschrift im Deuteronomoum?" *ZAW* 100 (1988): 65–88.

Pola, Thomas. *Die ursprüngliche Priesterschrift: Beobachtungen zur Literarkritik und Traditionsgeschichte von Pg.* WMANT 70. Neukirchen-Vluyn: Neukirchener Verlag, 1995.

Plöger, Otto. *Theokratie und Eschatologie.* WMANT 2. Neukirchen: Neukirchner Verlag, 1959.

Pury, Albert de. "Pg as the Absolute Beginning." Pages 99–128 in *Les dernières rédactions du Pentateuque, de l'Hexateuque et de l'Ennéateuque.* Edited by Thomas Römer and Konrad Schmid. BETL 203. Leuven: Peeters, 2007.

Rad, Gerhard von. *The Problem of the Hexateuch and Other Essays.* Translated by E. W. Trueman Dicken. New York: McGraw-Hill, 1966.

Rendtorff, Rolf. *Das überlieferungsgeschichtliche Problem des Pentateuch.* BZAW 147. Berlin: de Gruyter, 1977.

Römer, Thomas. "Der Pentateuch." Pages 52–166 in *Die Entstehung des Alten Testaments.* Edited by Walter Dietrich, Hans-Peter Mathys, Thomas Römer, and Rudolf Smend. Theologische Wissenschaft: Sammelwerk für Studium und Beruf 1. Stuttgart: Kohlhammer, 2014.

Rose, Martin. *Deuteronomist und Jahwist: Untersuchungen zu den berührungspunkten beider Literaturwerke.* ATANT 67. Zurich: TVZ, 1981.

Schmid, Hans H. *Der sogenannte Jahwist: Beobachtungen und Fragen zur Pentateuchforschung.* Zurich: TVZ, 1976.

Schmid, Konrad. "Genesis and Exodus as Two Formerly Independent Traditions of Origins of Ancient Israel." *Bib* 93 (2012): 187–208.

———. *Genesis and the Moses Story: Israel's Dual Origins in the Hebrew Bible.* Translated by James D. Nogalski. Siphrut 3. Winona Lake, IN: Eisenbrauns, 2010.

Schwartz, Baruch J. "Israel's Holiness: The Torah Traditions." Pages 47–59 in *Purity and Holiness: The Heritage of Leviticus.* Edited by Marcel Poorthuis and Joshua Schwartz. Jewish and Christian Perspectives Series 2. Leiden: Brill, 2000.

Ska, Jean-Louis. "Le récit sacerdotal: Une 'histoire sans fin'?" Pages 631–53 in *The Books of Leviticus and Numbers.* Edited by Thomas Römer. BETL 215. Leuven: Peeters, 2008.

Smith, Morton. *Palestinian Parties and Politics That Shaped the Old Testament.* 2nd ed. London: SCM, 1987.

Steck, Odil H. "Das Problem theologischer Strömungen in nachexilischer Zeit." *EvT* 28 (1969): 182–200.

Van Seters, John. *Abraham in History and Tradition.* New Haven: Yale University Press, 1975.

———. *The Life of Moses: The Yahwist as Historian in Exodus–Numbers.* Louisville: Westminster John Knox, 1994.

———. *Prologue to History: The Yahwist as Historian in Genesis.* Zurich: TVZ, 1992.

Weber, Max. *Das antike Judentum.* Vol. 3 of *Gesammelte Aufsätze zur Religionssoziologie.* Tübingen: Mohr Siebeck, 1921.

Weinberg, Joel. *The Citizen-Temple Community.* JSOTSup 15. Sheffield: JSOT Press, 1992.

Wellhausen, Julius. *Die Composition des Hexateuchs und der historischen Bücher des Alten Testaments.* 3rd ed. Berlin: Reimer, 1899.

Zenger, Erich. "Priesterschrift." *TRE* 27 (1997): 435–46.

Zenger, Erich, and Christian Frevel, eds. *Einleitung in das Alte Testament.* Kohlhammer Studienbücher Theologie 1.1. Stuttgart: Kohlhammer, 2012.

Textual, Historical, Sociological, and Ideological Cornerstones of the Formation of the Pentateuch

Konrad Schmid

Who wrote the Torah? In light of the ongoing disputes over this question in the wake of more than two hundred years of higher biblical criticism, the most precise answer to this question still is: we do not know.[1] The tradition claims it was Moses, but the Torah itself says otherwise. Only small portions within the Torah are traced back to him, such as Exod 17:14 (battle against Amalek); 24:4 (Covenant Code); 34:28 (Ten Commandments); Num 33:2 (wandering stations); Deut 31:9 (Deuteronomic law); and 31:22 (song of Moses).

On this question, no single, agreed-upon answer emerged from the proceedings of two major conferences of the research group "Convergence and Divergence in Pentateuchal Theory: Bridging the Academic Cultures of Israel, North America, and Europe," held in Jerusalem (2012–2013) at the Israel Institute of Advanced Studies.[2] It is fair to say that the second volume of conference papers produced by this group documents more

---

1. See, e.g., Thomas Römer, "Zwischen Urkunden, Fragmenten und Ergänzungen: Zum Stand der Pentateuchforschung," *ZAW* 125 (2013): 2–24; Römer, Jean-Daniel Macchi, and Christophe Nihan, eds., *Einleitung in das Alte Testament: Die Bücher der Hebräischen Bibel und die alttestamentlichen Schriften der katholischen, protestantischen und orthodoxen Kirchen* (Zurich: TVZ, 2013), 120–68; Römer, "Der Pentateuch," in *Die Entstehung des Alten Testaments*, ed. Walter Dietrich et al., Theologische Wissenschaft: Sammelwerk für Studium und Beruf 1 (Stuttgart: Kohlhammer, 2014), 52–166; Reinhard G. Kratz, "The Analysis of the Pentateuch: An Attempt to Overcome Barriers of Thinking," *ZAW* 128 (2016): 529–61; and Thomas B. Dozeman, *The Pentateuch: Introducing the Torah*, Introducing Israel's Scriptures (Minneapolis: Fortress, 2017).

2. Jan C. Gertz et al., eds., *The Formation of the Pentateuch: Bridging the Academic Cultures of Europe, Israel, and North America*, FAT 111 (Tübingen: Mohr Siebeck, 2016).

divergences than convergences among the positions in the field.³ The main benefit was apparently acknowledging our differences. Upon closer inspection, however, the situation in pentateuchal research is far from desperate, and there are indeed some basic statements that can be made regarding the formation of the Torah. This is what my present contribution is about. It is structured in the following three parts: (1) "The Textual Evidence of the Pentateuch," (2) "Sociohistorical Conditions for the Development of the Pentateuch," and (3) "Ideologies or Theologies of the Pentateuch in Their Historical Contexts."

1. The Textual Evidence of the Pentateuch

As with all exegetical questions, the initial questions are basic, yet crucial: What is the textual basis for the Pentateuch?⁴ What are the oldest manuscripts we have? At this point, one should mention the Codex Leningradensis.⁵ This manuscript of the Hebrew Bible dates to the year 1008 CE. It is a medieval text, but it is the oldest complete textual witness to the Pentateuch. This seems to leave us in a very awkward position: we are dealing with an allegedly 2,500-year-old text, but its earliest textual attestation is only 1,000 years old. Yet the situation is not hopeless.

First, there are ancient translations that significantly predate Codex Leningradensis. The oldest ones are the big codices of the translation of the Hebrew Bible into Greek, the earliest of which is the Codex Sinaiticus.⁶ While this text is not an original, it dates to the fourth century CE and is a good witness to the Hebrew text behind it. The Greek text of the Pentateuch shows differences from the Hebrew text, particularly in Exod 35–40. This issue was noted in 1862 by Julius Popper, who was the

---

3. This is especially true for the dispute between so-called neo-documentarian and redaction-critical approaches to the Pentateuch. See, e.g., the discussion between Joel S. Baden, "The Continuity of the Non-Priestly Narrative from Genesis to Exodus," *Bib* 93 (2012): 161–86; and Konrad Schmid, "Genesis and Exodus as Two Formerly Independent Traditions of Origins for Ancient Israel," *Bib* 93 (2012): 187–208.

4. Armin Lange, "From Many to One: Some Thoughts on the Hebrew Textual History of the Torah," in Gertz et al., *Formation of the Pentateuch*, 121–95.

5. Emanuel Tov, *Textual Criticism of the Bible*, 3rd ed. (Minneapolis: Fortress, 2012), 23–74.

6. David C. Parker, *Codex Sinaiticus: The Story of the World's Oldest Bible* (London: British Library, 2010).

first to deal extensively and deliberately with post-Priestly (or [post-]P) expansions in the Pentateuch.⁷

Second, there are older, preserved portions of the Pentateuch in Hebrew. Before 1947, the oldest extant fragment of a biblical text was the Nash Papyrus, which probably dates around 100 BCE and contains both the Decalogue and the beginning of the Shema from Deut 6.⁸

Much more important were the textual discoveries from the Dead Sea that began in 1947.⁹ Remnants of about nine hundred scrolls were discovered, among them many biblical texts. They date mainly from the second and first centuries BCE. Most of the texts are fragmentary, many of them no larger than a few square centimeters. All of the biblical fragments are accessible in Eugene Ulrich's *The Biblical Qumran Scrolls*.¹⁰

What do these Qumran texts reveal about the Pentateuch in the early, postbiblical period? The most important insight is the remarkable closeness of these fragments, as far as they have been preserved, to Codex Leningradensis. In the case of Gen 1:1–5 in 4QGen^b, no differences are present at all.¹¹

Nevertheless, the various scrolls seem to display affiliations to the traditionally known, post-70 CE textual families of the Pentateuch. Armin Lange gives the following estimate: 37.5 percent are proto-Masoretic, 5.0 percent are proto-Samaritan, 5.0 percent are proto-Septuagint, and 52.5 percent are independent.¹² In these figures, there is some prevalence of the proto-Masoretic strand, although one observes a significant number of independent readings. At times the differences are quite relevant, such as the reading of "Elohim" instead of "YHWH" in Gen 22:14 or of "Mount

---

7. Julius Popper, *Der biblische Bericht über die Stiftshütte: Ein Beitrag zur Geschichte der Composition und Diaskeue des Pentateuch* (Leipzig: Heinrich Hunger, 1862). See also Martha L. Wade, *Consistency of Translation Techniques in the Tabernacle Accounts of Exodus in the Old Greek*, SCS 49 (Atlanta: Society of Biblical Literature, 2003).

8. Tov, *Textual Criticism*, 111. However, this text is more liturgical than biblical in nature.

9. Armin Lange, *Die Handschriften biblischer Bücher von Qumran und den anderen Fundorten*, vol. 1 of *Handbuch der Textfunde vom Toten Meer* (Tübingen: Mohr Siebeck, 2009); and Géza G. Xeravits and Peter Porzig, *Einführung in die Qumranliteratur: Die Handschriften vom Toten Meer* (Berlin: de Gruyter, 2015), 23–47.

10. Eugene Ulrich, *The Biblical Qumran Scrolls: Transcriptions and Textual Variants*, VTSup 134 (Leiden: Brill, 2010), with the pentateuchal passages on 1–246.

11. Ulrich, *Biblical Qumran Scrolls*, 1–2.

12. Lange, *Die Handschriften*, 155.

Gerizim" instead of "Mount Ebal" in Deut 27:4 (although the latter fragment might be a forgery).[13] However, Emanuel Tov has stated the following about the large portion of proto-Masoretic texts: "The differences between these texts [the proto-Masoretic texts] and L [Codex Leningradensis] are negligible, and in fact their nature resembles the internal differences between the medieval manuscripts themselves."[14] The Qumran findings thus provide an important starting point for pentateuchal exegesis and corroborate the legitimacy of critically using the Masoretic Text (MT) in pentateuchal research. On the one hand, we can have considerable confidence in the Hebrew text of the Pentateuch, as attested in the medieval manuscript of Codex Leningradensis, which is the textual basis for most modern Bible editions. On the other hand, at the time, there was apparently not a fully stable text of the Pentateuch in terms of every single letter or word being fixed as part of a fully canonized Bible, as the differences between the scrolls show.[15]

In terms of the composition of the Pentateuch, another insight that we can deduce from Qumran is that the Pentateuch was basically finished no later than the second century BCE. Some of its texts are certainly much older, but probably none of them are later.

One epigraphical piece relating to our concerns should be mentioned: a quasi-biblical text from biblical times. The silver amulets from Ketef Hinnom, which can be dated anywhere between the seventh and the second centuries BCE, contain a text close to Num 6:24–26. However, this quasi-biblical text is not really a witness to the Bible.[16]

---

13. On Gen 22:14, see Thomas Römer, "Le 'sacrifice d'Abraham', un texte élohiste? Quelques observations à partir de Gn 22,14 et d'un fragment de Qumran," *Sem* 54 (2012): 163–72. On Deut 27:4, see Siegfried Kreuzer, *Geschichte, Sprache und Text: Studien zum Alten Testament und seiner Umwelt*, BZAW 479 (Berlin: de Gruyter, 2015), 151–54.

14. Emanuel Tov, "The Text of the Hebrew/Aramaic and Greek Bible Used in the Ancient Synagogues," in *The Ancient Synagogue from Its Origins until 200 C.E.: Papers Presented at an International Conference at Lund University, October 14–17, 2001*, ed. Birger Olsson and Magnus Zetterholm, ConBNT 39 (Stockholm: Almqvist & Wiksell, 2003), 237–59.

15. Lester L. Grabbe, "The Law, the Prophets, and the Rest: The State of the Bible in Pre-Maccabean Times," *DSD* 13 (2006): 319–38.

16. Angelika Berlejung, "Der gesegnete Mensch: Text und Kontext von Num 6,22–27 und den Silberamuletten von Ketef Hinnom," in *Mensch und König: Studien zur Anthropologie des Alten Testaments; Rüdiger Lux zum 60. Geburtstag*, ed. Angelika

2. Sociohistorical Conditions for the Development of the Pentateuch

How should we imagine the cultural-historical background of the Pentateuch's composition? A very insightful book by Christopher Rollston brings together all of the relevant evidence regarding writing and literacy in ancient Israel.[17] In addition, Matthieu Richelle and Erhard Blum have recently published important contributions that evaluate the evidence of scribal activities in early Israel and Judah.[18]

The first question here is: Who could actually read and write? We have different estimates for the ancient world, but they agree that probably not more than 5–10 percent of the population was literate to a degree that individuals could read and write texts of some length. Literacy was probably an elite phenomenon, and texts were circulated only within these circles, which were centered around the palace and the temple.[19] In biblical times, producing literature was an enterprise mainly restricted to professional scribes, and reading literature was generally limited to the same circles that produced it.

Berlejung and Raik Heckl, HBS 53 (Freiburg im Breisgau: Herder, 2008), 37–62; Berlejung, "Ein Programm fürs Leben: Theologisches Wort und anthropologischer Ort der Silberamulette von Ketef Hinnom," *ZAW* 120 (2008): 204–30.

17. Chris Rollston, *Writing and Literacy in the World of Ancient Israel*, ABS 11 (Atlanta: Society of Biblical Literature, 2010). See also Ron E. Tappy and P. Kyle McCarter, eds. *Literate Culture and Tenth-Century Canaan: The Tel Zayit Abecedary in Context* (Winona Lake, IN: Eisenbrauns, 2008).

18. Mattheiu Richelle, "Elusive Scrolls: Could Any Hebrew Literature Have Been Written Prior to the Eighth Century BCE?," *VT* 66 (2016): 556–94; and Erhard Blum, "Die altaramäischen Wandinschriften aus Tell Deir 'Alla und ihr institutioneller Kontext," in *Metatexte: Erzählungen von schrifttragenden Artefakten in der alttestamentlichen und mittelalterlichen Literatur*, ed. Friedrich-Emanuel Focken and Michael R. Ott, Materiale Textkulturen 15 (Berlin: de Gruyter, 2016), 21–52.

19. See, e.g., Rollston, *Writing and Literacy*, 127–33; David M. Carr, *Writing on the Tablet of the Heart: Origins of Scripture and Literature* (Oxford: Oxford University Press, 2005), 70–71, 165–66, 172–73, 187–91; Carr, *The Formation of the Hebrew Bible: A New Reconstruction* (Oxford: Oxford University Press, 2011), 128–29; and Catherine Hezser, *Jewish Literacy in Roman Palestine*, TSAJ 81 (Tübingen: Mohr Siebeck, 2001). Philip S. Alexander, "Literacy among Jews in Second Temple Palestine: Reflections on the Evidence from Qumran," in *Hamlet on a Hill: Semitic and Greek Studies Presented to Professor T. Muraoka on the Occasion of His Sixty-Fifth Birthday*, ed. Martin F. J. Baasten and W. Th. van Peursen, OLA 118 (Leuven: Peeters, 2003), 3–25, reckons with widespread literacy among members of the Qumran community.

Recently, Israel Finkelstein and others have claimed that the Lachish ostraca show at least six different hands, pointing to more widespread literacy even among soldiers in the early sixth century BCE.[20] But this kind of evidence remains debatable.

Othmar Keel, Richelle, and others have argued for a continuous literary tradition in Jerusalem from the Bronze Age city state to the early Iron Age.[21] While this perspective is probably not entirely wrong, it should not be overestimated. Abdi-Hepa's Jerusalem was quite different from David or Solomon's Jerusalem, and there was obviously a cultural break between Late Bronze and early Iron Age Jerusalem. A case in point would be the new Ophel inscription from Jerusalem, which exhibits a rather rudimentary level of linguistic education.[22]

A second question is: How did people write? Most of the inscriptions we have are on potsherds or stone, but this is only what has survived. For obvious reasons, texts on stone or clay last much longer than those on papyrus or leather, so we cannot simply determine what people wrote on in general from what archaeologists have found. (In fact, there is only a single papyrus sheet left from the time of the monarchy, Mur. 17).[23] In addition, we have an impressive number of seals and bullae from Jerusalem during the First Temple period with remnants of papyrus on them that prove that papyrus was a common medium for writing. Some of the bullae bear names such as Gemaryahu ben Shafan, who is mentioned in Jer 36:10, or Yehuchal ben Shelamayahu and Gedaliah ben Pashhur, whom we know from Jer 38:1.[24]

---

20. Shira Faigenbaum-Golovin et al., "Algorithmic Handwriting Analysis of Judah's Military Correspondence Sheds Light on Composition of Biblical Texts," *Proceedings of the National Academy of Sciences of the United States of America* 113 (2016): 4664–69.

21. Othmar Keel, *Die Geschichte Jerusalems und die Entstehung des Monotheismus*, 2 vols., Orte und Landschaften der Bibel 4.1 (Göttingen: Vandenhoeck & Ruprecht, 2007), 101–32; Rollston, *Writing and Literacy*; and Tappy and McCarter, *Literate Culture*.

22. Reinhard G. Lehmann and Anna E. Zernecke, "Bemerkungen und Beobactungen zu der neuen Ophel Pithosinschrift," in *Schrift und Sprache: Papers read at the 10th Mainz International Colloquium on Ancient Hebrew (MICAH), Mainz, 28–30 October 2011*, ed. Reinhard G. Lehmann and Anna E. Zernecke, Kleine Untersuchungen zur Sprache des Alten Testaments und seiner Umwelt 15 (Kamen: Spenner, 2013), 437–50.

23. Published in Pierre Benoit, J. T. Milik, and Roland de Vaux, *Les grottes des Murabba'at*, DJD 2 (Oxford: Clarendon, 1961), 93–100.

24. See the discussion in Richelle, *Elusive Scrolls*.

In all likelihood, the writing material for texts such as those in the Pentateuch was papyrus or leather. Longer books needed to be written on leather because papyrus sheets are fragile. The ink was composed of grime and metal. Scholars estimate that it took a professional scribe six months to copy a book the length of Genesis or Isaiah. If one adds the value of the sheep skins, it is evident how costly the production of such a scroll would have been.

In biblical times, copies of the books of the Bible were probably few in number. For the second century BCE, 2 Macc 2:13–15 provides evidence that the Jewish community in Alexandria, likely among the largest diaspora groups, did not possess a copy of every biblical book. This text quotes a letter from the Jerusalemites to the Jews in Alexandria that invites them to borrow a copy of those biblical books from Jerusalem that they do not possess. "Nehemiah…founded a library and collected the books about the kings and prophets, and the writings of David.… In the same way Judas [Maccabaeus] also collected all the books that had been lost on account of the war that had come upon us, and they are in our possession. So if you have need of them, send people to get them for you" (2 Macc 2:13–15).

But when was the Pentateuch composed? It is helpful at the outset to determine a time span in which its texts were written. In biblical scholarship, the terms *terminus a quo* and *terminus ad quem* are often used to delimit such a time span. The *terminus a quo* indicates the earliest point at which a text could have been written, while the *terminus ad quem* is the latest point at which it could have been written.

For the former (*terminus a quo*), an important clarification is needed. We can only determine the beginnings of the earliest *written* versions of a text. In other words, this does not include a text's oral prehistory. Many texts in the Bible, especially in the Pentateuch, go back to oral traditions that can be much older than their written counterparts. So the *terminus a quo* only determines the beginning of the written transmission of a text which, in turn, may have already been known as an oral tale or the like.[25] Unlike many prophetic texts, pentateuchal texts do not mention dates of authorship. One must therefore look for internal and external indicators in order to determine the date of their composition.

---

25. Odil H. Steck, *Old Testament Exegesis: A Guide to the Methodology*, trans. James D. Nogalski, RBS 33 (Atlanta: Scholars Press, 1995), 65–78. See also Harald-Martin Wahl, *Die Jakobserzählungen: Studien zu ihrer mündlichen Überlieferung, Verschriftung und Historizität*, BZAW 258 (Berlin: de Gruyter, 1997).

This basic observation is relevant for determining the *beginning* of the Pentateuch's literary formation. We can safely determine a historical break in the cultural development of Israel and Judah in the ninth and eighth centuries BCE. This point holds despite Richelle and Blum, who provide sufficient evidence to include the late ninth century as the beginning of this watershed with regard to the development of scribal culture in Israel and Judah.[26] By this point, a certain level of statehood and literacy was being achieved, and these two elements go together. That is, the more developed a state, the more bureaucracy and education are needed, especially in the area of writing.

When one considers the number of inscriptions found in ancient Israel and Judah, the numbers clearly increase in the eighth century, and this increase should probably be interpreted as indicating a cultural development in ancient Israel and Judah. This claim can be corroborated by looking at the texts that have been found that can be dated to the tenth century BCE, such as the Gezer calendar, the potsherd from Jerusalem, the Baal inscription from Beth Shemesh, the Tel Zayit abecedary, and the Qeiyafa ostracon.[27] All of them stem from or around the tenth century BCE. The modesty of their content and writing style alike are easy to discern.

If we move forward about one century to the ninth century BCE, then the evidence is much more telling, even if some of the evidence is in Aramaic and not Hebrew. The first monumental stela from the region is the Mesha stela, which is written in Moabite and which contains the first documented reference to YHWH and Israel as we know them.[28] Another monumental text is the Tel Dan stela in Aramaic, best known for mentioning the "Beth

---

26. Richelle, "Elusive Scrolls"; Blum, "Die altaramäischen Wandinschriften."

27. On the Gezer calendar, see, e.g., Dennis Pardee, "Gezer Calendar," *OEANE* 2:396–400; and Daniel Sivan, "The Gezer Calendar and Northwest Semitic Linguistics," *IEJ* 48 (1998): 101–5. On the Jerusalem potsherd, see Lehmann and Zernecke, "Bemerkungen und Beobactungen." On the Beth Shemesh inscription, see P. Kyle McCarter, Shelomoh Bunimovitz, and Zvi Lederman, "An Archaic Ba'l Inscription from Tel Beth-Shemesh," *TA* 38 (2011): 179–93. On the Tel Zayit abecedary, see Rollston, *Writing and Literacy*; Tappy and McCarter, *Literate Culture*. And on Qeiyafa, see Silvia Schroer and Stefan Münger, eds., *Khirbet Qeiyafa in the Shephelah: Papers Presented at a Colloquium of the Swiss Society for Ancient Near Eastern Studies Held at the University of Bern, September 6, 2014*, OBO 282 (Fribourg: Academic Press; Göttingen: Vandenhoeck & Ruprecht, 2017).

28. J. Andrew Dearman, ed., *Studies in the Mesha Inscription and Moab*, ABS 2 (Atlanta: Scholars Press, 1989).

David."[29] Still another piece of evidence is the eighth-century Aramaic wall inscription from Tell Deir ʿAlla, which mentions the prophet Balaam who appears in Num 22–24.[30] Balaam's story in the inscription is completely different from the narrative about him in the Bible, yet it remains one of the earliest pieces of evidence for a literary text in the vicinity of ancient Israel. Along with others, Blum has recently argued convincingly for interpreting the site of Tell Deir ʿAlla as a school, based on a late Hellenistic parallel to the building architecture that was found at Trimithis in Egypt (ca. fourth century CE).[31] This interpretation as a school might also be true for Kuntillet ʿAjrud, where we also have writing on the wall.[32]

The landmark set in the ninth and eighth centuries BCE by the large number and high quality of written texts in ancient Israel and Judah corresponds to another relevant feature. At this time, Israel begins to be perceived by its neighbors as a state. That is, not only internal changes in the development of writing, but also external, contemporaneous perceptions hint at Israel and Judah having reached a level of cultural development in the ninth and eighth centuries that enabled literary text production. Good examples are the mid-ninth century inscriptions from Assyria that mention Jehu, the man of Bit-Humri, which means Jehu of the house of Omri. The Black Obelisk even displays Jehu in a picture, bowing in front of the Assyrian king—the oldest extant image of an Israelite.[33]

---

29. George Athas, *The Tel Dan Inscription: A Reappraisal and a New Interpretation* (London: Continuum, 2005).

30. Helga Weippert and Manfred Weippert, "Die 'Bileam'-Inschrift von Tel Deir 'Alla," *ZDPV* 98 (1982): 77–103; Erhard Blum, "Verstehst du dich nicht auf die Schreibkunst…? Ein weisheitlicher Dialog über Vergänglichkeit und Verantwortung: Kombination II der Wandinschrift vom Tell Deir 'Alla," in *Was ist der Mensch, dass du seiner gedenkst? (Psalm 8,5): Aspekte einer theologischen Anthropologie; Festschrift für Bernd Janowski zum 65. Geburtstag*, ed. Michaela Bauks, Kathrin Liess, and Peter Riede (Neukirchen-Vluyn: Neukirchener Verlag, 2008), 33–53; and Blum, "Die Kombination I der Wandinschrift vom Tell Deir 'Alla: Vorschläge zur Rekonstruktion mit historisch-kritischen Anmerkungen," in *Berührungspunkte: Studien zur Sozial- und Religionsgeschichte Israels und seiner Umwelt; Festschrift für Rainer Albertz zu seinem 65. Geburtstag*, ed. Ingo Kottsieper, Rüdiger Schmitt, and Jakob Wöhrle, AOAT 350 (Münster: Ugarit, 2008), 573–601.

31. Blum, "Die altaramäischen Wandinschriften."

32. Zeev Meshel, ed., *Kuntillet ʿAjrud (Horvat Teman): An Iron Age II Religious Site on the Judah-Sinai Border* (Jerusalem: Israel Antiquities Authority, 2012).

33. Othmar Keel and Cristoph Uehlinger, "Der Assyrerkönig Salmanassar III. und Jehu von Israel auf dem Schwarzen Obelisken," *ZKT* 116 (1994): 391–420.

Based on these observations about the development of scribal culture in ancient Israel, we can assume that the earliest texts in the Pentateuch may have originated as literary pieces as early as the ninth and eighth centuries BCE. But, to repeat, this chronological claim pertains only to their literary shape, whereas the oral traditions behind them could be much older, perhaps at times reaching back into the second millennium BCE.

When was the Pentateuch finished? On this matter, three areas of evidence should be named. First, there is the translation into Greek, the Septuagint, which can be dated to the mid-second century BCE.[34] There are some differences, especially in the second account of the construction of the tabernacle in Exod 35–40, but the Septuagint basically points to a completed Pentateuch.[35] Second, the books of Chronicles and Ezra–Nehemiah, which probably date to the fourth century BCE, refer to a textual

---

34. See, e.g., Folker Siegert, *Zwischen Hebräischer Bibel und Altem Testament: Eine Einführung in die Septuaginta*, Münsteraner judaistische Studien 9 (Münster: Lit, 2001), 42–43; Manfred Görg, "Die Septuaginta im Kontext spätägyptischer Kultur: Beispiele lokaler Inspiration bei der Übersetzungsarbeit am Pentateuch," in *Im Brennpunkt: Die Septuaginta: Studien zur Entstehung und Bedeutung der Griechischen Bibel*, ed. Heinz-Josef Fabry and Ulrich Offerhaus, BWANT 153 (Stuttgart: Kohlhammer, 2001), 115–30; Siegfried Kreuzer, "Entstehung und Entwicklung der Septuaginta im Kontext alexandrinischer und frühjüdischer Kultur und Bildung," in *Septuaginta Deutsch: Erläuterungen und Kommentare zum griechischen Alten Testament*, ed. Martin Karrer and Wolfgang Kraus, 2 vols. (Stuttgart: Deutsche Bibelgesellschaft, 2011), 1:3–39; Stefan Krauter, "Die Pentateuch-Septuaginta als Übersetzung in der Literaturgeschichte der Antike," in *Die Septuaginta und das frühe Christentum; The Septuagint and Christian Origins*, ed. Thomas S. Caulley and Hermann Lichtenberger, WUNT 277 (Tübingen: Mohr Siebeck, 2011), 26–46; and Felix Albrecht, "Die alexandrinische Bibelübersetzung: Einsichten zur Entstehungs-, Überlieferungs- und Wirkungsgeschichte der Septuaginta," in *Alexandria*, ed. Tobias Georges, Felix Albrecht, and Reinhard Feldmeier, Civitatum orbis Mediterranei studia 1 (Tübingen: Mohr Siebeck, 2013), 209–43. The oldest manuscript of the Greek Pentateuch is P. Rylands 458, dating to the mid-second century BCE; see John W. Wevers, "The Earliest Witness to the LXX Deuteronomy," *CBQ* 39 (1977): 240–44; Kristin De Troyer, "When Did the Pentateuch Come into Existence? An Uncomfortable Perspective," in *Die Septuaginta: Texte, Kontexte, Lebenswelten, Internationale Fachtagung veranstaltet von Septuaginta Deutsch (LXX.D), Wuppertal 20.–23. Juli 2006*, ed. Martin Karrer and Wolfgang Kraus, WUNT 219 (Tübingen: Mohr Siebeck, 2008), 277; and Gilles Dorival, "Les origins de la Septante: La traduction en grec des cinq livres de la Torah," in *La Bible grecque de Septante*, ed. Gilles Dorival, Marguerite Harl, and Olivier Munnich (Paris: Cerf, 1988), 39–82.

35. E.g., John W. Wevers, "The Building of the Tabernacle," *JNSL* 19 (1993): 123–31.

body called either the "Torah of YHWH" or the "Torah of Moses." It is not clear whether this denotes an already-completed Pentateuch, but it at least points in this direction.³⁶ Third, the Pentateuch has no clear allusion to the fall of the Persian Empire in the wake of Alexander the Great's conquests.³⁷ The Persian Empire lasted from 539 to 333 BCE, a period perceived in ancient Israel as one of political stability, in some texts even marking the end of history. The loss of this political order was accompanied by numerous questions. Especially in prophetic literature, this event was interpreted as a cosmic judgment. But no text in the Pentateuch seems to allude to the event, either directly or indirectly. Therefore, the Pentateuch seems *basically* to be a pre-Hellenistic text, predating Alexander the Great and the Hellenization of the East.

However, there are a few exceptions to the pre-Hellenistic origins of the Pentateuch. The best candidate for a post-Persian, Hellenistic text in the Pentateuch seems to be the so-called small apocalypse in Num 24:14–24, which in verse 24 mentions the victory of the ships of the Kittim over Ashur and Eber. This text seems to allude to the battles between Alexander and the Persians, as some scholars have suggested.³⁸ Other post-Persian elements might be the specific numbers in the genealogies of Gen 5 and

---

36. Félix García López, "תורה," *ThWAT* 8:597–637, esp. 627–30; and Georg Steins, "Torabindung und Kanonabschluss: Zur Entstehung und kanonischen Funktion der Chronikbücher," in *Die Tora als Kanon für Juden und Christen*, ed. Erich Zenger, HBS 10 (Freiburg: Herder, 1996), 213–56.

37. Odil H. Steck, *Bereitete Heimkehr: Jesaja 35 als redaktionelle Brücke zwischen dem Ersten und dem Zweiten Jesaja*, SBS 121 (Stuttgart: Katholisches Bibelwerk, 1985), 52–54; Willem A. M. Beuken, *Jesaja 28–39*, HThKAT (Freiburg: Herder, 2010), 300–327; and Konrad Schmid, "Das kosmische Weltgericht in den Prophetenbüchern und seine historischen Kontexte," in *Nächstenliebe und Gottesfurcht: Beiträge aus alttestamentlicher, semitistischer und altorientalischer Wissenschaft für Hans-Peter Mathys zum 65. Geburtstag*, ed. Hanna Jenni and Markus Saur, AOAT 439 (Münster: Ugarit, 2016), 409–34.

38. See Hedwige Rouillard, *La péricope de Balaam (Nombres 22–24)*, EBib 2/4 (Paris: Gabalda, 1985), 467; Frank Crüsemann, *Die Tora: Theologie und Sozialgeschichte des alttestamentlichen Gesetzes* (Munich: Kaiser, 1992), 403; and Hans-Christoph Schmitt, "Der heidnische Mantiker als eschatologischer Jahweprophet: Zum Verständnis Bileams in der Endgestalt von Num 22–24," in *"Wer ist wie du, Herr, unter den Göttern?": Studien zur Theologie und Religionsgeschichte Israels; für Otto Kaiser zum 70. Geburtstag*, ed. Ingo Kottsieper (Göttingen: Vandenhoeck & Ruprecht, 1994), 185.

11.[39] These numbers build the overall chronology of the Pentateuch and differ significantly from one version to another. But these exceptions are minor. The substance of the Pentateuch seems to be pre-Hellenistic.

3. Ideologies or Theologies of the Pentateuch in Their Historical Contexts

If we can assume with some probability that the Pentateuch was written between the ninth and the fourth centuries BCE, how can we reconstruct its literary genesis in greater detail? We should begin by making a very general observation. Ancient Israel is part of the ancient Near East. Ancient Israel was a small political entitiy surrounded by greater, and much older, empires in Egpyt and Mesopotamia. It is therefore more than likely that Israel's literature was deeply influenced by its neighbors and their ideologies and theologies.[40] An extraordinary piece of evidence of cultural transfer is a fragment of the Gilgamesh Epic (dating to the fourteenth century BCE) found in Megiddo in northern Israel. The fragment proves that Mesopotamian literature was known and read in the Levant. Also noteworthy is the text of Darius's late-sixth-century Bisitun inscription both in Persia and in Egypt, where it existed as an Aramaic translation.

Of course, there are independent traditions in ancient Israel that are not paralleled in other ancient Near Eastern material. But some of the most prominent texts in the Pentateuch creatively adapt the ancient world's knowledge, and it is important to discern this background in order to understand the biblical texts and their own emphases properly.

Addressing this topic exhaustively is not possible at the moment. Instead, I will pick out two well-known examples to demonstrate how prominent biblical texts arose as receptions and adaptions of ancient Near Eastern imperial ideologies. That does not mean that the Bible is not an

---

39. See Jeremy Hughes, *Secrets of the Times: Myth and History in Biblical Chronology*, JSOTSup 66 (Sheffield: JSOT Press, 1990). See the reservations of Ronald Hendel, "A Hasmonean Edition of MT Genesis? The Implications of the Editions of the Chronology in Genesis 5," *HBAI* 1 (2012): 448–64, against dating the numbers in MT to the second century BCE.

40. Konrad Schmid, "Anfänge politikförmiger Religion: Die Theologisierung politisch-imperialer Begriffe in der Religionsgeschichte des antiken Israel als Grundlage autoritärer und toleranter Strukturmomente monotheistischer Religionen," in *Religion–Wirtschaft–Politik: Forschungszugänge zu einem aktuellen transdisziplinären Feld*, ed. Antonius Liedhegener, Andreas Tunger-Zanetti, and Stephan Wirz (Baden-Baden: Nomos, 2011), 161–77.

original text. What it does mean is that the Bible's originality and creativity are to be found not necessarily in the materials it contains but in its interpretive adaptations of these materials.

The first example of how the ancient Near East shaped the Pentateuch has to do with the Neo-Assyrian Empire, the preeminent power in the ancient world of the ninth and seventh centuries BCE.[41] Its ideology was based on the strict submission of the Assyrian king's subordinates as portrayed in this image: here, the Assyrian king is the master, and all other kings are to serve him.

The Assyrians secured their power through treaties with their vassals. These treaties usually have a three-part structure: an introduction, a corpus of stipulations, and a concluding section with blessings and curses. It is noteworthy that the book of Deuteronomy exhibits this same structure, apparently having been shaped according to the model of an Assyrian vassal treaty. But there is one big difference: The function of Assyrian vassal treaties was to oblige subdued people *to the Assyrian king* in terms of absolute loyalty. The book of Deuteronomy likewise demands absolute loyalty from the people of Israel, but *to God*, not the Assyrian king. So the book of Deuteronomy seems to take up both the structure and the basic concept of an Assyrian vassal treaty, which it reinterprets at the same time.[42] With Eckart Otto, Thomas Römer, Nathan MacDonald, and others, we therefore can maintain that at least a core of Deuteronomy originated in the late Neo-Assyrian period in an anti-Assyrian milieu of scribes.[43]

---

41. Angelika Berlejung, "The Assyrians in the West: Assyrianization, Colonialism, Indifference, or Development Policy?," in *Congress Volume Helsinki 2010*, ed. Martti Nissinen, VTSup 148 (Leiden: Brill, 2012), 21–60; and Eckart Otto, "Assyria and Judean Identity: Beyond the Religionsgeschichtliche Schule," in *Literature as Politics, Politics as Literature: Essays in Honor of Peter Machinist*, ed. David S. Vanderhooft and Abraham Winitzer (Winona Lake, IN: Eisenbrauns, 2013), 339–47.

42. See, e.g., Eckart Otto, *Das Deuteronomium: Politische Theologie und Rechtsreform in Juda und Assyrien*, BZAW 284 (Berlin: de Gruyter, 1999). For a more differentiated view, see Christoph Koch, *Vertrag, Treueid und Bund: Studien zur Rezeption des altorientalischen Vertragsrechts im Deuteronomium und zur Ausbildung der Bundestheologie im Alten Testament*, BZAW 383 (Berlin: de Gruyter, 2008); and, differently, Carly L. Crouch, *Israel and the Assyrians: Deuteronomy, the Succession Treaty of Esarhaddon, and the Nature of Subversion*, ANEM 8 (Atlanta: SBL Press, 2014).

43. Nathan MacDonald, "Issues in the Dating of Deuteronomy: A Response to Juha Pakkala," *ZAW* 122 (2010): 431–35. For a different view, see Reinhard G. Kratz, "Der literarische Ort des Deuteronomiums," in *Liebe und Gebot: Studien zum Deuteronomium;*

A second example of how the ancient Near East shaped the Pentateuch has to do with the Persian Empire. In 539 BCE, the Babylonian Empire was overthrown by the Persians, after which the Persians ruled the entire ancient world, as it was known in that part of the globe, for the next two hundred years. Persian rule was perceived by many people in the Levant as peaceful, with the era being seen as a quiet one, during which various peoples could live according to their own culture, language, and religion. In the Hebrew Bible, nearly every foreign nation is addressed with very harsh curses except for the Persians, probably due to their tolerant policy toward those whom they subdued.

In the Pentateuch, we can locate some indications of Persian imperial ideology. A very telling piece is the table of nations in Gen 10. This text explains the order or the world after the flood, and it structures the seventy people of the globe according to the offspring of Shem, Ham, and Japheth, including three, nearly identical refrains:[44]

בני יפת ... בארצתם איש ללשנו למשפחתם בגויהם
The sons of Japheth ... in their lands, with their own language, by their families, by their nations. (Gen 10:2, 5)

אלה בני־חם למשפחתם ללשנתם בארצתם בגויהם
These are the sons of Ham, by their families, by their languages, in their lands, and by their nations. (Gen 10:20)

אלה בני־שם למשפחתם ללשנתם בארצתם לגויהם
These are the sons of Shem, by their families, by their languages, in their lands, and by their nations. (Gen 10:31)

Festschrift zum 70. Geburtstag von Lothar Perlitt, ed. Reinhard G. Kratz and Hermann Spieckermann, FRLANT 190 (Göttingen: Vandenhoeck & Ruprecht, 2000), 101–20; Juha Pakkala, "The Date of the Oldest Edition of Deuteronomy," ZAW 121 (2009): 388–401; and Pakkala, "The Dating of Deuteronomy: A Response to Nathan MacDonald," ZAW 123 (2011): 431–36.

44. J. G. Vink, "The Date and the Origin of the Priestly Code in the Old Testament," in *The Priestly Code and Seven Other Studies*, OtSt 15 (Leiden: Brill, 1969), 61; Ernst A. Knauf, "Die Priesterschrift und die Geschichten der Deuteronomisten," in *The Future of the Deuteronomistic History*, ed. Thomas Römer, BETL 147 (Leuven: Peeters, 2000), 104–5; and Christophe Nihan, *From Priestly Torah to Pentateuch: A Study in the Composition of the Book of Leviticus*, FAT 2/25 (Tübingen: Mohr Siebeck, 2007), 383. See also Jacques Vermeylen, "La 'table des nations' (Gn 10): Yaphet figure-t-il l'Empire perse?," Transeu 5 (1992): 113–32.

At first glance, these texts may not look very interesting. But they are quite revolutionary insofar as they tell us that the world is ordered in a pluralistic way. After the flood, God intended humanity to live in different nations, with different lands and different languages. Genesis 10 is probably a Persian-period text reflecting this basic conviction of Persian imperial ideology. The same ideology is also attested, for example, in the Bisitun inscription, which was disseminated widely throughout the Persian Empire.[45] The Persian imperial inscriptions declare that every nation belongs to their specific region and has its specific cultural identities (see DNa 30–38; XPh 28–35; DB I 61–71). This structure results from the will of the creator deity, as Klaus Koch pointed out in his *Reichsidee und Reichsorganisation im Perserreich*, where he identifies this structure as *Nationalitätenstaat als Schöpfungsgegebenheit*.[46] Every people should live according to its own tradition and in its own place. This is a radically different political view when compared to the Assyrians and Babylonians, both of whom strove to destroy other national identities, especially by means of deportation. The Persians deported no one, and they allowed people to rebuild their own sanctuaries, such as the temple in Jerusalem that the Babylonians had destroyed.

Once again, though, Gen 10 is not merely a piece of Persian imperial propaganda. It also includes important interpretive changes. Specifically, it is not the Persian king who determines the world order; rather, the God of Israel allots every nation its specific place and language. Of course, the Pentateuch eventually makes clear that Israel has a specific function in the

---

45. Rüdiger Schmitt, *The Bisitun Inscriptions of Darius the Great: Old Persian Texts*, vol. 1 of *The Old Persian Inscriptions*, Corpus Inscriptionum Iranicarum (London: School of Oriental and African Studies, 1991); and Schmitt, *Die altpersischen Inschriften der Achämeniden: Editio minor mit deutscher Übersetzung* (Wiesbaden: Reichert, 2009).

46. Klaus Koch, "Weltordnung und Reichsidee im alten Iran und ihre Auswirkungen auf die Provinz Jehud," in *Reichsidee und Reichsorganisation im Perserreich*, 2nd ed., OBO 55 (Fribourg: Academic Press; Göttingen: Vandenhoeck & Ruprecht, 1996), 197–201; see 150–51: "Das Zurückführen von Göttern und Menschen an ihren, mit Städte- und Tempelnamen gekennzeichneten Ort (*ašru*) rühmen auch akkadische Königsinschriften, vom Prolog des Codex Hammurabi (Ia 65: 'restore' ANET 164; TUAT I 41) bis hin zum Kyros-Zylinder (Z. 32; ANET 316; TUAT I, 409). Doch gibt es dabei, soweit ich sehe, nirgends einen Hinweis auf Völker und Länder. Mit Dareios I. setzt also ein neuer, an der Nationenvielfalt ausgerichteter Schöpfungs- und Herrschaftsgedanke durch."

world, but it is important to see that the Bible acknowledges and allows cultural and religious variety in its world.

These examples highlight how the Bible interacts with imperial ideologies from the ancient Near East, a point that is crucial to see if we are to reconstruct its formation. But how do such different ideologies and theologies go together in the Bible? It is important to see that the Pentateuch in particular and the Bible in general are not uniform pieces of literature. They instead resemble a large cathedral that has grown over centuries. Its content is the result not of one but of many voices. And these different voices establish the overall beauty and richness of the Pentateuch.[47]

Bibliography

Albrecht, Felix. "Die alexandrinische Bibelübersetzung: Einsichten zur Entstehungs-, Überlieferungs- und Wirkungsgeschichte der Septuaginta." Pages 209–43 in *Alexandria*. Edited by Tobias Georges, Felix Albrecht, and Reinhard Feldmeier. Civitatum orbis Mediterranei studia 1. Tübingen: Mohr Siebeck, 2013.

Alexander, Philip S. "Literacy among Jews in Second Temple Palestine: Reflections on the Evidence from Qumran." Pages 3–25 in *Hamlet on a Hill: Semitic and Greek Studies Presented to Professor T. Muraoka on the Occasion of His Sixty-Fifth Birthday*. Edited by Martin F. J. Baasten and W. Th. van Peursen. OLA 118. Leuven: Peeters, 2003.

Athas, George. *The Tel Dan Inscription: A Reappraisal and a New Interpretation*. London: Continuum, 2005.

Baden, Joel S. "The Continuity of the Non-Priestly Narrative from Genesis to Exodus." *Bib* 93 (2012): 161–86.

Benoit, Pierre, J. T. Milik, and Roland de Vaux. *Les grottes des Murabba'at*. DJD 2. Oxford: Clarendon, 1961.

Berlejung, Angelika. "The Assyrians in the West: Assyrianization, Colonialism, Indifference, or Development Policy?" Pages 21–60 in *Congress Volume Helsinki 2010*. Edited by Martti Nissinen. VTSup 148. Leiden: Brill, 2012.

———. "Der gesegnete Mensch: Text und Kontext von Num 6,22–27 und den Silberamuletten von Ketef Hinnom." Pages 37–62 in *Mensch und*

---

47. Konrad Schmid, "Der Pentateuch und seine Theologiegeschichte," *ZTK* 111 (2014): 239–71.

König: Studien zur Anthropologie des Alten Testaments; Rüdiger Lux zum 60. Geburtstag. Edited by Angelika Berlejung and Raik Heckl. HBS 53. Freiburg im Breisgau: Herder, 2008.

———. "Ein Programm fürs Leben: Theologisches Wort und anthropologischer Ort der Silberamulette von Ketef Hinnom." *ZAW* 120 (2008): 204–30.

Beuken, Willem A. M. *Jesaja 28–39*. HThKAT. Freiburg: Herder, 2010.

Blum, Erhard. "Die altaramäischen Wandinschriften aus Tell Deir 'Alla und ihr institutioneller Kontext." Pages 21–52 in *Metatexte: Erzählungen von schrifttragenden Artefakten in der alttestamentlichen und mittelalterlichen Literatur*. Edited by Friedrich-Emanuel Focken and Michael R. Ott. Materiale Textkulturen 15. Berlin: de Gruyter, 2016.

———. "Die Kombination I der Wandinschrift vom Tell Deir 'Alla: Vorschläge zur Rekonstruktion mit historisch-kritischen Anmerkungen." Pages 573–601 in *Berührungspunkte: Studien zur Sozial- und Religionsgeschichte Israels und seiner Umwelt; Festschrift für Rainer Albertz zu seinem 65. Geburtstag*. Edited by Ingo Kottsieper, Rüdiger Schmitt, and Jakob Wöhrle. AOAT 350. Münster: Ugarit, 2008.

———. "Verstehst du dich nicht auf die Schreibkunst…? Ein weisheitlicher Dialog über Vergänglichkeit und Verantwortung: Kombination II der Wandinschrift vom Tell Deir 'Alla." Pages 33–53 in *Was ist der Mensch, dass du seiner gedenkst? (Psalm 8,5): Aspekte einer theologischen Anthropologie; Festschrift für Bernd Janowski zum 65. Geburtstag*. Edited by Michaela Bauks, Kathrin Liess, and Peter Riede. Neukirchen-Vluyn: Neukirchener Verlag, 2008.

Carr, David M. *The Formation of the Hebrew Bible: A New Reconstruction*. Oxford: Oxford University Press, 2011.

———. *Writing on the Tablet of the Heart: Origins of Scripture and Literature*. Oxford: Oxford University Press, 2005.

Crouch, Carly L. *Israel and the Assyrians: Deuteronomy, the Succession Treaty of Esarhaddon, and the Nature of Subversion*. ANEM 8. Atlanta: SBL Press, 2014.

Crüsemann, Frank. *Die Tora: Theologie und Sozialgeschichte des alttestamentlichen Gesetzes*. Munich: Kaiser, 1992.

Dearman, J. Andrew, ed. *Studies in the Mesha Inscription and Moab*. ABS 2. Atlanta: Scholars Press, 1989.

De Troyer, Kristin. "When Did the Pentateuch Come into Existence? An Uncomfortable Perspective." Pages 269–86 in *Die Septuaginta: Texte, Kontexte, Lebenswelten, Internationale Fachtagung veranstaltet von*

Septuaginta Deutsch (LXX.D), Wuppertal 20.–23. Juli 2006. Edited by Martin Karrer and Wolfgang Kraus. WUNT 219. Tübingen: Mohr Siebeck, 2008.

Dorival, Gilles. "Les origins de la Septante: La traduction en grec des cinq livres de la Torah." Pages 39–82 in *La Bible grecque de Septante*. Edited by Gilles Dorival, Marguerite Harl, and Olivier Munnich. Paris: Cerf, 1988.

Dozeman, Thomas B. *The Pentateuch: Introducing the Torah*. Introducing Israel's Scriptures. Minneapolis: Fortress, 2017.

Faigenbaum-Golovin, Shira, Arie Shaus, Barak Sober, David Levin, Nadav Na'aman, Benjamin Sass, Eli Turkel, Eli Piasetzky, and Israel Finkelstein. "Algorithmic Handwriting Analysis of Judah's Military Correspondence Sheds Light on Composition of Biblical Texts," *Proceedings of the National Academy of Sciences of the United States of America* 113 (2016): 4664–69.

García López, Félix. "תורה." *ThWAT* 8:597–637.

Gertz, Jan C., Bernard M. Levinson, Dalit Rom-Shiloni, and Konrad Schmid, eds. *The Formation of the Pentateuch: Bridging the Academic Cultures of Europe, Israel, and North America*. FAT 111. Tübingen: Mohr Siebeck, 2016.

Görg, Manfred. "Die Septuaginta im Kontext spätägyptischer Kultur: Beispiele lokaler Inspiration bei der Übersetzungsarbeit am Pentateuch." Pages 115–30 in *Im Brennpunkt: Die Septuaginta; Studien zur Entstehung und Bedeutung der Griechischen Bibel*. Edited by Heinz-Josef Fabry and Ulrich Offerhaus. BWANT 153. Stuttgart: Kohlhammer, 2001.

Grabbe, Lester L. "The Law, the Prophets, and the Rest: The State of the Bible in Pre-Maccabean Times." *DSD* 13 (2006): 319–38.

Hendel, Ronald. "A Hasmonean Edition of MT Genesis? The Implications of the Editions of the Chronology in Genesis 5." *HBAI* 1 (2012): 448–64.

Hezser, Catherine. *Jewish Literacy in Roman Palestine*. TSAJ 81. Tübingen: Mohr Siebeck, 2001.

Hughes, Jeremy. *Secrets of the Times: Myth and History in Biblical Chronology*. JSOTSup 66. Sheffield: JSOT Press, 1990.

Keel, Othmar. *Die Geschichte Jerusalems und die Entstehung des Monotheismus*. 2 vols. Orte und Landschaften der Bibel 4.1. Göttingen: Vandenhoeck & Ruprecht, 2007.

Keel, Othmar, and Cristoph Uehlinger. "Der Assyrerkönig Salmanassar III. und Jehu von Israel auf dem Schwarzen Obelisken." *ZKT* 116 (1994): 391–420.

Koch, Christoph. *Vertrag, Treueid und Bund: Studien zur Rezeption des altorientalischen Vertragsrechts im Deuteronomium und zur Ausbildung der Bundestheologie im Alten Testament.* BZAW 383. Berlin: de Gruyter, 2008.

Koch, Klaus. "Weltordnung und Reichsidee im alten Iran und ihre Auswirkungen auf die Provinz Jehud." Pages 134–337 in *Reichsidee und Reichsorganisation im Perserreich.* 2nd ed. OBO 55. Fribourg: Academic Press; Göttingen: Vandenhoeck & Ruprecht, 1996.

Knauf, Ernst A. "Die Priesterschrift und die Geschichten der Deuteronomisten." Pages 101–18 in *The Future of the Deuteronomistic History.* Edited by Thomas Römer. BETL 147. Leuven: Peeters, 2000.

Kratz, Reinhard G. "The Analysis of the Pentateuch: An Attempt to Overcome Barriers of Thinking." *ZAW* 128 (2016): 529–61.

———. "Der literarische Ort des Deuteronomiums." Pages 101–20 in *Liebe und Gebot: Studien zum Deuteronomium; Festschrift zum 70. Geburtstag von Lothar Perlitt.* Edited by Reinhard G. Kratz and Hermann Spieckermann. FRLANT 190. Göttingen: Vandenhoeck & Ruprecht, 2000.

Krauter, Stefan. "Die Pentateuch-Septuaginta als Übersetzung in der Literaturgeschichte der Antike." Pages 26–46 in *Die Septuaginta und das frühe Christentum; The Septuagint and Christian Origins.* Edited by Thomas S. Caulley and Hermann Lichtenberger. WUNT 277. Tübingen: Mohr Siebeck, 2011.

Kreuzer, Siegfried. "Entstehung und Entwicklung der Septuaginta im Kontext alexandrinischer und frühjüdischer Kultur und Bildung." Pages 3–29 in vol. 1 of *Septuaginta Deutsch: Erläuterungen und Kommentare zum griechischen Alten Testament.* Edited by Martin Karrer and Wolfgang Kraus. 2 vols. Stuttgart: Deutsche Bibelgesellschaft, 2011.

———. *Geschichte, Sprache und Text: Studien zum Alten Testament und seiner Umwelt.* BZAW 479. Berlin: de Gruyter, 2015.

Lange, Armin. *Die Handschriften biblischer Bücher von Qumran und den anderen Fundorten.* Vol. 1 of *Handbuch der Textfunde vom Toten Meer.* Tübingen: Mohr Siebeck, 2009.

———. "From Many to One: Some Thoughts on the Hebrew Textual History of the Torah." Pages 121–95 in *The Formation of the Pentateuch: Bridging the Academic Cultures of Europe, Israel, and North America.*

Edited by Jan C. Gertz, Bernard M. Levinson, Dalit Rom-Shiloni, and Konrad Schmid. FAT 111. Tübingen: Mohr Siebeck, 2016.

Lehmann, Reinhard G., and Anna E. Zernecke. "Bemerkungen und Beobactungen zu der neuen Ophel Pithosinschrift." Pages 437–50 in *Schrift und Sprache: Papers Read at the 10th Mainz International Colloquium on Ancient Hebrew (MICAH), Mainz, 28–30 October 2011.* Edited by Reinhard G. Lehmann and Anna E. Zernecke. Kleine Untersuchungen zur Sprache des Alten Testaments und seiner Umwelt 15. Kamen: Spenner, 2013.

MacDonald, Nathan. "Issues in the Dating of Deuteronomy: A Response to Juha Pakkala." *ZAW* 122 (2010): 431–35.

McCarter, P. Kyle, Shelomoh Bunimovitz, and Zvi Lederman. "An Archaic Ba'l Inscription from Tel Beth-Shemesh." *TA* 38 (2011): 179–93.

Meshel, Zeev, ed. *Kuntillet 'Ajrud (Horvat Teman): An Iron Age II Religious Site on the Judah-Sinai Border.* Jerusalem: Israel Antiquities Authority, 2012.

Nihan, Cristophe. *From Priestly Torah to Pentateuch: A Study in the Composition of the Book of Leviticus.* FAT 2/25. Tübingen: Mohr Siebeck, 2007.

Otto, Eckart. "Assyria and Judean Identity: Beyond the Religionsgeschichtliche Schule." Pages 339–47 in *Literature as Politics, Politics as Literature: Essays in Honor of Peter Machinist.* Edited by David S. Vanderhooft and Abraham Winitzer. Winona Lake, IN: Eisenbrauns, 2013.

———. *Das Deuteronomium: Politische Theologie und Rechtsreform in Juda und Assyrien.* BZAW 284. Berlin: de Gruyter, 1999.

Pakkala, Juha. "The Date of the Oldest Edition of Deuteronomy." *ZAW* 121 (2009): 388–401.

———. "The Dating of Deuteronomy: A Response to Nathan MacDonald." *ZAW* 123 (2011): 431–36.

Pardee, Dennis. "Gezer Calendar." *OEANE* 2:396–400.

Parker, David C. *Codex Sinaiticus: The Story of the World's Oldest Bible.* London: British Library, 2010.

Popper, Julius. *Der biblische Bericht über die Stiftshütte: Ein Beitrag zur Geschichte der Composition und Diaskeue des Pentateuch.* Leipzig: Heinrich Hunger, 1862.

Richelle, Mattheiu. "Elusive Scrolls: Could Any Hebrew Literature Have Been Written Prior to the Eighth Century BCE?" *VT* 66 (2016): 556–94.

Rollston, Chris. *Writing and Literacy in the World of Ancient Israel*. ABS 11. Atlanta: Society of Biblical Literature, 2010.

Römer, Thomas. "Der Pentateuch." Pages 52–166 in *Die Entstehung des Alten Testaments*. Edited by Walter Dietrich, Hans-Peter Mathys, Thomas Römer, and Rudolf Smend. Theologische Wissenschaft: Sammelwerk für Studium und Beruf 1. Stuttgart: Kohlhammer, 2014.

———. "Le 'sacrifice d'Abraham', un texte élohiste? Quelques observations à partir de Gn 22,14 et d'un fragment de Qumran." *Sem* 54 (2012): 163–72.

———. "Zwischen Urkunden, Fragmenten und Ergänzungen: Zum Stand der Pentateuchforschung." *ZAW* 125 (2013): 2–24.

Römer, Thomas, Jean-Daniel Macchi, and Christophe Nihan, eds. *Einleitung in das Alte Testament: Die Bücher der Hebräischen Bibel und die alttestamentlichen Schriften der katholischen, protestantischen und orthodoxen Kirchen*. Zurich: TVZ, 2013.

Rouillard, Hedwige. *La péricope de Balaam (Nombres 22–24)*. EBib 2/4. Paris: Gabalda, 1985.

Schmid, Konrad. "Anfänge politikförmiger Religion: Die Theologisierung politisch-imperialer Begriffe in der Religionsgeschichte des antiken Israel als Grundlage autoritärer und toleranter Strukturmomente monotheistischer Religionen." Pages 161–77 in *Religion–Wirtschaft–Politik: Forschungszugänge zu einem aktuellen transdisziplinären Feld*. Edited by Antonius Liedhegener, Andreas Tunger-Zanetti, and Stephan Wirz. Baden-Baden: Nomos, 2011.

———. "Genesis and Exodus as Two Formerly Independent Traditions of Origins for Ancient Israel." *Bib* 93 (2012): 187–208.

———. "Das kosmische Weltgericht in den Prophetenbüchern und seine historischen Kontexte." Pages 409–34 in *Nächstenliebe und Gottesfurcht: Beiträge aus alttestamentlicher, semitistischer und altorientalischer Wissenschaft für Hans-Peter Mathys zum 65. Geburtstag*. Edited by Hanna Jenni and Markus Saur. AOAT 439. Münster: Ugarit, 2016.

———. "Der Pentateuch und seine Theologiegeschichte." *ZTK* 111 (2014): 239–71.

Schmitt, Hans-Christoph. "Der heidnische Mantiker als eschatologischer Jahweprophet: Zum Verständnis Bileams in der Endgestalt von Num 22–24." Pages 180–98 in *"Wer ist wie du, Herr, unter den Göttern?": Studien zur Theologie und Religionsgeschichte Israels; für Otto Kaiser zum 70. Geburtstag*. Edited by Ingo Kottsieper. Göttingen: Vandenhoeck & Ruprecht, 1994.

Schmitt, Rüdiger. *Die altpersischen Inschriften der Achämeniden: Editio minor mit deutscher Übersetzung*. Wiesbaden: Reichert, 2009.

———. *The Bisitun Inscriptions of Darius the Great: Old Persian Texts*. Volume 1 of *The Old Persian Inscriptions*. Corpus Inscriptionum Iranicarum. London: School of Oriental and African Studies, 1991.

Schroer, Silvia, and Stefan Münger, eds. *Khirbet Qeiyafa in the Shephelah: Papers Presented at a Colloquium of the Swiss Society for Ancient Near Eastern Studies Held at the University of Bern, September 6, 2014*. OBO 282. Fribourg: Academic Press; Göttingen: Vandenhoeck & Ruprecht, 2017.

Siegert, Folker. *Zwischen Hebräischer Bibel und Altem Testament: Eine Einführung in die Septuaginta*. Münsteraner judaistische Studien 9. Münster: Lit, 2001.

Sivan, Daniel. "The Gezer Calendar and Northwest Semitic Linguistics." *IEJ* 48 (1998): 101–5.

Steck, Odil H. *Bereitete Heimkehr: Jesaja 35 als redaktionelle Brücke zwischen dem Ersten und dem Zweiten Jesaja*. SBS 121. Stuttgart: Katholisches Bibelwerk, 1985.

———. *Old Testament Exegesis: A Guide to the Methodology*. Translated by James D. Nogalski. RBS 33. Atlanta: Scholars Press, 1995.

Steins, Georg. "Torabindung und Kanonabschluss: Zur Entstehung und kanonischen Funktion der Chronikbücher." Pages 213–56 in *Die Tora als Kanon für Juden und Christen*. Edited by Erich Zenger. HBS 10. Freiburg: Herder, 1996.

Tappy, Ron E., and P. Kyle McCarter, eds. *Literate Culture and Tenth-Century Canaan: The Tel Zayit Abecedary in Context*. Winona Lake, IN: Eisenbrauns, 2008.

Tov, Emanuel. "The Text of the Hebrew/Aramaic and Greek Bible Used in the Ancient Synagogues." Pages 237–59 in *The Ancient Synagogue from Its Origins until 200 C.E.: Papers Presented at an International Conference at Lund University, October 14–17, 2001*. Edited by Birger Olsson and Magnus Zetterholm. ConBNT 39. Stockholm: Almqvist & Wiksell, 2003.

———. *Textual Criticism of the Bible*. 3rd ed. Minneapolis: Fortress, 2012.

Ulrich, Eugene. *The Biblical Qumran Scrolls: Transcriptions and Textual Variants*. VTSup 134. Leiden: Brill, 2010.

Vermeylen, Jacques. "La 'table des nations' (Gn 10): Yaphet figure-t-il l'Empire perse?" *Transeu* 5 (1992): 113–32.

Vink, J. G. "The Date and the Origin of the Priestly Code in the Old Testament." Pages 1–143 in *The Priestly Code and Seven Other Studies*. OtSt 15. Leiden: Brill, 1969.

Wade, Martha L. *Consistency of Translation Techniques in the Tabernacle Accounts of Exodus in the Old Greek*. SCS 49. Atlanta: Society of Biblical Literature, 2003.

Wahl, Harald-Martin. *Die Jakobserzählungen: Studien zu ihrer mündlichen Überlieferung, Verschriftung und Historizität*. BZAW 258. Berlin: de Gruyter, 1997.

Weippert, Helga, and Manfred Weippert. "Die 'Bileam'-Inschrift von Tel Deir 'Alla." *ZDPV* 98 (1982): 77–103.

Wevers, John W. "The Building of the Tabernacle." *JNSL* 19 (1993): 123–31.

———. "The Earliest Witness to the LXX Deuteronomy." *CBQ* 39 (1977): 240–44.

Xeravits, Géza G., and Peter Porzig. *Einführung in die Qumranliteratur: Die Handschriften vom Toten Meer*. Berlin: de Gruyter, 2015.

Contributions from Lay Scribal Circles in Yehud

The Relationship between Moses and Aaron and the Question of the Composition of the Pentateuch

Thomas Römer

There is no doubt that Moses is the most important human figure in the Torah, which could almost be understood, as suggested by Rolf Knierim, as a "biography of Moses."[1] Indeed, the book of Exodus starts with Moses's birth story in chapter 2, and the last chapter of the Pentateuch, Deut 34, reports the death of Moses, so that the books of Exodus to Deuteronomy are tied together by the life of Moses and cover, on the narrative level, the 120 years of his life. If the Pentateuch can be understood as a life of Moses, the book of Genesis would constitute a prologue of sorts to the Moses story.[2] There are, of course, other actors in the books of Exodus to Deuteronomy, especially Aaron, although he shows up only after Moses's call in Exod 4 and in a quite unexpected and unprepared way. The reader of Exod 4 may indeed be puzzled because the text had not yet mentioned that Moses had a brother. In Moses's birth story in Exod 2, there is no allusion at all to an older brother. On the contrary, Moses appears to be the firstborn. And it is also quite clear that the appearance of the sister in Exod 2 is due to a later redactor who wanted to show that Moses was not abandoned by his family when he was discovered by Pharaoh's daughter.[3] The

---

1. Rolf P. Knierim, "The Composition of the Pentateuch," in *Society of Biblical Literature 1985 Seminar Papers*, SBLSP 24 (Atlanta: Scholars Press, 1985), 393–415.

2. In the so-called final form of the Torah, this is certainly the case. Gen 15 already introduces a summary of the events described in the following books, and several texts in Genesis allude to the descent to Egypt, especially Gen 12:10–20 and Gen 37–50. When the term *Pentateuch* is used, it refers to the collection of five books that is the first part of the Hebrew Bible. The term *Torah* refers to the foundation document of nascent Judaism, which for some would have been a Hexateuch.

3. The verses mentioning Moses's daughter are quite commonly assumed to be

insertion of the sister into the story of Moses's adoption by the Egyptian princess creates a chronological problem because Moses receives his name only after his mother has brought him from nursing him, which normally takes several months. That means that the original story was told about a Moses without elder brothers or sisters. Interestingly, when Moses performs the miracle at the sea, so the Israelites can cross it in Exod 14, there is no mention at all of Aaron, although he is a main figure in the negotiations with Pharaoh and in the plague stories.

These observations may lead us to wonder whether there was an older and shorter narrative that told only about Moses, his birth, his flight to Midian, his call there by YHWH, and his return to Egypt, as well as his role as a miracle worker when parting the sea. If this is the case, one must ask why Aaron was introduced into this story and by whom. To complicate the issue, one must also take into account and explain the following fact: several texts in the books of Exodus, Leviticus, and Numbers present Aaron as being under the authority of Moses, whereas some other texts seem to confer upon him a much more important role. How should we explain the different types of relationship between Moses and Aaron? My hypothesis will be the following: behind the figures of Moses and Aaron we may detect different scribal groups that redacted and transmitted stories that were later combined in order to constitute the Pentateuch. To examine this hypothesis some remarks about the promulgation of the Torah are in order.

1. The Question of the Promulgation of the Torah

In the 1990s, Peter Frei postulated the existence of a Persian policy of "imperial authorization" of local law codes. He suggested that the central Achaemenid administration would occasionally have bestowed local legal documents with imperial authority.[4] The publication of the Pentateuch and its acceptance as law in Yehud should therefore be viewed as an exam-

---

an insertion by a later redactor; see, e.g., Werner H. Schmidt, *Exodus*, 2 vols., BKAT 2 (Neukirchen-Vluyn: Neukirchener Verlag, 1988–1999), 1:52–54; Meik Gerhards, *Die Aussetzungsgeschichte des Mose: Literar- und traditionsgeschichtliche Untersuchungen zu einem Schlüsseltext des nichtpriesterlichen Tetrateuch*, WMANT 109 (Neukirchen-Vluyn: Neukirchener Verlag, 2006), 52–54; and Thomas Römer, "Moses and the Women in Exodus 1–4," *Indian Theological Studies* 52 (2015): 245–46.

4. Peter Frei, "Zentralgewalt und Lokalautonomie im Achämenidenreich," in

ple of such imperial authorization. This practice would have encouraged Judeans to codify their traditional customs into an authoritative document, which they would subsequently have ratified. The general purpose of such imperial authorization would have been to prompt some form of institutional cooperation between the Persian Empire and the provinces, granting the latter some degree of local autonomy while simultaneously enforcing the king's rule in legal matters. Such an imperial authorization would also explain why the Pentateuch contains different and sometimes contradictory texts: the Persians would only allow one official document for the province of Yehud.

Several scholars have accepted the theory that such an imperial authorization instigated the publication of the Pentateuch.[5] However, more recently, this explanation has been strongly criticized.[6] In fact, the Pentateuch is not comparable to the evidence that has been claimed by Frei and others to exemplify the institution of imperial authorization. There are indeed quite a few inscriptions dealing with specific legal matters, which

---

Reichsidee und Reichsorganisation im Perserreich, ed. Peter Frei and Klaus Koch, 2nd ed., OBO 55 (Fribourg: Universitätsverlag; Göttingen: Vandenhoeck & Ruprecht, 1996), 33.

5. Frank Crüsemann, *Die Tora: Theologie und Sozialgeschichte des alttestamentlichen Gesetzes* (Munich: Kaiser, 1992), 404–6; Rainer Albertz, *Religionsgeschichte Israels in alttestamentlicher Zeit*, 2 vols., GAT 8 (Göttingen: Vandenhoeck & Ruprecht, 1992–1997), 2:497–504; Ernst A. Knauf, "Audiatur et altera pars: Zur Logik der Pentateuchredaktion," *BK* 53 (1998): 118–26; Joseph Blenkinsopp, "Was the Pentateuch the Civic and Religious Constitution of the Jewish Ethnos in the Persian Period?," in *Persia and Torah: The Theory of the Imperial Authorization of the Pentateuch*, ed. James W. Watts, SymS 17 (Atlanta: Society of Biblical Literature, 2001), 41–62; and Kyong-Jin Lee, *The Authority and Authorization of the Torah in the Persian Period*, CBET 64 (Leuven: Peeters, 2011).

6. Udo Rüterswörden, "Die persische Reichsautorisation der Thora: Fact or Fiction?," *ZABR* 1 (1995): 47–61; Josef Wiesehöfer, "'Reichsgesetz' oder 'Einzelfallgerechtigkeit'? Bemerkungen zu P. Freis Thesen von der achaemenidischen 'Reichsautorisation,'" *ZABR* 1 (1995): 36–46; Jean-Louis Ska, "'Persian Imperial Authorization': Some Question Marks," in Watts, *Persia and Torah*, 161–82; and Eckart Otto, "The Pentateuch in Synchronical and Diachronical Perspectives: Protorabbinic Scribal Erudition Mediating between Deuteronomy and the Priestly Code," in *Das Deuteronomium zwischen Pentateuch und Deuteronomistischem Geschichtswerk*, ed. Eckart Otto and Reinhard Achenbach, FRLANT 206 (Göttingen: Vandenhoeck & Ruprecht, 2004), 14–35. See also the contributions in Gary N. Knoppers and Bernard M. Levinson, eds., *The Pentateuch as Torah: New Models for Understanding Its Promulgation and Acceptance* (Winona Lake, IN: Eisenbrauns, 2007); and Uwe Becker, "Die Perser im Esra- und Nehemiabuch," *ZAW* 127 (2015): 607–27.

often are written in two or three languages. The only partial parallel would be with the so-called codification of Egyptian law under Darius I, but this latter case is quite different, and the text on which it is based makes no mention of the codification of law.[7]

One should therefore probably search for more internal explanations for its creation. In this context, the Pentateuch is often viewed as a document of compromise among different scribal schools in Jerusalem during the fourth century BCE or maybe even later.[8] Different groups agreed to collect the different traditions they regarded as authoritative—for example, the Priestly writing—and combine them in order to create a normative account or a foundation myth of the origins of Israel. That normative account, while it preserved conflicting views, was nevertheless unified by a comprehensive narrative framework stretching from the origin of the world (Gen 1) to the death of the divine mediator, Moses (Deut 34), with this Moses being its main figure.[9]

It is often claimed that the Torah was composed in Jerusalem. However, recent archaeological investigation of the population of Yehud and Jerusalem in the Persian period reveals that Jerusalem was only very sparsely inhabited during this time.[10] Of course, one cannot exclude that some priests and scribes around the temple were enough to compose the Pentateuch. But one should also take into account the political and economic strength of the Babylonian and the Egyptian diaspora. Even if the story of Ezra bringing a "law" from Mesopotamia to Jerusalem in Ezra 7 is totally invented, it reflects in one way or another the implication of the Babylonian diaspora in the compilation of the Torah.[11]

---

7. Donald B. Redford, "The So-Called 'Codification' of Egyptian Law Under Darius I," in Watts, *Persia and Torah*, 135–59.

8. Reinhard G. Kratz, "Temple and Torah: Reflections on the Legal Status of the Pentateuch Between Elephantine and Qumran," in Knoppers and Levinson, *Pentateuch as Torah*, 77–103.

9. Eckart Otto, *Das Gesetz des Mose* (Darmstadt: Wissenschaftliche Buchgesellschaft, 2007), esp. 197–204.

10. Oded Lipschits, "Demographic Changes in Judah between the Seventh and the Fifth Centuries B.C.E.," in *Judah and the Judeans in the Neo-Babylonian Period*, ed. Oded Lipschits and Joseph Blenkinsopp (Winona Lake, IN: Eisenbrauns, 2003), 323–76; and Israel Finkelstein, "The Territorial Extent and Demography of Yehud/Judea in the Persian and Early Hellenistic Periods," *RB* 117 (2010): 39–54.

11. See, e.g., Sebastian Grätz, *Das Edikt des Artaxerxes: Eine Untersuchung zum religionspolitischen und historischen Umfeld von Esra 7,12-26*, BZAW 337 (Berlin: de Gruyter, 2004).

The decision to prefer a Pentateuch to a Hexateuch and to end the Torah with Moses's death outside of the land (Deut 34) rather than with Joshua's conquest is best explained as a concession to the diaspora.[12] Moses's death, which happens according to the will of YHWH, shows that is not necessary to live inside the promised land; the most important thing is to accept YHWH's will and law. Defining the Torah as a *Pentateuch* rather than a Hexateuch means de facto acknowledging the reality and even the legitimacy of diaspora Judaism. Similarly, the Joseph story in Gen 37–50 was apparently a creation of the Jewish diaspora in Egypt or of an author who was sympathetic to this diaspora, which was later included in the Pentateuch as a concession to that diaspora.[13]

It is clear now that there was a (Yahwistic) sanctuary on Mount Gerizim that was built probably after the resettlement of Shechem ca. 480–475 BCE.[14] If so, the instruction in Deut 27:4 for building an altar on Mount Gerizim, found in the Samaritan Pentateuch and supported by one codex of the Old Latin, was most likely introduced at the time of the composition of the Pentateuch as a means of acknowledging the legitimacy of the newly built Samarian altar.[15]

---

12. For the debate between groups favoring a Hexateuch or wanting to construct a Pentateuch, see Thomas Römer and Marc Z. Brettler, "Deuteronomy 34 and the Case for a Persian Hexateuch," *JBL* 119 (2000): 401–19; Eckart Otto, *Das Deuteronomium im Pentateuch und Hexateuch: Studien zur Literaturgeschichte von Pentateuch und Hexateuch im Lichte des Deuteronomiumrahmens*, FAT 30 (Tübingen: Mohr Siebeck, 2000); and Rainer Albertz, *Exodus*, 2 vols., ZBK 2 (Zurich: TVZ, 2012–2015), 1:19–26.

13. On the Joseph story as written in the Egyptian diaspora, see Thomas Römer, "The Joseph Story in the Book of Genesis: Pre-P or Post-P?," in *The Post-Priestly Pentateuch: New Perspectives on Its Redactional Development and Theological Profiles*, ed. Federico Giuntoli and Konrad Schmid, FAT 101 (Tübingen: Mohr Siebeck, 2015), 185–201. On the notion that it was written by a written by an author in the land, but sympathetic to the Egyptian diaspora, see Bernd U. Schipper, "Joseph, Ahiqar, and Elephantine: The Joseph Story as a Diaspora Novella," *Journal of Ancient Egyptian Interconnections* 18 (2018): 71–84. According to Franziska Ede, *Die Josefsgeschichte: Literarkritische und redaktionsgeschichtliche Untersuchungen zur Entstehung von Gen 37–50*, BZAW 485 (Berlin: de Gruyter, 2016), the Joseph story was conceived from the beginning as a bridge between the patriarchs and the exodus.

14. Yitzhak Magen, "Mount Gerizim: Temple City," *Qad* 120 (2000): 74–118; Ephraim Stern and Yitzhak Magen, "Archaeological Evidence for the First Stage of the Samaritan Temple on Mount Gerizim," *IEJ* 52 (2002): 49–57; and Jan Dušek, "Mt. Gerizim Sanctuary, Its History and Enigma of Origin," *HBAI* 3 (2014): 111–33.

15. Cristophe Nihan, "Garizim et Ébal dans le Pentateuque: Quelques remarques

However, Jerusalem with its temple was perhaps the place in which the compilation of the first edition of the Torah was first decided, probably in contact and cooperation with groups from Samaria.[16] If we try now to identify more precisely the parties involved, we should logically think of the two main institutions in Persian-period Jerusalem: the temple and the lay council presiding over the temple assembly.[17]

The existence of a lay council alongside a priestly college seems to be attested in the correspondence between Jerusalem and the Judean/Israelite community of Elephantine, which mentions, besides the governor, "the high priest Jehohanan and his colleagues, the priests in Jerusalem" as well as "Ostanes, the brother of Anani and the leading men among the Jews."[18] The council of elders was composed of the ראשי האבות, the "heads of the fathers' [houses]," who are also mentioned in Ezra–Nehemiah. Ezra 3:12 (MT) makes the equation explicit with its phrase, ראשי האבות הזקנים, "the heads of the fathers' [houses], the elders." Significantly, in Deut 31:9–13, the Torah, after it is written by Moses, is entrusted to "the priests, the Levites, who bear the ark of the covenant of YHWH, as well as to the elders of Israel" (31:9), who have the task of reading it to the entire community every seven years (31:10–13). This looks like an attempt to bring together three major groups implicated in the promulgation of the Torah. According to Neh 8:13, three groups gather around Ezra "in order to discern [סכל *hiphil*] the words of the Law": these three groups are the ראשי האבות, the priests, and the Levites.

---

en marge de la publication d'un nouveau fragment du Deutéronome," *Sem* 54 (2011): 185–210. For a somewhat different view, see Detlef Jericke, "Der Berg Garizim im Deuteronomium," *ZAW* 124 (2012): 213–28.

16. Walter Houston, "Between Salem and Mount Gerizim: The Context of the Formation of the Torah Reconsidered," *JAJ* 5 (2014): 311–34; Benedikt Hensel, *Juda und Samaria: Zum Verhältnis zweier nach-exilischer Jahwismen*, FAT 110 (Tübingen: Mohr Siebeck, 2017), esp. 170–94.

17. Albertz, *Religionsgeschichte*, 502–4. For a similar idea, see Joel Weinberg, *The Citizen-Temple Community*, JSOTSup 151 (Sheffield: JSOT Press, 1992).

18. A. E. Cowley, *Aramaic Papyri of the Fifth Century B.C.* (Oxford: Clarendon, 1923), 30, lines 18–19; see also Bezalel Porten, *The Elephantine Papyri in English: Three Millennia of Cross-Cultural Continuity and Change*, 2nd ed., DMOA 22 (Leiden: Brill, 2011). For the social groups in Jerusalem and Samaria, see further Gard Granerød, *Dimensions of Yahwism in the Persian Period: Studies in the Religion and Society of the Judaean Community at Elephantine*, BZAW 488 (Berlin: de Gruyter, 2016).

On the other hand, however, various passages in the Pentateuch suggest an attempt by priestly groups to claim sole authority in the interpretation of the Torah. Thus, according to Deut 33:10, teaching (ירה) the Torah is the privilege of Levi, the priestly tribe among Jacob's sons.[19]

In Lev 10:10–11, Aaron and his sons are commanded to "separate" between "holy and profane, unclean and clean" (10:10) but also to "teach" (ירה) "*all* the statutes" (כל החקים) communicated to Moses by YHWH (10:11). Here the transition from the traditional duty reserved for the priests to the interpretation of the entire Torah is transparent. This passage is, along with Num 18, the only divine command in the Pentateuch that is addressed exclusively to Aaron.[20]

The conception of the Aaronides as teachers of the Law also plays an important role in writings from the Hellenistic period (see, e.g., Sir 45:17 or 11QT 56:2–6). At the end of the Persian period, the rapid decline in the influence of the Persian administration over the area appears to have led to the development of the power and status of priestly clergy in Jerusalem and particularly to political claims made by the high priest.[21]

This overview indicates that there are at least three competing groups that can be detected in the Pentateuch and that refer to different figures: Moses, who reflects in many cases the aspirations of the lay council, Aaron, who seems to represent the priestly line, and the Levites, who are related to the figure of Korah in some pentateuchal texts and claim their right to read and to teach the Torah.

2. Moses and Aaron

As already mentioned, in some texts of Exodus, Moses appears alone without his brother. In the texts where Moses and Aaron are mentioned together, Moses comes first in around 90 percent of these passages. Although Aaron appears as Moses's older brother, he is presented as Moses's spokesman or under the authority of Moses.

---

19. The Samaritan Pentateuch and Syriacus have a plural here, תורות.
20. See also Christophe Nihan, *From Priestly Torah to Pentateuch: A Study in the Composition of the Book of Leviticus*, FAT 2/25 (Tübingen: Mohr Siebeck, 2007), 591–92.
21. The first coin minted in the name of a high priest of Jerusalem, a certain Yohanan, is dated ca. 350 BCE. It indicates that coin minting, and therefore tax collection, came under the control of the high priest in Jerusalem at that time.

There are, however, some texts that claim a higher authority for Aaron, such as the genealogy in Exod 6:13–25, which is considered by most scholars a late priestly insert (P^s) into an older Priestly account (P^g) of Moses's call (6:2–8*), where Moses appears alone without any mention of Aaron.[22] The fact that we have to do here with an addition is also demonstrated by the *Wiederaufnahme* of verse 12 in verse 30. Verse 12 reads, "Moses spoke before YHWH, 'The Israelites have not listened to me; how then shall Pharaoh listen to me, I am uncircumcised of lips?'" and verse 30 reiterates, "Moses said before YHWH, 'I am uncircumcised of lips, how would Pharaoh listen to me?'"

This list, which looks at first glance as though it might be a genealogy of the twelve sons of Jacob, does not go further than Levi, born third, and pays special attention to Levi's offspring. Verse 20 presents Aaron indeed as Moses's older brother (without, however, mentioning Miriam). Interestingly, nothing is said about Moses's offspring, whereas Aaron's descendants are presented in a detailed way. The author of the list also shows interest for the Korahites who, in Num 16–17 appear in conflict with Moses and Aaron.[23] In Exod 6:14–25 Aaron, Moses, and Korah are all Levites, but the emphasis is put on Aaron and his line. This is particularly clear in the concluding remark in verse 26: "This is Aaron and Moses to whom YHWH said, 'Bring [sg.] the Israelites out of the land of Egypt, organized in armies.'" In this verse, Aaron, contrary to the majority of the texts in Exodus, appears as YHWH's privileged interlocutor, whom he commands to lead the Israelites out of Egypt, normally Moses's task. Interestingly, this has been corrected immediately in the following verse in MT, which reads: "It was they who spoke to Pharaoh king of Egypt to bring the Israelites out of Egypt, it was Moses and Aaron."[24] In MT, Moses is put in the first position; later redactors apparently wanted to emphasize Moses's superiority over Aaron.[25]

---

22. See recently Albertz, *Exodus*, 1:25–26 and 128, who attributes this genealogy to a very late postpriestly redactor, writing after the hexateuchal redactor.

23. On this, see Jaeyoung Jeon, "The Zadokites in the Wilderness: The Rebellion of Korach (Num 16) and the Zadokite Redaction," *ZAW* 127 (2015): 381–411.

24. See also Albertz, *Exodus*, 1:131.

25. LXX has the same order as in Exod 6:26. This could be due to stylistic considerations, or it could reflect the original texts. If the latter, MT would be a very late correction.

A similar phenomenon occurs in Num 18:1–24, which is, with Lev 10:8, the only text in the Torah in which YHWH speaks only to Aaron without mentioning Moses. In this speech, YHWH grants to Aaron and his sons a perpetual income and taxes from the sacrifices to be offered by the Israelites. This passage presupposes the foregoing story about Aaron's staff. According to this story, Aaron's staff was the only staff among those of the twelve tribes that sprouted overnight (Num 17:16–27). Here Aaron appears as representative of the tribe of Levi, whereas Num 18:1–24 clearly postulates the superiority of Aaron and his sons over the other Levites, who are said to be "assistants," but who cannot approach the utensils of the sanctuary or the altar (18:3).[26]

Interestingly, at the end of the chapter a passage was added (18:25–32), in which YHWH no longer speaks to Aaron but to Moses.[27] In a different way, this passage also stipulates the superiority of the Aaronides over the Levites, by claiming that the Levites should also receive a tithe from the Israelites, but that they should give also a tithe from their income to Aaron and his sons. The idea of a tithe of the Levites occurs in the Hebrew Bible only in Neh 10:39 and may reflect a reality of the Second Temple in the late Persian or Early Hellenistic period.[28] In Num 18, this topic is introduced by a speech of YHWH to Moses, so that, at the end of chapter 18, his leading position is confirmed again.

Exodus 6 and Num 18 seem to reflect a struggle between Aaron (and the group behind him) and Moses (and the group behind him). Both texts also affirm the superiority of Aaron and his offspring over the other Levites. There are, however, some texts in the Pentateuch that reflect attempts by the Levites to challenge the superiority of Aaron and his offspring.

---

26. According to Reinhard Achenbach, *Die Vollendung der Tora: Studien zur Redaktionsgeschichte des Numeribuches im Kontext von Hexateuch und Pentateuch*, BZABR 3 (Wiesbaden: Harrassowitz, 2003), 141–72, Num 18 is part of a theocratic redaction ("theokratische Bearbeitung") that belongs to the latest layers of the book of Numbers and was added when the Pentateuch was almost completed.

27. Ludwig Schmidt, *Das vierte Buch Mose: Numeri 10,11–36,13*, ATD 7.2 (Göttingen: Vandenhoeck & Ruprecht, 2004), 82–83.

28. Rudolf Meyer, "Levitische Emanzipationsbestrebungen in nachexilischer Zeit," *OLZ* 41 (1938): 722–28; Ulrich Dahmen, *Leviten und Priester im Deuteronomium: Literarkritische und redaktionsgeschichtliche Studien*, BBB 110 (Bodenheim: PHILO, 1996), 405–8; and Harald Samuel, *Von Priestern zum Patriarchen: Levi und die Leviten im Alten Testament*, BZAW 448 (Berlin: de Gruyter, 2014), 235–39.

3. Levites against the Aaronides

This conflict is apparent in Num 16, where the Levites associated with Korah are challenging Aaron's priestly prerogatives: Korah who is also mentioned in Exod 6 appears in Num 16 as the leader of the Levites, who claim the priesthood against Aaron, and who are harshly condemned by Moses:

> Then Moses said to Korah, "Hear now, you Levites! Is it too little for you that the God of Israel has separated you from the congregation of Israel, to allow you to approach him in order to perform the duties of the Lord's tabernacle, and to stand before the congregation and serve them? He has allowed you to approach him, and all your brother Levites with you; yet you seek the priesthood as well!" (Num 16:8–10)[29]

This chapter has recently been analyzed convincingly by Jaeyoung Jeon, who has shown that the Korah-Levites layer is the latest revision of Num 16 and that it reflects the rejection of attempts of Korahite Levites to obtain a priestly status.[30] This layer of Num 16 can therefore, as demonstrated by Jeon, be attributed to an Aaronide or a Zadokide redaction.[31] In Num 16, Moses and Aaron are in solidarity against attempts to challenge their special status and prerogatives.

There is, however, in the Pentateuch a text where the Levites are presented in a better light than Aaron: the story of the golden calf in Exod 32. In this story, Aaron appears in an ambiguous role (at best) because he is presented as the creator of the golden calf and the inventor of idolatry. Because of the clear intertextual relationship of this chapter to 1 Kgs 12, Aaron is even depicted as a forerunner of Jeroboam who according to the Dtr edition of the books of Kings committed the original sin of the Northern Kingdom by introducing idolatry and sanctuaries other than Jerusalem. In Exod 32:21, Moses also criticizes Aaron for bringing a sin over the people: "Moses said to Aaron, 'What did this people do to you

---

29. Biblical translations follow the NRSV, except that "the Lord" has been replaced by "YHWH."

30. Jeon, "Zadokites in the Wilderness," 381–411.

31. See also Jaeyoung Jeon, "The Zadokite and Levitical Scribal Conflicts and Hegemonic Struggles," in *Scripture as Social Discourse: Social-Scientific Perspectives on Early Jewish and Christian Writings*, ed. Jessica M. Keady, Todd E. Klutz, and Casey A. Strine (London: T&T Clark, 2018), 97–110.

that you have brought so great a sin upon them?'" In the parallel account of the story in Deut 9, it is even said that YHWH "was angry with Aaron and wanted to destroy him" and that he was rescued only through Moses's intercession (9:20).

In Exod 32, the negative image of Aaron is contrasted with the appearance of the Levites, who are presented as the only group who was on the side of YHWH and Moses: "Then Moses stood in the gate of the camp, and said, 'Who is on YHWH's side? Come to me!' And all the sons of Levi gathered around him" (32:6). Here the Levites, who appear belligerent and kill thousands of the idolatrous people, are opposed to the idolatrous Aaron. Moses then confirms the "ordination" of the Levites: "Moses said, 'Today you have ordained yourselves for the service of YHWH, each one at the cost of a son or a brother, and so have brought a blessing on yourselves this day.'" (32:29). What is translated here as "ordained" is מלאו ידכם "your hands have been filled" in Hebrew, and this is exactly the same expression used in Exod 28:41 for the ordination of Aaron and his sons.[32] That means that the passage in Exod 32 wants to claim for the Levites the same rights as for the Aaronides. One could therefore understand the rise of the Levites according to Exod 32 as "a replacement to the leadership of Aaron."[33] There is no consensus about the stratification and the date of Exod 32. The text is probably older than the harsh condemnation of the Levites in Num 16.[34] Its integration in the Exodus version of the story (interestingly, this episode is not mentioned in Deut 9–10) nevertheless also reflects the attempt to introduce critical notes about the Aaronide priesthood into the Torah. One may therefore suspect that Exod 32 was at least revised by the same Levitical group that is criticized in Num 16.

---

32. On this expression, see Konrad Rupprecht, "Quisquilien zur Wendung *ml'* (*'t*) *jd plnj* (jemand die Hand füllen) und zum Terminus *ml' jd* (Füllung)," in *Sefer Rendtorff: Festschrift zum 50. Geburtstag von Rolf Rendtorff*, ed. Konrad Rupprecht, DBAT 1 (Dielheim: printed by the authors, 1975), 73–93.

33. Thomas B. Dozeman, *Exodus*, ECC (Grand Rapids: Eerdmans 2009), 711. See also Jeon, "Zadokite and Levitical Scribal Conflicts," 101–2.

34. Thomas B. Dozeman, "The Composition of Ex 32 within the Context of the Enneateuch," in *Auf dem Weg zur Endgestalt von Genesis bis II Regum: Festschrift für Hans-Christoph Schmitt zu seinem 65. Geburtstag*, ed. Martin Beck and Ulrike Schorn, BZAW 370 (Berlin: de Gruyter, 2006), 175–89.

4. Moses's Superiority over Aaron

The introduction of Aaron as Moses's brother takes places in Exod 4:13–17, a passage that is part of 4:1–17, a post-Priestly supplement to the call of Moses in Exod 3.[35] This passage deals with Moses's doubts about the success of his mission. The first sign that YHWH performs for Moses, the transformation of his staff into a serpent prepares the reader for the prologue of the plague narrative, as does YHWH's announcement to Moses that the waters of the Nile will turn into blood. At the end, Moses is still not convinced and asks YHWH to find someone else. YHWH gets angry with Moses.

> Then the anger of YHWH was kindled against Moses and he said, "What of your brother Aaron the Levite? I know that he can speak fluently; even now he is coming out to meet you, and when he sees you his heart will be glad. You shall speak to him and put the words in his mouth; and I will be with your mouth and with his mouth, and will teach you what you shall do. He indeed shall speak for you to the people; he shall serve as a mouth for you, and you shall be God for him. Take in your hand this staff, with which you shall perform the signs." (Exod 4:14–17)

First of all, it is interesting that Aaron is described here as a Levite and not as a priest. Is this an attempt to downgrade Aaron or an attempt to integrate the Levites into the Israelite priesthood?[36] In any case, Aaron's function here is described as that of a prophet, a spokesman. Moses shall put YHWH's words that he receives into Aaron's mouth. This description of Aaron's role triggers the statement that Moses will be "god" for Aaron (Exod 4:16). The description of Aaron as Moses's prophet occurs also in Exod 7:1, where Moses is equally qualified as "god," but here in regard to Pharaoh: "YHWH said to Moses, 'See, I have made you God to Pharaoh, and your brother Aaron shall be your prophet.'" The qualification of Aaron as a prophet is related to texts in which Moses is described

---

35. Jan C. Gertz, *Tradition und Redaktion in der Exoduserzählung: Untersuchungen zur Endredaktion des Pentateuch*, FRLANT 186 (Göttingen: Vandenhoeck & Ruprecht, 1999), 305–27; and Thomas Römer, "Exodus 3–4 und die aktuelle Pentateuchdiskussion," in *The Interpretation of Exodus: Studies in Honour of Cornelis Houtman*, ed. Riemer Roukema, CBET 44 (Leuven: Peeters, 2006), 65–79.

36. Erhard Blum, *Studien zur Komposition des Pentateuch*, BZAW 189 (Berlin: de Gruyter, 1990), 362, speaks of a "bridge" between Aaron and the Levites.

not as a prophet (as, e.g., in Deut 18) but as standing over the prophets. This is especially the case in Num 12, which is a text where Aaron appears together with Miriam in conflict with Moses. In Num 12:6-8, YHWH puts Moses over all other mediations: "When there are prophets among you, I YHWH make myself known to them in visions; I speak to them in dreams. Not so with my servant Moses; he is entrusted with all my house. With him I speak face to face—clearly, not in riddles; and he beholds the form of YHWH" (Num 12:6-8). In the following story, when Miriam is struck with leprosy, Aaron, the priest, can only take note that Miriam has become leprous; he cannot even pronounce the quarantine. He asks Moses to heal her by calling him "my Lord" (אדני) in 12:11, so that only Moses can pray to YHWH, who instructs him about the time of exclusion from the camp. Aaron is depicted as unable to accomplish his priestly functions and dependent totally on Moses.[37]

One can therefore conclude that Exod 4:1-17 and Num 12 originated in the context of the lay group who considered Moses as their ancestor and as the only real mediator. In composing such texts, they apparently wanted to counter other texts such as Num 18, where Aaron receives direct divine communication and where his priestly function is presented as the most important in Israel.

Yet Num 12 transfers the priestly function to Moses, and a similar transfer can be observed in Exod 4:17, where Moses shall take a "staff" (מטה). The same staff that is mentioned in regard to Moses for the first time in Exod 4:2 appears in the hand of Moses in the account of the parting of the Sea as well, in Exod 14:16, where YHWH tells Moses to lift his staff and to raise his hands to divide the waters. In the rest of the story, however, Moses only raises his hand and the staff is never mentioned again. One can therefore conclude that this mention of the staff is a later insertion. In the plague story in Exod 7-8, the staff is clearly Aaron's staff, as also in Num 17:16-26. In late texts this priestly staff has been transferred to Moses in order to bestow him also with the symbol of priestly and magical power (see, e.g., Exod 9:23; 10:13; 17:5, 9).[38]

---

37. Thomas Römer, "Israel's Sojourn in the Wilderness and the Construction of the Book of Numbers," in *Reflection and Refraction: Studies in Biblical Historiography in Honour of A. Graeme Auld*, ed. Robert Rezetko, Timothy H. Lim, and W. Brian Aucker, VTSup 113 (Leiden: Brill, 2007), 439-41.

38. Gertz, *Tradition und Redaktion*, 313-14.

4. A Short Conclusion

External evidence from Elephantine and some biblical texts lead to the assumption that we should distinguish at least three main groups that were involved in the compilation of the Pentateuch, independently from Samaritan and Egyptian diaspora voices: (1) a lay group, which may be reflected in some texts which highlight the role of the elders and in others with the heads of the fathers' houses, and which considered Moses to be their founder; (2) a priestly group, which considered Aaron as its ancestor; and (3) a group of Levites, who tried to maintain their privileges.

The narrations about conflicts or tensions among Moses, Aaron, and the Levites seem to reflect tensions between these groups during the Persian period and perhaps early Hellenistic period. Most texts, especially those ascribed to P in Exodus and Leviticus, seem to reflect a compromise between the lay group and the priestly group. In those texts, Moses and Aaron act together, although Moses stands in almost every passage at first position. But there was apparently some disagreement about that compromise: in Exod 32 the Levites claim to be closer to Moses than the Aaronides. Numbers 16 strongly rejects Levitical claims and confirms Aaron's priestly prerogatives. The Aaronide group also made some attempts to put Aaron over Moses in late texts from the book of Numbers and in an addition to a P text in Exod 6. Other texts, probably written in the milieu of the lay group, responded to these texts by emphasizing Moses's superiority over Aaron, claiming that Moses was "god" to Aaron and Aaron his prophet. Numbers 12 also suggests that Aaron's priestly power needs support from Moses. The priestly power of Moses was finally emphasized by transforming Aaron's staff into Moses's staff.

The Pentateuch appears in this regard not only as a compromise but also as a record of scribal conflicts that were never totally resolved. The only solution was to maintain different claims inside the same document. Yet the epitaph about Moses as the incomparable mediator in Deut 34:10–12 makes the figure of Moses the most important human actor of the Torah, who can be overcome neither by Aaron nor by the Levites.

Bibliography

Achenbach, Reinhard. *Die Vollendung der Tora: Studien zur Redaktionsgeschichte des Numeribuches im Kontext von Hexateuch und Pentateuch*. BZABR 3. Wiesbaden: Harrassowitz, 2003.

Albertz, Rainer. *Exodus*. 2 vols. ZBK 2. Zurich: TVZ, 2012–2015.
———. *Religionsgeschichte Israels in alttestamentlicher Zeit*. 2 vols. GAT 8. Göttingen: Vandenhoeck & Ruprecht, 1992–1997.
Becker, Uwe. "Die Perser im Esra- und Nehemiabuch." *ZAW* 127 (2015): 607–27.
Blenkinsopp, Joseph. "Was the Pentateuch the Civic and Religious Constitution of the Jewish Ethnos in the Persian Period?" Pages 41–62 in *Persia and Torah: The Theory of the Imperial Authorization of the Pentateuch*. Edited by James W. Watts. SymS 17. Atlanta: Society of Biblical Literature, 2001.
Blum, Erhard. *Studien zur Komposition des Pentateuch*. BZAW 189. Berlin: de Gruyter, 1990.
Cowley, A. E. *Aramaic Papyri of the Fifth Century B.C.* Oxford: Clarendon, 1923.
Crüsemann, Frank. *Die Tora: Theologie und Sozialgeschichte des alttestamentlichen Gesetzes*. Munich: Kaiser, 1992.
Dahmen, Ulrich. *Leviten und Priester im Deuteronomium: Literarkritische und redaktionsgeschichtliche Studien*. BBB 110. Bodenheim: PHILO, 1996.
Dozeman, Thomas B. "The Composition of Ex 32 within the Context of the Enneateuch." Pages 175–89 in *Auf dem Weg zur Endgestalt von Genesis bis II Regum: Festschrift für Hans-Christoph Schmitt zu seinem 65. Geburtstag*. Edited by Martin Beck and Ulrike Schorn. BZAW 370. Berlin: de Gruyter, 2006.
———. *Exodus*. ECC. Grand Rapids: Eerdmans 2009.
Dušek, Jan. "Mt. Gerizim Sanctuary, Its History and Enigma of Origin." *HBAI* 3 (2014): 111–33.
Ede, Franziska. *Die Josefsgeschichte: Literarkritische und redaktionsgeschichtliche Untersuchungen zur Entstehung von Gen 37–50*. BZAW 485. Berlin: de Gruyter, 2016.
Finkelstein, Israel. "The Territorial Extent and Demography of Yehud/Judea in the Persian and Early Hellenistic Periods." *RB* 117 (2010): 39–54.
Frei, Peter. "Zentralgewalt und Lokalautonomie im Achämenidenreich." Pages 5–131 in *Reichsidee und Reichsorganisation im Perserreich*. Edited by Peter Frei and Klaus Koch. 2nd ed. OBO 55. Freiburg: Universitätsverlag; Göttingen: Vandenhoeck & Ruprecht, 1996.
Gerhards, Meik. *Die Aussetzungsgeschichte des Mose: Literar- und traditionsgeschichtliche Untersuchungen zu einem Schlüsseltext des nich-*

tpriesterlichen Tetrateuch. WMANT 109. Neukirchen-Vluyn: Neukirchener Verlag, 2006.

Gertz, Jan C. *Tradition und Redaktion in der Exoduserzählung: Untersuchungen zur Endredaktion des Pentateuch*. FRLANT 186. Göttingen: Vandenhoeck & Ruprecht, 2000.

Grätz, Sebastian. *Das Edikt des Artaxerxes: Eine Untersuchung zum religionspolitischen und historischen Umfeld von Esra 7,12–26*. BZAW 337. Berlin: de Gruyter, 2004.

Granerød, Gard. *Dimensions of Yahwism in the Persian Period: Studies in the Religion and Society of the Judaean Community at Elephantine*. BZAW 488. Berlin: de Gruyter, 2016.

Hensel, Benedikt. *Juda und Samaria: Zum Verhältnis zweier nach-exilischer Jahwismen*. FAT 110. Tübingen: Mohr Siebeck, 2017.

Houston, Walter. "Between Salem and Mount Gerizim: The Context of the Formation of the Torah Reconsidered." *JAJ* 5 (2014): 311–34.

Jeon, Jaeyoung. "The Zadokite and Levitical Scribal Conflicts and Hegemonic Struggles." Pages 97–110 in *Scripture as Social Discourse: Social-Scientific Perspectives on Early Jewish and Christian Writings*. Edited by Jessica M. Keady, Todd E. Klutz, and Casey A. Strine. London: T&T Clark, 2018.

———. "The Zadokites in the Wilderness: The Rebellion of Korach (Num 16) and the Zadokite Redaction." *ZAW* 127 (2015): 381–411.

Jericke, Detlef. "Der Berg Garizim im Deuteronomium." *ZAW* 124 (2012): 213–28.

Knauf, Ernst A. "Audiatur et altera pars: Zur Logik der Pentateuchredaktion." *BK* 53 (1998): 118–26.

Knierim, Rolf P. "The Composition of the Pentateuch." Pages 393–415 in *Society of Biblical Literature 1985 Seminar Papers*. SBLSP 24. Atlanta: Scholars Press, 1985.

Knoppers, Gary N., and Bernard M. Levinson, eds. *The Pentateuch as Torah: New Models for Understanding Its Promulgation and Acceptance*. Winona Lake, IN: Eisenbrauns, 2007.

Kratz, Reinhard G. "Temple and Torah: Reflections on the Legal Status of the Pentateuch Between Elephantine and Qumran." Pages 77–103 in *The Pentateuch as Torah: New Models for Understanding Its Promulgation and Acceptance*. Edited by Gary N. Knoppers and Bernard M. Levinson. Winona Lake, IN: Eisenbrauns, 2007.

Lee, Kyong-Jin. *The Authority and Authorization of the Torah in the Persian Period*. CBET 64. Leuven: Peeters, 2011.

Lipschits, Oded. "Demographic Changes in Judah between the Seventh and the Fifth Centuries B.C.E." Pages 323–76 in *Judah and the Judeans in the Neo-Babylonian Period*. Edited by Oded Lipschits and Joseph Blenkinsopp. Winona Lake, IN: Eisenbrauns, 2003.

Magen, Yitzhak. "Mount Gerizim: Temple City." *Qad* 120 (2000): 74–118.

Meyer, Rudolf. "Levitische Emanzipationsbestrebungen in nachexilischer Zeit." *OLZ* 41 (1938): 722–28.

Nihan, Cristophe. *From Priestly Torah to Pentateuch: A Study in the Composition of the Book of Leviticus*. FAT 2/25. Tübingen: Mohr Siebeck, 2007.

———. "Garizim et Ébal dans le Pentateuque: Quelques remarques en marge de la publication d'un nouveau fragment du Deutéronome." *Sem* 54 (2011): 185–210.

Otto, Eckart. *Das Deuteronomium im Pentateuch und Hexateuch: Studien zur Literaturgeschichte von Pentateuch und Hexateuch im Lichte des Deuteronomiumrahmens*. FAT 30. Tübingen: Mohr Siebeck, 2000.

———. *Das Gesetz des Mose*. Darmstadt: Wissenschaftliche Buchgesellschaft, 2007.

———. "The Pentateuch in Synchronical and Diachronical Perspectives: Protorabbinic Scribal Erudition Mediating between Deuteronomy and the Priestly Code." Pages 14–35 in *Das Deuteronomium zwischen Pentateuch und Deuteronomistischem Geschichtswerk*. Edited by Eckart Otto and Reinhard Achenbach. FRLANT 206. Göttingen: Vandenhoeck & Ruprecht, 2004.

Porten, Bezalel. *The Elephantine Papyri in English: Three Millennia of Cross-Cultural Continuity and Change*. 2nd ed. DMOA 22. Leiden: Brill, 2011.

Redford, Donald B. "The So-Called 'Codification' of Egyptian Law Under Darius I." Pages 135–59 in *Persia and Torah: The Theory of the Imperial Authorization of the Pentateuch*. Edited by James W. Watts. SymS 17. Atlanta: Society of Biblical Literature, 2001.

Römer, Thomas. "Exodus 3–4 und die aktuelle Pentateuchdiskussion." Pages 65–79 in *The Interpretation of Exodus: Studies in Honour of Cornelis Houtman*. Edited by Riemer Roukema. CBET 44. Leuven: Peeters, 2006.

———. "Israel's Sojourn in the Wilderness and the Construction of the Book of Numbers." Pages 419–45 in *Reflection and Refraction: Studies in Biblical Historiography in Honour of A. Graeme Auld*. Edited by

Robert Rezetko, Timothy H. Lim, and W. Brian Aucker. VTSup 113. Leiden: Brill, 2007.

———. "The Joseph Story in the Book of Genesis: Pre-P or Post-P?" Pages 185–201 in *The Post-Priestly Pentateuch: New Perspectives on Its Redactional Development and Theological Profiles*. Edited by Federico Giuntoli and Konrad Schmid. FAT 101. Tübingen: Mohr Siebeck, 2015.

———. "Moses and the Women in Exodus 1–4." *Indian Theological Studies* 52 (2015): 237–50.

Römer, Thomas, and Marc Z. Brettler. "Deuteronomy 34 and the Case for a Persian Hexateuch." *JBL* 119 (2000): 401–19.

Rupprecht, Konrad. "Quisquilien zur Wendung *ml'* (*'t*) *jd plnj* (jemand die Hand füllen) und zum Terminus *ml' jd* (Füllung)." Pages 73–93 in *Sefer Rendtorff: Festschrift zum 50. Geburtstag von Rolf Rendtorff*. Edited by Konrad Rupprecht. DBAT 1. Dielheim: printed by the authors, 1975.

Rütersworden, Udo. "Die persische Reichsautorisation der Thora: Fact or Fiction?" *ZABR* 1 (1995): 47–61.

Samuel, Harald. *Von Priestern zum Patriarchen: Levi und die Leviten im Alten Testament*. BZAW 448. Berlin: de Gruyter, 2014.

Schipper, Bernd U. "Joseph, Ahiqar, and Elephantine: The Joseph Story as a Diaspora Novella." *Journal of Ancient Egyptian Interconnections* 18 (2018): 71–84.

Schmidt, Ludwig. *Das vierte Buch Mose: Numeri 10,11–36,13*. ATD 7.2. Göttingen: Vandenhoeck & Ruprecht, 2004.

Schmidt, Werner H. *Exodus*. 2 vols. BKAT 2. Neukirchen-Vluyn: Neukirchener Verlag, 1988–1999.

Ska, Jean-Louis. "'Persian Imperial Authorization': Some Question Marks." Pages 161–82 in *Persia and Torah: The Theory of the Imperial Authorization of the Pentateuch*. Edited by James W. Watts. SymS 17. Atlanta: Society of Biblical Literature, 2001.

Stern, Ephraim, and Yitzhak Magen. "Archaeological Evidence for the First Stage of the Samaritan Temple on Mount Gerizim." *IEJ* 52 (2002): 49–57.

Weinberg, Joel. *The Citizen-Temple Community*. JSOTSup 151. Sheffield: JSOT Press, 1992.

Wiesehöfer, Josef. "'Reichsgesetz' oder 'Einzelfallgerechtigkeit'? Bemerkungen zu P. Freis These von der achaemenidischen 'Reichsautorisation.'" *ZABR* 1 (1995): 36–46.

The Elders Redaction (ER) in the Pentateuch: Scribal Contributions of an Elders Group in the Formation of the Pentateuch

Jaeyoung Jeon

In the current form of the Pentateuch, two clearly distinguished tents of meeting (אהל מועד) are erected in the wilderness of Sinai. The more well-known tent is the priestly wilderness sanctuary where the priestly ritual service is conducted (Exod 25–31), but another tent serves as a sort of prophetic tent where YHWH meets Moses personally (Exod 33:7–11).[1] Whereas the former was built as a national enterprise carried out by the wise craftsman Bezalel, its construction enabled through voluntary contributions of the people, the latter was a relatively simple structure erected by Moses only for himself and YHWH. This prophetic tent of meeting appears throughout the post-Sinaitic wilderness narrative especially in editorial passages (e.g., Exod 33:7–10; Num 11:16–17, 24b–30; 12:4–10a; Deut 31:14–15, 23). Earlier generations of pentateuchal scholarship attributed those passages either to the early, pre-Priestly source (J or E) or an old tradition or redaction (JE redaction) independent of J and E.[2] In more recent

---

1. For the prophetic nature of this tent, see e.g., Menahem Haran, "The Nature of the ''Ohel Mo'edh' in Pentateuchal Sources," *JSS* 5 (1960): 50–65; Jacob Milgrom, *Numbers*, JPS Torah Commentary (Philadelphia: Jewish Publication Society, 1990), 386; Israel Knohl, "The Priestly Torah Versus the Holiness School: Ideological Aspects," in *Proceedings of the Tenth World Congress of Jewish Studies: Jerusalem, August 16–24, 1989*, ed. David Asaf (Jerusalem: World Union of Jewish Studies 1990), 73–77.

2. For attribution to an early, pre-Priestly source, see, e.g., Abraham Kuenen, *An Historico-Critical Inquiry into the Origin and Composition of the Hexateuch (Pentateuch and Book of Joshua)*, trans. Philip H. Wiksteed (London: Macmillan, 1886), 158; H. Holzinger, *Numeri*, KHC 4 (Tübingen: Mohr Siebeck, 1903), 42; Otto Eissfeldt, *Hexateuch-Synopse: Die Erzählung der fünf Bücher Mose und des Buches Josua mit dem*

pentateuchal scholarship, these passages are considered part of a larger redactional/compositional layer and dated much later, in the exilic or Persian periods. Erhard Blum and John Van Seters, for instance, regard them as the core of a Deuteronomistic composition (KD) or late J, respectively, which they date to the exilic period.[3] Reinhard Achenbach attributes them to his post-Priestly Pentateuch redaction, dating it to the Persian period.[4] However, Antonius H. J. Gunneweg had already correctly viewed the texts as a separate redactional layer, yet without further identification or dating.[5] This position has been followed by Ranier Albertz, who attributes the layer to a separate, second phase of post-Priestly Deuteronomistic redaction.[6]

Anfange des Richterbuches (Leipzig: Hinrichs, 1922), 39, 57; Georg Fohrer, *Introduction to the Old Testament* (London: SPCK, 1984), 167; and Brevard S. Childs, *The Book of Exodus: A Critical, Theological Commentary*, OTL (Philadelphia: Westminster, 1974), 590–93. For attribution to a JE redaction, see Julius Wellhausen, *Die Composition des Hexateuchs und der historischen Bücher des Alten Testaments*, 3rd ed. (Berlin: Reimer, 1899), 101–2; George B. Gray, *A Critical and Exegetical Commentary on Numbers*, ICC 4 (Edinburgh: T&T Clark, 1912), 98–99; Hugo Gressmann, *Mose und seine Zeit: Ein Kommentar zu den Mose-Sagen*, FRLANT 18 (Göttingen: Vandenhoeck & Ruprecht, 1913), 240 n. 3; Martin Noth, *Numbers: A Commentary*, trans. James D. Martin, OTL (Philadelphia: Westminster, 1968), 83; Volkmar Fritz, *Israel in der Wüste: Traditionsgeschichtliche Untersuchung der Wüstenüberlieferung des Jahwisten*, Marburger Theologische Studien 7 (Marburg: Elwert, 1970), 17; and Wilhelm Rudolph, *Der "Elohist" von Exodus bis Josua*, BZAW 68 (Berlin: Töpelmann, 1938), 55. Martin Noth, *Exodus: A Commentary*, trans. J. S. Bowden, OTL (Philadelphia: Westminster, 1974), 254–55, regards the passages neither as J nor as secondary addition to J but as a special tradition taken up by J. Also, Tryggve N. D. Mettinger, *The Dethronement of Sabaoth: Studies in the Shem and Kabod Theologies*, ConBOT 18 (Lund: Gleerup, 1982), 81, attribute the tent texts in Exod 33 and Num 11–12 to an old premonarchical tradition of the tent of meeting.

3. Erhard Blum, *Studien zur Komposition des Pentateuch*, BZAW 189 (Berlin: de Gruyter, 1990), 76–88; John Van Seters, *The Life of Moses: The Yahwist as Historian in Exodus–Numbers* (Louisville: Westminster John Knox, 1994), 341–44.

4. Reinhard Achenbach, *Die Vollendung der Tora: Studien zur Redaktionsgeschichte des Numeribuches im Kontext von Hexateuch und Pentateuch*, BZABR 3 (Wiesbaden: Harrassowitz, 2003), 290–301. See also Eckart Otto, *Das Deuteronomium im Pentateuch und Hexateuch: Studien zur Literaturgeschichte von Pentateuch und Hexateuch im Lichte des Deuteronomiumrahmens*, FAT 30 (Tübingen: Mohr Siebeck, 2000), 188.

5. Antonius H. J. Gunneweg, "Das Gesetz und die Propheten: Eine Auslegung von Ex 33,7–11; Num 11,4–12,8; Dtn 31,14f.; 34,10," *ZAW* 102 (1990): 171–75.

6. Rainer Albertz, "Ex 33,7–11, ein Schlüsseltext für die Rekonstruktion der Redaktionsgeschichte des Pentateuch," *BN* 149 (2011): 13–43; Albertz, "The Late Exilic Book of Exodus (Exodus 1–34*): A Contribution to the Pentateuchal Discussion," in *The Pentateuch, International Perspectives on Current Research*, ed. Thomas B. Dozeman,

Against this backdrop, I will seek here to prove that those passages belong to a separate layer added to the Pentateuch at a relatively late post-P stage. It will also be suggested that some other passages can be assigned to the second phase of this redaction. The redactional layer(s) advocate(s) the religiopolitical interests of the lay leaders (elders) against the priestly group; I would therefore designate the layer(s) as an "Elders Redaction" (ER). After identifying two stages of ER (ER^1 and ER^2), the discussion will focus on the sociohistorical profile and background of ER in the context of the complex religiopolitical state of the Yahwistic community of Yehud in the Persian period. The last part of the essay will address ER's literary interactions with the different layers of the priestly scribal works.

1. Sociohistorical Perspective in the Persian Period

If we assume a complicated literary process especially during the Persian period, the social, economic, religious, and political states of Persian Yehud should be considered its background. Since Max Weber's seminal study of ancient Judaism (1921), the Yehud community has been perceived not as a unified society but as one that consists of conflicting social classes, groups, and parties. Recent developments in the study of this period, especially after the 1980s, have revealed more diverse socioreligious conflicts, such as conflicts between returnees from the *golah* and those who remained in the land; between different economic classes; between urban and rural; among priestly groups, lay intellectuals, and prophetic circles; between priestly and Levitical groups; between different Yahwistic communities in Jerusalem, Samaria, and the diaspora; and between pro-Persian and pro-Egyptian positions. It is now broadly admitted that various voices about identity and program for restoration, as well as various claims for leadership and hegemony in the community, are reflected in the biblical literature produced in this period. If any pentateuchal text is to be dated to the Persian period, the text can be examined in terms of the different voices and claims of the various social and religious groups and classes. This essay aims to examine possible debates among different scribal groups by analyzing a group of texts found primarily in Exodus, Numbers, and Deuteronomy, which I provisionally designate as the "Elders Redaction."

Konrad Schmid, and Baruch J. Schwartz, FAT 78 (Tübingen: Mohr Siebeck, 2011), 244–57; and Albertz, *Exodus*, 2 vols., ZBK 2 (Zurich: TVZ, 2012–2015), 1:23–25.

2. The Elders Redaction (ER¹)

2.1. Erecting the Tent of Meeting (Exod 33:7–11a)

Critics have recognized a group of texts that share elements such as the tent of meeting (אהל מועד) erected outside the camp and YHWH's occasional advent on it in the pillar of cloud. This motif first appears in a redactional passage, Exod 33:7–11a. In this passage, Moses erects the tent for his meeting with God outside of the Israelite camp after the people have transgressed by making the golden calf. The tent functions as a prophetic space where the people may seek YHWH and YHWH speaks to Moses "face to face" (פנים אל פנים). Neither priestly service nor ritual activity is supposed to take place in the tent. Contrary to the priestly tent, where YHWH resides (שכן) permanently in its innermost part, YHWH descends (ירד) on this prophetic tent temporarily in the pillar of cloud when Moses approaches it (Exod 33:9). This tent is therefore only the tent of meeting rather than the residence (משכן) of YHWH, as in P.

Previous generations of scholars often attributed this passage to an earlier, pre-Priestly literary tradition, yet an ample number of recent studies have indicated its lateness and dated it as post-Priestly.[7] The present passage presupposes Exod 33 and its issue of YHWH's presence among the people, which is more recently regarded as a post-Priestly addition as well.

---

7. For previous generations of scholars, see n. 2. For more recent readings, see Achenbach, *Die Vollendung*; Otto, *Das Deuteronomium*. See also, e.g, Jan C. Gertz, "Beobachtungen zu Komposition und Redaktion in Exodus 32–34," in *Gottes Volk am Sinai: Untersuchungen zu Ex 32–34 und Dtn 9–10*, ed. Matthias Köckert and Erhard Blum, Veröffentlichungen der Wissenschaftlichen Gesellschaft für Theologie 18 (Gütersloh: Gütersloher Verlagshaus, 2001), 88–106; and Friedhelm Hartenstein, "Das 'Angesicht Gottes' in Exodus 32–34," in Köckert and Blum, *Gottes Volk am Sinai*, 158–59. Erich Zenger, *Die Sinaitheophanie: Untersuchungen zum jahwistischen und elohistischen Geschichtswerk*, FB 3 (Wurzburg: Echter, 1971), 93–94, 107, e.g., assumes three layers in Exod 33:7–11 yet dates them post-P. For criticism of Zenger, see Michael Konkel, *Sünde und Vergebung: Eine Rekonstruktion der Redaktionsgeschichte der hinteren Sinaiperikope (Exodus 32–34) vor dem Hintergrund aktueller Pentateuchmodelle*, FAT 58 (Tübingen: Mohr Siebeck, 2008), 120 n. 81. For the unity of the passage, see Albertz, "Ex 33,7–11," 16–17 and Gunneweg, "Das Gesetz," 171–72. I see no reason to distinguish different layers in Exod 33:7–11a except the unexpected mention of Joshua in v. 11b. I will discuss this half verse shortly.

2.2. Appointment of the Elders (Num 11:16–17, 24b–25 [26–29], 30)

The non-Priestly tent of meeting reappears in Num 11, the story of the provision of quail in the wilderness. This story has a clear basic plot involving the greed of the people, miraculous provision, and punishment. The motif of the tent of meeting (vv. 16–17, 24b–25 [26–29], 30), however, deals with the issue of leadership of the community, an issue that is not necessarily connected to the basic plot of the story. In terms of the literary flow, these verses awkwardly interfere, disturbing the smooth flow of the narrative. Most critics therefore agree that those verses are either an originally separate strand or a secondary addition to the quail narrative.[8] The verses share major elements with the previous tent of meeting passage in Exod 33:7–11, elements such as the placement of the tent outside the camp (Num 11:30), YHWH's advent in the cloud (v. 25a), and a prophetic phenomenon (v. 25b).[9] The verses may therefore be assigned to the same redactional hand that produced Exod 33:7–11.

The major issue in those redactional passages in Num 11 is a shift of leadership of the community from the single individual Moses to a collec-

---

8. For arguments in favor of a separate source (E), see Kuenen, *Historico-Critical Inquiry*, 158; Bruno Baentsch, *Numeri*, HAT 1/2.2 (Göttingen: Vandenhoeck & Ruprecht, 1903), 276–77; Holzinger, *Numeri*, 42; Eissfeldt, *Hexateuch-Synopse*, 39, 57; Fohrer, *Introduction*, 167; Alan W. Jenks, *The Elohist and North Israelite Traditions*, SBLMS 22 (Missoula, MT: Scholars Press, 1977), 54–55; and Joel S. Baden, *J, E, and the Redaction of the Pentateuch*, FAT 68 (Tübingen: Mohr Siebeck, 2009), 109–10. For the view that the passage belongs to the Jehowist (JE redactor) or later addition, see Wellhausen, *Die Composition*, 101–3; Gray, *Critical and Exegetical Commentary*, 98–99; Gressmann, *Mose*, 240 n. 3; Fritz, *Israel*, 17; Rudolph, *Der "Elohist" von Exodus bis Josua*, 55; Philip J. Budd, *Numbers*, WBC 5 (Waco, TX: Word, 1984), 126; Noth, *Numbers*, 89; Achenbach, *Die Vollendung*; Horst Seebass, "Num XI, XII und die Hypothese des Jahwisten," *VT* 28 (1978): 214–23; and Seebass, *Numeri*, 3 vols., BKAT 4 (Neukirchen-Vluyn: Neukirchener Verlag, 1993–2003), 1:38–40. But Olivier Artus, "Moïse et la colère de Dieu en Nombres 11,4–34," in *Colères et repentirs divins: Actes du colloque organisé par le Collège de France, Paris, les 24 et 25 avril 2013*, ed. Jean-Marie Durand, Lionel Marti, and Thomas Römer, OBO 278 (Fribourg: Academic Press; Göttingen: Vandenhoeck & Ruprecht, 2015), 165–75 argues for the unity of Num 11. The last part of the passage, vv. 26–30, should be assigned to a second phase of the Elders Redaction (ER^2), which will be discussed shortly.

9. Numbers 11:30 reports that Moses and the elders returned to the camp after the division of the spirit of Moses among the elders. This verse presupposes that the tent is located outside the camp.

tive entity of the seventy elders. The layer begins with Moses's complaint about his overwhelming task to carry the people *alone* (vv. 14–15). As a response, YHWH assembles seventy members from the elders of Israel at the tent of meeting and divides the spirit of Moses upon them (vv. 24b–25a). The elders experience ecstatic prophecy (התנבא) upon the division of the spirit (v. 25b). In this way, the seventy elders are empowered to share Moses's responsibility and authority over the community.

2.3. Blame of Aaron and Miriam (Num 12:1*, 2, 4–8, 9*, 10a, 11b)

The motifs of the tent and YHWH's descent upon it continue to appear in the following chapter, Num 12, the narrative about Miriam's leprosy. There has been a general agreement in distinguishing the passages about the tent of meeting (Num 12:4–10a) from the basic narrative of Miriam accusing Moses of intermarriage with a Cushite woman followed by YHWH punishing her with leprosy (vv. 1, 2a, 9*, 10a, 13–15).[10] The controversial part of the source/layer division involves the passages containing Aaron (vv. 1* 2, 9* [only בם וילך], 10b–12). Some critics have attributed the Aaron passages to the basic Miriam story, while more recent studies assign them to a late addition.[11] In my view, Aaron is present in both strands: in the original Miriam story, Aaron appears as a mediator between Miriam and Moses (vv. 10b, 11a, 12), while the later addition depicts Aaron as a guilty party together with Miriam (vv. 1* [only ואהרון], 2a, 9* [only בם וילך], 11b).[12] The role of Aaron as the antagonist with Miriam appears to be an

---

10. For the source/redaction-critical assignments of the tent passage, see n. 11.

11. For the position that includes Aaron in the original story, see, e.g., Baentsch, *Numeri*, 510–14; Noth, *Numbers*, 92–96; George W. Coats, *Rebellion in the Wilderness: The Murmuring Motif in the Wilderness Traditions in the Old Testament* (Nashville: Abingdon, 1968), 261–64. See also Aaron Schart, *Mose und Israel im Konflikt: Eine redaktionsgeschichtliche Studie zu den Wüstenerzählungen*, OBO 98 (Freiburg: Universitätsverlag; Göttingen: Vandenhoeck & Ruprecht, 1990), 216–18. For the opposite position, see, e.g., Fritz, *Israel*, 75–79 and Achenbach, *Die Vollendung*, 267–301.

12. Aaron also appears in the original layer, yet he rather expectedly interferes between Miriam and Moses and makes petition for her (vv. 11a, 12), which presupposes the kinship between Miriam and Aaron (e.g., Exod 15:20; Num 26:59). Aaron's presence is justified by the fact that the original layer is characterized by family motifs. The original narrative treats a family issue such as Moses's marriage; the relationship between YHWH and Miriam is figuratively described as father and daughter (v. 14); motifs such as Miriam's birth, mother, and womb are used as the excuse for Miriam (v. 12).

integral part of the tent strand, as will be discussed below, and thus can be assigned to ER.[13]

The ER passages in Num 11 share the common features of the ER layer such as the tent of meeting outside the camp (v. 4), YHWH's descent in the pillar of cloud (v. 5a), and the issue of prophetic authority (v. 6).[14] Furthermore, the passage contains an expression of YHWH speaking to Moses "mouth to mouth" (פה אל פה, v. 8a) that is quite similar to YHWH speaking "face to face" (פנים אל פנים) in Exod 33:11a. Both expressions are used to indicate intimacy between YHWH and Moses.

The main focus of the ER layer in Num 12 is to emphasize Moses's superior authority over Aaron and Miriam. They challenge Moses's exclusive prophetic authority, claiming that YHWH spoke also to them (v. 2). Yet YHWH confirms Moses's higher authority by comparing YHWH's intimacy with Moses to YHWH's relationship with other prophets (vv. 6–8). The original Miriam story was probably selected as the place to insert the present content because Miriam is the only prophetic figure alongside Moses in Exodus–Numbers. Miriam thus represents prophetic authority in the present layer. Also the role of Aaron, notably, is altered from the mediator between Moses and Miriam in the earlier layer to that of the antagonist. The blame of Aaron and Miriam in the layer can be interpreted as polemic against both prophetic and priestly circles, as will be discussed shortly.

2.4. Moses's Exalted Prophetic Authority (Deut 34:10)

The ER layer skips the rest of the book of Numbers and reappears at the end of the Pentateuch. Deut 34:10–12, the concluding remark of the

---

13. Aaron is well embedded in the tent strand that deals with the prophetic issue (vv. 2–8): e.g., "with us" (גם בנו) in v. 2a; the names of Moses, Aaron, and Miriam and the expression "three of you" (or "them": שלשתכם and שלשתם) in v. 4; the names of Aaron and Miriam, as well as "two of them" (שניהם) in v. 5 followed by consistent use of plural such as שמעו־נא and נביאכם (v. 6), as well as יראתם (v. 8). Aaron's intercession for Miriam in vv. 10b–12 starts with Aaron's diagnosis of leprosy והנה מצרעת (v. 10b), which repeats the same report (והנה ... מצרעת) in v. 10a. The repetition in the verse supports the view that Aaron's petition in v. 11b belongs to the later layer. Aaron's petition for Miriam and himself (v. 11b), which imitates the style of v. 12, was probably intended to make leprosy the punishment for their challenge to Moses's prophetic authority (v. 2).

14. YHWH commands Moses, Aaron, and Miriam to "come out" (צאו) to the tent (v. 4ab), which presupposes the location of the tent outside the camp.

Pentateuch, has some features in common with ER. For instance, verse 10a describes Moses's superior prophetic authority, as it is the main focus of the ER text in Num 12. Also, the expression "face to face" (פנים אל פנים), which emphasizes the intimacy between YHWH and Moses (Exod 33:11a), recurs in Deut 34:10b (ידעו יהוה פנים אל פנים).[15] This expression rarely occurs in the Hebrew Bible.[16] By putting the verse at the very end of the Pentateuch, ER envelops the pentateuchal narratives from the Sinai narrative (Exod 33:7–11) to Deuteronomy.

3. The Second Phase of ER (ER²)

Some pentateuchal passages exhibit a close literary affinity to the previously discussed ER layer, yet simultaneously do not seem to have been added by exactly the same hand of ER. They probably stemmed from the identical scribal circle of elders in a later stage, so that we may assign them to a second phase of ER (ER²). The following passages may be attributed to ER².

The first is the introduction of Joshua at the tent of meeting in Exod 33:11b. Here Joshua is introduced as Moses's young assistant (משרתו) who permanently serves at the tent of meeting. This half verse is, however, not deeply embedded in the main body of the strand but appears to be a sort of postscript attached with its own purpose to foreshadow Joshua's succession of Moses.

Joshua is also identified as Moses's assistant in the story of the golden calf. When Moses is summoned to ascend the mountain of God, he is accompanied by Joshua his assistant (משרתו, Exod 24:13a). Together with the authorization of Aaron and Hur as ad hoc leaders of the community (Exod 24:14), the mention of Joshua is usually regarded as a late addition. Joshua appears once again in Exod 32:17–18, which is equally regarded as editorial.[17] Joshua is located somewhere between the mountaintop and the

---

15. Blum, *Studien*, 88.

16. Except the two occurrences, the expression appears only in Gen 32:31 and Ezek 20:35. But in the latter case, the expression is used in the context of judgement rather than divine intimacy.

17. See, recently, e.g., Gertz, "Beobachtungen," 97; Hans-Christoph Schmitt, "Die Erzählung vom Goldenen Kalb Ex. 32* und das Deuteronomistische Geschichtswerk," in *Rethinking the Foundations: Historiography in the Ancient World and in the Bible; Essays in Honour of John Van Seters*, ed. Thomas Römer and Steven L. McKenzie,

camp, misjudging the situation in a way that leads to Moses's right answer. The main purpose of this passage is most likely to save Joshua, the future leader, from the grave sin of making and worshiping the golden calf by locating him away from the crime scene. These verses (Exod 24:13*[only ויהושע משרתו], 14; 32:17–18) therefore share the identical subject matter with Exod 33:11b and can be attributed to ER².

The appearance of Joshua, Aaron, and Hur (Exod 24:14) together provides an obvious literary link to the account of the battle with Amalek (Exod 17:8–16). Also in this account, Aaron and Hur are introduced as the two major figures beside Moses (v. 12) as well as Joshua under the command of Moses (v. 9, 10, 13). Joshua unexpectedly appears here as a military leader rather than a mere assistant. Nevertheless, although Joshua is introduced as נער (often translated "boy") in Exod 33:11b, the term נער may also refer to a young professional such as a priest (e.g., Judg 18:12; 1 Sam 2:17) or a solder (e.g., 2 Sam 1:5; 2:14).

The literary connection between the aforementioned ER² passages in the golden calf story and the present account is markedly strong. Joshua is imagining a battle situation based on the sounds from the camp (קול מלחמה, Exod 32:17), which presupposes his military role. The expression for winning and losing in a battle in both texts stems from גבר and חלש, which are unique in the Pentateuch: גבר and ויחלש in Exod 17:11, 13; גבורה and חלושה in Exod 32:18.[18] Furthermore, YHWH's command to record the battle for Joshua (Exod 17:14) presupposes and emphasizes Joshua's future leadership, which is similar to the previously mentioned ER² passages.

Another ER² text is found in Num 11:26–29, where it is inserted into the ER¹ text. The ER² text tells a short story of Eldad and Medad, who remained in the camp while the seventy elders were at the tent of meeting. This passage is often regarded as a secondary addition, yet it has literary

---

BZAW 294 (Berlin: de Gruyter, 2000), 237; Reinhard Achenbach, "The Story of the Revelation at the Mountain of God and the Redactional Editions of the Hexateuch and the Pentateuch" in *A Critical Study of the Pentateuch: An Encounter between Europe and Africa*, ed. Eckart Otto and Jurie Le Roux, Altes Testament und Moderne 20 (Münster: Lit, 2005), 137. For an updated history of scholarship on the golden calf story, see Konrad Schmid, "Israel am Sinai: Etappen der Forschungsgeschichte zu Ex 32–34 in seinen Kontexten," in Köckert and Blum, *Gottes Volk am Sinai*, 9–39.

18. Blum, *Studien*, 152.

affinity with other ER² texts.¹⁹ First, Joshua appears when he has no clear relevance to the main strand of the story, namely, the empowering of the seventy elders. He is again introduced as the assistant of Moses "from his youth" (מבחריו, v. 28), which presupposes the previous ER² texts. Equally, the manner of narration—using dialogue form in order to allow Joshua's incorrect idea to lead Moses's answer (vv. 28–29)—is identical with the dialogue between them in the golden calf story (Exod 32:17–18, ER²). Critics often connect the passage to the late eschatological view of a universal idea of prophetic gifts found in Joel 3:1 (cf. Ezek 39:28–29).²⁰ This view, however, fails to consider that ER passages in Num 11 altogether are not about prophecy but about religiopolitical leadership structure.

The ER² layer finds its conclusion in Deut 31:14–15, 23, the account of Joshua's succession of Moses. In these verses, YHWH summons Joshua and Moses to the tent of meeting and appears in the pillar of cloud (vv. 14–15). Then YHWH commands Joshua to lead the people to the promised land (v. 23). Omitting the unexpected interference of YHWH's giving Moses a song (vv. 16–22), verses 14–15 smoothly connect to verse 23 with the use of "to command" (צוה) for appointing Joshua as the successor of Moses (ואצונו in v. 14a and ויצו in v. 23a). These verses are usually regarded as editorial.²¹ Notably, however, our passage says that YHWH is "seen" (וירא) in the pillar of cloud (v. 15a) rather than "descend" (ירד) as in ER¹ texts ([Exod 33:9] Num 11:25; 12:5). Use of the root ראה in *niphal* form

---

19. See, e.g., Noth, *Numbers*, 90; Olivier Artus, "Nb 11,26–29: Une critique prophétique préexilique du pouvoir politique et du culte?," *Transeu* 14 (1998): 79–89; Artus, "Moïse," 172–73; Seebass, *Numeri*, 2:38. Some critics, however, regard the passage as an integral part of the seventy elders layer. See, e.g., Fritz, *Israel*, 17; Achenbach, *Die Vollendung*, 262; Blum, *Studien*, 79–84, 194–95.

20. See, e.g., Blum, *Studien*, 194; Achenbach, *Die Vollendung*, 262; Artus, "Moïse," 174; John Strazicich, *Joel's Use of Scripture and the Scripture's Use of Joel: Appropriation and Resignification in Second Temple Judaism and Early Christianity*, BibInt 82 (Leiden: Brill, 2007), 212. Joel 3:1 is usually thought to be dependent upon Ezek 39:28–29; for this relationship, see Hans Walter Wolff, *Joel and Amos: A Commentary on the Books of the Prophets Joel and Amos*, ed. S. Dean McBride Jr., trans. Waldemar Janzen, S. Dean McBride Jr., and Charles A. Muenchow, Hermeneia (Philadelphia: Fortress, 1984), 66; Walther Zimmerli, *Ezekiel*, ed. Frank Moore Cross and Klaus Baltzer, trans. Ronald E. Clements and James D. Martin, 2 vols., Hermeneia (Philadelphia: Fortress, 1979–1983), 2:116, 566–68.

21. See, e.g., Blum, *Studien*, 85–88; Albertz, "Ex 33,7–11," 35–36; Gunneweg, "Das Gesetz," 179.

in descriptions of theophany is a priestly style,[22] which also prefers "glory of YHWH" as the subject (Lev 9:23 Num 14:10; 16:19; 17:7; 20:6). The appearance of this expression in our text (Deut 31:15) indicates that ER² has been influenced by those priestly texts.

I have assigned so far editorial passages such as Exod 17:8–16; 33:11b; 24:13*, 14; 32:17–18; Num 11:26–29; Deut 31:14–15, 23 to the second phase of ER (ER²). ER² takes a special interest in Joshua, and this interest is consistently reflected in its redactional passages. The sociopolitical agenda behind the emphasis on Joshua will be discussed below.

4. Literary Stratigraphy of ER

As we saw above, all of the passages assigned to the present layer appear as redactional additions to the existing texts. Yet their literary connection with other non-P texts is very weak, whereas, as we saw, the connection between them is markedly strong. The current layer is thus best understood as a separate redactional work that cannot be included in a larger redactional layer or literary source.

In terms of its nature, ER is not necessarily Deuteronomistic, as Blum and Albertz argue.[23] ER's central notions such as Moses's prophetic tent outside the camp and the seventy elders as a charismatic governing institution are not typically Deuteronomistic concepts. For instance, ER's notion of the prophetic tent is unknown for other texts often regarded as Deuteronomic/Deuteronomistic. The symbol of divine presence and guidance in the wilderness is still the ark (e.g., Num 10:33; 14:44);[24] the ark motif is combined with Levitical service of the Priestly tent in post-Priestly stages (e.g., Deut 10:8–9; 31:9, 25; cf. Num 4:1–20).[25]

---

22. I prefer the more general term *priestly* rather than capitalized *Priestly* in this context, as I assign the texts indicated the second half of the sentence to a priestly scribal circle later than $P^{(G)}$. For an exposition of the recent tendency to limit the extent of P, see the introduction to this volume.

23. See nn. 3, 6.

24. This passage is recently regarded as post-Priestly. See, e.g., Reinhard Achenbach, "Die Erzählung von der gescheiterten Landnahme von Kadesch Barnea (Numeri 13–14) als Schlüsseltext der Redaktionsgeschichte des Pentateuchs," *ZABR* (2003): 75–77.

25. For the post-Priestly nature of those verses, see Eckart Otto, *Deuteronomium 1–11*, HThKAT (Freiburg: Herder, 2012), 993–96; Otto, *Deuteronomium 12–34*, HThKAT (Freiburg: Herder, 2017), 2113–14, 2124–15.

Equally, the appointment of the seventy elders in the wilderness (Num 11) contradicts the Deuteronomistic account of the appointment of judges at Horeb (Deut 1:9–18). The critical difference between the two accounts is that the seventy elders are appointed directly by YHWH with a charismatic authorization, whereas the judges in Deut 1 are selected based on their personal qualities such as wisdom, understanding, and knowledge (v. 13) and appointed by Moses with the agreement of the people (v. 14). Furthermore, the ER layer of Num 12 produced a final text that conveys strong blame for the anti-intermarriage idea by criticizing Miriam and Aaron for their opposition to Moses's marriage with a Cushite woman. Although the marriage motif belongs to the earlier stratum, ER accepts the basic story and uses it for its own agenda. The pro-intermarriage nuance of the basic story has been left intact, and even justified, without any attempt to remove or reduce it. Such an attitude directly contradicts the anti-intermarriage sentiment of Deuteronomy.

Achenbach's Pentateuch Redaction also cannot satisfactorily explain the profile of the current redactional layer. He argues that the supreme authority of Moses demonstrated especially in Num 12 and Deut 34 aims to enhance the authority of the Pentateuch.[26] This argument, however, fails to consider the ER emphasis on the seventy elders who came to share Mosaic authority, forming a collective leadership rather than elevating only Moses's status. The supreme authority of Moses, according to ER, strengthens the status of the collective leadership of the elders who share his spirit. Focusing only on Moses's status may therefore be misleading about the real purpose of the redaction.

In spite of such difficulties, recent studies by Achenbach, Jan Christian Gertz, and Albertz seem to be correct in dating those texts as post-Priestly.[27] All our texts are found in the form of additions to texts recently regarded as post-P. The first phase of our layer (ER¹) starts with the addition to Exod 33, which has recently been regarded as a very late post-P composition.[28] The retold story of manna and quail in Num 11 also presupposes the Priestly version in Exod 16 and was probably composed as a midrashic

---

26. Achenbach, *Die Vollendung*, 281–85, 290–301. Albertz, "Ex 33,7–11," 36 similarly argues that this layer is about the authority of the laity in interpreting the Torah.

27. See above, nn. 4 and 6; and Gertz, "Beobachtungen," 103.

28. See, e.g., Gertz, "Beobachtungen" and Schmid, "Israel am Sinai." See also Hartenstein, "Das 'Angesicht Gottes,'" 158–59.

interpretation of the latter.²⁹ The basic layer of Num 12 has also recently been regarded as post-P.³⁰ Linguistically as well, יעד, the root for מועד in the expression "tent of meeting" (אהל מועד) is more prominent in P^g than any non-P layer. The post-P nature of ER is a clue to understanding ER as a scribal redaction and reaction against P^G, which will be discussed shortly.

My observation so far is that ER is not a part of larger source or redactional layer but a separate redactional work with its own purpose and one of multiple literary activities carried out on the pentateuchal horizon at a post-Priestly stage. Because our layer presupposes more or less the current form of the Pentateuch, it should be understood to represent a stage near the completion of the Pentateuch during the Persian period.

5. Purpose of the Layer

What, then, is the purpose of ER? Does it contain any social, religious, or political agendas reflecting the disunited community of Persian Yehud? A clue is found, first of all, in that ER is marked by its contradictions of the Priestly text. The present tent of meeting, for example, directly contradicts the priestly tent, namely, the tabernacle.³¹ The former is erected outside the camp, which is a ritually impure space according the Priestly concept (e.g., Exod 29:14; Lev 4:12; 13:46; Num 15:35).³² So priestly control does not reach this place, and, consequently, no priestly ritual is involved in it. Albertz rightly argues that the present passages intentionally named the tent "tent of meeting," which is originally a Priestly term, in order to polemicize the Priestly tent.³³ Also in Num 12, Aaron, who represents priestly authority, is denounced and humbled before the superior authority of Moses. In Num 12:1, as we saw, Aaron and Miriam claim that YHWH also spoke to them. It is, however, mainly the Priestly texts that say YHWH directly speaks to Aaron: YHWH often speaks to Moses

---

29. Thomas Römer, "Israel's Sojourn in the Wilderness and the Construction of the Book of Numbers," in *Reflection and Refraction: Studies in Biblical Historiography in Honour of A. Graeme Auld*, ed. Robert Rezetko, Timothy H. Lim, and W. Brian Aucker, VTSup 113 (Leiden: Brill, 2007), 436–40. Achenbach, *Die Vollendung*, 221–36 also assigns much of the original quail story to post-P hexateuchal redaction.

30. See, e.g., Achenbach, *Die Vollendung*, 267–301.

31. Gunneweg, "Das Gesetz," 171–75; Hartenstein, "Das 'Angesicht Gottes,'" 158–59; Gertz, "Beobachtungen," 103; and Albertz, "Late Exilic Book," 244–47.

32. Childs, *Book of Exodus*, 592; Albertz, "Ex 33,7–11," 33–34.

33. Albertz, "Ex 33,7–11," 33–34.

and Aaron together (e.g., Lev 11:1; 13:1; 15:1) and also only to Aaron (e.g., Lev 10:8; cf. Exod 4:27). Also, according to a Priestly notion, YHWH will present himself and speak on the mercy seat (כפרת) at the holy of holies of the priestly tabernacle (Exod 25:22; Num 17:19). The notion implies that the high priest would be the one who receives the divine revelation in the post-Mosaic period. ER nevertheless directly polemicizes Aaron's claim for authority equal to Moses's (Num 12:8). The present episode should thus be understood as a polemical counterhistory to P rather than an ancient tradition that survived in the current text.[34]

ER diminishes the authority of the prophets as well. In Num 12, as we saw, ER reshapes the original story of Miriam's challenge and punishment into a confirmation of Moses's superior authority over Aaron and Miriam and, more importantly, prophets in general (Num 12:6–8). As Aaron represents the priestly circle, Miriam the prophetess represents the prophets. The present passage polemicizes not only the priestly group but also prophetic circles.

On the contrary, the party esteemed in ER is that of the seventy elders. In Num 11, as we saw above, the elders receive the spirit from Moses and are assigned to share Moses's responsibility and leadership to carry the people to the promised land. The elders now have Moses's spirit, which has enabled him to exercise excellent charismatic leadership, so they have come to have Moses's leadership.

Because the elders experience ecstatic prophecy upon the division of the spirit, some critics argue for a historical group of ecstatic prophets behind our text.[35] However, our text clarifies that such an ecstatic prophecy did not continue (Num 11:25), so its main focus is neither prophetic vocation nor such authority. Rather, the ecstatic prophecy can be understood as an authorization of their political leadership. A parallel example is found in Saul's similar experience of ecstatic prophecy in 1 Sam 10 (vv. 5–13). For Saul, this experience is not a prophetic calling but a sign of divine authorization for his future kingship (see also 1 Sam 11:6). Similarly, the present

---

34. See, e.g., Marsha C. White, "The Elohistic Depiction of Aaron: A Study in the Levite-Zadokite Controversy," in *Studies in the Pentateuch*, ed. J. A. Emerton, VTSup 41 (Leiden: Brill, 1990), 157–58, who interprets the redactional layer of Num 12 as an Elohist's attack on the Zadokite (Aaronide) priesthood in Jerusalem. Although this view is based on the old hypothesis of the Elohist, which is no longer tenable, it correctly detects the polemical nature of the text.

35. See, e.g., Noth, *Numbers*, 89–90.

of the spirit of YHWH provides political leadership in the case of David (1 Sam 16:13), while its absence implies the loss of authentic leadership for Saul (v. 14). The spirit also enables Samson to be a judge with physical power (Judg 13:25). The description of the messianic leader in Isa 11 further emphasizes the role of the spirit of YHWH in enabling the political leadership of this figure (v. 2). Isa 11:2 and Num 11:25 correspond with each other linguistically as well in using the identical expression, נוח על combined with רוח. We have another example of transferring one's spirit to another as a sign of succession, namely, the transfer of Elijah's spirit to Elisha (2 Kgs 2:15), which signifies a succession of prophetic power. Our passage (Num 11) probably took the motif of the succession of the spirit from the case of Elisha and applied it to the seventy elders. The nature of the succession is nevertheless not the ability to do miracles as in Elisha's case (2 Kgs 2:14) but the divine affirmation of the elders' charismatic religiopolitical authority as in the cases of Saul, David, Samson, and the messianic figure.

If we consider the above features together, the subject matter of ER becomes clear. Moses has an incomparable authority which neither priests nor prophets may challenge, and this authority and leadership has been transferred to the seventy elders (ER[1]) and later also to Joshua (ER[2]).[36] Therefore, according to our layer, the true post-Mosaic leadership, which is divinely authorized, is the collective leadership of the elders and Joshua.[37] This is, in my view, an explicit scribal legitimation and support for the collective religopolitical leadership of the group of lay elders with their own representative, symbolized in the figure of Joshua, in the Yahwistic community of Persian Yehud.

---

36. For the close connection between the governing body of the laity and Joshua through the tent of meeting, see, Albertz, "Ex 33,7–11," 36.

37. This conclusion diverges from that of Gunneweg and Achenbach. Gunneweg, "Das Gesetz," 178, argues that the major purpose of this layer is to emphasize the superior authority of Torah over prophetic and priestly authorities. Following this position, Achenbach, *Die Vollendung*, 267–301 includes the layer in his PentRed and claims that its purpose is to elevate the status of Torah as an ultimate source of authority. However, this layer never mentions law, regulation, or any kind of Moses's writing, while both priestly and Deuteronomic/Deuteronomistic texts explicitly emphasize them. The only party directly authorized in the layer is the seventy elders.

6. Who Were the Seventy Elders?

Once it is recognized that ER represents the interests of the lay leadership in the Yahwistic community of Yehud, the next inquiry would be whether we are able to identify the group of elders behind this scribal activity. We are relatively better informed of the priestly circle in Yehud, yet we have only fragmentary knowledge about lay leadership, which hardly constitutes a unified picture.

Concerning the seventy elders in our texts, Martin Noth assumes a circle of ecstatic prophecy behind the account of Num 11.[38] As for the seventy elders in Ezek 8, Walther Zimmerli argues that they are an institution, sanctified by ancient tradition, distinguished from the elders of Judah in exile (Ezek 8:1), and probably opposed by the priestly group represented by Ezekiel.[39] Thomas B. Dozeman understands the passages about the seventy elders in Ezekiel and Numbers more generally, claiming that the texts reflect the "growing power of elders in governing the people and in public worship in the exilic period."[40] Yet Dozeman argues further that "a particular group of 'seventy elders' was active during the exilic period," and they were a charismatic group with their own leader, which may be linked to the Deuteronomistic group.[41] As we have discussed above, however, its link to a Dtr group should be denied. Equally, a historical connection between the literary presentation of the seventy elders and a specific cultic group is hard to prove. It seems to me that a more reasonable solution is to regard seventy as a symbolic number that signifies completeness, so that the seventy elders may be interpreted as a complete gathering of the important lay leaders of the community.

A remaining question is whether this group was an organized institution. This question requires further reflection, especially in connection with the Hellenistic *gerousia* or later Sanhedrin. It has usually been assumed based on later Jewish sources such as the Mishnah (e.g., m. Sanh. 11:2) that the origin of Sanhedrin (or כנסת גדולה in Hebrew) can be traced to the Persian period. This assumption has recently been challenged by critics. As David Goodblatt and others rightly point out, the

---

38. Noth, *Numbers*, 89.
39. Zimmerli, *Ezekiel*, 1:240–41.
40. Thomas B. Dozeman, *God on the Mountain: A Study of Redaction, Theology, and Canon in Exodus 19–24*, SBLMS 37 (Atlanta: Scholars Press, 1989), 181.
41. Dozeman, *God*, 182–83.

description of the Sanhedrin in the Mishnah indicates only the situation after the destruction of the temple (70 CE) and is therefore hardly a credible historical source.[42] Nevertheless, it is notable that different sources during the Hellenistic and Roman periods consistently mention a sort of council of elders, which cannot be simply ignored as fictional imagination. The Greek term for Sanhedrin, συνέδριον, is described as either a regional council (Josephus, *B.J.* 1.170; *A.J.* 14.91) or a regularly constituted council or senate, chaired by the high priest during the Roman period.[43] Also, the term βουλή, meaning an (advisory) council, is found in some references from the Roman period, indicating city councils or sometimes a body with authority much wider than the city of Jerusalem.[44]

Earlier sources from the Hellenistic period, such as Judith, the books of Maccabees, and others, commonly mention a γερουσία or "council of elders" that functioned as an organized body representing the Jews in Palestine in relationship with the Greeks as well as the Jews in diaspora.[45] The Jewish γερουσία had around seventy members, but at times the membership reached seventy-one or seventy-two.[46] Lester Grabbe suggests that συνέδριον, βουλή, and γερουσία refer to the same continuous institution of elders that functioned throughout the Hellenistic and Roman periods rather than three different institutions.[47] His observation of the continuity

---

42. David Goodblatt, *The Monarchic Principle: Studies in Jewish Self-Government in Antiquity*, TSAJ 38 (Tübingen: Mohr Siebeck, 1994), 113. See also Joshua Efron, *Studies on the Hasmonean Period*, SJLA 39 (Leiden: Brill, 1987), 298–99; Lester L. Grabbe, "Sanhedrin, Sanhedriyyot, or Mere Invention?," *JSJ* 39 (2008): 13–14.

43. See, e.g., Josephus, *A.J.* 14.163–184; Matt 5:22; 26:59; John 11:47; Mark 15:42–43; Luke 22:66; 23:50–51; and Acts 4–5, 22–23. See also Grabbe, "Sanhedrin," 17.

44. See, an alleged letter from Claudius in Josephus, *A.J.* 20.10–14 and a number of references in Josephus (*B.J.* 2.331, 336; see also 5.144, 532; 6.354). The Greek word is often used of city councils, and such usage even occurs in Josephus, *Vita* 12.64; 13.69; 34.169.

45. See, e.g., the decree of Antiochus III (Josephus, *A.J.* 12.138–146); 1 Macc 12:5–6; 2 Macc 1:10; 4:43–50; 11:27; 3 Macc 1:6–8; Jdt 4:6–8; 11:14; 15:8. For further discussion about the Jewish *gerousia*, see Lawrence H. Schiffman, *From Text to Tradition: A History of Second Temple and Rabbinic Judaism* (Hoboken, NJ: Ktav, 1991), 68–70; Efron, *Studies*, 303–6; Russell Gmirkin, *Berossus and Genesis, Manetho and Exodus: Hellenistic Histories and the Date of the Pentateuch*, LHBOTS 433 (London: T&T Clark, 2006), 250–54.

46. See n. 45.

47. Grabbe, "Sanhedrin," 17.

of the institution of the elders enables us to surmise that the Hellenistic γερουσία probably had a forerunner in the Persian period.

To be sure, we do not have concrete proof of a council of elders as an organized political institution before the Hellenistic period. In the Babylonian period, however, elders were regarded as major constituents of postmonarchic collective leadership, together with priests and prophets (e.g., Jer 29:1; Ezek 7:26). Ezek 7:26 says, "inquire of priests for Torah, and of the elders for counsel." During the Persian period, the lay leaders were variously designated by terms including חרים, זקנים, ראשי אבות, or arguably also סרים in Ezra–Nehemiah. Some of them represent the community to imperial authorities (e.g., Ezra 5:5, 9), and, from the latter's perspective, the elders are in charge of the temple building (Ezra 6:7, 8, 14). Also, Ezra 8:10 tells us that Ezra uses the authority of the counsel of the officers and elders (עצת השרים והזקנים) in his religious reform. The Nehemiah memoir provides the number of those influential lay people who participate in the daily meal of the Persian governor as 150. Although the historical accuracy of these accounts may be doubted, they indicate at least the possible existence of a loosely organized body of influential laity apart from the governor during the Persian period, which would develop as a more authoritative and institutionalized decision-making body. The Elders Redaction I have discussed so far probably represents and supports such an early stage of the development of a council of elders during the Persian period.

7. Scribal Debates with Priestly Scribal Works

The definition of this layer as a scribal work representing the elders group leads me to the question of its relationship with the priestly scribal activities. ER is not an isolated literary work but is found within a complicated fabric of scribal debates with the priestly scribal works. Already Ezekiel, a priest-prophet in exile, harshly criticizes the seventy elders of Israel (שבעים איש מזקני בית־ישראל) for making what he deems adulterous incense offerings at the Jerusalem temple being (Ezek 8:7–13). It is hard to confirm that the seventy elders in Ezekiel are the same ones in our redaction, or even that the number seventy is a historical figure. Nevertheless, at least on a literary level, our layer is responding to Ezekiel's criticism of the seventy elders. In Num 12, the prophecies inferior to Moses are described as revelations "in visions" (במראה) and "in riddles" (בחידת) (vv. 6, 8). Notably, the only prophet recorded in the Bible who spoke in riddles (חידה) is Ezekiel (Ezek 17:2), and the use of מראה as a means of prophetic revelation is dominant only in the writings of Ezekiel and the Ezekiel school (Ezek 1:16; 8:2; 10:1; 41:21; 42:11; 43:3). It is therefore plausible that our redactor had Ezekiel and his school, which was probably a priestly group, in his mind when he diminished the prophets' authority in Num 12. The addition of Aaron as the antagonist in the chapter, as we saw, further strengthens ER's polemical attitude toward the priestly circle.

The priestly scribal circle crafted a harsh polemic against the lay leadership of the community in Num 16. The story of 250 chieftains in this chapter, written by a relatively late priestly scribe, polemicizes against the lay leadership who were struggling with the priests for the religiopolitical hegemony in the temple of Jerusalem as well as in the community.[48] It is also to this priestly polemic that ER seems to respond. In Num 16, Aaron's leadership is guaranteed through the ordeal of incense at the priestly tent, while the lay leaders are punished by the fire from YHWH (v. 35). At the non-priestly tent of meeting in ER, on the contrary, it is Aaron who is humiliated (Num 12:8, 11), while the lay leaders are selected by YHWH as the community leadership to receive the divine spirit (Num 11:25). Such a symmetrical contradiction produced by ER suggests that we should read its text as a response to and refutation of the priestly polemic against the lay leaders.

We saw above that ER² places considerable emphasis on Joshua and the post-Mosaic lay leadership. The layer places Joshua, instead of the priests or Levites, in service of the tent of meeting from its erection (Exod 33:11). Joshua is saved from the national transgression (Exod 24:13* 32:17–18) of making the golden calf, while Aaron's status as a proper leader is significantly damaged in that account. At the end of Moses's career, Joshua is commissioned at the tent as the successor of Moses (Deut 31:14–15, 23). In ER's post-Mosaic political structure, therefore, the leadership truly authorized by YHWH is the collective lay leadership of the seventy elders and Joshua. Priests are not an important part of the leadership, which reflects the lay scribes' perspective on leadership structure of the Yehud community.

---

48. Jaeyoung Jeon, "The Zadokites in the Wilderness: The Rebellion of Korach (Num 16) and the Zadokite Redaction," *ZAW* 127 (2015): 381–411; also Thomas B. Dozeman and Jaeyoung Jeon, "From Sources to Redaction: Identifying the Authors of Numbers 16" in this volume.

Probably against ER, the later priestly scribes carried out another phase of redactional activity in the books of Numbers and Joshua, focusing on the political structure of the post-Mosaic period. Briefly summarizing the relevant features of the layer, it introduces Joshua already as a chief of the tribe of Ephraim and a faithful scout in the Scouts story (esp. Num 13:4–16; 14:6–9). This redactional phase saves Joshua from the cursed fate of the exodus generation that is to die in the wilderness (Num 14:30–32) and also provides him with justification for being the leader of the conquest. Otherwise it would have been illogical for the priestly scribe to suggest that a person from the exodus generation would still lead the people into the Cannanite land. Soon enough, however, at the account of his succession of Moses (esp. Num 27:19–21), Joshua is completely subordinated to the judgment of the אורים of Eleazar the high priest. The major decisions during the conquest and the division of the land are collectively assigned to Eleazar, Joshua, and elders who are the tribal leaders (ראשי האבות, Num 32:28–32; 34:16–29; Josh 14:1–5; 19:51; 21).[49] This layer also envisions the post-Mosaic collective leadership as does ER, yet with a critical difference: the lay leadership represented by Joshua and the elders is subordinate to the authority of the high priest. In other words, this late priestly redaction admits a certain degree of function for the lay leadership yet places the high priest as head of the religiopolitical structure. Such a description of political structure can be read as a response to the lay leadership group and their scribal work (ER).[50]

This late priestly layer constitutes a significant step toward a compromise between the two groups, the lay and priestly, although the priests are described as the supreme authority. A more complete compromise is evident in redactional verses in Exod 24 (esp. vv. 1a, 9–11).[51] In this passage, the seventy elders as well as the priestly family (Aaron and his sons Nadab and Abihu) are allowed to approach to YHWH's presence at Mount

---

49. With some differences in detail, critics have distinguished this layer as a very late, or probably the latest, priestly layer mainly found mainly in Numbers and Joshua. Achenbach, e.g., regards the layer a third phase of theocratic revision in the late Persian period.

50. Gunneweg, "Das Gesetz," 179 argues for the reverse order of literary response. He understands the appointment of Joshua (Deut 31:14–15, 23) as a reaction to the priestly text Num 27:18–23.

51. See, e.g., Noth, *Exodus*, 194; Jean-Louis Ska, *The Exegesis of the Pentateuch: Exegetical Studies and Basic Questions*, FAT 66 (Tübingen: Mohr Siebeck, 2009), 165–83.

Sinai. They are especially recognized by YHWH in that they see God and have a covenant meal in God's presence. The elders and the priestly family are together representatives of the people and venerated as the chiefs of Israel (אצילי בני ישראל, Exod 24:11).[52] Although the priests were named before the elders (vv. 1a, 9a), there is no clue that would suggest a hierarchy within the two groups.

Such a scribal compromise reflects a more stabilized religiopolitical reality in the community of Yehud during the mid- or late-Persian period, in which the elders and priestly groups agreed to coexist, probably after a long period of struggle for hegemony in the community. The Aramaic letters found at Elephantine reflect a similar collective leadership in late fifth-century Jerusalem. According to the letters, the Jerusalem leadership is represented by Johanan, the high priest of Jerusalem, a certain Ostanes (probably a lay representative like Joshua), and the other elders of the Jews.[53] This structure was probably the direct forerunner of the aforementioned γερουσία, which had a similar composition of priests and elders.

8. Conclusions

In this essay I have endeavored to identify literary layers of the Elders Redaction (ER[1] and ER[2]) and to prove that they must be regarded as separate literary works rather than parts of a larger literary source or redaction. The layers are found in a relatively late phase of the formation of the Pentateuch and presuppose more or less its current form, in which Deuteronomy is already connected to a certain part of Numbers. In pentateuchal stratigraphy, ER is post-Priestly and post-Deuteronomistic. ER was most likely produced by a scribal circle belonging to or advocating the interests of the lay leadership group in the Yahwistic community of Yehud during the Persian period. Often the lay leadership group in the exilic and

---

52. Baruch Levine, *Numbers 1–20: A New Translation with Introduction and Commentary*, AB 4 (New York: Doubleday, 1993), 339, e.g., finds a literary connection between the terms אציל (noun meaning "chef") in Exod 24:11 and אצל (verb meaning "to lay aside") in Num 11:17, 25 and argues that "what was alluded in Exod 24:11 is spelled out in Num 11:25." Nevertheless, although the two terms share a common root, אציל in Exod 24:11 includes the (Aaronite) priestly family, whereas אצל in Num 11:17, 25 should be applied only to the elders. The two passages envision two different political structures, so that the former should be regarded as a later stage than ER.

53. See *TAD* A4.7:18–19; A4.8:17–18.

Persian periods has been connected to the Deuteronomistic scribal circle. This essay, however, suggests that there was a lay leadership group that did not necessarily belong to the Deuteronomistic circle. This group worked on the Pentateuch either later than the Deuteronomistic circle or simultaneously with it.

ER presents its dynamic literary relationship with the different layers of priestly scribal works, often crafting a sharp polemic against the latter. We may therefore assume that the Pentateuch has been formulated for the most part through scribal debates among lay and priestly scribal groups. The debates are directly connected to the pursuit of hegemony by those groups in the political structure of the Yehud community.

Bibliography

Achenbach, Reinhard. "Die Erzählung von der gescheiterten Landnahme von Kadesch Barnea (Numeri 13–14) als Schlüsseltext der Redaktionsgeschichte des Pentateuchs." *ZABR* (2003): 56–123.

———. "The Story of the Revelation at the Mountain of God and the Redactional Editions of the Hexateuch and the Pentateuch." Pages 126–51 in *A Critical Study of the Pentateuch: An Encounter between Europe and Africa*. Edited by Eckart Otto and Jurie Le Roux. Altes Testament und Moderne 20. Münster: Lit, 2005.

———. *Die Vollendung der Tora: Studien zur Redaktionsgeschichte des Numeribuches im Kontext von Hexateuch und Pentateuch*. BZABR 3. Wiesbaden: Harrassowitz, 2003.

Albertz, Rainer. "Ex 33,7–11, ein Schlüsseltext für die Rekonstruktion der Redaktionsgeschichte des Pentateuch." *BN* 149 (2011): 13–43.

———. *Exodus*. 2 vols. ZBK 2. Zurich: TVZ, 2012–2015.

———. "The Late Exilic Book of Exodus (Exodus 1–34*): A Contribution to the Pentateuchal Discussion." Pages 244–57 in *The Pentateuch, International Perspectives on Current Research*. Edited by Thomas B. Dozeman, Konrad Schmid, and Baruch J. Schwartz. FAT 78. Tübingen: Mohr Siebeck, 2011.

Artus, Olivier. "Moïse et la colère de Dieu en Nombres 11,4–34." Pages 165–75 in *Colères et repentirs divins: Actes du colloque organisé par le Collège de France, Paris, les 24 et 25 avril 2013*. Edited by Jean-Marie Durand, Lionel Marti, and Thomas Römer. OBO 278. Fribourg: Academic Press; Göttingen: Vandenhoeck & Ruprecht, 2015.

———. "Nb 11,26–29: Une critique prophétique préexilique du pouvoir politique et du culte?" *Transeu* 14 (1998): 79–89.
Baden, Joel. *J, E, and the Redaction of the Pentateuch*. FAT 68. Tübingen: Mohr Siebeck, 2009.
Baentsch, Bruno. *Numeri*. HAT 1/2.2. Göttingen: Vandenhoeck & Ruprecht, 1903.
Blum, Erhard. *Studien zur Komposition des Pentateuch*. BZAW 189. Berlin: de Gruyter, 1990.
Budd, Philip J. *Numbers*. WBC 5. Waco, TX: Word, 1984.
Childs, Brevard S. *The Book of Exodus: A Critical, Theological Commentary*. OTL. Philadelphia: Westminster, 1974.
Coats, George W. *Rebellion in the Wilderness: The Murmuring Motif in the Wilderness Traditions in the Old Testament*. Nashville: Abingdon, 1968.
Dozeman, Thomas B. *God on the Mountain: A Study of Redaction, Theology, and Canon in Exodus 19–24*. SBLMS 37. Atlanta: Scholars Press, 1989.
Efron, Joshua. *Studies on the Hasmonean Period*. SJLA 39. Leiden: Brill, 1987.
Eissfeldt, Otto. *Hexateuch-Synopse: Die Erzählung der fünf Bücher Mose und des Buches Josua mit dem Anfange des Richterbuches*. Leipzig: Hinrichs, 1922.
Fohrer, Georg. *Introduction to the Old Testament*. London: SPCK, 1984.
Fritz, Volkmar. *Israel in der Wüste: Traditionsgeschichtliche Untersuchung der Wüstenüberlieferung des Jahwisten*. Marburger Theologische Studien 7. Marburg: Elwert, 1970.
Gertz, Jan C. "Beobachtungen zu Komposition und Redaktion in Exodus 32–34." Pages 88–106 in *Gottes Volk am Sinai: Untersuchungen zu Ex 32–34 und Dtn 9–10*. Edited by Matthias Köckert and Erhard Blum. Veröffentlichungen der Wissenschaftlichen Gesellschaft für Theologie 18. Gütersloh: Gütersloher Verlagshaus, 2001.
Gmirkin, Russell. *Berossus and Genesis, Manetho and Exodus: Hellenistic Histories and the Date of the Pentateuch*. LHBOTS 433. London: T&T Clark, 2006.
Goodblatt, David. *The Monarchic Principle: Studies in Jewish Self-Government in Antiquity*. TSAJ 38. Tübingen: Mohr Siebeck, 1994.
Grabbe, Lester L. "Sanhedrin, Sanhedriyyot, or Mere Invention?" *JSJ* 39 (2008): 1–19.
Gray, George B. *A Critical and Exegetical Commentary on Numbers*. ICC 4. Edinburgh: T&T Clark, 1912.

Gressmann, Hugo. *Mose und seine Zeit: Ein Kommentar zu den Mose-Sagen*. FRLANT 18. Göttingen: Vandenhoeck & Ruprecht, 1913.

Gunneweg, Antonius H. J. "Das Gesetz und die Propheten: Eine Auslegung von Ex 33,7–11; Num 11,4–12,8; Dtn 31,14f.; 34,10." *ZAW* 102 (1990): 169–80.

Haran, Menahem. "The Nature of the "Ohel Mo'edh' in Pentateuchal Sources." *JSS* 5 (1960): 50–65.

Hartenstein, Friedhelm. "Das 'Angesicht Gottes' in Exodus 32–34." Pages 157–83 in *Gottes Volk am Sinai: Untersuchungen zu Ex 32–34 und Dtn 9–10*. Edited by Matthias Köckert and Erhard Blum. Veröffentlichungen der Wissenschaftlichen Gesellschaft für Theologie 18. Gütersloh: Gütersloher Verlagshaus, 2001.

Holzinger, H. *Numeri*. KHC 4. Tübingen: Mohr Siebeck, 1903.

Jenks, Alan W. *The Elohist and North Israelite Traditions*. SBLMS 22. Missoula, MT: Scholars Press, 1977.

Jeon, Jaeyoung. "The Zadokites in the Wilderness: The Rebellion of Korach (Num 16) and the Zadokite Redaction." *ZAW* 127 (2015): 381–411.

Knohl, Israel. "The Priestly Torah Versus the Holiness School: Ideological Aspects." Pages 65–118 in *Proceedings of the Tenth World Congress of Jewish Studies: Jerusalem, August 16–24, 1989*. Edited by David Asaf. Jerusalem: World Union of Jewish Studies 1990.

Konkel, Michael. *Sünde und Vergebung: Eine Rekonstruktion der Redaktionsgeschichte der hinteren Sinaiperikope (Exodus 32–34) vor dem Hintergrund aktueller Pentateuchmodelle*. FAT 58. Tübingen: Mohr Siebeck, 2008.

Kuenen, Abraham. *An Historico-Critical Inquiry into the Origin and Composition of the Hexateuch (Pentateuch and Book of Joshua)*. Translated by Philip H. Wiksteed. London: Macmillan, 1886.

Levine, Baruch. *Numbers 1–20: A New Translation with Introduction and Commentary*. AB 4. New York: Doubleday, 1993.

Mettinger, Tryggve N. D. *The Dethronement of Sabaoth: Studies in the Shem and Kabod Theologies*. ConBOT 18. Lund: Gleerup, 1982.

Milgrom, Jacob. *Numbers*. JPS Torah Commentary. Philadelphia: Jewish Publication Society, 1990.

Noth, Martin. *Exodus: A Commentary*. Translated by J. S. Bowden. OTL. Philadelphia: Westminster, 1974

———. *Numbers: A Commentary*. Translated by James D. Martin. OTL. Philadelphia: Westminster, 1968.

Otto, Eckart. *Deuteronomium 1–11*. HThKAT. Freiburg: Herder, 2012.

———. *Deuteronomium 12–34*. HThKAT. Freiburg: Herder, 2017.
———. *Das Deuteronomium im Pentateuch und Hexateuch: Studien zur Literaturgeschichte von Pentateuch und Hexateuch im Lichte des Deuteronomiumrahmens*. FAT 30. Tübingen: Mohr Siebeck, 2000.
Römer, Thomas. "Israel's Sojourn in the Wilderness and the Construction of the Book of Numbers." Pages 419–45 in *Reflection and Refraction: Studies in Biblical Historiography in Honour of A. Graeme Auld*. Edited by Robert Rezetko, Timothy H. Lim, and W. Brian Aucker. VTSup 113. Leiden: Brill, 2007.
Rudolph, Wilhelm. *Der "Elohist" von Exodus bis Josua*. BZAW 68. Berlin: Töpelmann, 1938.
Schart, Aaron. *Mose und Israel im Konflikt: Eine redaktionsgeschichtliche Studie zu den Wüstenerzählungen*. OBO 98. Freiburg: Universitätsverlag; Göttingen: Vandenhoeck & Ruprecht, 1990.
Schiffman, Lawrence H. *From Text to Tradition: A History of Second Temple and Rabbinic Judaism*. Hoboken, NJ: Ktav, 1991.
Schmid, Konrad. "Israel am Sinai: Etappen der Forschungsgeschichte zu Ex 32–34 in seinen Kontexten." Pages 9–39 in *Gottes Volk am Sinai: Untersuchungen zu Ex 32–34 und Dtn 9–10*. Edited by Matthias Köckert and Erhard Blum. Veröffentlichungen der Wissenschaftlichen Gesellschaft für Theologie 18. Gütersloh: Gütersloher Verlagshaus, 2001.
Schmitt, Hans-Christoph. "Die Erzählung vom Goldenen Kalb Ex. 32* und das Deuteronomistische Geschichtswerk." Pages 235–50 in *Rethinking the Foundations: Historiography in the Ancient World and in the Bible; Essays in Honour of John Van Seters*. Edited by Thomas Römer and Steven L. McKenzie. BZAW 294. Berlin: de Gruyter, 2000.
Seebass, Horst. *Numeri*. 3 vols. BKAT 4. Neukirchen-Vluyn: Neukirchener Verlag, 1993–2003.
———. "Num XI, XII und die Hypothese des Jahwisten." *VT* 28 (1978): 214–23.
Ska, Jean-Louis. *The Exegesis of the Pentateuch: Exegetical Studies and Basic Questions*. FAT 66. Tübingen: Mohr Siebeck, 2009.
Strazicich, John. *Joel's Use of Scripture and the Scripture's Use of Joel: Appropriation and Resignification in Second Temple Judaism and Early Christianity*. BibInt 82. Leiden: Brill, 2007.
Van Seters, John. *The Life of Moses: The Yahwist as Historian in Exodus–Numbers*. Louisville: Westminster John Knox, 1994.

Wellhausen, Julius. *Die Composition des Hexateuchs und der historischen Bücher des Alten Testaments*. 3rd ed. Berlin: Reimer, 1899.
White, Marsha C. "The Elohistic Depiction of Aaron: A Study in the Levite-Zadokite Controversy." Pages 149–59 in *Studies in the Pentateuch*. Edited by J. A. Emerton. VTSup 41. Leiden: Brill, 1990.
Wolff, Hans Walter. *Joel and Amos: A Commentary on the Books of the Prophets Joel and Amos*. Edited by S. Dean McBride Jr. Translated by Waldemar Janzen, S. Dean McBride Jr., and Charles A. Muenchow. Hermeneia. Philadelphia: Fortress, 1984.
Zenger, Erich. *Die Sinaitheophanie: Untersuchungen zum jahwistischen und elohistischen Geschichtswerk*. FB 3. Wurzburg: Echter, 1971.
Zimmerli, Walther. *Ezekiel*. Edited by Frank Moore Cross and Klaus Baltzer. Translated by Ronald E. Clements and James D. Martin. 2 vols. Hermeneia. Philadelphia: Fortress, 1979–1983.

J's Problem with the East:
Observations on the So-Called Yahwistic Texts in Genesis 1–25

Jürg Hutzli

The cardinal direction east appears often in the book of Genesis, much more so than in other biblical books.[1] The east serves as a place of intrigue for the story in Gen 2:4b–3:24, the narrative of Jacob and Laban, and probably also the story of the tower of Babel. Furthermore, the east often appears as the position of a main protagonist: the cherubim and the fiery ever-turning sword guarding the tree of life are situated at the east of the garden of Eden, and Cain, too, lives east of Eden. Lot chooses the region of the plain and the city of Sodom, located in the east, as a place to live. Finally, Abraham sends all of his sons borne by concubines to the east, away from his favorite son, Isaac. How can one explain this concentration of references to the cardinal direction east in the book of Genesis?

Analysis of all these texts will reveal different if not contradictory images and appraisals of the east. One reason for the great number of texts mentioning the east seems to be the disagreement between the biblical authors on this point. This article seeks to clarify what is at stake in this disagreement and the role the latter played in the process of the formation of the primeval history and the Abraham narrative.

I would like to thank Monica Biberson for her careful English translation of the original French text of this contribution.

1. Two expressions mean "east": קדם (קדמה) and מזרח. The first appears particularly in the book of Genesis (Gen 2:8; 3:24; 4:16; 11:2; 12:8 [x2]; 13:11; 25:6; 29:1) but also in Num 23:7; 34:11; Deut 33:15, 17. The second appears especially in the books of Numbers and Deuteronomy (Exod 38:13; Num 2:3; 3:38; 21:11; 32:19; 34:15; Deut 3:17, 27; 4:41, 47, 49) and almost always refers to Transjordan.

1. Genesis 2–3: At Which Cardinal Point Does the Garden of Eden Lie?

The story in Gen 2–3 takes place in a garden, which is situated in Eden (עדן). This name means "bliss, delight," and it makes sense that we should remember the delicious fruits found in the garden. The name עדן, with a slightly different vocalization, also refers to the small Aramean state of Bīt Adini. The garden and Eden are located in "the east" (2:8, cf. 2:14). 2:8: "YHWH God planted a garden in Eden, in the east [גן בעדן מקדם], and placed there the man whom he had formed." Going against the common opinion, Terje Stordalen has suggested the meaning "in primeval times, in the olden days" instead of "in the east."[2] Indeed, the temporal sense of the noun מקדם is attested, but I see two arguments against Stordalen's interpretation.

First, the story already gives a temporal indication at the beginning: ביום עשות יהוה אלהים ארץ ושמים, "In the day when Yahweh God made earth and heaven." In principle, a second temporal indication is not impossible. However, because the planting of the garden follows the creation of humans (cf. 2:7), we would expect מקדם, based on the temporal indication, to be linked to the first work of the creator God. Second, in the Hebrew Bible, in the story genre, temporal indications are normally given at the beginning, not the end, of a sentence (Gen 1:1; 2:4b; 9:2; 14:1; 15:1; Judg 1:1; Ruth 1:1; etc.). For these reasons, in my opinion, the primary sense of the phrase is definitely "east."

With regard to the location of the garden in the east, we are surprised to read at the end of the story that the position of the couple expelled from the garden is to "the east" of the latter: "He [YHWH God] drove the man out, and placed east of the garden of Eden [מקדם לגן עדן] the cherubim and the fiery ever-turning sword, to guard the way to the tree of life" (Gen 3:24). This verse implies that the man and the woman must live to the east of the garden of Eden. It seems bizarre that the author of this elaborate story should use the same cardinal point east to refer to both the position of the garden of Eden and that of the expelled couple.

Furthermore, in the story of Cain and Abel, we learn that Cain, son of the banished couple, settles in the land of Nod, "east of Eden": "Then Cain went out from the presence of YHWH and settled in the land of Nod, east

---

2. Terje Stordalen, *Echoes of Eden: Genesis 2–3 and Symbolism of the Eden Garden in Biblical Hebrew Literature* (Leuven: Peeters, 2000), 261–70. Unless otherwise indicated, all biblical translations are mine.

of Eden [קדמת עדן]" (Gen 4:16). This indication of place goes well with the one I have just discussed (Gen 3:24): the expelled couple and Cain, the vagabond, live east of Eden. But the two locations do not tally with the first one. Suddenly, from the point of view of those who were chased out, the garden of Eden is *in the west*.

How can this incoherence be explained? A seductive theory has been put forward by Hartmut Gese and Jan Christian Gertz.[3] According to them, the author (or, rather, the redactor) who composed the two verses, 3:24 and 4:16, would have been influenced by the layout of the Jerusalem temple.[4] Indeed, the only entrance to the temple was on its eastern side (1 Kgs 7:39; Ezek 47:1). This geography is congruent with Ezekiel's motif of the mythological river flowing out of the Jerusalem temple *toward the east*: "Then he brought me back to the door of the house; behold, water was flowing from under the threshold of the house *toward the east* [קדימה], for the forefront of the house stood toward the *east* [קדים]. And the water was flowing down from under, from the right side of the house, from south of the altar" (Ezek 47:1; see also Joel 4:18; cf. Zech 14:8). According to Gertz, a redactor of the story in Gen 2–3, inspired by the "theology" of the Jerusalem temple, added Gen 3:24 and 4:16b as well as the passage at 2:10–14, making Eden "compatible" with Jerusalem or even identifying the two sites.[5] One telling element that favors Gertz's idea regarding Gen 3:24 and 4:16b is the motif of the cherubim watching over the garden (Gen 3:24). The cherubim were an important architectural feature in Solomon's temple. Thus by adding 3:24 and 4:16b, the redactor contradicts and, in a way, corrects the location of the garden of Eden in the story at Gen 2–3* by moving it from the east to the west and, in doing so, perhaps identifying it with Jerusalem.

Another clue corroborates Gertz's redaction-critical reading of Gen 3:24. This verse does indeed seem to be a redactional addition, a doublet of the

---

3. Hartmut Gese, "Der bewachte Lebensbaum und die Heroen: Zwei mythologische Ergänzungen zur Urgeschichte der Quelle J," in *Festschrift für Karl Elliger zum 70. Geburtstag*, ed. Hartmut Gese and Hans Peter Rüger, AOAT 18 (Kevelaer: Butzon & Bercker, 1973), 82; Jan C. Gertz, "Von Adam zu Enosch: Überlegungen zur Entstehungsgeschichte von Gen 2–4," in *Gott und Mensch im Dialog: Festschrift für Otto Kaiser zum 80. Geburtstag*, ed. Markus Witte, BZAW 345 (Berlin: de Gruyter, 2004), 225–27.

4. Genesis 4:16 is not taken into consideration by Gese, "Der bewachte Lebensbaum."

5. Gertz, "Von Adam zu Enosch," 225–27.

previous verse, which also refers to the primordial couple's departure from the garden: "YHWH God sent him out [וישלחהו] from the garden of Eden to cultivate the ground from which he was taken. He drove the man out [ויגרש] and placed east of the garden of Eden the cherubim and the fiery ever-turning sword, to guard the way to the tree of life" (Gen 3:23–24). The two verbs used to refer to the primordial couple's exit from the garden have different meanings: שלח in verse 23 means "to send; to send out," while the *piel* form of גרש in verse 24 means "to expel, to drive out." As rightly noted by Gertz, Gen 3:23 picks up the leitmotif of Gen 2:5 ("and there was no man to cultivate the ground") according to which, at the beginning, there was no one to cultivate the land on earth; it therefore marks a satisfactory framing and culmination of the intrigue.[6] It is therefore probable that the primary story ended with the statement at Gen 3:23. Verse 24 would then be a dramatizing reinterpretation of it: man (and woman) has (have) to leave the garden under threat, and the way back is barred by the cherubim and the fiery sword.

This reinterpretation fits well with another passage that emphasizes the opposition between God and the primal couple, a passage that could belong to the same redactional layer. God's severe judgment in Gen 3:13–19, the condemnation of the three protagonists, stands in tension with its context—in particular, the man's praise of Eve in verse 20 and God's observation that "the man has become like one of us."[7] There are clues that the transgression lying at the center of the story, the couple eating the forbidden fruit, was initially seen as a necessary or even positive act. We will come back to this point later.

2. The East in the J (Non-P) Stratum

The eastern location of the primordial humans who were expelled and punished (the primordial couple, Cain) goes hand in hand with the attribution

---

6. Gertz, "Von Adam zu Enosch," 225.

7. The following scholars point to the tension between Gen 3:13–19 and 3:20: Paul Humbert, *Études sur le récit du paradis et de la chute dans la Genèse*, Mémoires de l'Université de Neuchatel 14 (Neuchâtel: University, 1940), 159; Gordon J. Wenham, *Genesis 1–15*, WBC 1 (Waco, TX: Word, 1979), 84; Christoph Levin, *Der Jahwist*, FRLANT 157 (Göttingen: Vandenhoeck & Ruprecht, 1991), 83; Jürg Hutzli, "Transgression et initiation: Tendances idéologiques et développement littéraire du récit de Genèse 2–3," in *Tabou et transgressions: Actes du colloque organisé par le Collège de France, Paris, les 11–12 avril 2012*, ed. Jean-Marie Durand, Michaël Guichard, and Thomas Römer, OBO 274 (Fribourg: Academic Press; Göttingen: Vandenhoeck & Ruprecht, 2015), 120–21, 125–27.

of this cardinal point to certain foreign tribes or peoples in the J stratum. One occurrence of מקדם is in the story of the tower of Babel (Gen 11:1–9). The meaning of this indication is not clear, and two translations of it in verse 2 have been suggested: "And it came about as they journeyed from the east/eastward [ויהי בנסעם מקדם] that they found a plain in the land of Shinar and settled there." Given Gen 13:11, where the exact same phrase is used and where only "eastward" makes sense, I would be inclined to adopt the second interpretation, "eastward."[8]

In the text of Gen 13:11, which is part of the patriarchal narrative, we read that Lot, having separated from Abraham, emigrates *eastward*, toward the cities of Sodom and Gomorrah whose inhabitants "were wicked, great sinners against YHWH" (Gen 13:13). Verse 11 reads: "So Lot chose for himself the whole plain of the Jordan, and Lot journeyed *eastward* [ויסע מקדם]." We can see that the two phrases (11:2 and 13:11) are constructed the same way (using the verb נסע and the spatial adverb מקדם).

Finally, another verse fits well with the assertions just discussed. Next in the patriarchal narrative we read that Abraham sent the sons he had with his concubines away from his favorite son Isaac "eastward, to the land of the east": "To the sons of his concubines Abraham gave gifts while he was still living, and he sent them away from his son Isaac *eastward, to the land of the east* [קדמה אל־ארץ קדם]" (Gen 25:6). It is striking to note that, in all these texts, a negative type of behavior or a certain problem is attributed to people living "in the east": the primordial couple, Cain, the builders of the tower of Babel, the inhabitants of Sodom and Gomorrah, and the sons of Abraham's concubines who are Isaac's potential rivals. This insistence on the connection between the east and "problem" is undoubtedly not due to chance. It is interesting to note that all these texts are non-Priestly (or J, following the terminology of classical documentary hypothesis). Reinhard G. Kratz attributes all these texts to a basic J[G] narrative, with the exception of the last one (Gen 25:6), which is supposed to belong to a secondary J layer, whether J[S] or R[JP].[9]

It seems likely to me that this insistence on an eastern location is connected to the eastern location of Eden in Gen 2–3 (cf. 2:8). The authors of J intervened in a targeted way in the story of Gen 2–3 and

---

8. BDB, s.v. "קֶדֶם."
9. Reinhard G. Kratz, *Die Komposition der erzählenden Bücher des Alten Testaments: Grundwissen der Bibelkritik* (Göttingen: Vandenhoeck & Ruprecht, 2000), 278, 280.

other texts: they rejected the idea that the east (seen elsewhere as the cradle of wisdom, as in 1 Kgs 5:10) could be the location of God's garden. These regions are devalued to the benefit of the land of promise (Canaan, Israel); it is here that the fathers of Israel will see their blessing realized (cf. Gen 12:1–3).

3. Focus on the Story of the Tower of Babel and the Table of Nations

According to my interpretation of Gen 11:2, the protagonists in the story of Gen 11:1–9 went *to* the east. In my opinion, this allows us to understand the various easterly indications (in this presupposed J stratum) in a coherent way: the primordial humans (the first couple, Cain, the ancestors of Babylon) gradually and continually move farther away from the garden of Eden to the east. It is only later that Abraham, with the guidance of YHWH, is able to set off in the opposite direction, to the west, to the land of Canaan (Gen 12:1–3).

Perhaps this interpretation, placing the story of the tower of Babel "in the east," could find one confirmation by comparing the account with the composition that precedes it, the table of nations (Gen 10). The cardinal point east also plays a significant role there, where it is represented by the sons of Shem. Genesis 11:1–9, through its eastern location, possibly relates to it.

In general, as several scholars have recently noted, the story in Gen 11:1–9 shares certain points with the table of nations (Gen 10). Apart from certain common phrases and motifs, the two compositions share above all the theme of humanity's dispersal and its ethnic ramifications. On the other hand, they contradict each other, as the cause of humanity's dispersion and expansion is different in the two texts. According to Gen 10, this development seems neutral or positive. According to the account in Gen 11:1–9, however, it is the result of the humans' hubris, their attempt to reach the divine realm and to "make themselves a name." This overly ambitious enterprise triggers God's immediate countermeasure, which is to confuse people's language and scatter them across the world.

What is the literary-historical relationship between the two compositions? Does one of them depend closely on the other and react to it? Before I can answer this question, I need to make a few observations on the composition of the table of nations and its internal structure. Most scholars agree on the distinction between two literary layers (P and J/non-P) in

Gen 10.[10] Unlike the J stratum, the Priestly layer is an autonomous and homogenous composition. According to most recent analyses, it is the P stratum that forms the primary composition, while the J passages are secondary additions.[11] In the following, the most important characteristics of this presumably original composition are outlined. Genesis 10 (P version) lists the descendants of Noah's three sons up to the third (Japheth, Shem) or fourth generation (Ham). Many of the nations mentioned here have been identified. Only for a few names is the identification is uncertain.[12] One enigmatic name is "Arpachshad" (ארפכשד). It probably is an allusion to Ur-Chasdim (אור כשדים, Gen 11:28, 31, see the graphic similarity) and refers to Babylon.

What is the internal organization of the Priestly composition? The three ancestors Japheth, Ham, and Shem represent the three main regions of the world. The tripartite division of the world seems to be made according to two criteria. The first is geographical position: Noah's three sons correspond to the northern (Japheth), southern (Ham), and eastern or central (Shem) regions. As for the second criterion, each of these three names seems to allude, through its meaning, to a certain trait of the nations affiliated with it; thus, they are evocative names. Such a function seems obvious to me in the case of two of the three names and conceivable for the third: Ham (חָם) should be associated with "warmth, heat" (חֹם) and "warm, hot" (חָם).[13] Indeed, Ham's world region comprises nations all situated in the hot regions of the south (Egypt, Sudan, the Arabian Penin-

---

10. The Priestly stratum includes Gen 10:1–7, 20, 22–23, 31–32, while the non-Priestly (J^c) stratum consists of Gen 10:8–19, 21, 24–30.

11. Wenham, *Genesis 1–15*, 215; Israel Knohl, "Nimrod, Son of Cush, King of Mesopotamia, and the Dates of P and J," in *Birkat Shalom: Studies in the Bible, Ancient Near Eastern Literature, and Postbiblical Judaism Presented to Shalom M. Paul on the Occasion of His Seventieth Birthday*, ed. Chaim Cohen et al., 2 vols. (Winona Lake, IN: Eisenbrauns, 2008), 1:47–48; Markus Witte, *Die biblische Urgeschichte: Redaktions- und theologiegeschichtliche Beobachtungen zu Genesis 1,1–11,26*, BZAW 265 (Berlin: de Gruyter, 1998), 110–16; and Christophe Nihan, "L'écrit sacerdotal entre mythe et histoire," in *Ancient and Modern Scriptural Historiography; L'historiographie biblique, ancienne et moderne*, ed. George J. Brooke and Thomas Römer, BETL 207 (Leuven: Peeters, 2007), 180–82.

12. There are only three names—three of Aram's four sons—for which scholars have not been able to suggest identifications.

13. For חֹם "warmth, heat," see Gen 8:22; 18:1; 1 Sam 11:9, 11; 21:7; 2 Sam 4:5; Neh 7:3; Isa 18:4; and *KAI* 200:10–11. For חָם "warm, hot," see Josh 9:12 and Job 37:17.

sula, Libya). The name Shem (שם) could be interpreted as "(great) name, reputation." This interpretation makes sense to the extent that Shem is the ancestor of five nations (regions) that were very important in the Levant in the period between roughly the ninth and sixth centuries BCE: Elam, Assyria, Arpachshad (Babylonia), Lydia (in western Anatolia), and Aram. Gerhard von Rad highlighted the important role the nations attributed to Shem played at that time.[14] The inclusion of Lydia (לוד) among Shem's sons despite the fact that it does not really correspond to its geographical position (as part of Anatolia, Lydia is situated in the north) makes sense from the point of view of the second criterion (the name's meaning), because Lydia was a very powerful empire around 700–550 BCE. As for the name Japheth (יפת), we can perhaps associate it with "beauty, beautiful" (root יפי), an interpretation that could draw on several points common to the table of nations and the poem about Tyre's decline in Ezek 27. Tyre's beauty (יפי) is a keyword in this chapter, where we find it three times (Ezek 27:3–4, 11). According to this text, Tyre's beauty is due to excellent products and craftwork associated with certain nations with which the port city has trade relations. It is striking to note that, among these trade partners, several "sons of Japheth" are mentioned: the coastlands of Cyprus (Kittim, v. 6), Elishah (v. 7), Tarshish (v. 12), Javan (v. 13), Tubal (v. 13), Meshech (v. 13), and Beth-togarmah (v. 14). With regard to these commonalities, one is tempted to assume a common tradition-historical background of Gen 10 (P) and Ezek 27. It could therefore be that, for the author of the table of nations, the most salient trait of the northern nations was the beauty (יפי) of their craftwork. Two considerations may favor the interpretation of the names of Shem, Ham, and Japheth as evocative names proposed here: first, they are absent from the *onomasticon* of the ancient Near East and, second, the three suggested meanings fit the three so-called world regions.

I now return to the literary-historical relationship between Gen 10 and Gen 11:1–9. Scholars who have looked at it believe that the story of the tower of Babel presupposes and reacts against the table of nations (Priestly

---

14. Gerhard von Rad, *Das erste Buch Mose: Genesis*, 2nd ed., ATD 2.4 (Göttingen: Vandenhoeck & Ruprecht, 1950), 118. Aram may be included among the nations of "renown" due to its political importance, as it is also attested in historical reports of the Bible; for Aram-Damascus, see 1 Kgs 11:25; 15:18; 19:15; 20; 22; 2 Kgs 5:1–5; 6; 7; 8–13 (Hazael); 15–16 (Rezin). But it may also be due to the important role played by the Aramaic language (ארמית) in the ancient Near East from the eighth century BCE onward.

stratum of Gen 10): the author of Gen 11:1–9 casts the development and ethnic ramifications shown in Gen 10* in a bad light.[15] Something that is described in the table of nations as a neutral or positive trait of humanity—its dispersion and ethnic ramification—appears in the account of Gen 11:1–9 as a consequence of hubris and disagreement between God and people. What could also be significant for the comparison of the two compositions is the motif of wanting to "make for ourselves a name [שם]": "And they said, 'Come, let us build for ourselves a city, and a tower whose top will reach into heaven, and let us make for ourselves a name [שם] lest we be scattered abroad over the face of the whole earth'" (Gen 11:4). It is conceivable that, by using this phrase and attributing it to an eastern nation (Babylon), the author of the story in Gen 11:1–9 refers to the table of nations, where Shem's sons, the eastern nations, are characterized by "reputation, renown." The reply coming from the story in Gen 11:1–9 emphasizes the pointlessness of the search for fame.

Perhaps the message of the story in Gen 11:1–9 should be understood in the context of the short passage in Gen 12:1–3, which is also often attributed to the J layer: "'And I will make you a great nation, And I will bless you, And make your name [שמך] great; And so you shall be a blessing'" (Gen 12:2). We see that "reputation, renown" should not be the object of human efforts. On the contrary, this quality is a gift from YHWH that is meant for the one whom the deity has chosen (Abraham).

4. Implications of the Conflicting Images of the East in Genesis 1–25 for the Literary History of the Texts Involved

In this overview I tried to show different images of the east in the book of Genesis. I started with the story of paradise (Gen 2–3). Here, the east seems to be the cradle not only of humanity but of wisdom as well. Recent

---

15. Witte, *Die biblische Urgeschichte*, 90; Erich Bosshard-Nepustil, *Vor uns die Sintflut: Studien zu Text, Kontexten und Rezeption der Fluterzählung Genesis 6–9*, BWANT 9/5 (Stuttgart: Kohlhammer, 2005), 210–12; Andreas Schüle, *Der Prolog der hebräischen Bibel: Der literar- und theologiegeschichtliche Diskurs der Urgeschichte (Gen 1–11)*, ATANT 86 (Zurich: TVZ, 2006), 402–3; and Albert de Pury, "P^g as the Absolute Beginning," in *Die Patriarchen und die Priesterschrift: Gesammelte Studien zu seinem 70. Geburtstag; Les patriarches et le document sacerdotal; Recueil d'articles, à l'occasion de son 70e anniversaire*, ed. Jean-Daniel Macchi, Thomas Römer, Konrad Schmid, ATANT 99 (Zurich: TVZ, 2010), 30–32.

analyses have brought to light the link between Gen 2–3 and the Hebrew Bible's wisdom texts. The tree of the knowledge of good and evil plays a central role in the intrigue of the story: the latter deals with the acquisition of the capacity for cognitive judgment and life wisdom by the protagonist couple. The connection between the east and wisdom is further reflected in other biblical texts. In the story of Balaam (Num 22–24), the east, more concretely Aram, is the homeland of the wise Balaam (Num 23:7), and the text at 1 Kgs 5:10 states: "And Solomon's wisdom surpassed the wisdom of all the sons of the East and all the wisdom of Egypt." The table of nations (Priestly layer) presents the east in a neutral way as a region made up of several great, renowned nations.

Several texts belonging to the J/non-P layer seem to react against the texts showing positive or neutral images of the east. Firstly, the redactor who intervenes in the text at Gen 2–3 rejects the idea that the east could be the location of God's garden—this place is devalued to the benefit of Jerusalem (Gen 3:24). The same author-redactor (or perhaps other authors who shared the same ideology) intervene(s) in other stories and compose(s) other texts (Gen 4:16; 11:2; 13:11; 25:6). Here the east appears as a place for transgressors, people ruled by vain ambitions, and potential rivals of Abraham's chosen line. Traditionally, all these texts polemicizing against the east are attributed to the Yahwist (J) source.

According to von Rad and others, the Yahwist composed this large work—starting with the creation of humans and going all the way to the conquest of the promised land—at the time of Solomon.[16] This dating has been largely abandoned today. Important analyses carried out by John Van Seters, Martin Rose, Christoph Levin, and others have tried to prove that J is a much more recent work composed during the exilic or postexilic period.[17] A growing number of scholars have gone further by abandoning the hypothesis of a Yahwist document altogether as they contest the linguistic and conceptional coherence of the texts in ques-

---

16. Gerhard von Rad, "Das formgeschichtliche Problem des Hexateuch," in *Gesammelte Studien zum Alten Testament*, ed. Rudolf Smend (Munich: Kaiser, 1958), 75–81; and Rad, *Das erste Buch Mose*, 10–17.

17. Martin Rose, *Deuteronomist und Jahwist: Untersuchungen zu den Berührungspunkten beider Literaturwerke*, ATANT 67 (Zurich: TVZ, 1981); John Van Seters, *Prologue to History: The Yahwist as Historian in Genesis* (Zurich: TVZ, 1992); Van Seters, *The Life of Moses: The Yahwist as Historian in Exodus–Numbers* (Louisville: Westminster John Knox, 1994); and Levin, *Der Jahwist*, 1991.

tion.¹⁸ Nevertheless, these commentators opposed to the J theory agree on the fact that J's stories in Gen 1–11 are linked and form a more or less homogeneous stratum; instead of J, they often call it the non-P layer and contrast it with the P layer (the Priestly composition).¹⁹ Certain scholars consider all the J/non-P stories in Gen 1–11 as post-P additions.²⁰

According to my analysis, the J/non-P texts presuppose the proto-Priestly accounts in Gen 1*; 6–9*; 10*; and 11:27–25:8*, but not the genealogies in Gen 5 and 11, both of which belong to the Priestly composition.²¹ To those texts in Gen 1–11 attributed to J we could perhaps add the hinge text in Gen 12:1–4, another late redactional text, as well as the texts in Gen 13 and 18–19, all of which have important points in common with the J stories in Gen 1–11. As for the terminology, given that the Tetragrammaton appears in all of the texts and that YHWH as unique deity intervenes in primeval and pre-Israelite history—which for the primarily national deity YHWH is not evident, the Yahwist (J) designation seems appropriate. A dominant motif appearing in most of the J texts in Gen 1–25 is that of humans' transgression and God's punishment:²² The primordial man and his wife eat of the forbidden fruit, and the primordial couple is punished (cursed) by YHWH and cast out of the garden (Gen 2:4b–3:24). Cain kills and is cursed and expelled by YHWH (Gen 4). Angels and women marry, and YHWH limits human lifespan (Gen

---

18. Rolf Rendtorff, *Das überlieferungsgeschichtliche Problem des Pentateuch*, BZAW 147 (Berlin: de Gruyter, 1976); Erhard Blum, *Die Komposition der Vätergeschichte*, WMANT 57 (Neukirchen-Vluyn: Neukirchener Verlag, 1984); and Blum, *Studien zur Komposition des Pentateuch*, BZAW 189 (Berlin: de Gruyter, 1990).

19. The thesis put forward by Frank Crüsemann, "Die Eigenständigkeit der Urgeschichte: Ein Beitrag zur Diskussion um den 'Jahwisten,'" in *Die Botschaft und die Boten: Festschrift H. W. Wolff*, ed. Jörg Jeremias and Lothar Perlitt (Neukirchen-Vluyn: Neukirchener Verlag, 1981), 11–29 about the autonomy of the J or pre-P primeval history has resonated with many scholars, including Joseph Blenkinsopp, "A Postexilic Lay Source in Genesis 1–11," in *Abschied vom Jahwisten: Die Komposition des Hexateuch in der jüngsten Diskussion*, ed. Jan C. Gertz, Konrad Schmid, and Markus Witte, BZAW 315 (Berlin: de Gruyter, 2002), 49–61; Martin Arneth, *Durch Adams Fall ist gänzlich verderbt...: Studien zur Entstehung der alttestamentlichen Urgeschichte*, FRLANT 217 (Göttingen: Vandenhoeck & Ruprecht, 2007).

20. Blenkinsopp, "Post-exilic Lay Source"; Bosshart-Nepustil, *Vor uns die Sintflut*, 178–218; Schüle, *Der Prolog*, esp. 24–30; Arneth, *Durch Adams Fall*; and Pury, "P^g," 28–32.

21. Jürg Hutzli, *Origins of P* (forthcoming).

22. In one case, the curse is pronounced by a human (Noah) instead of God.

6:1–4). People are wicked, so God decides to destroy the creatures by flood (Gen 6:5–8). Ham sees his father, Noah, naked, and Noah curses Canaan, Ham's son (Gen 9:20–27). The tower of Babel is built out of overweening ambition, and people are dispersed by YHWH (Gen 11:1–9). And the inhabitants of Sodom are wicked and perverse, so the city of Sodom is destroyed by YHWH (Gen 13,12; 19).

The texts containing this theme, well defined by its two elements of transgression and punishment, have several typical phrases in common.[23] The theme never reappears in the following sections (the narratives of Jacob-Esau and Jacob-Laban, the narrative of Joseph, Exodus). By relating this motif, these stories reveal a very similar theology: humans are viewed negatively, and YHWH is described as a severe, punishing god who metes out sanctions for people's transgressions. According to J's theology, humans, because of their ontological vileness, are not able to properly manage their lives. Certainly, there are exceptional characters, such as Noah and Abra(ha)m, who achieve this feat but only because they have been guided by YHWH: they have "found favor in the eyes" of the latter (Gen 6:8 and 18:3) who chose them. It is significant that, according to the J layer and in contradiction to P, Abram leaves his homeland not by choice but because YHWH has instructed him to do so (Gen 12:1). J's anthropology is also expressed in the episode of the separation between Lot and Abram after their arrival in the land of Canaan. After some deliberation, Lot chooses the plain of Jordan and Sodom as a place to live, which will prove to be an exceedingly poor choice. On the other hand, Abram does not make a choice; consequently, it is YHWH who offers him the whole of the land of Canaan, which will turn out to be a very advantageous option (Gen 13:14–17).[24] It is very interesting to note that J's negative anthropology is diametrically opposed to the ideal of autonomy expressed in the

---

23. The texts in question share several phrases related to this theme: אח "brother" used in an ethical sense: Gen 4:2, 8, 9 (2x), 10, 11; 9:22, 25; 13:8; 19:7; איה "where" in a question asked by Yahweh: Gen 3:9; 4:9; 16:8 (2x); 18:9; מצא חן בעיני "to find favor in the eyes of Yahweh": Gen 6:8; 18:3; 19:9; צעקה/צעק "to cry": Gen 4:10; 18:20, 21; 19:13; יהוה ראה "Yahweh saw": Gen 2:19; 6:5; 11:5; 18:21; רעע "to be bad, evil" and רעה "wickedness": Gen 6:5 (2x); 8:21; 13:13; 19:7, 9. See the more comprehensive list in Levin, *Der Jahwist*, 399–408.

24. Genesis 13:14–17 is sometimes considered an insertion, but Matthias Köckert, "Wie wurden Abraham- und Jakobüberlieferung zu einer 'Vätergeschichte' verbunden?," *HBAI* 3 (2014): 49, 55–57, has shown that the text is closely linked to Gen 12:1–4 and 28:13–14, which are traditionally attributed to J; see Martin Noth, *Über-*

primary version of the story in Gen 2-3. An overview of the occurrences of the phrase "knowledge of good and evil"—a central motif in the original story—in the Hebrew Bible shows that it is a basic and indispensable life management skill.[25] It is a trait of adult life that, in contrast, neither underage children nor the very old possess (Deut 1:39; 2 Sam 19:36).[26] Thus, in the pre-Yahwist account in Gen 2-3, the primordial couple's transgression is seen as positive: by acquiring the capacity for judgment, humans become autonomous beings. As already noted, God's strong condemnation of the transgressive act in Gen 3:13-19 probably belongs to the redactional (J) layer.[27] The idea of human autonomy and emancipation from God allows us to draw a parallel between the story in Gen 2-3* and the Greek myth of Prometheus.[28] The J redactor thus goes against the grain of the primary narrative in Gen 2-3 with regard not only to the eastern motif but also to the story's central idea of human autonomy.

5. Preliminary Stratification and Setting(s) of the J Stratum in Genesis 1-25

Even though J's texts in Gen 1-25 seem theologically coherent, there are clues supporting the idea that these stories were composed in two or more stages. Recent studies have put forward three alternative hypotheses concerning the formation of the non-Priestly primeval history in Gen 2-11. According to the first model, the primary non-P narrative includes the elements of creation, increase in violence, and culmination in the flood

---

lieferungsgeschichte des Pentateuchs, 2nd ed. (Stuttgart: Kohlhammer, 1960), 29-30; Kratz, *Die Komposition*, 268.

25. Deut 1:39; 2 Sam 14:17; 19:36; 1 Kgs 3:9.

26. Cf. Rainer Albertz, "'Ihr werdet sein wie Gott': Gen 3,1-7 vor dem Hintergrund des alttestamentlichen und sumerisch-babylonischen Menschenbildes," *WO* 24 (1993): 89-111; Konrad Schmid, "Loss of Immortality? Hermeneutical Aspects of Genesis 2-3 and Its Early Receptions," in *Beyond Eden: The Biblical Story of Paradise (Genesis 2-3) and Its Reception History*, ed. Konrad Schmid and Christoph Riedweg, FAT 2/34 (Tübingen: Mohr Siebeck, 2008), 61.

27. See the first paragraph of this article.

28. For a parallel with the myth of Prometheus, see Philippe Borgeaud and Thomas Römer, "Mythologie de la Méditerranée et du Proche-orient ancient: Regards croisés sur l'origine de l'humanité," in *Religions antiques: Une introduction comparée*, ed. Philippe Borgeaud and Francesca Prescendi (Geneva: Labor et Fides, 2008), 121-48.

(Gen 2–4*; 6–8*). The sequence of the themes of creation as myth and flood as antimyth has an ancient Near Eastern counterpart in the epic of the "exceedingly wise" Atraḫasis.²⁹ The second model highlights clues suggesting a primary non-P composition that does not yet contain the flood story. The account in Gen 2–4* is supposed to continue with the story of the tower of Babel.³⁰ The two hypotheses draw on arguments relating to narrative and linguistic coherence. Other authors renounce all J (non-P) stratigraphy, considering J to be a unified post-Priestly layer within Gen 1–11.³¹ The following arguments come in support of the second of these models: Firstly, the profile of the J passages in the flood account strongly deviates from that of the J texts in Gen 2:4b–3:24; 4*; 11:1–9. While the latter consists of complete, autonomous stories, the J (non-P) layer of the flood account is fragmentary and dependent on the Priestly stratum. Here J reuses the vocabulary typical of the P stratum, imitates the P style, and is influenced by Priestly theology.³²

Furthermore, Gen 2–4* does not seem to lead up to the flood story. Rather, it is the story of the tower of Babel (Gen 11:1–9) that continues Gen 2–4*, given that its beginning is connected to Gen 4:16 (by picking up the keyword "east"; cf. 11:2). There are clues suggesting that this original Yahwist primeval story was composed after the proto-P units that deal with the primeval history (the creation account in Gen 1*; the flood account in Gen 6–9*; the table of nations in Gen 10*), probably as a

---

29. Witte, *Die biblische Urgeschichte*; Jan C. Gertz, "The Formation of the Primeval History," in *The Book of Genesis: Composition, Reception, and Interpretation*, ed. Craig A. Evans, Joel N. Lohr, and David L. Petersen, VTSup 152 (Leiden: Brill, 2012), 107–35.

30. Kratz, *Die Komposition*, 252–62; Konrad Schmid, *Literaturgeschichte des Alten Testaments: Eine Einführung* (Darmstadt: Wissenschaftliche Buchgesellschaft, 2008), 153–56.

31. Blenkinsopp, "Post-exilic Lay Source"; Bosshart-Nepustil, *Vor uns die Sintflut*, 178–218; and Arneth, *Durch Adams Fall*.

32. As for vocabulary, I should mention the verb ברא (Gen 6:7), the Priestly terms for the designation of animals: מאדם עד בהמה עד רמש ועד עוף השמים, "from man to animals to creeping things and to birds of the sky" (6:7: see also 7:2–3 and 7:23), and the cultic expression ריח הניחח, "soothing aroma," (8:21) which occurs only in P, H, and Ezekiel. A stylistic feature is the typical Priestly correspondence between order and fulfillment found in 7:5 ("And Noah did according to all that YHWH had commanded him"; cf. 6:22 P). A theological theme with great importance in P, H, and Ezekiel is the distinction between clean and unclean animals (see 7:2; 8:20). See Hutzli, *Origins*; Schmid, *Literaturgeschichte*, 154–55.

competing narrative (e.g., Gen 11:1–9 reacts to Gen 10 [P], on which see above).³³ The compositions climax—the (unsuccessful) founding of a city and the dispersion of humanity (Gen 11:1-9)—may also be understood as a polemical response to the Sumerian King List, which has a strong focus on the primordial cities as seats of kingship.³⁴ The other J texts in Gen 1–11 were probably added only after the two narrative compositions, proto-P and J, were merged; indeed, they are mostly redactional elements that complete the Priestly account of the flood and the table of Nations (P).³⁵

The formation of the Abraham narrative in Gen 11:27–25:10 seems similar. According to a minority point of view, which I nevertheless share, the J/non-P stories presuppose the P (proto-P) Abraham narrative.³⁶ But they probably do not all belong to the same literary layer. The J stories in Gen 12–13*; 18–19* are distinct from other J (non-P) texts to the extent that they form a big continuous Abraham-Lot narrative.³⁷ Perhaps it was

---

33. Hutzli, *Origins*.

34. Thorkild Jacobsen, *The Sumerian King List*, AS 11 (Chicago: University of Chicago Press, 1939).

35. Genesis 5:29b; 6:5–8; 7:1–5, 10, 12, 17, 21–23; 8:2b, 8–13, 20–22; 9:18–19; 10:8–19, 21, 24–30.

36. Pury, "P^g," 32–37; Pury, "Genèse 12–36," in *Introduction à l'Ancien Testament*, ed. Thomas Römer, Jean-Daniel Macchi, and Christophe Nihan, 2nd ed. (Geneva: Labor et Fides, 2009), 217–38; Pury, Thomas Römer, and Konrad Schmid, *L'Ancien Testament commenté: La Genèse* (Geneva: Labor et Fides; Montrouge: Bayard, 2016), 104–6; Hutzli, *Origins*.

37. Hermann Gunkel, *Genesis*, 3rd ed., HKAT (Göttingen: Vandenhoeck & Ruprecht, 1922), 173; Blum, *Die Komposition*, 280–89; Irmtraud Fischer, *Die Erzeltern Israels: Feministischtheologische Studien zu Genesis 12–36*, BZAW 222 (Berlin: de Gruyter, 1994), 339; Thomas Römer, "Genèse 15 et les tensions de la communauté juive postexilique dans le cycle d'Abraham," *Transeu* 7 (1994): 111; Konrad Schmid, *Genesis and the Moses Story: Israel's Dual Origin in the Hebrew Bible*, trans. James D. Nogalski, Siphrut 3 (Winona Lake, IN: Eisenbrauns, 2010), 96. Genesis 13 and 18–19 have in common the two protagonists Abram/Abraham and Lot, as well as the toponyms "grove of Mamre" and "Sodom." The plot seems coherent: At its beginning, the narrative deals with the separation between Lot and Abram and their settlement in Sodom and Mamre, respectively. In chapters 18–19, which are located in Mamre and Sodom, respectively, the reader is told how Abraham and Lot acquire offspring. The Abraham-Lot story highlights the origins of the three neighboring nations of Israel, Moab, and Ammon, the offspring of Abraham and Lot. The strong cohesion between Gen 13 and 18 is indicated in 18:1, which refers to Abraham only with a suffix and seems to depend on the final statement of chapter 13 (13:18a), also located in Mamre.

meant to play the role of a competing story in relation to the proto-Priestly Abraham narrative. There are, of course, still questions that remain open. The Abraham-Lot story has no satisfying beginning or end; Gen 12:1–4a opens quite abruptly. It is not clear how the Yahwist primeval narrative and the J stratum in Gen 12–25 were or became connected. Perhaps Gen 2:4b–3:24; 4*; 11:1–9 can be considered the first nucleus (J^g) of a Yahwist compositional layer covering Gen 2–25 or beyond (J^c).[38] The latter, although possibly composed by several authors, is marked by strong thematic, linguistic, and ideological coherence.

When and where were the J texts composed? In the absence of clear clues, scholars are prudent about this question and often content themselves with retracing the influence that various existing literary works had on J.[39] The internal stratification of the J stratum makes this question all the more difficult. I will tackle it by focusing first and foremost on what is probably the oldest J nucleus, namely, the stories in Gen 2:4b–4:24; 11:1–9 (= J^g, the first Yahwist *Grundschrift*).

First, J^g expresses a theology close to that of Deuteronomistic texts. Shared themes include divine election/nonelection, obedience/nonobedience to God, God's punishment, and, more concretely, forced exile. The expulsion of the primordial couple from the garden of Eden eastwards forms an inclusion with the deportation of Jerusalem's and Judah's elite to Babylon in the wake of the Neo-Babylonian conquest of Jerusalem. It thus seems obvious that the J^g texts presuppose the Deuteronomistic texts and redactions in the Former Prophets (and beyond). In fact, we can interpret J^g's primeval history as a backward extension of the Deuteronomistic History.[40] The history of Israel and, in particular, the loss of the land and the exile in the east are universalized; they are illuminated by J^g's pessimistic anthropology.[41]

---

38. According to Kratz, *Die Komposition*, 249–80, this layer would extend from Gen 2 through 35. The identification of J texts in Gen 26–35, however, is less evident to me.

39. Blenkinsopp, "Post-exilic Lay Source," 52, 60 and Schmid, *Literaturgeschichte*, 155–56.

40. The term "Deuteronomistic History" is used here to refer to a multilayered redaction covering the books Deuteronomy–2 Kings; see Thomas Römer, *The So-Called Deuteronomistic History: A Sociological, Historical and Literary Introduction* (London: T&T Clark, 2007).

41. Similarly, Van Seters, *Prologue to History*, 330–31; Schmid, *Literaturgeschichte*, 156; Cynthia Edenburg, "From Eden to Babylon: Reading Gen 2–4 as a Paradigmatic

Second, the J^g stories react to the proto-P units in Gen 1–9, the latter showing a rather universalistic tendency. For example, among them, the stories referring to the world's origins (Gen 1; 6–9 [P]) do not allude to Israel.⁴² In contrast, the primeval history presented by J^g has a tendency towards "Israelization."⁴³ The deity's name (YHWH) is that of the national god. The garden of Eden is moved from the east to the west, possibly in order to identify it with Jerusalem. In this respect, J^g goes with late Deuteronomistic texts which depict YHWH, Israel's God, as creator God and "the only 'real' God of the universe" (Deut 4 and 10:14–22).⁴⁴

Third, J^g presupposes Hebrew wisdom texts and reacts to them. In particular, it is the story in Gen 2–3 that is marked by several motifs and phrases typical of this literary genre: "tree of life" (cf. Prov 3:18; 11:30; 13:12; 15:4), "the knowledge of good and evil" (cf. Deut 1:39; 2 Sam 14:17; 19:36; 1 Kgs 3:9), "intelligent" (ערום, cf. Job 5:12; Prov 12:23; 13:6; 14:8, 15, 18; 22:3; 27:12), and "acquiring discernment" (שכל hiphil, cf. Prov 1:3; 10:5; 14:35; 15:24; 16:20, 23; 17:2; 21:11, 12, 16; Dan 1:4, 17; 9:13, 22, 25; 11:33, 35; 12:3, 10, et al.).⁴⁵ This is due to the fact that J^g, working here as a redactor, took up and reworked an already existing "wisdom story."⁴⁶ By giving a negative connotation to the story's central idea, the acquisition of human autonomy, he gave it the opposite interpretation, as already noted above.

According to most modern interpreters, however, the autonomy acquired by humans in Gen 2–3 was not seen in a negative way by its author; rather, it was an ambiguous achievement. Having gained the ability to know good and evil, humans have become like God—suffering, in

---

Narrative," in *Pentateuch, Hexateuch, or Enneateuch: Identifying Literary Works in Genesis Through 2 Kings*, ed. Thomas Dozeman, Thomas Römer, and Konrad Schmid, AIL 8 (Atlanta: Society of Biblical Literature, 2011), 155–67.

42. The allusion to the Sabbath in Gen 2:2–3 does not belong to the original account.

43. See also Kratz, *Die Komposition*, 269.

44. Römer, *So-Called Deuteronomistic History*, 173–74, quote 173.

45. Cf. Konrad Schmid, "Die Unteilbarkeit der Weisheit: Überlegungen zur sogenannten Paradieserzählung und ihrer theologischen Tendenz," *ZAW* 114 (2002): 21–39; Blenkinsopp, "Post-exilic Lay Source," 54–55.

46. Schmid, *Literaturgeschichte*, 155–56, although he sees Gen 2:4–3:24 as closely related to the stories in Gen 4 and 11:1–9, he recognizes the theological distinctiveness of this opening unit, which he considers to be unified.

return, the loss of paradise and estrangement from God.⁴⁷ This interpretation is certainly not incorrect, and it is especially appropriate for the primary version of the story. In my opinion, however, these commentators too easily overlook the passages containing God's condemnation of the serpent, the woman, and the man (Gen 3:13–19) and the couple's expulsion from the garden (3:24). Here the J^g redactor adopts a clear position against transgression and its consequence, namely, the autonomy acquired by humans. Furthermore, other J texts clearly show that J^g's anthropological ideal *is not* human autonomy—reasonings and decisions of the main protagonists lead to catastrophe in both Gen 4 and 11:1–9—but rather obedience to and willingness to be guided by YHWH (Gen 2:16–17; 4:7; 12:1–4a). With David M. Carr, one may even see in Gen 2:4b–3:24 (final text) an "anti-wisdom story."⁴⁸

To summarize, I would like to note that the stories of the J^g stratum presuppose different schools of thought present especially in the late writings of the Hebrew Bible. This fact excludes an early date for J^g in the monarchic period, as still suggested today by several scholars.⁴⁹ We should preferably look to the Persian period, also because the J^g units apparently found almost no echo in other writings of the Hebrew Bible.⁵⁰ For instance, the first explicit references to Gen 2–3 appear in early Jewish literature from the second and first centuries BCE (Sir 25:24; Wis 2:23–24).⁵¹ The particular affinity of the J^g texts in Gen 1–25 to Deuteronomistic ideology may indicate that their authors came from the same milieu. Recent global treatments of Deuteronomistic texts have highlighted evidence indicating

---

47. Schmid, "Unteilbarkeit," 21–39; Thomas Krüger, "Sündenfall? Überlegungen zur theologischen Bedeutung der Paradiesgeschichte," in Schmid and Riedweg, *Beyond Eden*, 95–109.

48. David M. Carr, "The Politics of Textual Subversion: A Diachronic Perspective on the Garden of Eden Story," *JBL* 112 (1993): 577, 591–93, sees in Gen 2–3 an "anti-wisdom story." Other J passages that are close to wisdom texts are the statements in the J flood story on the "evilness" or "badness" of the human heart and thoughts (Gen 6:5; 8:21 cf. Eccl 9:3 and 8:6 MT, 11). According to Thomas Krüger, *Qohelet: A Commentary* (Minneapolis: Fortress, 2004), 170, Ecclesiastes is dependent on the non-Priestly flood narrative.

49. See, e.g., Kratz, *Die Komposition*, 269.

50. Blenkinsopp, "Post-exilic Lay Source" and Schmid, *Literaturgeschichte*, 156.

51. Cf. Schmid, "Loss," 65. Gerhard von Rad, *Die Theologie der geschichtlichen Überlieferungen Israels*, vol. 1 of *Theologie des Alten Testaments*, 9th ed. (Munich: Kaiser, 1987), 163–64, was also aware of this striking fact.

that a large number of these were composed or edited in the Persian era.[52] As for the J^g texts, the devaluation of the east (in particular Babylon) in favor of Jerusalem pleads for a setting in Jerusalem. Given the absence of specific Priestly themes, their authors should be assigned to lay circles within the Jerusalem elite in the Persian period.[53]

Bibliography

Albertz, Rainer. "'Ihr werdet sein wie Gott': Gen 3,1–7 vor dem Hintergrund des alttestamentlichen und sumerisch-babylonischen Menschenbildes." *WO* 24 (1993): 89–111.
Arneth, Martin. *Durch Adams Fall ist gänzlich verderbt…: Studien zur Entstehung der alttestamentlichen Urgeschichte*. FRLANT 217. Göttingen: Vandenhoeck & Ruprecht, 2007.
Blenkinsopp, Joseph. "A Post-exilic Lay Source in Genesis 1–11." Pages 49–61 in *Abschied vom Jahwisten: Die Komposition des Hexateuch in der jüngsten Diskussion*. Edited by Jan C. Gertz, Konrad Schmid, and Markus Witte. BZAW 315. Berlin: de Gruyter, 2002.
Blum, Erhard. *Die Komposition der Vätergeschichte*. WMANT 57. Neukirchen-Vluyn: Neukirchener Verlag, 1984.
———. *Studien zur Komposition des Pentateuch*. BZAW 189. Berlin: de Gruyter, 1990.
Borgeaud, Philippe, and Thomas Römer. "Mythologie de la Méditerranée et du Proche-orient ancient: Regards croisés sur l'origine de l'humanité." Pages 121–48 in *Religions antiques: Une introduction comparée*. Edited by Philippe Borgeaud and Francesca Prescendi. Geneva: Labor et Fides, 2008.
Bosshard-Nepustil, Erich. *Vor uns die Sintflut: Studien zu Text, Kontexten und Rezeption der Fluterzählung Genesis 6–9*. BWANT 9.5. Stuttgart: Kohlhammer, 2005.
Carr, David M. "The Politics of Textual Subversion: A Diachronic Perspective on the Garden of Eden Story." *JBL* 112 (1993): 577–95.

---

52. Raymond F. Person Jr., *The Deuteronomic School: History, Social Setting, and Literature*, SBLStBL 2 (Atlanta: Society of Biblical Literature, 2002); Römer, *So-Called Deuteronomistic History*, 165–83.

53. Thus Blenkinsopp, "Post-exilic Lay Source," 60. But, although a single text, the J flood story, seems to be influenced by Priestly theology and language (see above, n. 32), this text probably belongs to a later J stratum (P^s).

Crüsemann, Frank. "Die Eigenständigkeit der Urgeschichte: Ein Beitrag zur Diskussion um den 'Jahwisten.'" Pages 11–29 in *Die Botschaft und die Boten: Festschrift H. W. Wolff*. Edited by Jörg Jeremias and Lothar Perlitt. Neukirchen-Vluyn: Neukirchener Verlag, 1981.

Edenburg, Cynthia. "From Eden to Babylon: Reading Gen 2–4 as a Paradigmatic Narrative." Pages 155–67 in *Pentateuch, Hexateuch, or Enneateuch: Identifying Literary Works in Genesis through 2 Kings*. Edited by Thomas Dozeman, Thomas Römer, and Konrad Schmid. AIL 8. Atlanta: Society of Biblical Literature, 2011.

Fischer, Irmtraud. *Die Erzeltern Israels: Feministischtheologische Studien zu Genesis 12–36*. BZAW 222. Berlin: de Gruyter, 1994.

Gertz, Jan C. "The Formation of the Primeval History." Pages 107–35 in *The Book of Genesis: Composition, Reception, and Interpretation*. Edited by Craig A. Evans, Joel N. Lohr, and David L. Petersen. VTSup 152. Leiden: Brill, 2012.

———. "Von Adam zu Enosch: Überlegungen zur Entstehungsgeschichte von Gen 2–4." Pages 215–36 in *Gott und Mensch im Dialog: Festschrift für Otto Kaiser zum 80. Geburtstag*. Edited by Markus Witte. BZAW 345. Berlin: de Gruyter, 2004.

Gese, Hartmut. "Der bewachte Lebensbaum und die Heroen: Zwei mythologische Ergänzungen zur Urgeschichte der Quelle J." Pages 77–85 in *Festschrift für Karl Elliger zum 70. Geburtstag*. Edited by Hartmut Gese and Hans Peter Rüger. AOAT 18. Kevelaer: Butzon & Bercker, 1973.

Gunkel, Hermann. *Genesis*. 3rd ed. HKAT. Göttingen: Vandenhoeck & Ruprecht, 1922.

Humbert, Paul. *Études sur le récit du paradis et de la chute dans la Genèse*. Mémoires de l'Université de Neuchatel 14. Neuchâtel: University, 1940.

Hutzli, Jürg. *Origins of P*. Forthcoming.

———. "Transgression et initiation: Tendances idéologiques et développement littéraire du récit de Genèse 2–3." Pages 113–33 in *Tabou et transgressions: Actes du colloque organisé par le Collège de France, Paris, les 11–12 avril 2012*. Edited by Jean-Marie Durand, Michaël Guichard, and Thomas Römer. OBO 274. Fribourg: Academic Press; Göttingen: Vandenhoeck & Ruprecht, 2015.

Jacobsen, Thorkild. *The Sumerian King List*. AS 11. Chicago: University of Chicago Press, 1939.

Knohl, Israel. "Nimrod, Son of Cush, King of Mesopotamia, and the Dates of P and J." Pages 45–52 in vol. 1 of *Birkat Shalom: Studies in the Bible,*

Ancient Near Eastern Literature, and Postbiblical Judaism Presented to Shalom M. Paul on the Occasion of His Seventieth Birthday. Edited by Chaim Cohen, Victor Avigdor Hurowitz, Avi Hurvitz, Yochanan Muffs, Baruch J. Schwartz, and Jeffrey H. Tigay. 2 vols. Winona Lake, IN: Eisenbrauns, 2008.

Köckert, Matthias. "Wie wurden Abraham- und Jakobüberlieferung zu einer 'Vätergeschichte' verbunden?" *HBAI* 3 (2014): 43–66.

Kratz, Reinhard G. *Die Komposition der erzählenden Bücher des Alten Testaments: Grundwissen der Bibelkritik*. Göttingen: Vandenhoeck & Ruprecht, 2000.

Krüger, Thomas. *Qohelet: A Commentary*. Minneapolis: Fortress, 2004.

———. "Sündenfall? Überlegungen zur theologischen Bedeutung der Paradiesgeschichte." Pages 95–109 in *Beyond Eden: The Biblical Story of Paradise (Genesis 2–3) and Its Reception History*. Edited by Konrad Schmid and Christoph Riedweg. FAT 2/34. Tübingen: Mohr Siebeck, 2008.

Levin, Christoph. *Der Jahwist*. FRLANT 157. Göttingen: Vandenhoeck & Ruprecht, 1993.

Nihan, Christophe. "L'écrit sacerdotal entre mythe et histoire." Pages 151–90 in *Ancient and Modern Scriptural Historiography; L'historiographie biblique, ancienne et moderne*. Edited by George J. Brooke and Thomas Römer. BETL 207. Leuven: Peeters, 2007.

Noth, Martin. *Überlieferungsgeschichte des Pentateuchs*. 2nd ed. Stuttgart: Kohlhammer, 1960.

Person Jr., Raymond F. *The Deuteronomic School: History, Social Setting, and Literature*. SBLStBL 2. Atlanta: Society of Biblical Literature, 2002.

Pury, Albert de. "Genèse 12–36." Pages 217–38 in *Introduction à l'Ancien Testament*. Edited by Thomas Römer, Jean-Daniel Macchi, and Christophe Nihan. 2nd ed. Geneva: Labor et Fides, 2009.

———. "P^g as the Absolute Beginning." Pages 13–42 in *Die Patriarchen und die Priesterschrift: Gesammelte Studien zu seinem 70. Geburtstag; Les patriarches et le document sacerdotal; Recueil d'articles, à l'occasion de son 70e anniversaire*. Edited by Jean-Daniel Macchi, Thomas Römer, Konrad Schmid. ATANT 99. Zurich: TVZ, 2010.

Pury, Albert de, Thomas Römer, and Konrad Schmid. *L'Ancien Testament commenté: La Genèse*. Geneva: Labor et Fides; Montrouge: Bayard, 2016.

Rad, Gerhard von. *Das erste Buch Mose*. 2nd ed. ATD 2.4. Göttingen: Vandenhoeck & Ruprecht, 1950.

———. "Das formgeschichtliche Problem des Hexateuch." Pages 9–86 in *Gesammelte Studien zum Alten Testament*. Edited by Rudolf Smend. Munich: Kaiser, 1958.

———. *Die Theologie der geschichtlichen Überlieferungen Israels*. Vol. 1 of *Theologie des Alten Testaments*. 9th ed. Munich: Kaiser, 1987.

Rendtorff, Rolf. *Das überlieferungsgeschichtliche Problem des Pentateuch*. BZAW 147. Berlin: de Gruyter, 1977.

Römer, Thomas. "Genèse 15 et les tensions de la communauté juive postexilique dans le cycle d'Abraham." *Transeu* 7 (1994): 107–21.

———. *The So-Called Deuteronomistic History: A Sociological, Historical and Literary Introduction*. London: T&T Clark, 2007.

Rose, Martin. *Deuteronomist und Jahwist: Untersuchungen zu den Berührungspunkten beider Literaturwerke*. ATANT 67. Zurich: TVZ, 1981.

Schmid, Konrad. *Genesis and the Moses Story: Israel's Dual Origins in the Hebrew Bible*. Translated by James D. Nogalski. Siphrut 3. Winona Lake, IN: Eisenbrauns, 2010.

———. *Literaturgeschichte des Alten Testaments: Eine Einführung*. Darmstadt: Wissenschaftliche Buchgesellschaft, 2008.

———. "Loss of Immortality? Hermeneutical Aspects of Genesis 2–3 and Its Early Receptions." Pages 58–78 in *Beyond Eden: The Biblical Story of Paradise (Genesis 2–3) and Its Reception History*. Edited by Konrad Schmid and Christoph Riedweg. FAT 2/34. Tübingen: Mohr Siebeck, 2008.

———. "Die Unteilbarkeit der Weisheit: Überlegungen zur sogenannten Paradieserzählung und ihrer theologischen Tendenz." *ZAW* 114 (2002): 21–39.

Schüle, Andreas. *Der Prolog der hebräischen Bibel: Der literar- und theologiegeschichtliche Diskurs der Urgeschichte (Gen 1–11)*. ATANT 86. Zurich: TVZ, 2006.

Stordalen, Terje. *Echoes of Eden: Genesis 2–3 and Symbolism of the Eden Garden in Biblical Hebrew Literature*. Leuven: Peeters, 2000.

Van Seters, John. *The Life of Moses: The Yahwist as Historian in Exodus–Numbers*. Louisville: Westminster John Knox, 1994.

———. *Prologue to History: The Yahwist as Historian in Genesis*. Zurich: TVZ, 1992.

Wenham, Gordon J. *Genesis 1–15*. WBC 1. Waco, TX: Word, 1979.

Witte, Markus. *Die biblische Urgeschichte: Redaktions- und theologiegeschichtliche Beobachtungen zu Genesis 1,1–11,26*. BZAW 265. Berlin: de Gruyter, 1998.

Contributions from Priestly Scribal Circles in Yehud

Formulae That Equate the גר and the Israelite: Literary Activity in the Priestly Writings

Itamar Kislev

The Hebrew Bible גר, usually understood to represent a stranger who does not own land, is afforded extra protection in many pentateuchal commandments. This view of the גר as a dependent, impoverished member of agrarian society, found in many other parts of the Hebrew Bible, is reflected in the usual translation of גר as "resident alien" or along similar lines.[1] There is a disparity, however, with the Priestly legislation, where the גר is also portrayed as wealthy enough to own an Israelite slave (Lev 25:47) or to bring an expensive sacrifice (see esp. Num 15:14).[2] This disparity is one of the elements fueling the debate on the socioeconomic

---

1. See, e.g., BDB, s.v. "גר"; *HALOT*, s.v. "גר"; Dieter Kellermann, "גור," *TDOT* 2:439–40; and Jan Joosten, *People and Land in the Holiness Code: An Exegetical Study of the Ideational Framework of the Law in Leviticus 17–26*, VTSup 67 (Leiden: Brill, 1996), 54–73.

2. Some scholars point to several other cases according to which the גר enjoys a decent socioeconomic status, such as Lev 17:8–9; 22:18–19; see, e.g., Dieter Vieweger, "Vom 'Fremdling' zum 'Proselyt': Zur sakralrechtlichen Definition des גר im späten 5. Jahrhundert v. Chr.," in *Von Gott reden: Beiträge zur Theologie und Exegese des Alten Testaments; Festschrift für Siegfried Wagner zum 65. Geburtstag*, ed. Dieter Vieweger and Ernst-Joachim Waschke (Neukirchen-Vluyn: Neukirchener Verlag, 1995), 274–75. As some scholars note, Deut 28:43–44 illustrates the unexpected nature of the situation in which the גר achieves higher socioeconomic status than the Israelite; see, e.g., Joosten, *People and Land*, 62. This distinctive socioeconomic status of the גר led scholars to place the historical background of this change in the Persian period; see Christophe Nihan, "Resident Aliens and Natives in the Holiness Legislation," in *The Foreigner and the Law: Perspectives from the Hebrew Bible and the Ancient Near East*, ed. Reinhard Achenbach, Rainer Albertz, and Jakob Wöhrle, BZABR 16 (Weisbaden: Harrassowitz, 2011), 131–33, but cf. Joosten, *People and Land*, 62–63.

status of the גר in the Priestly writings (P).³ A more significant difference between references to the גר in the Priestly writings and elsewhere in the Pentateuch is the relatively frequent appearance in P of formulae that equate the גר and the Israelite. Found about twenty times in the Torah, twice in the book of Joshua, and twice in Ezekiel, these formulae are the topic of this essay.⁴

The ostensibly different social and religious status of the גר in the Priestly writings has led some scholars to suggest that the גר in this context is not a resident alien as in the other parts of the Pentateuch but an Israelite from the north, a Judahite, or a Samaritan. Others retain the usual conception that, even in these texts, the גר is a resident alien.⁵ Also disputed is the question of the scope of the parity between the גר and the Israelite in the eyes of the Priestly authors. In other words: what is the meaning of these equating formulae? Until the last third of the twentieth century, the prevailing consensus was that the גר achieves full religious communion with Israel in the Priestly writings.⁶ Since that time, some scholars have noted the differences between the גר and the Israelite in the Priestly writings, concluding that it was not their intention to completely equalize the religious status of the גר and the Israelite. Arguing that the equating formulae

---

3. Joosten, *People and Land*, 54–73; and Nihan, "Resident Aliens and Natives," 117, 129–32.

4. In treating the גר in the Priestly writings or in the Holiness legislation (H) in general, other scholars categorize the occurrences of the גר but usually do not include all the formulae that equate the גר and the Israelite in one group; see, e.g., Cristiana van Houten, *The Alien in Israelite Law*, JSOTSup 107 (Sheffield: JSOT Press, 1991), 120–21.

5. See the survey in Joosten, *People and Land*, 55–58 and, more recently Nihan, "Resident Aliens and Natives," 113–14.

6. The usual equivalent of גר in the LXX is προσήλυτος, which first appears there. Many scholars think that it means religious conversion to Judaism in the LXX; see, e.g., Houten, *Alien*, 179–83, but cf. Abraham Geiger, *Urschrift und Übersetzungen der Bibel in ihrer Abhängigkeit von der innern Entwickelung des Judentums* (Breslau: Hainauer, 1857), 353–54. In modern times, Alfred Bertholet, *Die Stellung der Israeliten und der Juden zu den Fremden* (Freiburg: Mohr, 1896), 152–78 is considered the first to suggest that the term גר in H had become a technical term for a religious convert, but cf. Morton Smith, *Palestinian Parties and Politics That Shaped the Old Testament*, 2nd ed. (London: SCM, 1987), 136–39; Christoph Bultmann, *Der Fremde im antiken Juda: Eine Untersuchung zum sozialen Typenbegriff 'ger' und seinem Bedeutungswandel in der alttestamentlicher Gesetzgebung*, FRLANT 153 (Göttingen: Vandenhoeck & Ruprecht, 1992), 176.

do not mean complete parity between גר and Israelite, these scholars offer a variety of alternative theories regarding the organizing principles that explain both the details of the units in which these formulae appear and the larger, more complex picture.[7]

This disputed point raises a related question. Some of these equating formulae seem to be general statements that create full equity between the גר and the Israelite (e.g., Exod 12:49: "There shall be one law [תורה אחת] for the native born and for the גר who dwells among you"; cf. Lev 24:22; Num 9:14, 15:15–16).[8] On the other hand, many legal units contain equating formulae that are explicitly related only to the specific context. In still other legal units, such formulae do not appear, and there is no reference to the גר at all. More than the inconsistency, one wonders whether these general statements are intended to fully equalize the גר and the Israelite, as some scholars think, or whether they are perhaps valid only with regard to the topic of the legal unit in which they appear, as others maintain.[9]

The equating formulae treated here are found in some twenty pentateuchal legal units but never appear in the core P law code: Lev 1–16 (aside from the sole occurrence in Lev 16:29, long recognized as part of a secondary passage bearing features of H).[10] Eleven occurrences of equating

---

7. See, e.g., Moshe Weinfeld, "Theological Currents in Pentateuchal Literature," *PAAJR* 37 (1969): 135–39; Jacob Milgrom, "Religious Conversion and the Revolt Model for the Formation of Israel," *JBL* 101 (1982): 170–71; and Nihan, "Resident Aliens and Natives," 114–29.

8. A similar general formula appears in Num 15:29. In this case, however, the verse explicitly states that the equation relates only to "anyone who acts in error." On this verse, see below. Some scholars indeed try to find differences between these general formulae; see, e.g., Reinhard Achenbach, "*gêr–nåkhrî–tôshav–zår*: Legal and Sacral Distinctions regarding Foreigners in the Pentateuch," in Achenbach, Albertz, and Wöhrle, *Foreigner and the Law*, 41–42.

9. See, e.g., Bertholet, *Die Stellung*, 167–68, who applies these general statements with regard to all religious laws. In contrast, Milgrom, "Religious Conversion," 170 emphasizes that these general sentences apply "only to the case given in the context; it is not a generalization."

10. See, e.g., Israel Knohl, *The Sanctuary of Silence: The Priestly Torah and the Holiness School* (Minneapolis: Fortress, 1995), 27–28; Christophe Nihan, *From Priestly Torah to Pentateuch: A Study in the Composition of the Book of Leviticus*, FAT 2/25 (Tübingen: Mohr Siebeck, 2007), 347–50. The following are the units; some are subunits. In some cases, more than one such equating formula occurs in a unit. The verses in which the equating formula appear are noted in parentheses: Exod 12:15–20 (19),

formulae are found in Lev 17–26, which is considered the core of H, two in Exodus, and seven in Numbers. This distribution of the equating formulae relates to the general discussion of how to define the Priestly units outside Leviticus. Whereas some researchers connect them to H, others see them as late layers of P or even as part of the redaction of the Pentateuch.[11] Scholars tend to determine which texts should discussed in relation to the גר based on their attitudes about this question.

This study examines these equating formulae, bringing philological evidence to bear on the argument that the majority of these formulae are secondary additions. Recognition of their secondary status is a necessary first step toward understanding the intention and meaning of these Israelite-גר equating formulae. This recognition also has important ramifications for clarifying some crucial issues related to the process of the formation of the Pentateuch.

Before proceeding to the heart of the discussion, I note three cases from the Deuteronomistic context in which we find the גר as an integral part of the Israelite community: Deut 29:10; 31:12; Josh 8:35. Although, as formulated, these verses seem to be interrelated and attest to an underlying notion of some equalization of the גר with the Israelite, the exact scope of that equalization remains unclear, as does the nature of the connection between these three cases and the less ambiguous Priestly formulae that equate the גר and the Israelite, which are the topic of this essay.[12]

43–49 (48–49); Lev 16:29–34 (29); 17:8–9 (8), 10–12 (10, 12), 13–14 (13), 15–16 (15); 18:1–30 (26); 19:33–34 (33–34); 20:1–4 (2); 22:17–25 (18); 24:13–16 (16), 17–22 (22); Num 9:9–14 (14); 15:1–16 (14–16), 22–26 (26), 27–29 (29), 30–31 (30); 19:1–22 (10); 35:9–34 (15). In Lev 17:3 only the LXX has an equating formula, and this is discussed below. Such formulae also appear in Josh 8:33; 20:9; Ezek 14:7; 47:22 (see below).

11. Knohl, *Sanctuary*, 21; Rainer Albertz, "From Aliens to Proselytes: Non-Priestly and Priestly Legislation Concerning Strangers," in Achenbach, Albertz, and Wöhrle, *Foreigner and the Law*, 53–69; and Nihan, "Resident Aliens and Natives," 111–12.

12. Some scholars believe that the reference to the גר in Deut 29:10, according to which he takes part in the covenant, is a late addition; see Reinhard Achenbach, "Der Eintritt der Schutzbürger in den Bund (Dtn 29,10–12): Distinktion und Integration von Fremden im Deuteronomium," in *Gerechtigkeit und Recht zu üben (Gen 18,19): Studien zur altorientalischen und biblischen Rechtsgeschichte, zur Religionsgeschichte Israels und zur Religionssoziologie; Festschrift für Eckart Otto zum 65. Geburtstag*, ed. Reinhard Achenbach and Martin Arneth, BZABR 13 (Weisbaden: Harrassowitz, 2009), 247–48. In Deut 31:12, it seems that the גר who comes to the temple with the entire Israelite nation "that they may hear, and that they may learn ... and observe to do all the words of this law" is completely integrated in the Isra-

1. Establishing the Secondary Character of the Equating Formulae: The Most Definitive Cases

I begin by examining four cases in which the evidence suggests most conclusively, in my opinion, that the equating formulae are secondary. Subsequently, I investigate the philological evidence to back my contention that there are additional cases in which it is likely that the equating formulae are also secondary. Finally, given the extensive nature of this phenomenon, I further suggest that, even in the absence of direct evidence, the few remaining cases of equating formulae are also secondary. In each section I follow the scriptural order.

Case 1, Exod 12:48–49

וכי יגור אתך גר ועשה פסח ליהוה המול לו כל זכר ואז יקרב לעשתו והיה כאזרח הארץ וכל ערל לא יאכל בו תורה אחת יהיה לאזרח ולגר הגר בתוככם

Should a גר who resides among you wish to perform [ועשה] the paschal sacrifice to YHWH, all his males must be circumcised; then he shall be admitted to offer it; he shall be as a native born of the country. But no uncircumcised person may eat of it. There shall be one law for the native born and for the גר who resides among you.

These verses appear at the end of a supplementary passage regarding the Passover offering (vv. 43–49).[13] Some puzzling questions arise in relation

---

elite religious and sacral community, although he still has a distinct social status. Some scholars, however, hesitate to draw the full conclusions from this verse (as from Deut 29:10); see, e.g., S. R. Driver, *A Critical and Exegetical Commentary on Deuteronomy*, ICC 5 (Edinburgh: T&T Clark, 1902), 336: "All are to be assembled ... the resident foreigner because ... he should be instructed in the practical duties and responsibilities which his position lays upon him"; cf. Kellermann, "גור," 445. With respect to Josh 8:35, while the connection between this verse and Deut 31:12 is clear, the character of the entire passage (vv. 30–35) is harder to determine, as it exhibits a heavy Deuteronomistic flavor together with the clearly Priestly expression כגר כאזרח in v. 33. The meaning of the appearance of the clearly Priestly expression כגר כאזרח in v. 33 is disputed; see George A. Cooke, *The Book of Joshua: in the Revised Version; with Introduction and Notes*, Cambridge Bible for Schools and Colleges (Cambridge: Cambridge University Press, 1918), 73; Christophe Nihan, "The Torah between Samaria and Judah: Shechem and Gerizim in Deuteronomy and Joshua," in *The Pentateuch as Torah: New Models for Understanding Its Promulgation and Acceptance*, ed. Gary N. Knoppers and Bernard M. Levinson (Winona Lake, IN: Eisenbrauns, 2007), 217–22.

13. See Bruno Baentsch, *Exodus—Leviticus—Numeri*, HKAT (Göttingen: Van-

to the appearance of the גר in this pericope. First, only in the case of the Passover offering is circumcision demanded as a condition for the גר's participation in the ceremony (Exod 12:48). Even the pericope in Num 9:1–14, which deals with this offering and equates the גר and the Israelite (v. 14), does not mention the prerequisite of circumcision. We can argue that the commandment in Exod 12:48 underlies the law in Num 9:9–14; the demand of circumcision would thus be required according to the latter unit as well. Alternatively, it is possible that circumcision is a basic condition for participation by the גר in any aspect of Israelite religious life.[14] We must then ask why this requirement appears only in the context of the Passover offering and why it is not mentioned in Num 9. Another option is that there is a disagreement between these verses, with one demanding circumcision for performing the paschal sacrifice (Exod 12:48) and the other not (Num 9:14).

Another difficulty that arises regarding the passage in Exod 12:43–49 is the difference between גר and תושב ושכיר. According to this legal unit, a circumcised slave can partake in the Passover meal (v. 44), whereas תושב ושכיר are not allowed to do so (v. 45). The continuation of the passage states that a circumcised גר can also eat the Passover offering. Several answers have been proposed to the question of what constitutes the difference between גר and the תושב ושכיר.[15]

Moreover, there is tension in this unit. The general statement with which it opens—כל בן נכר לא יאכל בו (v. 43)—forbids a non-Israelite from eating the Passover offering. Similarly, the statement in verse 47, כל עדת ישראל יעשו אתו, designates the law only for the Israelites. These are incon-

---

derhoeck & Ruprecht, 1903), 108, who considers the passage as a supplement to P (P^s). Note that v. 51 is a resumptive repetition of v. 41, which indicates that the intervening passage is late.

14. See Smith, *Palestinian Parties and Politics*, 138; Nihan, "Resident Aliens and Natives," 115 n. 17; and Achenbach, "gêr—nåkhrî—tôshav—zâr," 40–41, who thinks that the גר's circumcision for the Passover sacrifice is a "benchmark to signal the degree of integration." There is no evidence, however, that the demand of circumcision relates to other commandments in addition to the Passover rite. Others hold the opposite view; see Sara Japhet, "The Term גר and the Concept of Religious Conversion in the Bible" [Hebrew], in *The Wisdom of the Sages: Biblical Commentary in Rabbinic Literature, Presented to Hananel Mack*, ed. Avigdor Shinan and Israel J. Yuval (Jerusalem: Carmel, 2019), 215.

15. See, e.g., Joosten, *People and Land*, 73–74; Bultmann, *Der Fremde*, 200–205; Albertz, "From Aliens to Proselytes," 62; Nihan, "Resident Aliens and Natives," 118.

sistent with the different general statement that concludes the passage: וכל ערל לא יאכל בו, "but no uncircumcised person may eat of it" (v. 48). Should we understand these requirements as supplementary, which means that an uncircumcised Israelite is not allowed to participate in the Passover meal? Or should we understand them as contradictory, with the later prohibition וכל ערל לא יאכל בו meaning that a circumcised non-Israelite can participate in the Passover ritual? According to the view that the requirements are complementary, only an Israelite can eat the Passover sacrifice. (And, as the property of an Israelite, the circumcised slave is exceptional.) How, then, is the circumcised גר allowed to take part in the Passover ceremony? Is he considered an Israelite?[16] That this line of thought seems to have led some scholars to suggest that the גר in this context is either a Judahite from Yehud or elsewhere in the diaspora, or a Samaritan.[17]

Several points suggest that Heinrich Holzinger is correct in claiming that verses 48–49 soften the message of verses 43–45: (1) the superfluity of the command כל ערל לא יאכל בו (v. 48) in relation to the prohibition כל בן נכר לא יאכל בו (v. 43)—after all, according to Priestly legislation every Israelite male should be circumcised (Gen 17:10–14; 12:3); (2) the similar formulation of both prohibitions; and (3) the difference between them.[18] This leads in turn to the conclusion that verses 48–49 are an addition to the original pericope intended to enable the גר to take part in the Passover meal even though he is not included in עדת ישראל. There is indeed a real contradiction between this addition and the prohibition against the שכיר and תושב eating the Passover offering, caused because the interpolator deliberately sought to change the original injunction and to include the גר in the ritual. He therefore added these verses and inserted a different general statement: כל ערל לא יאכל בו (v. 48), which enables a non-Israelite

---

16. The slave is indeed an exception. Although a non-Israelite, the slave is allowed to eat the paschal sacrifice. It seems that he is considered part of the family because he was purchased with money (מקנת כסף) and is circumcised like an Israelite; see S. R. Driver, *The Book of Exodus* (Cambridge: Cambridge University Press, 1918), 103 and cf. Lev 22:11.

17. For a survey of the literature, see note 4 above. According to Pierre Grelot, "La dernière étape de la rédaction sacerdotale," *VT* 6 (1956): 177, among others, Exod 12:43–48 is a key pericope for understanding the meaning of the Priestly גר.

18. H. Holzinger, *Exodus*, KHC (Tübingen: Mohr Siebeck, 1900), 40. Other commentators also have doubts regarding the relationship between vv. 48–49 and 44–45; see, e.g., William H. Propp, *Exodus 1–18*, AB 2 (New York: Doubleday, 1999), 419.

to share in the offering on condition that he is circumcised.[19] The wording of this general sentence toward the end of the unit is very similar to that of the statement with which the passage opens: כל בן נכר לא יאכל בו (v. 43). Clearly, the interpolator formulated his new general statement (v. 48) in line with the original opening of the pericope (v. 43). His aim was that the reader would interpret the original phrase at the beginning of the paragraph in light of the second, new utterance, which prohibits the non-Israelite from taking part in the Passover meal because he is uncircumcised, not because he is a non-Israelite; hence, the גר could participate in this ceremony on condition that he has been circumcised. This invented prerequisite was derived from verse 44, which stipulates that an Israelite who wants his slave to eat the Passover offering must circumcise his slave. The addition of the question of the גר to this unit, which is the only instance in which circumcision appears as a prerequisite even before the addition of the גר, is the reason why this demand is found here and only here. The assumption that verses 48–49 were added to the unit therefore renders all the attempts to find a distinction between the גר, on the one hand, and the תושב and שכיר, on the other superfluous.

Case 2, Lev 16:29
והיתה לכם לחקת עולם בחדש השביעי בעשור לחדש תענו את נפשתיכם וכל מלאכה לא תעשו האזרח והגר הגר בתוככם
And this shall be for you a law for all time; in the seventh month, on the tenth day of the month you shall practice self-denial, and you shall do no work, neither the native born nor the גר who resides among you.

The passage in Lev 16:1–28, with its detailed description of a purgation ritual, is followed in verse 29 by a formula that equalizes the גר and the Israelite. This is the opening verse of an H-style passage in verses 29–34a

---

19. If we posit that vv. 48–49 are not part of the original passage, its structure becomes apparent. After the general statement כל בן נכר לא יאכל בו (v. 43), the law presents a single exception to this rule: the slave, on condition he is circumcised (v. 44). Then the author emphasizes that even תושב and שכיר are not allowed to eat the paschal offering (v. 45). Verse 46 is a detail about eating the offering, and v. 47 concludes the unit with another general statement: כל עדת ישראל יעשו אתו, which repeats the statement in v. 43 using different wording, כל בן נכר לא יאכל בו, and creates a nice closure to the unit. According to this reconstruction, there is only one, not two exceptions to the rule, which do not appear together in proximity as in the current form of the passage.

that was added to the P unit in verses 1–28, as many scholars have correctly recognized.[20] Parallel statements (vv. 29, 34a) in which the expression והיתה (זאת) לכם לחקת עולם appears frame this passage. The appointed date of the purgation, which is explicitly stated in verse 29, is expressed in verse 34a as אחת בשנה. This means that both parts of the framework were intentionally formulated in a similar manner, thematically and linguistically. Accordingly, the difference in the definition of the group to which the law applies is significant: in verse 29 the גר and the native born (אזרח), whereas the phrase לכפר על בני ישראל מכל חטאתם, "to effect purgation on behalf of the Israelites for all their sins" in verse 34a reveals that the plural לכם at the beginning of the verse (והיתה זאת לכם) refers to the Israelites; this contradicts the first part of the framework, which refers to גר and Israelite as addressees of the law. It thus stands to reason that the words האזרח והגר הגר בתוככם—namely, the formula that equates the גר and the Israelite in vere 29—is secondary, inserted in order to apply the instructions for the purgation day to the גר as well.[21]

Case 3, Num 19:10
וכבס האסף את אפר הפרה את בגדיו וטמא עד הערב והיתה לבני ישראל ולגר הגר בתוכם לחקת עולם
He who gathers up the ashes of the cow shall also wash his clothes and be unclean until evening; this shall be a permanent law for the Israelites and for the גר who resides among you.

This verse, found in the pericope treating the red heifer, contains another formula that equates the גר and the Israelite. The placement of this sentence is difficult to understand because it immediately follows a similar statement in verse 9: "This shall be kept for the Israelite community for water of lus-

---

20. E.g., Jacob Milgrom, *Leviticus 1–16*, AB 3A (New York: Doubleday, 1998), 1064–65; Nihan, *From Priestly Torah to Pentateuch*, 346–50. Verse 34b is connected to v. 28, as Milgrom rightly comments, because the singular verb in this phrase relates to Aaron the priest, who is referred to in vv. 2–28, and not to the Israelites, who are the subject of vv. 29–34a. Note that the Syriac version has the plural here.

21. It is hard to decide on the basis of the current wording of v. 29 alone whether the interpolators who added the words האזרח והגר הגר בתוככם wanted the גר only to engage in no work on the purgation day or to practice self-denial, too; see Alfred Bertholet, *Leviticus*, KHC 3 (Tübingen: Mohr Siebeck, 1901), 56; Milgrom, *Leviticus 1–16*, 1055–56. The ambiguity on this point may indicate the clumsiness ensuing from an interpolation and therefore may indicate this verse's lack of uniformity.

tration." This statement stipulates that the complicated preparation of the ashes of the cow with its other ingredients is intended for the Israelites. Not only does the sentence in verse 10b contradict verse 9 with regard to the group to which the statute applies, its function as a concluding sentence is also unnecessary, as the statement in verse 9 already serves this function.

This proximity between two sentences so similar to one another has troubled commentators since the mid-nineteenth century, leading some to understand verse 10b as the opening sentence of the following passage.[22] Yet this notion seems forced because this statement's formulation is not that of an opening sentence; similar formulations do function not as the beginning of units but as their conclusions (Exod 29:9; 40:15; Num 27:11).[23] Moreover, the general statement in verse 10b separates the masculine noun אפר הפרה in verse 10a from the word בו in verse 12, to which its masculine suffix refers.[24] These considerations suggest that the sentence in verse 10b is a secondary insertion to the original law. Its interpolator sought to equate the status of the גר and the Israelite regarding purification from human corpse contamination. The existing contradiction between verses 9b and 10b implies that the interpolators initially intended to replace the similar statement in verse 9, but both verses eventually remained in the received text. The addition of verse 10b thus created a disturbing double conclusion (in vv. 9 and 10), a contradiction regarding the group to which the law refers, and disjunction between verse 10a and verse 12.[25]

---

22. August W. Knobel, *Numeri, Deuteronomium und Josua*, Kurzgefasstes exegetisches Handbuch zum Alten Testament 13 (Leipzig: Hirzel, 1861), 99; Carl Friedrich Keil, *Leviticus, Numeri und Deuteronomium*, BKAT (Leipzig: Dörffling & Franke, 1862), 285; H. Holzinger, *Numeri*, KHC (Tübingen: Mohr Siebeck, 1903), 80; and Martin Noth, *Numbers: A Commentary*, trans. James D. Martin, OTL (Philadelphia: Westminster, 1968), 141.

23. On the lateness of Exod 12:14 (which is formulated similarly to Num 19:10) and its function as a transition between two unrelated legal units, see Shimon Gesundheit, *Three Times a Year: Studies on Festival Legislation in the Pentateuch* (Winona Lake, IN: Eisenbrauns, 2012), 76–80. A similar case is Lev 16:29, which opens a secondary, concluding pericope, as discussed above, but there only the formula that equates the גר with the Israelite was added and not the entire opening verse.

24. See Jacob Milgrom, *Numbers*, JPS Torah Commentary (Philadelphia: Jewish Publication Society, 1990), 160, who correctly comments on the relationship between בו in v. 12 and אפר הפרה in v. 10.

25. The continuation of the unit also refers only to the Israelites. The phrase ונכרתה הנפש ההוא מישראל "that person shall be cut off from Israel" (v. 13) supports the above assumption that the law of the red cow did not originally relate to the גר.

In the middle of the developed law on the cities of refuge (Num 35:9–34), we find a formula that equates the גר and the Israelite (v. 15).

> Case 4, Num 35:15
> לבני ישראל ולגר ולתושב בתוכם תהיינה שש הערים האלה למקלט לנוס שמה כל מכה נפש בשגגה
> These six cities shall serve the Israelites and the גר and the תושב among them as a place of refuge, so that anyone who kills a person unintentionally may flee there.

I have discussed this legal unit elsewhere and presented evidence that Num 35:13–15 are secondary, based on the argument that these verses interrupt the original sequence in which verse 16 immediately followed verse 12.[26] Verse 12 states that the murderer will receive temporary asylum "until he stands before the עדה for judgment," and the passage starting with verse 16 lays out the criteria for permanent residence in an asylum city. Thus verses 12 and 16–23 grapple with the same topic: the killer's trial before the authorities. In contrast, the interim passage (vv. 13–15) addresses another topic: the number and array of the cities of refuge. Furthermore, verse 15 stands out in the unit because it addresses the Israelites in the third person, whereas the previous verses do so in the second person. This leads to the assumption that verses 13–15 were added to the unit in one or two stages and that the purpose of the insertion of verse 15 was to equate the גר with the Israelite concerning the cities of refuge.

A similar formula appears in Josh 20:9

> Case 5, Josh 20:9
> אלה היו ערי המועדה לכל בני ישראל ולגר הגר בתוכם לנוס שמה כל מכה נפש בשגגה
> Those were the cities designated for all the Israelites and for the גר residing among them, to which anyone who killed a person unintentionally might flee.

Knohl, *Sanctuary*, 92–93 claims that vv. 10b–13 are a secondary addition. While there is no decisive backing for his suggestion, the connection between v. 10a and v. 12 leads to the supposition that only v. 10b is an interpolation.

26. For the full discussion see Itamar Kislev, "The Cities of Refuge Law in Numbers 35:9–34: A Study of Its Sources, Textual Unity and Relationship to Deuteronomy 19:1–13," *ZABR* 26 (2020): 151–59.

It seems likely that this formula was composed after the addition to Num 35:15, as the entire passage in Josh 20:1–9 in its original form, as reflected in the Septuagint, was framed as the direct fulfillment of the injunction in Num 35:9–15.[27]

2. Two Composite Units

This section treats two complex cases—the handling of animal blood in Lev 17 and inadvertent and intentional wrongdoing in Num 15:22–31—each of which is composed of several sections that contain formulae equating the גר and the Israelite. In order to arrive at definitive conclusions, these multibranched laws require comprehensive, detailed discussion.

Cases 6–10 are in Lev 17. This chapter, which is devoted to the proper handling of animal blood, contains several occurrences of formulae that equate the גר and the Israelite (vv. [3 in LXX,] 8, 10, 12, 13, 15). There are five sections in the chapter (vv. 1–7, 8–9, 10–12, 13–14, 15–16), in four of which the MT includes such formulae (excluding the first unit), but equating formulae appear in all of the sections in the LXX. Two formulae (vv. 10, 12) are found in the third unit of the chapter, which deals with the prohibition of consuming blood (vv. 10–12), and the formulation of the second occurrence is unusual: "Therefore I said to the Israelites: No person among you shall ingest blood, neither shall any גר that resides among you ingest blood." The uniqueness of this formulation lies in the separation of the verse into two clauses, one aimed at the Israelites (נפש מכם) and the other at the גר. Such a separate formulation is unnecessary and has no parallel; the injunction could easily be formulated in one sentence, like similar formulae in the Priestly legislation: *כל נפש מכם ומן הגר הגר בתוככם לא תאכל דם, "No person among you and the גר that resides among you shall ingest blood." The distinctive double formulation raises the possibility that the second part of the verse, which addresses the גר, is not original. Moreover, such a formula is missing from the similar sentence at the end of the fourth paragraph, which treats covering the blood of hunted animals: "therefore I said to the Israelites: You shall not ingest the blood of any flesh; for the life of all flesh is its blood; anyone who ingests it shall be cut off" (v. 14). Both verses include an explicit self-quotation of the divine words: אמרתי (v. 12) and ואמר (v. 14), whose source is the divine statement about the penalty

---

27. Kislev, "Cities of Refuge Law," 251 n. 7, 253 n. 14.

for consuming blood in v. 10: "And if anyone of the house of Israel, or of the גר that resides among them, ingests any blood, I will set my face against the person who ingests blood, and I will cut him off from his people."[28] This creates an uncomfortable inconsistency with regard to the mentions of the גר: why did the authors of the passage mention the גר twice in the third paragraph, at the beginning (v. 10) and again at the end (v. 12) but only once at the beginning (v. 13) of the fourth paragraph, without mentioning him again at its end? This structural inconsistency, together with the unusual duplication in verse 12, implies that the mention of the גר at the end of verse 12 is secondary. Clearly, this addition was fueled by the tension between the beginning of the paragraph (v. 10), which relates to the Israelite and the גר together, and its end (v. 12), which, without the addition, refers only to the Israelites: על כן אמרתי לבני ישראל כל נפש מכם לא תאכל דם "Therefore I said to the Israelites: No person among you shall ingest blood."

Similar tension exists between verse 14, which quotes the divine prohibition against ingesting blood as applying to the Israelites alone—ואמר לבני ישראל דם כל בשר לא תאכלו, "therefore I said to the Israelites: '*You* shall not ingest the blood of any flesh' "—and verse 10, the source of that quotation, which includes the גר in this commandment. This double tension between the heading of the prohibition in verse 10 that mentions the גר and the two quotations of it regarding the ingesting of blood—in verse 12 in its original form and in verse 14 even in its current form, which apply the prohibition found in verse 10 only to Israelites—suggests that the inclusion of the גר at the beginning of verse 10 is secondary. The evidence from the quotations of the prohibition in verses 12 and 14 is stronger than the testimony from the opening heading of the paragraph containing the prohibition itself (v. 10) because we would expect an interpolator to pay special attention to the heading of a unit but not necessarily to all of its details, leaving some tensions and discrepancies. I surmise, therefore, that the formulae that equalize the גר and the Israelite in verses 10 and 12 are secondary.

We can also posit secondary status for the formula in verse 13 that opens the fourth paragraph, which treats covering the blood of hunted animals. As cited in this paragraph (v. 14), the reason for draining the blood onto the earth and covering it with dust is the prohibition against

---

28. Baruch J. Schwartz, "The Prohibitions Concerning the 'Eating' of Blood in Leviticus 17," in *Priesthood and Cult in Ancient Israel*, ed. Gary A. Anderson and Saul M. Olyan, JSOTSup 125 (Sheffield: Sheffield Academic, 1991), 45–46, 61.

ingesting blood. This does not quite make sense because, as seen above, the original prohibition against ingesting blood applies only to Israelites. But, according to verse 13, the injunction in the fourth paragraph refers to the גר as well, and it seems illogical that a commandment for the גר and the Israelite would be designed to prevent just the Israelite from ingesting blood.[29] This incompatibility indicates that the mention of the גר in verse 13 is secondary as well. Note that the references to the גר in verses 10 and 13 are identical: ומן הגר הגר בתוכם; this reinforces the supposition that both originated from the same source, namely, from the same interpolator.

Similarly, we can argue that the formula that equates the גר and the Israelite in the LXX version of verse 3, the prohibition of the profane slaughter of domestic quadrupeds, is not original because verse 5, which provides its rationale, mentions the Israelites alone: "this is in order that the *Israelites* may offer their sacrifices ... before YHWH, to the priest."[30] It appears unlikely that, if the LXX version of verse 3 was original, the motivational verses would refer to the Israelites alone; the formula that equates the גר and the Israelite reflected in the LXX to verse 3 is thus most likely an addition to the original text. This addition was written either by the same authors who inserted the formulae that equalize the גר and the Israelite in verses 10, 12, and 13 as analyzed above but was erroneously omitted when copying from the MT,[31] or it was written by a later author who wanted to make all the passages in the chapter similar with regard to the equation of the גר and the Israelite, and this interpolation penetrated only the *Vorlage* of the LXX.[32]

This leaves two formulae in chapter 17, in verses 8, 15. Although the above discussion raises suspicions that these formulae are also secondary, direct philological support for this supposition is lacking. Nevertheless, some general considerations favor this conjecture. The prohibition against

---

29. The hypothetical notion that the גר, who is allowed to ingest blood according to the above analysis, should cover the blood in order to prevent the Israelite from ingesting blood seems unlikely.

30. A clear determination of the exact nature of the prohibition in Lev 17:3-7 is not crucial for my argument here. On that issue see, e.g., Baruch A. Levine, *Leviticus*, JPS Torah Commentary (Philadelphia: Jewish Publication Society, 1989), 112-13; Baruch J. Schwartz, "'Profane' Slaughter and the Integrity of the Priestly Code," *HUCA* 67 (1996): 18-26.

31. Karl Elliger, *Leviticus*, HAT (Tübingen: Mohr Siebeck, 1966), 219.

32. MT's shorter text is preferred by, e.g., John E. Hartley, *Leviticus*, WBC (Dallas, TX: Word, 1992), 261.

ingesting blood is already found in P in Gen 9:4, where it applies to all of humanity, including גרים, making it unlikely that, in Lev 17:10–12, H (in its original form) opposes P's conception and allows ingestion of blood with the exception of Israelites. The plain explanation for the disregard of the גרים and other non-Israelites in this passage is that the legislator of the law in its original form did not conceive of the גרים as a group to which the law should relate. He addressed the law to his target audience, the Israelites, whom he wanted to influence; the גרים are not at all in his purview. The mentions of the גר in some paragraphs in the chapter are thus incompatible with that notion. Furthermore, as Baruch Schwartz has shown in detail, the entire chapter has a balanced, structured design with thematic connections among its elements; this makes it reasonable to assume that the chapter is not an arbitrary collection of different, unrelated laws.[33] Given this orderly, organized structure, the inconsistency created by the mentions of the גר in this chapter stands out, suggesting that all the references to the גר in the chapter are late insertions.[34]

Based on the absence of the גר from the first paragraph in the MT, some scholars argue that this is an example of a distinction between the גר and the Israelite: Israelites are not allowed to slaughter an edible domestic quadruped (i.e., cattle) outside the sanctuary, but the גר is permitted to do so. These scholars offer various theories to explain that difference.[35] Note, however, that according to the MT there is a disturbing lacuna in the law. As some commentators rightly observe, the unifying theme of the entire chapter is the prohibition against ingesting blood, and the law rules out in advance any option that Israelites can consume blood: in the case of edible domestic quadrupeds, the animal must be sacrificed in the sanctuary and

---

33. Schwartz, "Prohibitions," 36–43.

34. We cannot rule out the possibility that the second paragraph, which prohibits decentralized sacrifice (vv. 8–9), is entirely a harmonistic addition. Scholars have discussed the need for the appearance of this prohibition after the prohibition concerning profane slaughter (vv. 3–7); see, e.g., Martin Noth, *Leviticus*, trans. J. E. Anderson, OTL (London: SCM, 1965), 131. It is possible that the purpose of this paragraph is to guide readers how to interpret the first paragraph. The contradiction between the first passage, which prohibits profane slaughter, and Deut 12, which permits such slaughter, would have led a late author to seek a solution whereby the readers could interpret the prohibition in vv. 3–7 according to the prohibition in vv. 8–9 and prohibit only decentralized sacrifice but not profane slaughter.

35. See Joosten, *People and Land*, 65–66; Jacob Milgrom, *Leviticus 17–22*, AB 3A (New York: Doubleday, 2000), 1453.

its blood dashed on the altar (vv. 3–4, 7–8); in case of hunting, there is an injunction to cover the blood with earth (v. 13).³⁶ According to the MT, the גר can engage in so-called profane slaughter; there are, however, no instructions as to what the גר should do with the blood in that case. In line with the supposition that the גר was not mentioned in the original form of the chapter—because the legislators had only Israelites, not גרים, on their minds—the problem disappears. This points to an imperfect implementation of the insertion of the גר into Lev 17; thus, either the interpolator wrote the formula in order to insert it into the text, but it penetrated only the first paragraph in the LXX but not the MT, or the interpolator missed the first paragraph for some reason.

Cases 11–13 are in Num 15:22–31. This law of inadvertent and intentional wrongdoing has three sections. The first two, which deal with inadvertent sin, are preceded by an introduction (vv. 22–23). The first section treats inadvertent sinning by the community (vv. 24–26); the second, an individual who sins inadvertently (vv. 27–29); and the third, intentional transgressions (vv. 30–32). A formula that equates the גר and the Israelite appears in each section (vv. 26, 29, 30) except for the introduction, but these are formulated differently and appear in different locations in these units. The absence of such a formula in the introduction, where it would be strongly expected, together with the differences in wording and location of the formulae, implies that the three equalization formulae were not formulated concurrently with the basic form of the law.

Moreover, the first unit begins with the description of the case: "If this was done unwittingly, through the inadvertence of the community [העדה]" (v. 24). According to this verse, the עדה is the group that has sinned and needs expiation through sacrifice. But who is this עדה? Verse 25a seems to reveal the answer: "The priest shall make expiation for the whole Israelite community [עדת בני ישראל], and they shall be forgiven." This verse explicitly states that the עדה is עדת בני ישראל, namely, the Israelites; accordingly, the law applies to the Israelites alone. There is tension, however, between the notion manifested in verses 24–25 and the formula that equates the גר and the Israelite in verse 26, because verse 26 also includes the גר. The appearance of the גר alongside the עדה in verse 26 is a surprising twist because until that point only the עדה has been mentioned. Furthermore, many similarities exist between verses 25a and 26 as table 1 demonstrates.

---

36. See, e.g., Schwartz, "'Profane' Slaughter," 17.

Table 1: Comparison of Num 15:25 and 26

Num 15:25a	Num 15:26
וכפר הכהן	
על כל עדת בני ישראל ונסלח להם	ונסלח לכל עדת בני ישראל
	ולגר הגר בתוכם
כי שגגה היא	כי לכל העם בשגגה
The priest shall make expiation for the whole Israelite community,	The whole Israelite community and the גר residing among them
and they shall be forgiven;	shall be forgiven,
for it was an error	for it happened to the entire people through error

Both verses share the term עדת בני ישראל, the verb ונסלח, and a causal clause that opens with כי and includes the word שגגה. Actually, in terms of content, verse 26 does not add anything to verse 25 but the גר, and this could be easily integrated into verse 25 itself. This suggests that verse 26 is a late insertion that was formulated in line with verse 25 in order to apply this part of the law of inadvertent and intentional wrongdoing to the גר as well and that perhaps verse 26 was supposed to replace the parallel part in verse 25.[37]

Both units that treat inadvertent sin, of the community (vv. 24–26) and of an individual (vv. 27–29), share a similar structure and a common vocabulary. As we would expect, each section opens with a description of the case of unintentional sin, using the words אם and שגגה, and goes on to describe the sacrifice that should be offered using the word לחטאת (vv. 24, 27). The second verse in both units cites the results of the offering using the phrases וכפר הכהן על, "the priest shall make expiation" and ונסלח ל, "shall be forgiven" (vv. 25, 28). The third verse in both sections relates to the גר and includes the word בשגגה (vv. 26, 29). Based on my conclusion that the third verse in the first paragraph (v. 26), which refers to the גר, is

---

37. On verse 26 as a late insertion, see Horst Seebass, *Numeri II*, BKAT 4.1 (Neukirchen-Vluyn: Neukirchener Verlag, 1995), 144; cf. George Buchanan Gray, *Numbers*, ICC (Edinburgh: T&T Clark, 1903), 181: "The verse adds nothing to what has been said in v. 25, and may consist of glosses."

secondary, it is likely that this is the case for the second paragraph as well. Yet we could postulate that, because including the גר is especially important in the case of an individual sinner, the equating formula is therefore original in verse 29 but secondary in verse 26. Consideration of the third unit, however, shows this to be untenable.

The location of the equating formula in the third unit, in verse 30, which deals with intentional sin, differs from its previous two appearances. Here, in the passage that treats the intentional sinner, it comes at the beginning with the presentation of the sinner, whereas in the previous sections it was placed at the end. Unlike what we saw for the previous units, this formula is part of the opening sentence and does not stand alone in a separate verse. As in the second part of the law, the legislative text here deals with the individual sinner. Thus there is no reason to differentiate between these two sections of the same law with regard to the גר. If the first reference to this issue, in verse 29, is original, it should be original in the second paragraph, in verse 30, as well. But, if this is indeed the case, why are the references to the גר in these two subunits placed in different locations? There is no apparent explanation for why the equating sentence appears at the end of the first paragraph, whereas it is found in the opening in the second. Actually, it would be more natural for the formula to be placed at the beginning rather than the end of the section, as the reader expects to know from the start to which group the law applies. Accordingly, it is not clear why the formula is found at the end of the first subunit. The different locations of the formulae in the two units on the individual sinner suggest that at least one of them is secondary. But, because there is no apparent reason to equate the גר and the Israelite in only one of these sections, it seems preferable to infer that both formulae are secondary.

Moreover, because it is formulated as a general statement with a restriction relevant to the case in that given context, the final clause of the intermediate paragraph is unique: "For the native among the Israelites and for the גר who resides among them—you shall have one תורה for anyone who acts in error" (v. 29). Such generalizations are found among the equating formulae (Exod 12:49; Lev 24:22; Num 9:14; 15:15–16) but never with a restriction. As noted above, some scholars interpret these sentences as a complete equation of the גר and the Israelite, whereas others claim that they relate only to the specific issue at hand.[38] Nothing in the

---

38. See note 9.

formulations themselves, however, points to the narrow interpretation. Numbers 15:29 is the only case that explicitly states that the generalization applies to the law in the given context, but the uniqueness of this case may indicate the multistep process by which this verse was formed. In light of the discussion above concerning the lateness of the reference to the גר in this legislation, it appears reasonable to assume that the words לעשה בשגגה, "for anyone who acts in error," at the end of verse 29 were originally the direct continuation of verse 28. The addition of the equating formula in verse 29 probably caused the separation of the words לעשה בשגגה from their beginning, creating this special formulation. Possibly the result of a scribal mistake made in copying the added sentence from the margin to the main text, this may also explain the shift from plural (לכם) to singular (לעשה) at the end of verse 29.

Now, the reconstruction of the original placement of the words לעשה בשגגה reveals a resemblance between the assumed original closings of both paragraphs (vv. 24–26, 27–29) treating inadvertent sin. In verse 25, the expression ונסלח להם is followed by the explanation כי שגגה היא. At the end of verse 28, however, such reasoning is absent after the words ונסלח לו. But, according to the proposed reconstruction of the original closing of the second paragraph, the words לעשה בשגגה immediately followed ונסלח לו and functioned as a kind of explanation for the forgiveness granted, similar to what was stated in the first paragraph.

It seems that interpolators who sought to apply the entire three-part law to the גר added the formulae that equate the גר and the Israelite to each section of the law. Because they did so at a secondary stage, they could not formulate it in the same manner but adapted their interpolations to the existing legislation, avoiding changes in the original text. Alternatively, it is possible that the references to the גר in this law were inserted not by the same interpolator but by different glossators in two or three stages and that this explains the varied formulations and locations of the equation of the גר and the Israelite in this case.

3. Analysis of Additional Texts with Formulae Equating the גר and the Israelite

The cases examined above, in which I concluded that the formulae that equate the גר and the Israelite were secondary, led to consideration of additional texts containing such formulae. In this section, I discuss some other instances of equating formulae for which, in my opinion, there is some philological evidence to justify the suspicion that they are secondary additions, even though the evidence is not decisive.

Case 14 is Exod 12:19. A formula that equates the גר and the Israelite also appears in a passage treating the prohibition against eating leavened products during the Festival of Unleavened Bread (vv. 14–20): "whoever eats what is leavened shall be cut off from Israel's community, whether a גר or a native born of the land" (v. 19). From this verse, we can conclude that the גר is part of עדת ישראל, and some scholars think that this was indeed the original intention of the verse.[39] Yet this seems implausible because, in the other cases, there is an emphatic, consistent distinction between the גר and בית ישראל or בני ישראל (e.g., Lev 20:2; 22:18; Num 35:15).[40] Moreover, even in a case where the גר is included in העם, the distinction between the גר and עדת ישראל is retained: ונסלח לכל עדת בני ישראל ולגר הגר בתוכם כי לכל העם בשגגה (Num 15:26).[41] It therefore seems reasonable to surmise that the words בגר ובאזרח הארץ in Exod 12:19 are secondary and were added to the text by an interpolator who also wanted to apply the prohibition against eating leavened products during the Festival of Unleavened Bread to the גר and did not pay attention to the fact that, according to the final form of the verse, an unexpected and unwitting conclusion can be drawn, that the גר is part of עדת ישראל.

Actually, verse 19 is parallel and similar to verse 15, as shown in table 2.

Table 2: Comparison of Exod 12:15 and 19

Exod 12:15	Exod 12:19
שבעת ימים מצות תאכלו	שבעת ימים
אך ביום הראשון תשביתו שאר מבתיכם	שאר לא ימצא בבתיכם
כי כל אכל חמץ	כי כל אכל מחמצת
ונכרתה הנפש ההוא מישראל	ונכרתה הנפש ההוא מעדת ישראל

---

39. Nihan, "Resident Aliens and Natives," 130 n. 69.

40. This consistent separation between Israelites and גרים was discussed by José E. Ramírez Kidd, *Alterity and Identity in Israel: The גר in the Old Testament*, BZAW 283 (Berlin: de Gruyter, 1999), 53.

41. In Num 15:15, the גר is part of הקהל, but that might be the result of a copyist's error, namely, dittography of the following word, חקה, as some scholars have suggested; see note a in the BHS apparatus to Num 15:15.

מיום הראשן עד יום השבעי

בגר ובאזרח הארץ

Seven days you will eat unleavened bread	Seven days
Even on the first day you will eliminate leaven from your houses	leaven will not be found in your houses
whoever eats what is leavened shall be cut off from Israel	whoever eats what is leavened shall be cut off from Israel's community
from the first day until the seventh day	
	whether a גר or a native born of the land

It seems clear that verse 19 was formulated in line with verse 15, but the fact that the equating formula appears only in verse 19 requires attention.[42] The unusual inclusion of the גר in עדת ישראל in this verse reinforces my doubts regarding the formula's originality. Looking at the deviation of the equating formula from the overall similarity between verses 19 and 15, it seems preferable not to explain the uniqueness of the message of the current text of Exod 12:19 as an especially innovative notion. It is better explained in light of the repeated phenomenon of inserted formulae that equate the גר and the Israelite as a composite verse, with the end of the verse, the words בגר ובאזרח הארץ, being a late addition.[43]

Case 15 is Lev 19:33–34. This passage deals entirely with the גר and enjoins that he is not to be treated unfairly (לא תונו) and should be loved like the native born (אזרח). This is the sole case in the Priestly writings in which a formula that equates the גר and the Israelite appears in a social context and considers the inferior situation of the גר.[44] Scholars correctly connect this passage to Exod 22:20 and Deut 10:19, but there are closer

---

42. See Gesundheit, *Three Times a Year*, 84–88, who claims that Exod 12:18–20 is a very late stratum in that chapter, later than vv. 13–17.

43. Even if we do not accept the above argumentation, the formula is part of a very late Priestly stratum in Exod 12, as Gesundheit, *Three Times a Year*, 84–88 claims.

44. In analyzing Lev 19:33–34, some scholars argue that the equating formula in v. 34aα comes from a late hand. This assumption is based not on textual considerations but on a presupposition that it was inserted by an author who sought to integrate some groups in the land of Israel in his day; see Henri Cazelles, "La mission d'Esdras," *VT* 4 (1954): 126–27; Grelot, "La dernière étape," 177–78; Alfred Cholewinski, *Heiligkeitsgesetz und Deuteronomium: Eine vergleichende Studie*, AnBib 66 (Rome: Biblical Insti-

connections to statutes in the Holiness legislation itself, in Lev 19:18 and 25:14, 17.⁴⁵ The parallels in the Holiness legislation probably refer only to Israelites. Leviticus 19:18 applies the imperative of love to רעך ("your fellow"), namely, another Israelite, as some commentators rightly observe.⁴⁶ Similarly, in Lev 25:14, 17, which prohibits unfair treatment, the fellow is called עמית or אח, which means another Israelite. This is certainly the case with respect to land sales such as those found in Lev 25:14, 17; after all, according to the Holiness legislation, only Israelites can be landowners in the land of Israel. The short passage in Lev 19:33–34 thus adjures the Israelite to love not only the Israelite but also the גר and not to treat him unfairly. Accordingly, there is tension between this passage and the verses (Lev 19:18; 25:14, 17) that refer only to the Israelite. This tension, together with the uniqueness of the application of the equating formula to a social issue, suggests that the short unit in Lev 19:33–34 is not original in the Holiness legislation, which probably initially dealt only with the Israelites in this context, but a late addition aimed at including the גר in some of its social injunctions.⁴⁷

---

tute Press, 1976), 50–51; and Bultmann, *Der Fremde*, 177. There is no justification, however, for such an assumption, which must be backed by philological arguments.

45. On links to Exod 22:20 and Deut 10:19, see, e.g., Joosten, *People and Land*, 61, who also draws attention to Exod 23:9, where the phrase כי גרים הייתם בארץ מצרים appears as in Exod 22:20 and Lev 19:34. On the connection with Lev 19:18, see Baruch J. Schwartz, *The Holiness Legislation: Studies in the Priestly Code* [Hebrew] (Jerusalem: Magnes, 1999), 358.

46. Milgrom, *Leviticus 17–22*, 1655 follows in the wake of Gordon J. Wenham, *Leviticus*, NICOT (Grand Rapids: Eerdmans, 1979), 266–67, who noted the deliberate use of different words for the "fellow" in the unit in Lev 19:11–18. The alternation of the words shows that they all have the same meaning for the author, whereas the use of עמיך (v. 16) and בני עמך (v. 18) reveals that all signify Israelites.

47. Cf. Julius Wellhausen, *Die Composition des Hexateuchs und der historichen Bücher des Alten Testaments*, 3rd ed. (Berlin: Reimer, 1899), 154; Elliger, *Leviticus*, 250. Nihan, *From Priestly Torah to Pentateuch*, 460–76 discusses the structure of Lev 19 and remarks that vv. 33–34 are part of the sophisticated structure of the chapter, being parallel to vv. 13–14, 17–18 in the chapter's first part. Although his concept has several flaws, it provides the best explanation for the current form of the chapter. Given the tension—almost a contradiction—between v. 18, which relates to the Israelite as the object of the commandment on love, and vv. 33–34, which add the גר as an additional object of this commandment, it is unlikely that the same author penned both of these injunctions.

Case 16 is Num 9:14. In this case, a formula that equalizes the גר and the Israelite appears at the end of a legal unit that focuses on second Passover (vv. 9–14). According to that statute, a person who was unable to take part in the Passover ceremony on the fourteenth day of the first month, either because he was impure or on a long journey, can do so a month later. It seems, however, that the formula in verse 14 deals not with second Passover specifically but with the paschal sacrifice in general: "should a גר who resides among you wish to perform [ועשה] the paschal sacrifice to YHWH, he must offer it in accordance with the rule of the paschal sacrifice and according to its regulations." It is not clear why this statement regarding the participation of the גר in the Passover sacrifice follows the second Passover statute, because it would be more suited to a passage that deals with the principal Passover sacrifice.[48] This is the case for Exod 12:48–49, which, as mentioned above, enables the גר to participate in this ceremony. Other passages that deal with the basic Passover sacrifice in the Priestly legislation are Exod 12:25–27; Lev 23:4–8; and Num 28:16–25.[49]

Furthermore, as many commentators correctly note, the phrase ועשה פסח ליהוה, which occurs twice in this passage (as well as in Exod 12:48) in relation to second Passover (v. 10) and in relation to the גר (v. 14), means "and *wish* to perform the paschal sacrifice."[50] Accordingly, the גר has no obligation to perform the sacrifice; that depends on his free will. Numbers 9:14 thus states that the גר who wants to perform the sacrifice shall do so in accordance with the regular rules of the Passover offering. This verse, however, immediately follows a sentence that imposes a כרת penalty on one who is present and able to perform the sacrifice at its proper time but does not do so (v. 13). The commitment underlying this verse does not apply to the גר, who is not at all obligated to perform the sacrifice. The equation of the גר with the Israelite regarding the Passover offering is thus incomplete, and the application of the formula is not clear in this context. The problematic location of the reference to the equation of the גר and the

---

48. The difficulty of understanding that formula in relation to second Passover is articulated by medieval Jewish commentators such as Ibn Ezra and Nahmanides to Num 9:14.

49. On the attribution of Exod 12:25–27 to a P layer, see Gesundheit, *Three Times a Year*, 58–73.

50. Baruch A. Levine, *Numbers 1–20*, AB 4A (New York: Doubleday, 1993), 297; Simeon Chavel, *Oracular Law and Priestly Historiography in the Torah*, FAT 71 (Tübingen: Mohr Siebeck, 2014), 109–11.

Israelite just after a sentence that does not apply to him raises suspicions regarding the originality of verse 14. It seems reasonable to assume that here, too, the formula that equates the גר and the Israelite was added to the end of the unit and that the statute originally ended with the penalty announced in verse 13. The formula was attached to the passage in order to include the גר in the Passover ceremony without paying attention to its unsuitable location.[51]

This conjecture could explain the difference between this verse and Exod 12:48, which requires that the גר be circumcised in order to eat the Passover sacrifice. Because the prerequisite of circumcision is not mentioned in Num 9:14, this raises the questions of whether there is a disagreement between these verses, one demanding circumcision for those performing the paschal sacrifice and the other not, or whether the injunction in Exod 12:48 underlies the law in Num 9:9–14, and the requirement of circumcision therefore applies to this unit as well. Some scholars even think that the prerequisite of circumcision applies to all cases in which the גר is included in legal passages, as noted above.[52] This naturally raises the question of why this prerequisite of circumcision appears explicitly only in Exod 12:48. In line with my conclusion that both equating formulae are secondary additions, it is easy to understand that there is no systematic, coherent way to articulate the notion of equalization of the גר and the Israelite. Circumcision is mentioned in Exod 12:48 because it is required there for the slave whose owner wants him to eat the sacrifice (v. 44), as proposed above. The interpolator realized that, if a slave must be circumcised in order to consume the Passover offering, there is then no reason to allow an uncircumcised גר to partake of the offering. But circumcision receives no mention in the context of Num 9:14, which suggests that this issue had not occurred to the interpolator when he added the formula that equates the גר and the Israelite there.

Case 17 is Num 15:14–16. This passage, which contains stacked formulae that equate the גר and the Israelite, appears at the end of a unit about the cereal and wine offerings that accompany animal sacrifices (vv. 1–12). In between the sections we find an exceptional, highly superfluous verse: "Every native born, when presenting an offering by fire of pleasing

---

51. Holzinger, *Numeri*, 35 implies that this case, in which reference is made to the equation of the גר with the Israelite, is part of a broader phenomenon, but I was unable to find another treatment by him of this phenomenon.

52. See note 14.

odor to YHWH, shall do so with them" (v. 13). This verse applies all that was said previously in verses 1–12 to the Israelite. Apart from the fact that no such verse appears again in the Priestly legislation, there is no need to state that the law applies to the Israelites; after all, to whom else could it apply?[53] All the laws were given to the Israelites and refer to them unless explicitly noted otherwise. Moreover, the opening of the unit explicitly states that the law is aimed at the Israelites: "speak to the Israelites" (v. 2). It seems that verse 13 is a secondary addition that functions only as a transitional link to the next passage, which equates the גר and the Israelite in this regard (vv. 14–16). Feeling that the previous statute refers to the Israelites alone, the authors of verses 14–16 wrote verse 13, too, in order to enable the inclusion of the גר in this instruction. Verse 13, together with the beginning of verse 14, which opens with the imperfect (יגור), eases the inclusion of the גרים in this legal issue because, according to that transitional link, the first part of the law (vv. 1–12) indeed deals only with the Israelites. Now, according to the last passage of the unit (vv. 14–16), in the future, when גרים will reside in Israel, they will have to act as the Israelites do with regard to sacrifices. If the inclusion of גרים in this law were original, it would have been formulated without the notable exceptionality of verse 13. The presence of verse 13 can be explained by the process of insertion of a new matter to the pericope. The singularity and redundancy of verse 13 and its close and inseparable connection to verses 14–16 suggest that the entire passage (vv. 13–16) is a late insertion intended to include the גר in this law.

The above discussion illustrates that, for most of the pentateuchal formulae that equate the גר and the Israelite, there is sufficient reason to think—and sometimes strong evidence to support—that the formula is secondary. Before examining the ramifications of this statement, a look at the two occurrences of equating formulae in Ezekiel is instructive.

4. The Formulae in Ezekiel

Case 1 is Ezek 14:7. This is the first appearance of an equating formula in the book of Ezekiel: "for any of those of the house of Israel, or of the גר who resides in Israel." This unique formula in the book of Ezekiel, which resembles some formulae in the Priestly writings (cf. Lev 17:8, 10, 13; 20:2;

---

53. For a discussion of Lev 23:42, see below.

22:18), opens a statement that God will harshly punish those who think about idols. The equating clause appears in the middle of a prophecy, which extends from verses 1 to 11, concerning people who believe in idols and come to the prophet to hear a divine message. Apart from the question of the relevance of a גר in the exile, there is another difficulty. The addressees of this prophecy are mentioned five times in the passage (vv. 4, 5, 6, 7, 11). Whereas בית ישראל, the house of Israel, appears each time, the גר appears only once, in verse 7. Moreover, a sentence with very similar wording and content appears in verse 4 but makes no reference to the גר. There is no apparent reason for the difference between these verses, and some scholars note this irregularity.[54] These considerations, together with the almost complete absence of such formulae from the book of Ezekiel and the similarity to the pentateuchal ones, suggest that this formula was added to Ezek 14:7 under the influence of similar formulae in the Pentateuch.[55]

Case 2 is Ezek 47:22–23. The second occurrence of a formula that equates the גר and the Israelite in the book of Ezekiel states:

> and this shall be [והיה] you shall appropriate it as an inheritance for yourselves and for the גרים who reside among you and have begotten children among you. They shall be to you as native born of Israel; they shall join with you in appropriating the land as an inheritance among the tribes of Israel. In whatever tribe the גר resides, there you shall assign them their inheritance, says the Lord YHWH.

This developed statement is a part of a long prophecy dealing with a futuristic division of the land between the tribes of Israel that starts at Ezek 47:13 and ends in 48:29. The message of these verses takes a further step in the process of equalization of the גר with the Israelite because, in this case, the גר would inherit land as an Israelite, a right that is found neither in the Priestly writings in the Pentateuch nor elsewhere in the Hebrew Bible.[56]

---

54. See Moshe Greenberg, *Ezekiel 1–20*, AB 22 (Garden City, NY: Doubleday, 1983), 249: "The old formula is kept despite its inappropriateness for the exilic community to lend the pronouncement the aura of ancient, general authority and applicability."

55. Cf. the analysis of Bultmann, *Der Fremde*, 196–200.

56. The condition that the גרים who receive an inheritance in the promised land will "have begotten children among you" seems to restrict the equalization of the גר with the Israelite. But the exact meaning of this limitation is not clear; see, e.g., Daniel Isaac Block, *Ezekiel 25–48*, NICOT (Grand Rapids: Eerdmans, 1998), 718; Lisbeth S. Fried, "From Xeno-Philia to -Phobia: Jewish Encounters with the Other,"

Yet there are some good reasons to think that these verses are secondary, as some commentators note.⁵⁷

First, the inner dynamic of the entire prophecy (Ezek 47:13–48:29) does not move toward the גרים sharing in the allotment of the land. Just the opposite: the heading of the prophecy states that the land is intended for "the twelve tribes of *Israel*" (47:13). The next verse states: "You shall share it equally; as I swore to give it to your fathers, so this land shall fall to you as your inheritance." This verse makes it clear that the land that was promised to the fathers would be given to *their* sons. Moreover, after the description of the boundaries of the land (47:15–20) we find the following: "So you shall divide this land for yourselves among the tribes of *Israel*" (v. 21). And again at the end of the unit: "This is the land that you shall allot as an inheritance among the tribes of *Israel*" (48:29). The integration of the גר in the allotment of the land in verses 22–23 is therefore a surprising twist.

Second, the irregular opening of verse 22 with the word והיה may mark lack of continuity and indicate the artificial binding of verses 22–23 to the previous section.⁵⁸ Third, these two verses interrupt the sequence between verse 21—"So you shall divide this land for yourselves among the tribes of Israel"—and the details of this division in Ezek 48, right after verses 22–23. The end of verse 23, נאם אדני יהוה, represents this interruption well because there is no need for such a postscript before the account of the division itself in Ezek 48, as it would be expected according to verse 21. Fourth, at the end of the detailed description of the division of the land

---

in *A Time of Change: Judah and Its Neighbours in the Persian and Early Hellenistic Periods*, ed. Yigal Levin, LSTS 65 (London: T&T Clark, 2007), 184. For his part, Smith, *Palestinian Parties and Politics*, 136–37 focuses on the fact that these verses are part of a prophecy of the future, "but meanwhile there was nothing to do."

57. Walther Eichrodt, *Ezekiel*, trans. Charles W. C. Quin, OTL (Philadelphia: Westminster, 1970), 592; Walther Zimmerli, *Ezekiel 2*, trans. James D. Martin; Hermeneia (Philadelphia: Fortress, 1983), 526. Some of the considerations in the following discussion were proposed by them in short.

58. S. R. Driver, *A Treatise on the Use of the Tenses in Hebrew and Some Other Syntactical Questions*, 3rd ed. (Oxford: Clarendon, 1892), § 121, 147–48 mentions this case together with Ezek 47:10 as the only instances of והיה that precede a verb, that serve "as a mere introductory formula." The ancient versions and the modern translations illustrate the doubts experienced by the translators. Taking into account the reasonable version which is reflected in the LXX—וחיה at the end of 47:9 instead of והיה at the beginning of v. 10 in the MT; see Zimmerli, *Ezekiel 2*, 507—its appearance in v. 22 is most exceptional.

according to tribes in Ezek 48, we find a developed postscript: "This is the land that you shall allot as an inheritance among the tribes of Israel, and these are their portions, declares the Lord YHWH [נאם אדני יהוה]." This postscript refers to the entire land and to the specific allotments, namely, to Ezek 47:15–20 and 48:1–28 respectively; the postscript at the end of 47:23 therefore not only interrupts the sequence but is superfluous. Fifth, the heading of the pericope in Ezek 48:1–29, "These are the names of the tribes" (48:1), is perplexing because the following passage does not list the tribes but describes the division of the land according to tribes. Actually, this point does not directly relate to the verses about the גר, but, together with the previous three points, it illustrates the clumsiness in the transitions from the description of the boundaries of the land (Ezek 47:13–21) to the verses that note the inclusion of גרים in the division of the land (Ezek 47:22–23), and from these verses to the section that describes the division of the land according to tribes (Ezek 48:1–29).

Sixth, at the end of verse 22 we find the phrase אתכם יפלו בנחלה. The expression נפ"ל בנחלה usually means to allocate as an inheritance, as Moshe Greenberg has persuasively shown.[59] In all of these cases, the syntactic subject of the phrase is land or the like. This expression appears in the context of the division of the land in Ezek 45:1; 47:14, and even at the beginning of verse 22, with its usual meaning in all of them. This meaning cannot, however, be applied to the phrase אתכם יפלו בנחלה, which probably means "they shall join with you in appropriating the land as an inheritance."[60] In this case alone, the syntactic subject of the expression is "people" (גרים). This shift in meaning may indicate the work of another author who was not familiar with the exact meaning and use of the phrase נפ"ל בנחלה.[61]

Accordingly, it is highly probable that verses 22–23 are a secondary insertion intended to equate the status of גרים to that of Israelites by grant-

---

59. Moshe Greenberg, "The Terms נפל and הפיל in the Context of Inheritance," in *Ki Baruch Hu: Ancient Near Eastern, Biblical and Judaic Studies in Honor of Baruch A. Levine*, ed. Robert Chazan, William W. Hallo, and Lawrence H. Schiffman (Winona Lake, IN: Eisenbrauns, 1999), 251–59.

60. Greenberg, "Terms נפל and הפיל," 258; cf. Block, *Ezekiel 25–48*, 707.

61. In this case, there is no difference if we punctuate the word תפלו in the *qal* pattern as in the MT or *hiphil* as some scholars propose; e.g., Block, *Ezekiel 25–48*, 707. In any case, the phrase here has a special meaning. On the problematic interpretation of this phrase, see Greenberg, "Terms נפל and הפיל," 258.

ing them a legal inheritance in the land of Israel. Because the addition of these verses interrupts the sequence between Ezek 47:21 and 48:1, a new heading was needed for Ezek 48. The current heading: "These are the names of the tribes" in 48:1 is presumably a late abortive attempt to create such an opening to the chapter as a kind of resumptive repetition.[62]

It is therefore a reasonable conclusion that both formulae (in Ezek 14:7; 47:22–23) that equalize the גר and the Israelite in the book of Ezekiel are secondary. The original mentions of the גר in this book deal with him only as a person of low socioeconomic status (22:7, 29).

5. The Remaining Pentateuchal Formulae

The discussion up to this point makes it apparent that literary activity operated in the Priestly writings and Ezekiel that involved the addition of many, albeit differently worded, formulae that equate the גר and the Israelite. This determination, together with the above analysis, suggests that the remaining formulae, namely, those few remaining cases not treated in the discussion above for which we lack direct evidence of their secondary character, were also part of this activity. In all of these cases, the formulae can be removed without damaging the remaining text.

There is, of course, the possibility that, in the absence of local philological evidence that the formula is not original, and notwithstanding the above-noted general phenomenon of the insertion of such formulae in Priestly texts, some of the formulae that equate the גר and the Israelite are not secondary in their immediate context. In these cases, it is possible that the entire passage in which the formula appears is late, and discussion of the occurrences of the equating formulae in Lev 24:10–23 (vv. 16, 22), which presents the case of the blasphemer and the legislation that follows it, illustrates the various options. Although there is no apparent evidence that the occurrences of these equalization statements in this unit are secondary, removal of both formulae that equate the גר and the Israelite does not interrupt the sequence. Some scholars, however, postulate that what drives the passage, including the narrative part, is the applicability of the laws to the גר, as the blasphemer was half-Egyptian and half-Israelite, namely, a גר.[63] Even if we accept this notion—and it is by no means unequivocal, as

---

62. Ezekiel 47:21 concludes with לשבטי ישראל, and 48:1 opens with ואלה שמות השבטים.

63. See, e.g., Baentsch, *Exodus—Leviticus—Numeri*, 420; Kidd, *Alterity and Iden-*

Simeon Chavel convincingly argues—there are good reasons to think that the entire passage is secondary, both because it is unrelated to the nearby context of chapters 23–25 and, because this is the only narrative section in the Holiness chapters (Lev 17–26).[64] It is possible that the author who incorporated this pericope took for granted the parity between the גר and the Israelite with respect to observing the commandments and therefore included the formulae in writing the whole passage.

The above discussion leads to the overall understanding of all the formulae that equate the גר and the Israelite as late. This applies to the cases in which only the formula itself is secondary in its context, as well as to the cases in which the entire passage in which the formula appears is secondary.

6. Concluding Remarks

The suggestion that all of these formulae are secondary and late can explain the inconsistent appearance of these formulae in the Priestly legislation. As stated above, some scholars attempt to identify general principles that explain their appearance and their absence.[65] But, if we understand all of these formulae as secondary, this obviates the need to seek theoretical organizing principles that explain what seems to be the inconsistency in their occurrence. As an activity of interpolators who inserted their additions into an extant text, rather than planned, organized writing, it is doubtful whether we can draw general conclusions from the absence of such formulae in some cases or find a general explanation for the presence of all the existing formulae. Glossators usually do not do their job perfectly. We can postulate that they sought to completely equate the legal status of the גר and the Israelite and therefore inserted as many equating formulae as they could but did not cover all possible cases. We must also take into consideration the possibility that there were some failures to incorporate such formulae into the existing text. It may be that some formulae were written in the margins of the scroll but did not penetrate the transmitted text. Perhaps Lev 17:3, which presents a difference between MT and LXX

---

tity, 54; and Jacob Milgrom, *Leviticus 23–27*, AB 3B (Garden City, NY: Doubleday, 2001), 2111, 2119.

64. Chavel, *Oracular Law*, 38–44. On its place in the Holiness chapters, see Nihan, *From Priestly Torah to Pentateuch*, 512–13, *contra* Chavel, *Oracular Law*, 88–92.

65. See note 7.

such that only the Septuagint reflects an equating formula, is such a case of partial penetration of a formula.

The conclusion that the equating formulae are secondary insertions also has the ability to explain the inconsistencies regarding the injunctions concerning forbidden sexual relations and the prohibition against offering children to Molech, which appear together twice, in Lev 18 and 20. A general equating formula appears in Lev 18:26 with respect to all the commandments in the chapter, including forbidden sexual relations (vv. 7–20, 22–23) and the prohibition against offering children to Molech (v. 21), whereas in Lev 20 such a formula occurs only in relation to Molech (v. 2). The explanation that the author did not want to reiterate the formula equating the גר with the Israelite is not relevant in this case. It seems that this consideration did not bother the author, because the entire collection of commandments in Lev 20 is very much a repetition of Lev 18. Moreover, why did he designate a special, additional equation of the גר and the Israelite only with reference to the prohibition against offering children to Molech? The understanding of these formulae as secondary easily explains this inconsistency, because we cannot expect a glossator to act with full consistency.

It appears, then, that the glossators' goal was to equate the legal status of the גר with the Israelite. We should, however, say that, even according to the inserted formulae, the obligation of the גר to observe the laws is not complete; in some cases, the glossators leave the participation of the גר in the Israelites' religious life to his good will. This is the case for the Passover offering (Exod 12:48; Num 9:14) and voluntary sacrifices (Num 15:14), as shown by the use of the form ועשה, which means "wish to perform" as mentioned above. It seems that this incomplete imposition of commitment on the גר probably reflects the inability to enforce such a legal system on the גרים in light of historical circumstances.

Some scholars, indeed, cite Lev 23:42, which explicitly states כל האזרח בישראל ישבו בסכת, "all natives-born in Israel shall live in booths," as evidence that, notwithstanding the general tendency to equate the גר and the Israelite, there are still differences between them.[66] Alfred Bertholet, however, persuasively suggests that in the original version of the verse the גר was part of the statement and was omitted during the lengthy process of

---

66. See, e.g., Kellermann, "גור," 446; Milgrom, *Leviticus 23–27*, 2051–52.

textual transmission. He supports his argument with the claim that אזרח never appears without גר in the Priestly writings.⁶⁷

According to this view, all the general statements that equate the גר and the Israelite, such as "there shall be one law [תורה אחת] for the native born and for the גר who dwells among you" (Exod 12:49; cf. Lev 24:22; Num 9:14; 15:15–16) should be interpreted literally, namely, as full equalization sentences. The formulae that were added to the law about inadvertent and intentional wrongdoing (Num 15:22–31) support this claim. The formulae in this legislative unit apply to the גר the law that deals with all the commandments, as explicitly stated in the condition in the opening of the pericope: וכי תשגו ולא תעשו את כל המצות האלה, "In the event you inadvertently fail to perform all of these commandments" (v. 22). This suggests that, according to the inserted formulae in this passage, the גר is committed to all the commandments.

7. Historical Background

Even though they did not recognize the secondary nature of the formulae, many scholars connect these equalizations to Yehud in the Persian period and the burning question of identity at that time.⁶⁸ In line with the conclusion that the formulae equating the גר and the Israelite are mainly late, even scholars that attribute the Priestly writings to the period of the monarchy can agree that these formulae could have been inserted in the Persian period. This phenomenon is related to the tendency during that period to be tolerant of foreigners, against which Ezra acted decisively. As many scholars have noted, this tendency is manifested in some biblical writings from that period, such as the book of Ruth or Isa 56 as well as in the Pentateuch, particularly in the Priestly writings.⁶⁹ Here we find a phenomenon

---

67. Bertholet, *Die Stellung*, 171–72. I surmise that the omission was the result of homoioteleuton; the original phrase would have been והגר (הגר) בישראל (cf. Lev 20:2; 22:18; Ezek 14:7).

68. Fried, "From Xeno-Philia to -Phobia," 196 thinks that this attitude of equality reflects Mesopotamian ideas, especially for the Achaemenid period.

69. See, e.g., Smith, *Palestinian Parties and Politics*, 113–46; Moshe Weinfeld, "Universalistic and Particularistic Trends during the Exile and Restoration," in *Normative and Sectarian Judaism in the Second Temple Period*, LSTS 54 (London: T&T Clark, 2005), 251–66; Itamar Kislev, "P, Source or Redaction: The Evidence of Numbers 25," in *The Pentateuch: International Perspectives on Current Research*, ed. Thomas

that is part of a larger literary tendency to embody the stranger in the life of the community and the cult in Yehud during the Persian period.

In the book of Chronicles, we find explicit use of the term גרים to refer to the foreign population in the land of Israel (1 Chr 22:2; 2 Chr 2:16; 30:25), as Sara Japhet has convincingly shown.[70] In 2 Chr 30:25, these גרים come to Jerusalem and participate in the Passover ceremony in Hezekiah's day. The Chronicler, surely following the Pentateuch, accepts the tendency to equate the religious status of the גר and the Israelite and describes the fulfillment of this tendency in the history of the monarchy. Undoubtedly, and certainly at the end of the Persian period or the beginning of the Hellenistic period, the Chronicler views the foreigners in the country in his day as גרים and grants them equal status with the Israelites in his description of Hezekiah's reign.

8. Implications for Questions about the Composition of the Pentateuch

Notwithstanding the lateness of this literary activity, because it is reflected only in the Priestly writings—or, more accurately, in the Holiness legislation in Lev 17–26, other Priestly legal passages outside the book of Leviticus, and Lev 16:29—it appears not to be connected to the composition of the entire Torah.[71] Some scholars indeed link all of these units to H because they all display its characteristic features.[72] The observation that the addition of the equating formulae is an inner-Priestly phenomenon *not* connected to the redaction of the Pentateuch has some important ramifications. First, the fact that the inserting activity is found only in Priestly writings probably testifies that the formulae were added at a stage when the Priestly writings still existed as a separate document. This can contribute to the ongoing debate about the nature of the Priestly writings and contrasts with the opinions of those who hold that P is only a redactional layer in the Pentateuch.[73] If this inserting process had taken part during

---

B. Dozeman, Konrad Schmid, and Baruch J. Schwartz, FAT 78 (Tübingen: Mohr Siebeck, 2011), 398–99.

70. Japhet, "Term גר," 226–27.

71. The appearance of such formulae in the book of Joshua (8:33; 20:9) will be discussed separately in note 79.

72. See, e.g., Knohl, *Sanctuary*, 21, 87 n. 81, 93 n. 111, 108.

73. For a survey of the debate on this issue, see Ernest W. Nicholson, *The Pentateuch in the Twentieth Century: The Legacy of Julius Wellhausen* (Oxford: Clarendon, 1998), 197–218; David M. Carr, "Changes in Pentateuchal Criticism," in *The Twentieth Century: From Modernism to Post-Modernism*, vol. 3.2 of *Hebrew Bible/Old Testament:*

the formative, compositional process of the Torah, we would expect to find such formulae in other parts of the Pentateuch.

Second, the fact that these formulae were not added to the basic stratum of the Priestly legislation (Lev 1–16) indicates that the glossators considered these legislative chapters a completed composition that should not be touched; therefore, they did not allow themselves to insert formulae there. The addition in Lev 16:29 is the exception that proves the rule, because it is placed at the very end of the long unit of P in Lev 1–16, in a late passage that includes some features of H, as many scholars have recognized.[74] With regard to the passages into which the formulae were inserted, I postulate that the glossators felt that these materials were still fluid and, as such, that they could embed their additions in them, because all the passages in which the formulae were inserted are probably later than the main P legislation in Lev 1–16. Note, for example, that in Lev 11, where food taboos are discussed, and which was edited by the H redactor as many scholars have correctly observed, no formula appears that equates the גר and the Israelite.[75] It seems that the interpolators of the equating formulae, who hesitated to insert their additions to the core P legislation, acted differently from and later than other H authors and redactors.[76]

Third, some of the formulae appear in passages outside the core of the Holiness legislation (Lev 17–26) but always in P-like sections (the attribution of some of them is disputed), and this suggests that all these pericopes were nevertheless part of the independent Priestly source. This is an important conclusion, especially in relation to the passages in the book of Numbers, because there is a strong contemporary trend to consider the Priestly materials in this book as very late and as part of the process of the composition of the Torah, written after Deuteronomy was already

---

The History of Its Interpretation, ed. Magne Sæbø (Göttingen: Vandenhoeck & Ruprecht, 2015), 454–64.

74. See note 20.

75. On the attribution of Lev 11:43–45 to H, see, e.g., Knohl, *Sanctuary*, 69; Milgrom, *Leviticus 1–16*, 691–98; Nihan, *From Priestly Torah to Pentateuch*, 293–99. The same is true for Lev 15:31, which was recognized as an addition by H; see Knohl, *Sanctuary*, 70; Milgrom, *Leviticus 1–16*, 946–47; and Nihan, *From Priestly Torah to Pentateuch*, 283.

76. Alternatively, it is possible that glossators tried to insert equating formulae into some P passages, but these did not penetrate the text in the continuation of the process of textual transmission, perhaps because P's code was already fixed.

incorporated into the composition.⁷⁷ This argument seems not to take into account the possibility that P continued to develop before it was incorporated into a combined composition. This ramification is also relevant in the context of the heated discussion of the nature of the entire book of Numbers.⁷⁸ According to the conclusions reached here, a significant portion of the P-like sections in Numbers are part of an independent Priestly source; this reinforces the view that the compositional process of the book of Numbers is more or less the same as and part of the three previous books. The passages discussed may be dated to a very late period but were still part of an independent Priestly document.

The Priestly materials were available to these glossators when they inserted their additions. We can therefore surmise that they were members of a late Priestly school. In this school, the writers probably treated not only the Priestly materials in what is now the Torah and the book of Joshua, but also the book of Ezekiel, because it includes two inserted formulae that equalize the גר and the Israelite which are similar to the pentateuchal formulae.⁷⁹ The Priestly materials and the book of Ezekiel were apparently both set out in this school in a nonfinal form on which the authors could still make their mark. In other words, this school was

---

77. See, e.g., Reinhard Achenbach, *Die Vollendung der Tora: Studien zur Redaktionsgeschichte des Numeribuches im Kontext von Hexateuch und Pentateuch*, BZABR 3 (Wiesbaden: Harrassowitz, 2003); Thomas Römer, "Israel's Sojourn in the Wilderness and the Construction of the Book of Numbers," in *Reflection and Refraction: Studies in Biblical Historiography in Honour of A. Graeme Auld*, ed. Robert Rezetko, Timothy H. Lim, and W. Brian Aucker (Leiden: Brill, 2007), 419–45.

78. Jean-Louis Ska, "Old and New in the Book of Numbers," *Bib* 95 (2014): 102–16; Christian Frevel, "The Book of Numbers—Formation, Composition, and Interpretation of a Late Part of the Torah: Some Introductory Remarks," in *Torah and the Book of Numbers*, ed. Christian Frevel, Thomas Pola, and Aaron Schart (Tübingen: Mohr Siebeck, 2013), 1–37.

79. We should devote more attention to the two formulae in the book of Joshua (8:33 and 20:9). As noted above (note 13), there is a dispute regarding the appearance of the words כגר כאזרח in Josh 8:33. In any case, the expression seems very late. The formula in Josh 20:9 depends on Num 35:15, as I remarked above, and the earlier version of this chapter as reflected in LXX^B has only priestly characters; see Alexander Rofé, "Joshua 20: Historico-literary Criticism Illustrated," in *Empirical Models for Biblical Criticism*, ed. Jeffrey H. Tigay (Philadelphia: University of Philadelphia Press, 1985), 134–47. It supports the evidence that this chapter, like other Priestly units in the book of Joshua, was placed on the desk of this school as part of the independent Priestly document.

the place in which the P source and the book of Ezekiel received their final (or almost final) form, and it stands to reason that this school is at least partly a source for some of the similarities between the book of Ezekiel and P. This final observation, as well as the three previous ramifications, certainly merit separate discussion, and further evidence is needed in order to arrive at a deeper understanding of the extent and the process of formation of the Priestly document.

Bibliography

Achenbach, Reinhard. "Der Eintritt der Schutzbürger in den Bund (Dtn 29,10–12): Distinktion und Integration von Fremden im Deuteronomium." Pages 240–55 in *Gerechtigkeit und Recht zu üben (Gen 18,19): Studien zur altorientalischen und biblischen Rechtsgeschichte, zur Religionsgeschichte Israels und zur Religionssoziologie; Festschrift für Eckart Otto zum 65. Geburtstag*. Edited by Reinhard Achenbach and Martin Arneth. BZABR 13. Weisbaden: Harrassowitz, 2009.

———. "gêr–nåkhrî–tôshav–zår: Legal and Sacral Distinctions regarding Foreigners in the Pentateuch." Pages 29–52 in *The Foreigner and the Law: Perspectives from the Hebrew Bible and the Ancient Near East*. Edited by Reinhard Achenbach, Rainer Albertz, and Jakob Wöhrle. BZABR 16. Weisbaden: Harrassowitz, 2011.

———. *Die Vollendung der Tora: Studien zur Redaktionsgeschichte des Numeribuches im Kontext von Hexateuch und Pentateuch*. BZABR 3. Wiesbaden: Harrassowitz, 2003.

Albertz, Rainer. "From Aliens to Proselytes: Non-Priestly and Priestly Legislation Concerning Strangers." Pages 53–69 in *The Foreigner and the Law: Perspectives from the Hebrew Bible and the Ancient Near East*. Edited by Reinhard Achenbach, Rainer Albertz, and Jakob Wöhrle. BZABR 16. Weisbaden: Harrassowitz, 2011.

Baentsch, Bruno. *Exodus—Leviticus—Numeri*. HKAT. Göttingen: Vanderhoeck & Ruprecht, 1903.

Bertholet, Alfred. *Leviticus*. KHC 3. Tübingen: Mohr Siebeck, 1901.

———. *Die Stellung der Israeliten und der Juden zu den Fremden*. Freiburg: Mohr, 1896.

Block, Daniel Isaac. *Ezekiel 25–48*. NICOT. Grand Rapids: Eerdmans, 1998.

Bultmann, Christoph. *Der Fremde im antiken Juda: Eine Untersuchung zum sozialen Typenbegriff 'ger' und seinem Bedeutungswandel in der alttestamentlicher Gesetzgebung.* FRLANT 153. Göttingen: Vandenhoeck & Ruprecht, 1992.

Carr, David M. "Changes in Pentateuchal Criticism." Pages 433–66 in *The Twentieth Century: From Modernism to Post-Modernism.* Vol. 3.2 of *Hebrew Bible/Old Testament: The History of Its Interpretation.* Edited by Magne Sæbø. Göttingen: Vandenhoeck & Ruprecht, 2015.

Cazelles, Henri. "La mission d'Esdras." *VT* 4 (1954): 113–40.

Chavel, Simeon. *Oracular Law and Priestly Historiography in the Torah.* FAT 71. Tübingen: Mohr Siebeck, 2014.

Cholewinski, Alfred. *Heiligkeitsgesetz und Deuteronomium: Eine vergleichende Studie.* AnBib 66. Rome: Biblical Institute Press, 1976.

Cooke, George A. *The Book of Joshua: In the Revised Version; with Introduction and Notes.* Cambridge Bible for Schools and Colleges. Cambridge: Cambridge University Press, 1918.

Driver, S. R. *The Book of Exodus.* Cambridge: Cambridge University Press, 1918.

———. *A Critical and Exegetical Commentary on Deuteronomy.* ICC 5. Edinburgh: T&T Clark, 1902.

———. *A Treatise on the Use of the Tenses in Hebrew and Some Other Syntactical Questions.* 3rd ed. Oxford: Clarendon, 1892.

Eichrodt, Walther. *Ezekiel.* Translation by Charles W. C. Quin. OTL. Philadelphia: Westminster, 1970.

Elliger, Karl. *Leviticus.* HAT. Tübingen: Mohr Siebeck, 1966.

Frevel, Christian. "The Book of Numbers—Formation, Composition, and Interpretation of a Late Part of the Torah: Some Introductory Remarks." Pages 1–37 in *Torah and the Book of Numbers.* Edited by Christian Frevel, Thomas Pola, and Aaron Schart. Tübingen: Mohr Siebeck, 2013.

Fried, Lisbeth S. "From Xeno-Philia to -Phobia: Jewish Encounters with the Other." Pages 179–204 in *A Time of Change: Judah and Its Neighbours in the Persian and Early Hellenistic Periods.* Edited by Yigal Levin. LSTS 65. London: T&T Clark, 2007.

Geiger, Abraham. *Urschrift und Übersetzungen der Bibel in ihrer Abhängigkeit von der innern Entwickelung des Judentums.* Breslau: Hainauer, 1857.

Gesundheit, Shimon. *Three Times a Year: Studies on Festival Legislation in the Pentateuch.* Winona Lake, IN: Eisenbrauns, 2012.

Gray, George Buchanan. *Numbers.* ICC. Edinburgh: T&T Clark, 1903.

Greenberg, Moshe. *Ezekiel 1–20*. AB 22. Garden City, NY: Doubleday, 1983.

———. "The Terms נפל and הפיל in the Context of Inheritance." Pages 251–59 in *Ki Baruch Hu: Ancient Near Eastern, Biblical and Judaic Studies in Honor of Baruch A. Levine*. Edited by Robert Chazan, William W. Hallo, and Lawrence H. Schiffman. Winona Lake, IN: Eisenbrauns, 1999.

Grelot, Pierre. "La dernière étape de la rédaction sacerdotale." *VT* 6 (1956): 174–89.

Hartley, John E. *Leviticus*. WBC. Dallas, TX: Word, 1992.

Holzinger, H. *Exodus*. KHC. Tübingen: Mohr Siebeck, 1900.

———. *Numeri*. KHC. Tübingen: Mohr Siebeck, 1903.

Houten, Cristiana van. *The Alien in Israelite Law*. JSOTSup 107. Sheffield: JSOT Press, 1991.

Japhet, Sara. "The Term גר and the Concept of Religious Conversion in the Bible" [Hebrew]. Pages 213–29 in *The Wisdom of the Sages: Biblical Commentary in Rabbinic Literature, Presented to Hananel Mack*. Edited by Avigdor Shinan and Israel J. Yuval. Jerusalem: Carmel, 2019.

Joosten, Jan. *People and Land in the Holiness Code: An Exegetical Study of the Ideational Framework of the Law in Leviticus 17–26*. VTSup 67. Leiden: Brill, 1996.

Kellermann, Dieter. "גור." *TDOT* 2:439–49.

Keil, Carl Friedrich. *Leviticus, Numeri und Deuteronomium*. BKAT. Leipzig: Dörffling & Franke, 1862.

Kislev, Itamar. "The Cities of Refuge Law in Numbers 35:9–34: A Study of Its Sources, Textual Unity and Relationship to Deuteronomy 19:1–13." *ZABR* 26 (2020): 249–64.

———. "P, Source or Redaction: The Evidence of Numbers 25." Pages 387–399 in *The Pentateuch: International Perspectives on Current Research*. Edited by Thomas B. Dozeman, Konrad Schmid, and Baruch J. Schwartz. FAT 78. Tübingen: Mohr Siebeck, 2011.

Knobel, August W. *Numeri, Deuteronomium und Josua*. Kurzgefasstes exegetisches Handbuch zum Alten Testament 13. Leipzig: Hirzel, 1861.

Knohl, Israel. *The Sanctuary of Silence: The Priestly Torah and the Holiness School*. Minneapolis: Fortress, 1995.

Levine, Baruch A. *Leviticus*. JPS Torah Commentary. Philadelphia: Jewish Publication Society, 1989.

———. *Numbers 1–20*. AB 4A. New York: Doubleday, 1993.

Milgrom, Jacob. *Leviticus 1–16*. AB 3A. New York: Doubleday, 1998.

———. *Leviticus 17–22*. AB 3A. New York: Doubleday, 2000.
———. *Leviticus 23–27*. AB 3B. Garden City, NY: Doubleday, 2001.
———. *Numbers*. JPS Torah Commentary. Philadelphia: Jewish Publication Society, 1990.
———. "Religious Conversion and the Revolt Model for the Formation of Israel." *JBL* 101 (1982): 169–76.
Nicholson, Ernest W. *The Pentateuch in the Twentieth Century: The Legacy of Julius Wellhausen*. Oxford: Clarendon, 1998.
Nihan, Christophe. *From Priestly Torah to Pentateuch: A Study in the Composition of the Book of Leviticus*. FAT 2/25. Tübingen: Mohr Siebeck, 2007.
———. "Resident Aliens and Natives in the Holiness Legislation." Pages 135–55 in *The Foreigner and the Law: Perspectives from the Hebrew Bible and the Ancient Near East*. Edited by Reinhard Achenbach, Rainer Albertz, and Jakob Wöhrle. BZABR 16. Weisbaden: Harrassowitz, 2011.
———. "The Torah between Samaria and Judah: Shechem and Gerizim in Deuteronomy and Joshua." Pages 187–223 in *The Pentateuch as Torah: New Models for Understanding Its Promulgation and Acceptance*. Edited by Gary N. Knoppers and Bernard M. Levinson. Winona Lake, IN: Eisenbrauns, 2007.
Noth, Martin. *Leviticus*. Translation J. E. Anderson. OTL. London: SCM, 1965.
———. *Numbers: A Commentary*. Translated by James D. Martin. OTL. Philadelphia: Westminster, 1968.
Propp, William H. *Exodus 1–18*. AB 2. New York: Doubleday, 1999.
Ramírez Kidd, José E. *Alterity and Identity in Israel: The גר in the Old Testament*. BZAW 283. Berlin: de Gruyter, 1999.
Rofé, Alexander. "Joshua 20: Historico-literary Criticism Illustrated." Pages 131–47 in *Empirical Models for Biblical Criticism*. Edited by Jeffrey H. Tigay. Philadelphia: University of Philadelphia Press, 1985.
Römer, Thomas. "Israel's Sojourn in the Wilderness and the Construction of the Book of Numbers." Pages 419–45 in *Reflection and Refraction: Studies in Biblical Historiography in Honour of A. Graeme Auld*. Edited by Robert Rezetko, Timothy H. Lim, and W. Brian Aucker. Leiden: Brill, 2007.
Schwartz, Baruch J. *The Holiness Legislation: Studies in the Priestly Code* [Hebrew]. Jerusalem: Magnes, 1999.

———. "'Profane' Slaughter and the Integrity of the Priestly Code." *HUCA* 67 (1996): 18–26.

———. "The Prohibitions Concerning the 'Eating' of Blood in Leviticus 17." Pages 34–66 in *Priesthood and Cult in Ancient Israel*. Edited by Gary A. Anderson and Saul M. Olyan. JSOTSup 125. Sheffield: Sheffield Academic, 1991.

Seebass, Horst. *Numeri II*. BKAT 4.1. Neukirchen-Vluyn: Neukirchener Verlag, 1995.

Ska, Jean-Louis. "Old and New in the Book of Numbers." *Bib* 95 (2014): 102–16.

Smith, Morton. *Palestinian Parties and Politics That Shaped the Old Testament*. 2nd ed. London: SCM, 1987.

Vieweger, Dieter. "Vom 'Fremdling' zum 'Proselyt': Zur sakralrechtlichen Definition des גר im späten 5. Jahrhundert v. Chr." Pages 271–84 in *Von Gott reden: Beiträge zur Theologie und Exegese des Alten Testaments; Festschrift für Siegfried Wagner zum 65. Geburtstag*. Edited by Dieter Vieweger and Ernst-Joachim Waschke. Neukirchen-Vluyn: Neukirchener Verlag, 1995.

Wellhausen, Julius. *Die Composition des Hexateuchs und der historichen Bücher des Alten Testaments*. 3rd ed. Berlin: Reimer, 1899.

Weinfeld, Moshe. "Theological Currents in Pentateuchal Literature." *PAAJR* 37 (1969): 117–39.

———. Restoration." Pages 251–66 in *Normative and Sectarian Judaism in the Second Temple Period*. LSTS 54. London: T&T Clark, 2005.

Wenham, Gordon J. *Leviticus*. NICOT. Grand Rapids: Eerdmans, 1979.

Zimmerli, Walther. *Ezekiel 2*. Translation by James D. Martin. Hermeneia. Philadelphia: Fortress, 1983.

From Sources to Redaction: Identifying the Authors of Numbers 16

Thomas B. Dozeman and Jaeyoung Jeon

The composition of the book of Numbers and its relationship to the literature throughout the Pentateuch have long posed central questions in the source-critical study of the Pentateuch. The reason is that the literature of Numbers departs from the books of Genesis and Exodus in both form and organization; as a result, Numbers has often functioned on the periphery of source-critical research on the Pentateuch. But in the present debate between source- and redaction-critical methods over the composition of the Pentateuch, Numbers has emerged from the shadows. Christian Frevel points out that the literary character of Numbers highlights central questions among recent researchers about the viability of source criticism as a working model for the composition of Numbers.[1] He notes further that the problems of composition and the identification of authors linger even if one adheres to the presence of the P source in the Pentateuch, because a growing number of researchers now judge the P source to end with the priestly cultic system in Exodus or Leviticus. The absence of the P source in Numbers forces interpreters to reevaluate the diverse literature in Numbers that is priestly in character as post-Priestly compositions originating in the postexilic period.[2] Thomas Römer summarizes

---

1. Christian Frevel, "The Book of Numbers—Formation, Composition, and Interpretation of a Late Part of the Torah: Some Introductory Remarks," in *Torah and the Book of Numbers*, ed. Christian Frevel, Thomas Pola, and Aaron Schart, FAT 2/62 (Tübingen: Mohr Siebeck, 2013), 1–37, esp. 2–3.

2. The ending of the P source has been regularly located in either Josh 18–19 or Deut 34. For Josh 18–19, see, e.g., Joseph Blenkinsopp, *The Pentateuch: An Introduction to the First Five Books of the Bible*, AYBRL (New Haven: Yale University Press, 1992), 237–39. For Deut 34, see, e.g., Martin Noth, *A History of Pentateuchal*

the growing research surrounding the composition and authorship of Numbers as having brought the book from the periphery to the center of pentateuchal studies.[3]

Numbers 16 is a central narrative in the book of Numbers. The conflict over priestly, Levitical, and lay leadership in Num 16 has played an important role throughout the modern critical period in identifying the different authors, while the central role of the narrative in the book has also provided interpreters with a window into the composition of Numbers as a whole. The present study will focus on Num 16 in order to engage the issues of composition and authorship that dominate the study of the book of Numbers. The interpretation will proceed in two stages. First, a review of two representative studies of source and redaction criticism will clarify a range of contrasts between these methods concerning the function of the book of Numbers in the formation of the Pentateuch, which results in the identification of different authors in the composition of Num 16. The broad study of methodology will set the stage for a more focused illustration of the ongoing debate among redaction critics over the social context and identity of the postexilic authors of Num 16.

Traditions, trans. Bernhard W. Anderson (Englewood Cliffs, NJ: Prentice-Hall, 1972), 8-19 and, more recently, Peter Weimar, *Studien zur Priesterschrift*, FAT 56 (Tübingen: Mohr Siebeck, 2008), 16-17 and Christian Frevel, *Mit dem Blick auf das Land die Schöpfung erinnern: Zum Ende der Priestergrundschrift*, HBS 23 (Freiburg: Herder, 2000). The traditional ending of the P source with the death of Moses (Deut 34) or with the distribution of the land by Joshua (Josh 18-19) is increasingly being shortened in scope so that the document ends within the context of the Sinai narrative, although interpreters disagree on the precise ending. The solutions range widely, and the following are samples of the literature for each one: Eckart Otto, "Forschungen zur Priesterschrift," *TRu* 62 (1997): 1-50 for Exod 29:46; Thomas Pola, *Die ursprüngliche Priesterschrift: Beobachtungen zur Literarkritik und Traditionsgeschichte von Pg*, WMANT 70 (Neukirchen-Vluyn: Neukirchener Verlag, 1995), 103 for Exod 40:33b; Reinhard Gregor Kratz, *The Composition of the Narrative Books of the Old Testament*, trans. John Bowden (London: T&T Clark, 2000) for Exod 40:34; Erich Zenger, *Einleitung in das Alte Testament* (Stuttgart: Kohlhammer, 1995), 95 for Lev 9:26; and Christophe Nihan, *From Priestly Torah to Pentateuch: A Study in the Composition of the Pentateuch*, FAT 2/25 (Tübingen: Mohr Siebeck, 2007) 340-94 for Lev 16.

3. Thomas Römer, "De la périphérie au centre: Les livres du Lévitique et des Nombres dans le débat actuel sur le Pentateuque," in *The Books of Leviticus and Numbers*, ed. Thomas Römer, BETL 215 (Leuven: Peeters, 2008), 3-34.

1. Source and Redaction Criticism in the Interpretation of Numbers 16

Martin Noth provided the point of departure for comparing and contrasting source and redaction methodologies in the interpretation of Num 16 and in the book of Numbers as a whole when he wrote: "If we compare Numbers with the other books of the Pentateuch, what strikes us most of all here is the lack of longer complexes."[4] What he meant is that the sections of the book and the individual stories do not clearly form a larger narrative plot, as is the case in Genesis and Exodus. The camp legislation (1:1–10:10) is tied more closely to Exodus and Leviticus than to the second stage of the wilderness journey (10:11–21:35). The events in the wilderness journey present further problems of literary unity. The conflict over prophetic leadership (Num 11–12), for example, is not closely tied to the loss of the land (Num 13–14) or to the conflict over priestly leadership (Num 16). This led Noth to a further conclusion: "If we were to take the book of Numbers on its own, then we would think not so much of 'continuous sources' (e.g., J, E, and P) as of an unsystematic collection of innumerable pieces of tradition."[5]

The hypothesis of continuous sources in classical source criticism assumes that the wilderness stories in Numbers are part of the formation of the Pentateuch at all stages of composition, because the journey from Sinai is an episode within each source. The authors in this case range in time from the monarchic to the postexilic periods as they compose different versions of the entire pentateuchal story. The interpretation of Numbers as a collection of "innumerable pieces of tradition" challenges the assumption that some form of the wilderness journey in Numbers was always part of the pentateuchal story, which, in turn, raises new questions about the function of Numbers within the formation of the Pentateuch and the identification of the authors of Num 16.

This section will explore the implications of Noth's different conceptions of the book of Numbers by comparing the interpretations of Num 16 in classical source criticism and contemporary redaction criticism. Although there are many examples of source criticism, as well as a growing body of redaction-critical studies on Num 16, the comparison will focus on the source-critical commentary of George Buchanan Gray and

---

4. Martin Noth, *Numbers: A Commentary*, trans. James D. Martin, OTL (Louisville: Westminster John Knox, 1968), 4.
5. Noth, *Numbers*, 4.

the redaction-critical study of Reinhard Achenbach.⁶ The comparison will highlight three areas of research: (1) the contrasting conceptions of the book of Numbers coupled with distinct views of its function in the formation of the Pentateuch; (2) the implication of the larger view of Numbers for describing the composition of Num 16; and (3) the identification of distinct authors within Num 16. The study will illustrate significant overlap in the literary study of Num 16, yet distinct conceptions of the literature in Numbers and of its function in the formation of the Pentateuch lead to divergent literary processes to describe the composition of Num 16 and the identification of its authors.

1.1. George Buchanan Gray and Source Criticism

George Buchanan Gray published *A Critical and Exegetical Commentary on Numbers* in the International Critical Commentary series in 1903. In the preface, he situates his commentary in the context of German source-critical research, citing in particular his debt to the late nineteenth-century critical commentaries on Numbers by August Dillmann and D. Hermann Strack.⁷ Gray states that his aim is "to enable the reader to look at and interpret the Book of Numbers from these new standpoints."⁸

1.1.1. Function of Numbers in the Formation of the Pentateuch

The origin of the book of Numbers, according to Gray, begins with the composition of a Judean edition of the wilderness journey (J) from the ninth century BCE and a parallel northern version (E) from the eighth

---

6. The source-critical research on Num 16 is extensive. For the most recent and comprehensive source-critical study, see Horst Seebass, *Numeri 10,1–22,1*, BKAT 4.2 (Neukirchen-Vluyn: Neukirchener Verlag, 2003). For bibliography on redaction-critical studies, see the recent study by Jaeyoung Jeon, "The Zadokites in the Wilderness: The Rebellion of Korach (Num 16) and the Zadokite Redaction," *ZAW* 127 (2015): 381–411. See also George Buchanan Gray, *A Critical and Exegetical Commentary on Numbers*, ICC (Edinburgh: T&T Clark, 1903); Reinhard Achenbach, *Die Vollendung der Tora: Studien zur Redaktionsgeschichte des Numeribuches im Kontext von Hexateuch und Pentateuch*, BZABR 3 (Wiesbaden: Harrassowitz, 2003).

7. August Dillmann, *Die Bücher Numeri, Deuteronomium und Josua*, 2nd ed. (Leipzig: Hirzel, 1886); Hermann Strack, *Die Bücher Genesis, Exodus, Leviticus und Numeri* (Munich: Beck'she Verlagsbuchlanung, 1984).

8. Gray, *Critical and Exegetical Commentary on Numbers*, vii.

century. These separate sources were combined (JE) so thoroughly in the seventh century that it is no longer possible to separate them. The JE source contains ancient poetry (e.g., the priestly blessing in Num 6:24–26, the ark song in 10:35–36; the songs in 21:14–15, 17–18; and the Balaam poems in chapters 22–24*), but the sources constitutes the earliest version of Numbers as an account of the wilderness journey from the divine mountain (10:29–34) to the land of Moab (25:1–5). The content of the earliest version of Numbers (JE) may be illustrated in the following diagram (although Gray concedes that the order of the episodes may not be original).

JE Source: ninth–seventh centuries BCE
Scope: Hexateuch (Genesis–Exodus–Numbers–Joshua)

10:29–34	Departure
11–12	Moses
13–14*	Spies
16*	Dathan and Abiram
20:14–21	Edom's Refusal of Israel's Travel Request
21:1–3	War against Arad
21:4–9	Serpent
21:10–20	Travel
21:21–35	Sihon and Og
22–24*	Balaam and Balak
25:1–5	Moab at Shittim

The wilderness journey in JE was an episode in a larger hexateuchal narrative (Genesis, Exodus, Numbers, Joshua) that begins with the ancestors (Genesis), continues through the account of salvation from Egypt (Exodus), and concludes with the conquest of the land (Joshua). In this way, Gray reads the wilderness journey from Sinai in Numbers as an intrinsic theme in the formation of the Pentateuch from the earliest hexateuchal sources written during the period of the monarchy. He writes: "Numbers (and more especially that part of it which is contained in 10:11–25) is, like Genesis and Exodus, mainly derived from two earlier works."[9]

The content and the growth of Numbers undergo transformation in the history of composition. The Priestly source (P^g) is an independently

---

9. Gray, *Critical and Exegetical Commentary on Numbers*, xxx.

written composition of the wilderness journey from the early postexilic period (ca. 500 BCE).[10] Unlike the JE source, the P source is a combination of narrative and law that incorporates prior independent laws (e.g., camp laws in Num 5:5–6:20, tassels on garments in 15:37–41, and the law of the red heifer in chapter 19),[11] while it also frames the wilderness journey with the promulgation of laws at Sinai (e.g., Num 1–4; 5:1–4; and part of 6:21–27) and on the plains of Moab (e.g., 22:1; 26*; 27:12–23; 34). The result is a divergent structure from the JE source in three parts: (1) camp law at Sinai linking the wilderness journey closely with the revelation of the tabernacle cult in Exodus (e.g., Exod 25–31), the wilderness journey focusing on the leadership of Moses and Aaron, and (3) the promulgation of law to the second generation on the plains of Moab. Central themes of P^g include the institution of the Levites, the census of the tribes and the establishment of the camp, and the leading of Aaron and Moses in the wilderness.[12] The P source in Numbers may be illustrated in the following manner.

P^g Source: 500 BCE
Scope: Pentateuch (Genesis–Exodus–Leviticus–Numbers–Deut 34)
1. Camp Law
    1–4   Census, Camp, Levites
    5:1–4   Camp Law
    6:21–27   Priestly Blessing
2. Wilderness Journey
    10:11   Date and Departure
    13–14*   Spies
    15*   Law
    16–18*   Korah and the 250 Leaders
3. Plains of Moab
    20:1–13   Moses and Aaron Disobey
    20:22–29   Death of Aaron
    22:1   Plains of Moab
    26*   Census
    27:12–23   Moses Prepares to Die, Succession of Joshua
    34   Land Borders

---

10. Gray, *Critical and Exegetical Commentary on Numbers*, xxxiv.
11. Gray, *Critical and Exegetical Commentary on Numbers*, xxxiii–xxxiv.
12. Gray, *Critical and Exegetical Commentary on Numbers*, xxiv.

The revelation of law and the wilderness journey in P^g remain an episode within the larger story of the ancestors (Genesis) and the salvation from Egypt (Exodus), as was the case in JE. The literary scope of the Priestly source (P^g), however, is not a Hexateuch as it was for JE, because there is no account of the conquest of land. Instead, P^g is confined to the life of Moses. The end of the document is anticipated with the announcement of the death of Moses (Num 27:12–23) and concludes with the fulfillment (Deut 34).[13]

The identification of the P^g in Numbers is complicated by a history of priestly supplements (P^s) over an extended period of time in the postexilic period (ca. 500–250 BCE). Gray leaves open whether P^s was added to the independent P source (P^g) or to the combined text (JE, D, and P^g), although the commentary appears to favor the former, evident in his interpretation of Num 16, where the challenge of lay leaders to Moses and Aaron over holiness (P^g) becomes an inner-priestly debate between Aaron and Levites (P^s). In spite of the influence of priestly supplements in the narrative of Num 16, Gray concludes that the majority of P^s material is confined to the legal sections that frame the wilderness journey, as illustrated in the following diagram.

P^s Redaction: 500–250 BCE
Scope: Pentateuch (Genesis–Exodus–Leviticus–Numbers–Deut 34)
1. Camp Law
    7–8   Offerings of the Levites
    9:1–14   Passover
2. Wilderness Journey
    9:15–23   Cloud and Travel
    10:12–28   Departure
    16–17*   Korah and the Levites
3. Plains of Moab
    26*   Census
    27:1–11   Daughters of Zelophehad
    28–30   Offering Vows
    31   War with Midian
    32*   Division of Transjordan
    33:1–49   Travel
    35:1–8   Cities of Refuge

---

13. Gray, *Critical and Exegetical Commentary on Numbers*, xxxvii.

The list clarifies the concentration of priestly supplements in the legal sections of the Priestly source. Camp law is expanded to include instruction on Levitical offerings (Num 7:8) and Passover (Num 9:1–14), while the law given in Moab is enlarged even further to include a range of new legislation concerning life in the promised land.

The history of composition disrupts the plot of the book of Numbers. The result of the extended legal supplementation in particular is that the present form of Numbers lacks unity of subject matter and that its content is linked only through a "geographical and chronological skeleton."[14] Gray states further that Num 1:1–10:10 is best interpreted as an appendix to Exodus–Leviticus, while Num 33:50–36:13 contains laws and instructions related to Deuteronomy (sharing the same setting near the Jordan, laws aimed at settlement, and similar subject matter).[15] The conclusion suggests that one function of Numbers in its present form is to relate priestly law in Exodus and Leviticus with the legislation in Deuteronomy, although this was not the original aim of the JE source, which sought to relate the wilderness journey from Sinai (in Numbers) into the land (in Joshua).

1.1.2. Composition of Numbers 16

The composition of Num 16 is closely related to the formation of the book of Numbers, because the narrative includes literature from each phase of the book's development. Gray identifies the history of the composition of Num 16 by examining the cast of characters involved in the conflict over leadership (Num 16:1–2), which includes Moses, Aaron, Korah, Dathan, Abiram, and 250 additional men.[16] "It would in the abstract be conceivable," writes Gray, that so many characters functioned together in a single conflict, but he separated Korah and the 250 leaders from Dathan and Abiram, noting that "the two parties always act separately, and are finally cut off by entirely different acts of God."[17] Gray notes further that the separation of characters is reinforced in Deut 11:6, where Dathan and Abiram

---

14. Gray, *Critical and Exegetical Commentary on Numbers*, xxii–xxiii, quote from xxiii.

15. Gray, *Critical and Exegetical Commentary on Numbers*, xxiii–xxiv.

16. Gray, *Critical and Exegetical Commentary on Numbers*, 186–218.

17. Gray, *Critical and Exegetical Commentary on Numbers*, 187.

are also mentioned alone.[18] The cluster of characters reveals three stages of composition that mirror the formation of the book of Numbers as a whole: the combined sources of J and E (JE), the independently composed Priestly source (P^g), and post-Priestly additions (P^s). Gray's literary analysis of Num 16 assumes that JE is nearly complete and freestanding (although he questions whether the introduction to the story is missing and whether a scene is absent between Num 16:1–2 and 12–15).[19] The P^g source is also an independent version of the story, but it is obscured by P^s additions that transform Korah and his company into Levites, which was not their identification in P^g.[20] The literary analysis may be illustrated in table 1.

Table 1: Gray's Composition of Numbers 16

	JE	P^g	P^s
Scope	16:1–2*, 12–15, 25, 26a*b*, b, 27b–32a, 33 (minus last line), 34	16:1–2*, 3–7a, 18–23, 24 (tent of Yahweh), 26a*a*, 27a (tent of Yahweh), 35	16:1a, 7b, 8–11, 16–17; 17:1–5
Characters	Dathan and Abiram Moses 16:1–2*	Korah and 250 Lay Leaders Moses and Aaron 16:12*	Korah and Levites Aaron 16:8
Complaint	Leadership of Moses 16:12–15	Lay Holiness 16:3	Status of Levites 16:9–11
Confrontation	Natural/Unnatural Death 16:25, 26b, 27b–30	Censers, Incense, Fire 16:4–7 minus Levites	Censers, Incense 16:16–17
Result	Swallowed by Ground 16:31–32a, 33aba, 34	Death by Fire 16:18–23, 24 (tent of Yahweh), 26a, 27 (tent of Yahweh), 35	Censers as Plates on Altar 17:1–5

---

18. Gray, *Critical and Exegetical Commentary on Numbers*, 187.
19. Gray, *Critical and Exegetical Commentary on Numbers*, 189.
20. Gray, *Critical and Exegetical Commentary on Numbers*, 192.

The JE version narrates a conflict over social authority between Moses and the Reubenites, Dathan and Abiram, who complain about the failed leadership of Moses in the wilderness and his status "to lord (his leadership) over them" (Num 13:13). The conflict is resolved at the tents of Dathan and Abiram, when the ground swallows their entire households (13:31–32).[21]

The theme of authority shifts in topic from Moses (JE) to lay holiness in the Priestly source (P^g), when Korah and the 250 lay leaders challenge both Aaron and Moses: "You have gone too far? All the congregation are holy, every one of them, and Yahweh is among them. So why, then, do you exalt yourselves above the assembly of Yahweh?" (16:3). In this version, the dispute over holiness is clarified through a cultic ritual at the tent of meeting with incense burners, in which divine fire destroys the 250 lay leaders (16:35).[22]

The Priestly source (P^g) is overwritten with additions (P^s) that transform the conflict once again, into an innerpriestly debate between Korah (now a Levite with additional Levites) and Aaron: "Then Moses said to Korah, 'Hear now, you Levites?'...Who is Aaron that you should rail against him?" (Num 16:8, 11). The death by fire in the Priestly source is extended in this version so that the censers of the Levites are hammered into plates as coverings on the altar as a warning about the holy status of the Aaronide priests, separate from Levites (17:1–5).[23]

1.1.3. Identification of Authors

Who are the authors of Numbers in general and Num 16 in particular remains vague in Gray's research. The wilderness journey from Sinai and the conflict over leadership between Moses and the Reubenite leaders, Dathan and Abiram (Num 16), is embedded in the earliest source documents from the period of the monarchy: the Judean J source (ninth century BCE); the northern E source (eighth century); and the JE combination (seventh century, at the time of Hezekiah). But more detailed information on authorship and social conflict in the monarchy period is not provided.

---

21. Gray, *Critical and Exegetical Commentary on Numbers*, 189–91.
22. Gray, *Critical and Exegetical Commentary on Numbers*, 191–92.
23. Gray, *Critical and Exegetical Commentary on Numbers*, 192–93.

The debate over leadership in Num 16 remains a central topic in the independent P source (P^g), written by a single author approximately 500 BCE. Gray notes that the theme is the challenge of lay holiness to priestly leadership, but he does not elaborate on the social circumstances that may have given rise to such a conflict in the early postexilic period. He adds that priestly authority continues to undergo revision within the "Priestly school" (P^s): "The inserted passages (in Numbers 16) reflect some struggle, of which we have no direct record, between the priests and the Levites."[24] Gray notes changing ritual practices such as the altar of incense that may have occasioned conflict. In support of this conclusion, Gray cites the research of Heinemann Vogelstein on conflicts between the priests and Levites in the book of Ezekiel during the sixth century, but he also cites Abraham Kuenen approvingly on the point that the struggle between Levite and priest continued into a much later time in the postexilic period (as late as 250 BCE), when Levites appear to lose authority.[25]

1.2. Reinhard Achenbach and Redaction Criticism

Reinhard Achenbach published *Die Vollendung der Tora: Studien zur Redaktionsgeschichte des Numeribuches im Kontext von Hexateuch und Pentateuch* in 2003 as a revision of his Habilitationsschrift for the Ludwig-Maximilian University in München. In the preface, he situates his monograph within emerging redaction-critical research on the formation of the Pentateuch. He cites in particular his debt to Eckart Otto, who identified a two-stage process of redaction in the formation of the Pentateuch, in which the literary corpus of Deuteronomy and Joshua first merged with Priestly and non-Priestly literature to form a Hexateuch, after which the Joshua was separated from the Hexateuch to form the Torah.[26] Achenbach's aim is to explore the formation of the book of Numbers within Otto's theory of the formation of the Pentateuch.

---

24. Gray, *Critical and Exegetical Commentary on Numbers*, 193.

25. Gray, *Critical and Exegetical Commentary on Numbers*, 193. See Hermann Vogelstein, *Der Kampf zwischen Priestern und Leviten seit den Tagen Ezechiels—Eine historischkritische Untersuchung* (Stettin: Nagel, 1889).

26. Achenbach, *Die Vollendung*, preface. For the research of Eckart Otto on the formation of the Pentateuch, see in particular *Das Deuteronomium im Pentateuch and Hexateuch: Studien zur Literaturgeschichte von Pentateuch und Hexateuch im Lichte des Deuteronomiumrahmens*, FAT 30 (Tübingen: Mohr Siebeck, 2000).

1.2.1. The Function of Numbers in the Formation of the Pentateuch

Achenbach presents a very different concept of the book of Numbers and its function in the formation of the Pentateuch than Gray's the source-critical model. Gray's commentary was based on Noth's description of Numbers as made up of "continuous sources"; Gray identified the origin of Numbers in the JE account of the wilderness journey with a parallel version in the P source; both sources wove the literature of Numbers into all stages of the formation of the Pentateuch. Achenbach, on the other hand, illustrates Noth's contrasting vision of the book as a collection of "innumerable pieces of tradition." As a consequence, sources play no role in the composition of Numbers as far as Achenbach is concerned.

There is no JE source linking literature from Genesis, Exodus, Numbers, and Joshua that might allow for the identification of an early version of the wilderness journey in the formation of the Pentateuch. Nor is there even a Priestly source in Numbers, because Achenbach locates the conclusion of the Priestly source in the revelation of the tabernacle cult at Sinai, either in Exod 29 or 40 or Lev 9 or 16.[27] Thus, for Achenbach, the origin of the wilderness journey in Numbers could not possibly be an old narrative tradition taken up in different sources from the period of the monarchy onward. He concedes the possibility of independent wilderness stories, perhaps as early as the late monarchy.[28] The origin of Numbers, however, derives from late post-Priestly redactions that are intended to address legal disputes in the postexilic period. The redactions in Numbers relate the previously separate legal traditions in Genesis–Leviticus and in Deuteronomy–Joshua; the first of these redactions creates the Hexateuch, while a subsequent redaction fashions the Pentateuch.[29] The function of Numbers, as a bridge between Priestly law and the legislation in Deuteronomy, echoes Gray's conclusion about the function of the final form of Numbers in the wake of the extensive Priestly supplements (P^s). For Achenbach, however, what Gray recognized in the present form of Numbers becomes the key for recovering the entire history of the composition of the book. The goal of Achenbach, therefore, is to describe the entire editorial development of the legal and narrative material in the book of

---

27. Achenbach, *Die Vollendung*, 14–22, esp. 21.
28. Achenbach, *Die Vollendung*, 181–83, 203–9, 267–85, et passim.
29. Achenbach, *Die Vollendung*, 34–35.

Numbers and to place this process within the larger context of the formation of the Pentateuch.[30]

Achenbach identifies three successive stages of post-Priestly composition in the formation of Numbers, each of which is aimed at relating Priestly legislation with law in Deuteronomy–Joshua. The earliest composition of the book of Numbers is the Hexateuchal Redaction (HexRed) composed in the fifth century BCE; its intended audience is the new generation after the Babylonian exile. This composition incorporates wilderness stories, including the departure in Num 10:29b–32*, the complaint story in chapter 11*, Moses's Cushite wife in 12:1b, a version of the spy story in chapters 13–14*, the confrontation with Edom in chapter 20, perhaps the war against Arad in 21:1–3*, the story of poisonous snakes in 21:6–9*, and the war against Sihon in 21:21–34, 27–30*. In spite of the array of independent stories, HexRed constitutes the first version of the wilderness journey from Sinai, fashioned as a history of disobedience to divine commands. The wilderness journey from Sinai provides a literary bridge between Priestly law and the legislation in Deuteronomy–Joshua, emphasizing the themes of Mosaic prophetic authority and the promise of land, thus creating the Hexateuch.[31] The literary structure of Numbers in HexRed may be illustrated as follows:

Hexateuchal Redaction: (HexRed): fifth century BCE (pre-Nehemiah)
Scope: Hexateuch (relates Exodus–Leviticus to Deuteronomy–Joshua)

10:29, 33, 35	Departure
11*	Complaint
12*	Challenge of Moses
13–14*	Spies
16*	Dathan and Abiram
20:1b, 14b, 15–16, 22a	Edom
20:12b, 14–20*	Travel
21:21–35*	Sihon andOg
32*	Land East of the Jordan
25:1–5	Moab at Shittim
22–24*	Balaam

---

30. Achenbach, *Die Vollendung*, 34.
31. Achenbach, *Die Vollendung*, 629–30.

The Pentateuchal Redaction (PentRed) is a revision of the wilderness journey in Numbers, priestly in orientation and composed most likely by Zadokite priests in the wake of the mission of Nehemiah at the close of the fifth century BCE. PentRed severs the book of Joshua from the Hexateuch with its emphasis on the theme of land, creating an early version of the Pentateuch. The central themes of PentRed are cultic, including the nature of revelation, the *kavod* YHWH, the role of the high priest, the sanctuary as the tent of meeting, and the holiness of the people.[32] The literary structure of Numbers in PentRed is as follows:

Pentateuchal Redaction: (PentRed): fifth century BCE (post-Nehemiah)
Scope: Pentateuch (separates Joshua and relates Exodus–Leviticus to Deuteronomy)

10:11–12, 33*	Departure Date
11*	Complaint
12*	Unique Moses
13–14*	Spies
16*	250 Leaders and Moses
20:1–13*	Failure of Moses and Aaron
20:22b–29	Death of Aaron
22–24*	Balaam and the Donkey, etc.

The Theocratic Revision (ThB) is not a single literary stratum like HexRed and PentRed but consists of multiple instances of overwriting in the literature of Numbers in the fourth century BCE, after the mission of Ezra. The central themes of the multiple revisions include the authority of the Zadokite high priest as the transmitter of torah, the limited authority of the Levites, and matters of purity. The revisions that constitute ThB are concentrated in the legislation of Numbers, both in the camp legislation at the outset of the wilderness journey and in the legislation on the plains of Moab at the conclusion of the wilderness.[33] The literary structure of Numbers in ThB may be illustrated as follows:

---

32. Achenbach, *Die Vollendung*, 32–33, 631–32.
33. Achenbach, *Die Vollendung*, 632–34.

Theocratic Revision: (ThB, multiple revisions): fourth century BCE (post-Ezra)
Scope: Pentateuch
1. Camp Law
    1:1–10:10   Camp Legislation
2. Wilderness Journey
    10:11–28   Departure
    13–14*   Spies
    15   Law
    16–18*   Korah and Levites
    19   Red Heifer
    20:12b,14–20*   Travel
3. Plains of Moab
    25:6–18   Phinehas in Midian
    26–[32*]–36   Legislation

Achenbach would likely agree with Gray's assessment of the present form of Numbers as containing miscellaneous content structured in a "geographical and chronological skeleton" that is intended to relate Priestly law with legislation in Deuteronomy. But the composition of Numbers, conceived as a series of post-Priestly redactions, clarifies that what Gray identified as the function of the present form of the book, has become for Achenbach the key for recovering the entire history of composition of Numbers. For Achenbach, Numbers is a postexilic composition aimed at clarifying institutional conflicts and legal debates in Yehud during the Persian period.

1.2.2. Composition of Numbers 16

Achenbach's redaction-critical study of Num 16(–18) follows the contours of Gray's source analysis. Like Gray, the large cast of characters in Num 16:1–2 provides insight into the history of composition, which is further reinforced by the separate reference to Dathan and Abiram in Deut 11:6 and Ps 106:17.[34] Achenbach also concludes that the present cluster of characters constitutes three stages of composition: the Hexateuchal Redaction

---

34. Achenbach, *Die Vollendung*, 42–43, 46, 52–54. For discussion of "overwriting," see Cynthia Edenburg, *Dismembering the Whole: Composition and Purpose in Judges 19–21*, AIL 24 (Atlanta: Scholars Press, 2017).

(HexRed), the Pentateuchal Redaction (PentRed), and the Theocratic Revision(s) (ThR). The history of composition emerges from the combination of literary and thematic comparisons within the narrative, which bring to light the process of supplementation in Num 16 as overwriting (or rewriting).[35] The redaction-critical details of Num 16 may be generalized in the following diagram:

Table 2: Achenbach's Composition of Numbers 16

	HexRed	PentRed	ThB
Scope	16:1b*, 2*, 12–15, 25, 26, 27b*, 28–32a, 33ab^a, 34	16:1a*, 2a^b, 3–4, 16a^a*g, 17–18, 19b, 23–24a, 27a, 35; 17:11–13, 14–15	16:1a*, 5–7*, 8–11, 16*, 19a, 20–22, 24b, 27b*, 32*, 33b^b; 17:1–5, 27–28; 18:1–7*
Characters	Dathan and Abiram Moses 16:2*	250 Lay Leaders Moses and Aaron 16:2ab	Korah and Levites Aaron 16:1
Complaint	Leadership of Moses 16:12–15	Lay Holiness 16:3	Status of Levites 16:5–7*, 8–11
Confrontation	Natural/Unnatural Death 16:25, 26, 27b*–30	Censers, Incense, Fire 16:4, 16a^a*b, 17 (7ab), 18, 19b	Mediation for the Innocent 16:16*, 19a, 20–22
Result	Swallowed by the Ground 16:31–32a, 33ab^a, 34	Death by Fire 16:23–24a, 27a, 35	Death Limited to Guilty 16:24b, 27b*, 32*, 33bb

HexRed narrates a conflict between Moses and the Reubenites, Dathan and Abiram, over Mosaic authority and the leadership of Moses to fulfill the promise of land (Num 16:12–15). The challenge is addressed at the door of the tents of Dathan and Abiriam (16:26) with a test requiring

---

35. Achenbach, *Die Vollendung*, 37.

their unnatural death (16:28–29). The ground swallows the households of Dathan and Abiram, thus vindicating Moses.[36]

PentRed focuses on the conflict between Moses and Aaron, on the one hand, and the 250 leaders, on the other, independent of Korah; the leaders complain about the restriction of holiness to Aaron, claiming that "all the congregation are holy" (Num 16:3). This redaction changes the setting of the confrontation from the door of the tents of Dathan and Abiram to the door of the tent of meeting (16:18); it also reshapes the narrative into the pattern of rebellion (16:3), intercession through prostration (16:4), theophany (16:17) and punishment of the rebels (16:35). The test of holiness is signaled using a ritual with censors (16:7, 17), which results in the death of the 250 leaders from divine fire (16:35).

ThB consists of multiple additions to the narrative. The most important change in character is the addition of Korah as the leader of the Levites (16:1a*). The conflict shifts from lay holiness to the relationship of Aaronide priests and Levites (16:8–11), which is also resolved with the test of censers at the tabernacle, when fire destroys Korah's company and their censers become warning signs attached to the sanctuary (17:1–5).[37]

1.2.3. Identification of Authors

Achenbach's redaction criticism, in which the story is modified and reshaped over time, results in a more complex narrative in Num 16 than Gray's source criticism. The reason is that the interwoven motifs in the present form of the story cannot be separated into distinct sources. Yet identifying the authors of the different compositions becomes more important in Achenbach's research, because the redaction-critical process of composition is anchored directly in specific conflicts within the institutional history of Yehud in the Persian period.[38] All stages of the composition of Num 16, moreover, presuppose a completed Priestly source extending from Genesis through Exod 29 or 40 or Lev 9 or 16. In view of this, the post-Priestly redactions represent debates over authority in three specific time periods: (1) the postexilic period up to Nehemiah, (2) the period after Nehemiah through Ezra under Atraxerxes II, and (3) the post-Ezra period, when the torah becomes more constitutive for people with regard

---

36. Achenbach, *Die Vollendung*, 51.
37. Achenbach, *Die Vollendung*, 66–75.
38. Achenbach, *Die Vollendung*, 37.

to cult. The latter phase continues to the pre-Chronicles period, during which the text is enriched with legends and other supplemental material.[39]

The cultic history reflected in the composition of Num 16 may be summarized in the following manner. HexRed addresses the theme of Mosaic authority in the account of Dathan and Abiram's conflict with Moses; the audience is the first generation of Babylonian exiles to return to Yehud in the fifth century BCE prior to the mission of Nehemiah. PentRed is a Zadokite response in the fifth century to the emphasis on lay holiness that accompanied the mission of Nehemiah; this theme is evident in the conflict between Moses and Aaron, on the one hand, and the 250 lay leaders, on the other; Korah is not yet a character in the narrative. ThB overwrites the story with the character of Korah as the leader of Levites in a conflict with Aaron; the conflict is intended to emphasize the power of the Zadokite high priest with two aims: (1) to underscore the distinction between Aaronide priests and Levites and (2) to stress the authority of the high priest over the twelve tribes of Israel. ThB is not a single literary stratum but represents a sequence of disputes in the mid-to-late Persian period.

1.3. Summary

The interpretations of Num 16 by Gray and Achenbach allow us to compare and contrast source and redaction criticisms. Achenbach agrees with a number of Gray's conclusions with regard to the interpretation of Num 16: (1) Numbers 16 is the central text for identifying the composition of Numbers.[40] (2) The cast of characters confronting Moses and Aaron is unusually large, and careful study of the different groups will reveal both the history of the composition of the narrative and of the book of Numbers as a whole. (3) Comparison to Deuteronomy aids in recovering the history of composition. (4) The literary analysis of Num 16 involves three stages of composition, representing three distinct conflicts over authority. And (5) the development of the theme of authority follows the same general pattern from Moses, to lay holiness, and finally to the status of the Levites over against Aaronide priests. The two methodologies diverge, however, in their conception of the book of Numbers, in their understanding of the function of Numbers in the formation of the Pentateuch, in their

---

39. Achenbach, *Die Vollendung*, 35, 629–33.
40. Achenbach, *Die Vollendung*, 34.

sense of the time period in which the book of composed, and finally in their identification of authors.

2. Reflections on Achenbach's Model

Whereas the validity of classical source criticism, upon which Gray's thesis is based, has been widely questioned in recent decades, Achenbach's model requires some further reflections. The latter is fully in accord with the recent development of European pentateuchal scholarship, which is marked by the confined extent of $P^{(G)}$ and post-P dating of an increasing number of texts. Achenbach fills the gap between the short P (Creation–Sinai pericope) and Deuteronomy (partly also Joshua) with the model of HexRed, PentRed, and ThB. His sophisticated and precise literary-critical analysis, as well as his discussion of the social context for composition and redaction, makes Achenbach's work a significant contribution to current scholarship on the Pentateuch. The contextual analyses presented in this article also have much in common with his work. Nevertheless, there are several issues with Achenbach's model to be discussed before we proceed to the questions of authorship and the social and religious circumstances in which the text was written.

Achenbach's model is largely based upon Otto's attractive model of Hexateuch and Pentateuch redactions. According to Otto, HexRed connects the two literary clusters of the Priestly redactional work (Genesis–Exodus) and the Moabite redaction (Deuteronomy–Joshua) that produced an earlier form of the Hexateuch. The following PentRed separated the Pentateuch from the Hexateuch, adding a number of redactional passages into the Pentateuch. The current form of the Pentateuch was therefore formulated by PentRed. For Otto, both HexRed and PentRed are post-Priestly, so he does not strictly apply the classical criteria that distinguish between Priestly, non-Priestly, and Deuteronomistic texts for his reconstruction of HexRed and PentRed. For instance, Otto assigns much of the classical JE to HexRed and P to PentRed. Yet in his redaction analysis of Num 13–14 in particular, Otto assigns to HexRed most of the verses previously regarded as part of the Priestly narrative strand, while he attributes to PentRed verses with priestly and Deuteromonistic flavor.[41] Achenbach, however, extensively revises Otto's reconstruction of

---

41. Otto, *Das Deuteronomium*, 26–109 assigns to HexRed Num 13:1, 2a, 2bα, 3a,

the redaction history of Num 13–14, generally assigning the nonpriestly passages to HexRed and the passages with priestly flavor to PentRed and ThB.[42] Such a classical division between the priestly and nonpriestly texts is more persistent in Achenbach's modified HexRed and PentRed than those of Otto.

Still, Achenbach puts texts with different linguistic and conceptual characteristics together in one redactional phase. An example is found in Num 16. Achenbach assigns the appearance of the glory of YHWH at the entrance of the tent of meeting (Num 16:9b; see also Num 14.10b) to PentRed.[43] The motif of the appearance of glory of YHWH begins to appear properly in the inaugural service for the tabernacle in Lev 9,[44] which presupposes the Priestly tent of meeting (tabernacle) commanded and constructed in Exod 25–31 and 35–40. To the same PentRed, however, Achenbach assigns also passages such as Num 11:16–17, 24–30; 12:2–8 that presuppose the non-Priestly tent of meeting erected by Moses outside the camp (Exod 33:7–11).[45] As is further discussed in the article "The Elders Redaction" in this volume, this tent of meeting is obviously distinguished form the Priestly tent of meeting. The latter is built by the whole people at the center of the Israelite camp for the purpose of ritual service of the community by the priests; the non-Priestly tent is erected by Moses outside the camp for the purpose of individual prophetic revelation

---

21–22aβ, 25–27bα, 28bβ, 29, 32–33; 14:1a, 2–10, 26–27b, 29aα, 31, 35, 37–38, 44b; Josh 14:6–15. To PentRed he attributes Num 13:2bβ, 3b–17a; 14:11–25, 27a, 29*, 30, 32–34, 36, 39. Whereas the list of the spies in Num 13:3b–17a is broadly admitted as a priestly text, whether P^g or P^s, the divine speech in Num 14:11–25 is nonpriestly in nature.

42. Reinhard Achenbach, "Die Erzählung von der gescheiterten Landnahme von Kadesch Barnea (Numeri 13–14) als Schlüsseltext der Redaktionsgeschichte des Pentateuchs," *ZABR* 9 (2003): 56–123 assigns to HexRed the strand of Num 13:17b–20, 22–24, 26a, 27*–28, 30–31; 14:1b, 11a, (21a*), 23b–24, 40–45*; Deut 1:19b, 27b–31, 36–38, 46; Josh 14:6–15*; 15:13–19*. To PentRed, he attributes Num 13:1, 2a*, 3a, 21, 25–26*, 32–33; 14:1a, 2–5a, 10b, 11b–22, 25a, 26–29a*b, 30a, 31–37, 39; Deut 1:32–33,39aa*. To ThB, he assigns Num 13:2b, 3b, 4–16, 17a*, 29; 14:5b, 6–10a, 25a, 29b*, 30b, 38.

43. Achenbach, *Die Vollendung*, 63; Achenbach, "Die Erzählung."

44. The verses mentioning the glory of YHWH (e.g., vv. 4*, 5b, 6b, 23) are conventionally regarded as editorial additions; see, e.g., Martin Noth, *Exodus: A Commentary*, trans. John Stephen Bowden (Philadelphia: Westminster, 1974), 233. See further Nihan, *From Priestly Torah to Pentateuch*, 104–5.

45. Achenbach, *Die Vollendung*, 237–51, 290–301.

to Moses. It is only Joshua, not the priests, who serves in this tent (Exod 33:11). The two concepts of the tent of meeting are incompatible with each other and hardly could have been formulated by a single redactor. The notion of the Pentateuch redaction or the final redaction in the classical source criticism has often been criticized as a hodgepodge of the passages cannot be assigned to any source document. It is doubtful if the currently suggested new models are free from this sort of criticism.

Achenbach's notion of ThB should also be admitted with caution. He assumes that behind this redactional phase lies a dominant priestly power in the mid-to-late Persian period, largely depending on James Vanderkam's reconstruction of the priesthood in the Second Temple period.[46] But Vanderkam bases his argument largely upon Josephus's description of the dominant priestly power in Yehud, the historicity of which is generally doubted. In contrast to Vanderkam's maximal reconstruction of priestly power, many critics argue that the high priest had neither governmental authority nor absolute autonomy in religious matters; Yehud was governed primarily by the the provincial governors appointed by the empire.[47] Judges and magistrates were more likely to be Persians, and the primary legal basis for their judgments was the *dāta* of the Persian king or the satraps rather than Mosaic law.[48] The imperial authority also usually exercised control over local temples throughout the empire, and there is

---

46. James C. Vanderkam, *From Joshua to Caiaphas: High Priests after the Exile* (Minneapolis: Fortress; Assen: Van Gorcum, 2004). Josephus, *C.Ap.* 2.165 first suggested using the term *theocracy* to describe this period. In modern scholarship, the notion has been employed by Julius Wellhausen, *Prolegomena zur Geschichte Israels* (Berlin: Reimer, 1883), 55, 82, 422, etc.

47. See, e.g., Deborah W. Rooke, *Zadok's Heirs: The Role and Development of the High Priesthood in Ancient Israel* (Oxford: Clarendon, 2000), 125–174; Joachim Schaper, *Priester und Leviten im achamenidischen Juda: Studien Zur Kult- und Sozialgeschichte Israels in Persischer Zeit*, FAT 31 (Tübingen: Mohr Siebeck, 2000), 221–45; Lisbeth S. Fried, *The Priest and the Great King: Temple-Palace Relations in the Persian Empire*, Biblical and Judaic Studies 10 (Winona Lake, IN: Eisenbrauns, 2004), 8–107; and Jeremiah W. Cataldo, *A Theocratic Yehud? Issues of Government in a Persian Province*, LHBOTS 498 (New York: T&T Clark, 2009), 33–117. For further discussion, see Jon L. Berquist, *Judaism in Persia's Shadow: A Social and Historical Approach* (Minneapolis: Fortress, 1995), 131–46; Cataldo, *Theocratic Yehud*, 175–92.

48. Lisbeth S. Fried, "You Shall Appoint Judges: Ezra's Mission and the Rescript of Artaxerxes," in *Persia and Torah: The Theory of Imperial Authorization of the Pentateuch*, ed. James W. Watts (Atlanta: Scholars Press, 2001), 63–89, esp. 88–89.

no evidence that Yehud was an exception.[49] Some of the Aramaic papyri from Elephantine reveal that the governors of Samaria (and Yehud) made decisions for the type of ritual sacrifice in the rebuilt temple in Elephantine (*TAD* A4.9–10). It is also a royal decree that sets the date of a religious festival such as the Passover (*TAD* A4.1). Nehemiah, too, reforms the temple with his imperial authority. Deborah Rooke recently reviewed the arguments about a strong priesthood in Yehud and concluded that priestly power was not so dominant until the early Hellenistic period.[50] The status of the priests (or the high priest) in Persian Yehud is still at best a controversial issue. Achenbach rightly observes that some late passages that are priestly in flavor advocate the interests of the priestly circle in Persian Yehud, the Zadokites in particular. Yet the notion of theocratic revision (ThB) is more persuasive as an ideological orientation rather than a reflection of the existing, powerful theocracy by the Zadokite family.

In spite of these reservations, however, we are in agreement with Achenbach's analysis of Num 16 on some crucial points, especially involving the two layers with priestly flavor. (1) The two more recent layers, involving the 250 chieftains and Korah, bear priestly imprint but should be dated post-$P^{(G)}$. (2) The two layers reflect the interests of the priests in the social and religious circumstances of Persian Yehud.[51] Although the limited space of this articles does allow us to present a detailed redaction-critical analysis of the text, the issue of the social and religious contexts of the two layers, involving the 250 chieftains and Korah, will be elaborated in what follows. The two layers contain harsh polemics and conflicts among different groups, including the priests, elders, and Levites. The following section will prove that the conflicts and the necessity of the polemics are best explained in the social and religious context of Persian Yehud.

3. The Social and Religious Context of the Two Strands with Priestly Flavor

Since Julius Wellhausen and Kuenen, there has been consensus that Num 16 contains three different strands, but scholars disagree about the original

---

49. John M. Cook, *The Persian Empire* (London: Dent, 1983), 49; Cataldo, *Theocratic Yehud*, 175–92.

50. Rooke, *Zadok's Heirs*.

51. For further discussion of these three points, Jeon, "Zadokites," 381–411.

place of Korah.⁵² As discussed above, Gray and others put Korah together with the 250 chieftains; the majority, including Achenbach, places Korah in the final redaction with the Levites.⁵³ Korah is a prominent Levitical ancestor in biblical texts from the Persian period and should therefore be understood as a representative of the Levites rather than other lay leaders. This point will be discussed momentarily. Our reconstruction of the redactional history of Num 16 is therefore in accordance with the majority view with slight differences: Dathan and Abiram are in verses 1*, 2* (only ויקמו לפני משה), 12–15, 25, 26* (without וידבר אל העדה לאמר), 27b, 28–31, 32* (without אשר לקרח ואת כל הרכוש), 33–34. The 250 chieftains are in verses 2 (without ויקמו לפני משה), 3–4, 6* (without קרח וכל עדתו), 7* (without רב לכם בני לוי), 18, 35. And Korah and the Levites are in 1a, 5, 6bβ, 7b, 8–11, 16–17, 19–24, 26* (only וידבר אל העדה לאמר), 27a, 32b.⁵⁴

---

52. Abraham Kuenen, "Bijdragen tot de critiek van Pentateuch en Jozua: IV. De opstand van Korach, Dathan en Abiram," *ThT* 12 (1878): 139–62; Julius Wellhausen, *Die Composition des Hexateuchs und der historischen Bücher des Alten Testaments* (Berlin: Reimer, 1885), 179–80.

53. For those who put Korah with the 250 chieftains, see, e.g., Gray, *Critical and Exegetical Commentary on Numbers*, 186–90. Gray finds in the chapter JE (Dathan and Abiram), P⁽ᴳ⁾ (Korah and 250), and supplements to P⁽ᴳ⁾ (the Levites). Similarly, Jacob Milgrom, *Numbers*, JPS Torah Commentary (Philadelphia: Jewish Publication Society, 1990), 414–18 suggests two redactional phases: the earlier redaction of the stories of Dathan and Abiram, Korah, and the 250 chieftains and the final redaction with the Levites. For more references for this position, see Jacob Liver, *Studies in Bible and Judean Desert Scrolls* [Hebrew] (Jerusalem: Bialik, 1971), 12 n. 7. On the placement of Korah in the final redaction, see Bruno Baentsch, *Numeri*, HAT 1/2.2 (Göttingen: Vandenhoeck & Ruprecht, 1903), 539–41; Heinrich Holzinger, *Numeri*, KHCAT 4 (Tübingen: Mohr, 1903), 65–68; Wilhelm Rudolph, *Der "Elohist" von Exodus bis Josua*, BZAW 68 (Berlin: Töpelmann, 1938), 81–83; Philip J. Budd, *Numbers*, WBC 5 (Waco, TX: Word, 1984), 181–84; Noth, *Numbers*, 120–24; Antonius H. J. Gunneweg, *Leviten und Priester: Hauptlinien der Traditionsbildung und Geschichte des Israelitisch-Jüdischen Kultpersonals*, FRLANT 89 (Göttingen: Vandenhoeck & Ruprecht, 1965), 175–80; S. E. Loewenstamm, "Korach, Sons of Korach, Korachites" [Hebrew], *Encyclopedia Miqrait* 7:261; Olivier Artus, *Etudes sur le livre des Nombres: Récit, histoire et loi En Nb 13,1–20,13*, OBO 157 (Göttingen: Vandenhoeck & Ruprecht, 1997), 160–65; Israel Knohl, *The Sanctuary of Silence: The Priestly Torah and the Holiness School* (Minneapolis: Fortress, 1995), 73–75; David Frankel, *The Murmuring Stories of the Priestly School: A Retrieval of Ancient Sacerdotal Lore*, VTSup 89 (Leiden: Brill, 2002), 212–24. Baruch A. Levine, *Numbers 1–20: A New Translation with Introduction and Commentary*, AB 4 (New York: Doubleday, 1993), 405–10 admits a complex development in P without providing details.

54. For the redactional analysis underlying this, see Jeon, "Zadokites," 383–95.

3.1. The Layer of the 250 Chieftains and the Council of Elders

A number of biblical and extrabiblical sources reveal that lay leaders or elders of family clans played a major role in the process of restoration in Persian Yehud.[55] According to the cultural memory of the early Persian period found in Ezra 5–6, the rebuilding of the temple was completed by the collective leadership of the elders of the Jews (שבי יהודיא or שביא, Ezra 5:5; 6:14), although it was initiated by Zerubbabel and Jeshua the high priest (Ezra 5:2). The elders also represented the community to the Persian delegates (Ezra 5:9).[56] The lay leaders were variously grouped or designated, but they undeniably had significant functions in decision making and implementation for the community. Examples include the חורים (Neh 2:16; 4:8, 13; 5:7; 7:5), the elders of the Jews (שבי יהודיא, Ezra 5:5, 9; 6:7, 8, 14), and the heads of families (ראשי האבות, Ezra 2:68; 4:2, 3; 8:1; Neh 8:13; 11:13, etc.).

The Aramaic papyri from Elephantine also reveal the significant role of such lay leadership in Persian Yehud in the late fifth century BCE. In the petition to Bagoas, the Persian governor in Yehud, lay leaders such as Ostanes and Avastana, who are the brothers of Annani, and the nobles of Yehud are mentioned as representatives of the community (Jerusalem) together with the priestly group (*TAD* A4.7:18–19; A4.8:17–18). Those letters indicate that the local authority of Yehud was a collective of priests and lay leaders. Joel Weinberg therefore claims that Jerusalem in the Persian period was a citizen-temple community "self-administered by elders and judges."[57] In spite of recent criticism of this model, Weinberg's observation of the significant role of the elders still seems to be unchallenged.[58]

---

55. Parts of this and the next section will summarize the main points already presented in Jeon, "Zadokites," 395–403.

56. It is controversial if the priests were possibly among the representatives. Kyung-Jin Min, *The Levitical Authorship of Ezra-Nehemiah*, JSOTSup 409 (New York: T&T Clark, 2004), 125–30 develops this point, suggesting that this change indicates a change in the Persian policy from support for the priest to support for the elders after the ban on the building of walls.

57. Joel Weinberg, *The Citizen-Temple Community*, trans. Daniel L. Smith-Christopher, JSOTSup 151 (Sheffield: JSOT Press, 1992), 134.

58. See, e.g., Lester L. Grabbe, *Yehud: A History of the Persian Province of Judah*, vol. 1 of *A History of the Jews and Judaism in the Second Temple Period*, LSTS 47 (London: T&T Clark, 2004), 143–45; Hugh G. M. Williamson, *Studies in Persian Period History and Historiography* (Tübingen: Mohr Siebeck, 2004), 25–27.

The sociohistorical studies of Otto Plöger, Morton Smith, Ranier Albertz, and others likewise indicate the significance of the elders or their rivalry with the dominant priestly group in Persian Yehud.[59]

The influence of the elders in religious issues is also related to the financial state of the temple. The rebuilding of the temple in Jerusalem was initiated and enabled by the political and financial support of Persia, probably driven by Darius's policy of reorganizing the local religions of the provinces in the empire.[60] Nevertheless, since the early fifth-century reign of Xerxes, who refused financial support for local temples, the maintenance and service of the temple in Jerusalem came to be largely dependent upon the financial contributions of the community's laity.[61] This situation likely provided the elders or lay leaders more power and influence in temple politics.

The lay leaders seem to have constituted a sort of collegial body for religious and civil issues in the community. Ezra promoted his reform not only by his imperial authority but also by depending on the "council of chieftains and elders" (בעצת השרים והזקנים, Ezra 10:8). The body of lay leaders probably developed as a permanent institution that was later recognized as the *gerousia* (council of elders) in the early Hellenistic period.[62] A prominent group of elders also made scribal contributions to the Penta-

---

59. Otto Plöger, *Theokratie und Eschatologie*, WMANT 2 (Neukirchen-Vluyn: Neukirchner Verlag, 1959), 129–32; Morton Smith, *Palestinian Parties and Politics That Shaped the Old Testament*, 2nd ed. (London: SCM, 1987), 75–80; Rainer Albertz, *From the Exile to the Maccabees*, vol. 2 of *A History of Israelite Religion in the Old Testament Period*, trans. by John Bowden, 2 vols. (Louisville: Westminster John Knox, 1994), 471–79. See also Frank Crüsemann, "Israel in der Perserzeit: Eine Skizze in Auseinandersetzung mit Max Weber," in *Max Webers Sicht des antiken Christentums: Interpretation und Kritik*, ed. Wolfgang Schluchter (Frankfurt am Main: Suhrkamp, 1985), 205–32; Erhard S. Gerstenberger, *Israel in the Persian Period* (Atlanta: Society of Biblical Literature, 2011), 102–3; and Achenbach, *Die Vollendung*, 54–65. The leadership of the elders is not a phenomenon specific to Persian Yehud but is also observable already in the exilic period among the exiles. It is apparent in Ezekiel, for instance, that the leadership of the exilic community was collectively exercised by a group of people designated as elders of Israel (זקני ישראל: e.g., Ezek 14:1; 20:1, 3).

60. Berquist, *Judaism*, 59–63.

61. Berquist, *Judaism*, 113.

62. See, e.g., the Decree of Antiochus III in Josephus, *A.J.* 12.138–46; 1 Macc 12:5–6; 2 Macc 1:10; 4:43–50; 11:27; 3 Macc 1:6–8; Jdt 4:6–8; 11:14; 15:8 and Jeon, "Elders' Redaction" in this volume.

teuch. The elders group and their scribal activities are further discussed in "The Elders Redaction" in this volume.

The episode of the 250 chieftains describes the lay leaders of Israel challenging the exclusive religiopolitical authority of Moses and Aaron and claiming that the whole congregation is holy for YHWH is among them (Num 16:3). The narrative develops to the ordeal of the incense offering, which is the major motif of this strand. The narrative as a whole indicates that the lay leaders' claim was about their right to participate in temple rituals such as incense offering. In the monarchic and early exilic periods, sacrificial ritual was not the exclusive domain of the priests. The Judean kings performed rituals in their royal temple (e.g., 1 Kgs 8:62–63), and Ezek 8 describes how the seventy elders of Israel make incense sacrifices (Ezek 8:11). Ezekiel harshly reproaches this ritual activity as an abomination (Ezek 8:12), yet the focus is the worship of idols rather than the legitimacy of the incense offering made by nonpriestly laity. This passage indicates that, until the Babylonian period, the right to make incense offerings in the temple was not exclusively preserved for the priests.[63] The book of Jeremiah also testifies that incense offerings in individual households were widely practiced in Judah during the late monarchic and early exilic periods (e.g., Jer 6:20; 17:26; 41:5). Incense offering became increasingly popular in later periods, such that rabbinic authorities eventually legitimized lay incense offering outside of Jerusalem (e.g., Tanh., Ahare 9; Tanh. B, 14). Even in our text, the incense offering by the elders (Num 16:18) is not described as illegitimate at the moment of ordeal.[64]

The Judahite community in Elephantine likewise demonstrates that temple and sacrificial issues were not decided exclusively by priests even in the mid-Persian period. Stephen Rosenberg made an archaeological survey of the temple area in Elephantine and suggested that, due to the location of the temple so close to the residential area, it is possible that the laity participated in the rituals within the temple.[65] Furthermore, some of the papyri from their archive reveal that Bagoas and Delaiah, the Persian governors of Judah and Samaria, respectively, gave detailed instructions

---

63. Menahem Haran, *Temples and Temple-Service in Ancient Israel: An Inquiry into the Character of Cult Phenomena and the Historical Setting of the Priestly School* (Oxford: Clarendon, 1978), 231.

64. Haran, *Temples and Temple-Service*, 232.

65. Stephen G. Rosenberg, "The Jewish Temple at Elephantine," *NEA* 67 (2004): 4–13, esp. 12.

for the kinds of sacrifices that should be offered in the rebuilt temple, namely, only meal and incense offerings are allowed without burnt offerings (*TAD* A4.9). Yedoniah and his colleagues therefore make another petition probably to Arsames, the Persian satrap in Egypt, to request a permission to make burnt offerings (*TAD* A4.10). The texts mentioned above together indicate that, at least until the mid-Persian period, temple and sacrificial issues in Judahite communities were controlled not only by priests but also by the Persian governors and lay leaders. Worship was a matter for the whole people; there was no fundamental division between laity and priests about it.[66]

The lay leaders were influential in the temple and ritual issues and had a custom of making incense offerings both in the temple and in individual households from the late monarchic period. There is no reason to expect that they voluntarily gave up their traditional right in the rebuilt temple. It is thus probable that, at least in early or mid-Persian-period Jerusalem, the lay leaders still claimed the right to participate in temple rituals like incense offering. This situation seems to be the context of the episode of 250 chieftains. In the episode, the lay leaders of the community make incense offering to YHWH at the entrance of the tent of meeting, which turns out to be illegitimate and a transgression punishable by death. This is a stark warning against the offering of incense by laity. The epilogue of the episode (Num 17:1–5a [NRSV 16:36–40]) perpetuates the warning by providing an etiology for the bronze altar of the tabernacle covered by the censers of the chieftains (Num 17:4 [NRSV 16:39]). The purpose of the whole episode is clarified in the last sentence: "no outsider, who is not of the descendants of Aaron, shall approach to offer incense before the Lord" (Num 17:5a [NRSV 16:40]). Obviously, therefore, through the composition of this episode, the priestly scribes in Jerusalem endeavored to prohibit the old custom of lay incense offering in the temple and to establish a new order of exclusive priestly right for the temple service.

3.2. Korah and the United Levites

The redaction of the Korah layer produced the current form of the narrative, combining the two strands of Dathan and Abiram and 250 chieftains.

---

66. Albertz, *From the Exile to the Maccabees*, 475.

The Korah layer, however, is not a complete narrative strand but uses the major narrative elements of the two previous strands such as the rebellion, incense ordeal, and two punishments, being consumed by fire and the earth. The redaction establishes the guilts and punishments of the earlier layers to be imposed upon Korah and the Levites in several ways.[67] What is intrinsic to this redaction is that Moses blames the Levites for seeking the priesthood (Num 16:8–10), and this is its major focus. Like the previous layer of the 250 chieftains, the Korah redaction is best understood as a polemic against the Levites who, probably from the perspective of the dominant priestly group, challenged exclusive priestly rights.

Nevertheless, the person of Korah is known little in the Pentateuch, and only in late redactional passages such as the incomplete genealogy in Exod 6:14–27 and later passages that mention the present text (Num 26:9–11; 27:3; cf. 27:58). In Chronicles, however, Korah is described as the ancestor of several influential Levitical families that were responsible for the three main tasks of the Levites: singing, gatekeeping, and ancillary temple service (1 Chr 9:19, 31; 26:1, 19; 2 Chr 20:19). Provided that the books of Chronicles are Levitical literary products, such honorable depictions of Korah demonstrate that he was an important ancestral figure especially among the Levites. The fact that the present redaction takes Korah as the representative of the Levites reflects the late priestly redactor's knowledge of the Levitical genealogy more or less as found in Chronicles.

The well-established genealogy of the Levites leads us to consider the growth of Levitical groups in the mid-to-late Persian period. The Levites as the second-tier temple personnel were not a strong or influential group in the historical memory of the early and mid-Persian period. The lists of the first returnees (late sixth century BCE) in Ezra 2 and Neh 7 report that there were only 74 Levites among them (Ezra 2:40; Neh 7:43) besides the 128 singers and 139 gatekeepers (Ezra 2:40–42; Neh 7:43–45), whereas the number of the priests was 4,342 (Ezra 2:36–39; Neh 7:39–42). Ezra himself could invite only 38 Levites to Jerusalem (Ezra 8:18) besides the 220 temple servants (נתנים; Ezra 8:20). Nehemiah reports an increased number, that is, 284 Levites in Jerusalem (Neh 11:18, cf. v. 20). The status of the Levites in Jerusalem, even though second tier, seems to have been improved by the reform of Nehemiah (445–430 BCE). According to the Nehemiah memoir, he appointed the Levites, singers, and gatekeepers

---

67. For further discussion, see Jeon, "Zadokites," 390.

and supported them with the temple tithe, which was not immediately accepted by local authorities of Yehud such as the priests and officials (Neh 7:1; 13:5, 10–13).[68] The priests in this period seem to have been in strong alliance with influential foreigners such as Tobiah and Sanballat (Neh 13:4, 28), such that Nehemiah could not rely solely on them for his reform.[69] Probably this was a good reason for Nehemiah to appoint and consistently support other groups of temple personnel such as the Levites, singers, and gatekeepers, seeking a new order and power balance in the temple (Neh 7:1; 13:10–13). As a result, as Joachim Schaffer observes, the Levites were allied with Nehemiah and, with imperial support, they came to have "a new field of activity escaping from priestly authority."[70]

The second-tier Levites, singers, and gatekeepers were originally separate groups, yet they came to be united in the course of time and eventually appear in Chronicles as branches of the Levite family with well-established genealogies (1 Chr 9:14–44; 24–26). The Chronicler imagines and projects the much elevated status of those united Levites in the monarchic period, which is so powerful and influential as to take control over temple administration, sacrificial and liturgical processes, and security (e.g., 1 Chr 15; 16; 23–26).[71]

To be sure, one should not take the description of the Levites in Chronicles as historical. Nevertheless, the pro-Levite passages in Chronicles and the so-called Levitical psalms in the Hebrew Bible indicate that the Levites acquired scribal capability in the course of time as well as access to the scrolls such as the Pentateuch and DtrH.[72] The capability of a scribal group requires infrastructure for education and economic support for

---

68. See further, Jaeyoung Jeon, "The Levites (OT/Hebrew Bible)," *EBR* (forthcoming).

69. Not only the priests but also the local Judean aristocrats had strong connections with them (Neh 6:10–14, 17–19).

70. Schaper, *Priester und Leviten*, 230.

71. Schaper, *Priester und Leviten*, 290 defines the growth of the Levites as "Levitical reform" introduced in mid- and late Persian period. Cf. Juha Pakkala, *Ezra the Scribe: The Development of Ezra 7–10 and Nehemia 8*, BZAW 347 (Berlin: de Gruyter, 2004), 268–70.

72. Chronicles exhibit a detailed knowledge of both the Pentateuch and DtrH. Also, e.g., the Levitical psalms in Neh 9 and Ps 78 among the Asaphite psalms particularly reflect their knowledge of the Pentateuch. Furthermore, the Levitical scribes were probably responsible for the compiling and editing of the book of Psalms. For a concise presentation of the "Levitical-Singer-Hypothesis" for the compiling of the psalms, see, S. E. Gillingham, "The Levites and the Editorial Composition of the Psalms," in

professional scribes, which presupposes a certain degree of available social and economic resources. Furthermore, the production of a pro-Levite text such as Chronicles indicates that they developed a sort of class consciousness, understanding themselves as distinguished from the priests as a significant clan in the community.[73] The infrastructure that makes scribal work at this level possible is hardly expected from a group in a marginalized state but reflects stronger Levites with a stable socioeconomic status.

The growth of the Levites and their possible challenge to the priesthood seems to be the most probable context of the Korah redaction. As we saw above, the redaction endeavors to blame the Levites, represented by Korah, for claiming the priesthood. The motif of the ordeal of incense has been taken from the 250 chieftains layer and reproduced in the current redaction (Num 16:16–17). Most likely, the present redactor was from the dominant priestly circle and endeavored to defend the exclusive priestly prerogatives in temple service from the growing power of the Levites. Achenbach argues this is the Theocratic Revision that was made in the late fourth century, when the Zadokites were strong enough to pursue a theocracy.[74] It seems, however, that the current redaction reflects a different situation, in which the Levites grew stronger to a degree that the priests felt necessity to respond to their challenge. If the priests were already powerful, there would have been no challenge to their authority or need to defend it.

4. The Zadokites in Jerusalem

In the above discussion, we concluded that the layers of the 250 chieftains and Korah represent two stages of priestly scribal struggle with other rival groups, namely, the lay leaders and the Levites. We also briefly mentioned that the two layers could most probably be attributed to two generations of, most probably, the Zadokite priestly group in Jerusalem. This argument is based on research that the Zadokites were, arguably, the most prominent priestly clan holding office in the Jerusalem temple during the Persian period and that the power struggle in the two layers among

---

The Oxford Handbook of the Psalms, ed. William P. Brown (New York: Oxford University Press, 2014), 201–13.

73. See further Jaeyoung Jeon, "Seeking the Hegemony: Scribal Rivalry between the Zadokites and Levites," in *The Bible and Social Sciences*, ed. Todd Klutz (Sheffield: Sheffield Phoenix, forthcoming).

74. Achenbach, *Die Vollendung*, 66–81.

the priests, lay leaders, and Levites is best explained in that context.[75] As we discussed above, from the late monarchic and early exilic periods, the incense offerings were made by elders in the Jerusalem temple; biblical and extrabiblical sources reveal that the local authority of Yehud was a collective type consisting of both priests and lay leaders. Also, the claim of the 250 chieftains for general holiness (Num 16:3) is rooted in Deuteronomistic ideology (כל קדשים כלם העדה, Num 16:3; see also Exod 19:6; Deut 7:6; 14:2, 21; 26:19; 28:9), which was arguably preserved and developed by the returnees from the exile.[76] Morton Smith already argued that the postexilic lay leaders of the returnees (בני גולה) were successors of the late preexilic "YHWH-alone party," which promoted Deuteronomic reform under Josiah and was later exiled to Babylonia. In the Persian period, according to Smith, some members of the party who were from the upper classes of Jerusalem succeeded in gaining high positions in the Persian court. With support from the imperial authority, they were able to lead the rebuilding of the temple and became the most significant political group in Yehud.[77] Similarly, Albertz maintains that the Deuteronomic reform group, mostly the high officials in the Jerusalem court, was succeeded by the lay groups who produced DtrG and JerD, as well as Deuteronomistic ideas about religion and society in the exilic period. The Deuteronomistic ideas were accepted by the lay leaders of Persian Yehud and functioned as the base for their program of restoration.[78] If

---

75. For the detailed genealogy of the Zadokite high priests in Persian Yehud, see Vanderkam, *From Joshua to Caiaphas*. For the critical reflection of the priesthood in Yehud, see Rooke, *Zadok's Heirs*.

76. Albertz, *From the Exile to the Maccabees*, 47 maintains that the late heirs of the Deuteronomic reformers took over the Deuteronomic idea of "holy people" (עם קדוש: Deut 7:6; 14:2, 21; 26:19; 28:9; Exod 19:6), "but understood it literally as a special religious consecration which all Israel had received from God: the covenant with Yahweh qualified Israel as a 'kingdom of priests'." Cf. Achenbach, *Die Vollendung*, 56–57. For further discussion of the literary aspect of the claim of the chieftains (Num 16:3) and its relationship with the Deuteronomistic and radical priestly concept of general holiness, see Jeon, "Zadokites," 399–400.

77. Smith, *Palestinian Parties and Politics*, 62–95.

78. Albertz, *From the Exile to the Maccabees*, 195–242, 369–492. Based on Blum's Deuteronomistic Composition (KD) theory, Albertz claims that the pre-Priestly Pentateuch (KD) is a work of the scribes who belong to this group. Recently, however, Ranier Albertz, *Exodus 1–18* (Zürich: TVZ, 2012), 19–26 dates the D layer of the Pentateuch (late Deuteronomistic redaction) later than two major stages of Priestly reworking (PB1/PB2).

the lay leaders in our text had Deuternomistic ideals, the context of the struggle was hardly a Yahwistic temple other than that in Jerusalem.

The struggle with the Levites in the Korah layer also indicates a close connection with the Zadokites through the Aaronide lineage. The truncated genealogy of the Levites in Exod 6:14-25, which can also be assigned to the current redactor, focuses on the Korahite family (v. 24) and the Aaronide line with special emphasis on Phinehas (v. 25). Phinehas is remembered as the supervisor of the Levites, especially the Korahites (1 Chr 9:19-20), as well as the direct ancestor of Zadok (1 Chr 6:1-15, 49-53). The emphasis on Phinehas in the genealogy in Exod 6 is again connected to the covenant of the eternal priesthood for him at Baal Peor (Num 25:6-15), which can also be understood as an effort on the part of the Zadokite scribes to perpetuate their exclusive priestly rights. The three pentateuchal passages in Exod 6; Num 16; and Num 25 share the interest of the Zadokites and can be assigned to the redaction by the Zadokite scribes.[79]

The struggle between the Zadokites and the Levites is found not only in the Pentateuch but also in Ezek 44. Unequivocally in favor of the Zadokites, the passage limits the priesthood to the Zadokites and degrades the rest of the Levitical priests to the status of second-tier temple personnel (vv. 10-14); as a consequence, the legitimate priesthood remains exclusively among the Zadokites (vv. 15-16). These verses are increasingly regarded as a late addition that advocates the Zadokites' exclusive priesthood in the struggle among different priestly groups in Persian-period Jerusalem.[80] It is also suggested that there was a mutual literary influence between Ezek

---

79. See further Jeon, "Zadokites," 403-6. For further explication of the fusion of the Aaronides and Zadokites during the mid- to late Persian period, see Jaeyoung Jeon, *From the Reed Sea to Kadesh: Formation of the Pentateuchal Wilderness Narrative*, FAT (Tübingen: Mohr Siebeck, forthcoming).

80. See, e.g., Hartmut Gese, *Der Verfassungsentwurf des Ezechiel (Kap. 40-48): Traditionsgeschichtlich untersucht*, BHT 25 (Tübingen: Mohr Siebeck, 1957), 52-57; Gunneweg, *Leviten und Priester*, 188; Paul D. Hanson, *The Dawn of Apocalyptic: The Historical and Sociological Roots of Jewish Apocalyptic Eschatology*, rev. ed. (Philadelphia: Fortress, 1983), 220-28; Joachim Schaper, "Rereading the Law: Inner-Biblical Exegesis of Divine Oracles in Ezekiel 44 and Isaiah 56," in *Recht und Ethik im Alten Testament: Beiträge des Symposiums "Das Alte Testament und die Kultur der Moderne" anlässlich des 100. Geburtstags Gerhard von Rads (1901–1971), Heidelberg, 18.–21. Oktober 2001*, ed. Bernard M. Levinson and Eckart Otto, Altes Testament und Moderne 13 (Münster: Lit, 2004), 125-44; Nathan MacDonald, *Priestly Rule: Polemic and*

44 and Num 16–18.⁸¹ Whatever the literary relationship between the two texts, it is significant for our purpose that Ezek 44 shares with the Korah redaction the same attitude against the (other) Levites and specifies the Aaronides/Zadokites as the legitimate priests.

To be sure, we cannot entirely dismiss the possibility that the second-tier Levites existed in other temples or sanctuaries in the postexilic period. The Ezra memoir mentions a certain "place Casiphia" (Ezra 8:17; cf. LXX ἐν ἀργυρίῳ τοῦ τόπου), where he could recruit some Levites and temple servants, although the existence of a temple or sanctuary is not explicitly mentioned. It is also not impossible that the temple of Gerizim was a Zadokite temple in terms of its priesthood, if its building was connected to Sanballat the Horonite for his son-in-law, a grandson of Eliashib the high priest of Jerusalem.⁸² Some of the inscriptions found at the temple site, from the Persian and Hellenistic periods, contain the title "priests" (כהנים or כהניא) and names such as Eleazar and Phinehas.⁸³ Josephus reports that many priests and Levites from Jerusalem were involved in the temple of Gerizim (A.J. 11.335).⁸⁴ He mentions another Yahwistic temple in Egypt where the Zadokites were in office, the temple of Onias at Leontopolis in the Hellenistic period. He explicitly reports the service of the Levites at this temple (A.J. 13.62–73). Nevertheless, even if the second-tier Levites served in the temples of Gerizim and Leontopolis, that must have been

---

Biblical Interpretation in Ezekiel 44, BZAW 476 (Berlin: de Gruyter, 2015), 19–55. For a brief summary of the research on Ezekiel 44, see, MacDonald, *Ezekiel 44*, 4–10.

81. See esp. MacDonald, *Ezekiel 44*, 44–47.

82. For this hypothesis, see Yitzakh Magen, "The Dating of the First Phase of the Samaritan Temple on Mt. Gerizim in Light of Archaeological Evidence," in *Judah and the Judeans in the Fourth Century BCE*, ed. Oded Lipschitz, Gary N. Knoppers, and Rainer Albertz (Winona Lake, IN: Eisenbrauns, 2007), 157–211, esp. 182. Magen argues that, after Nehemiah's expulsion of Eliashib's grandson (Neh 13:28), Sanballat the Horonite built a temple at Mount Gerizim for his son-in-law. Magen claims that Josephus's account of the building of the temple in the Hellenistic period (A.J. 11.335) was his error of the period.

83. See further Yitzhak Magen, Haggai Misgav, and Levana Tsfania, *The Aramaic, Hebrew and Samaritan Inscriptions*, vol. 1 of *Mount Gerizim Excavations* (Jerusalem: Staff Officer of Archaeology, 2004), 67 no. 24, 68 no. 25, 253–54 no. 382, 257–59 nos. 388–89; Magen, "Dating," 166–67.

84. Gary N. Knoppers, *Jews and Samaritans: The Origins and History of Their Early Relations* (Oxford: Oxford University Press, 2013), 129, however, points out that, unlike the situation with reference to the priests as a group, there are no attested references to the Levites as a group (e.g., לוים or הלוים).

implemented in those temples following the Jerusalemite system of the Zadokite-Levite hierarchy. We have no indication of the presence of a Levitical group nor a struggle between the Zadokites and the Levites in temples other than Jerusalem. Based on all these considerations, the two layers in Num 16 should be assigned to Zadokite scribes in Jerusalem.

5. Conclusion

In this essay we reviewed the history of research on Num 16, comparing Gray's classical source-critical interpretation with Achenbach's more recent redaction-critical study. In the first portion we compared the two approaches with regard to the composition and authorship of Num 16. In the second half we explored further developments in the identification of the authors in the composition of Num 16.

Redaction-critical study of Num 16 has identified two layers of composition with priestly flavor, those of the 250 chieftains and of Korah and the Levites; both represent the agenda of the dominant priestly group in two historical stages of their power struggle with rival groups in the Jerusalem temple. In the earlier stage, most likely a Jerusalemite priest-scribe endeavored to ban the custom of lay incense offering in the temple. Because the lay leaders were influential in temple politics and probably even cosupervised the temple (e.g., Neh 13:10–13), the priestly group must have taken pains to establish the new order. The redaction of Korah and the Levites reflects a later stage when the Levites grew strong enough to challenge the priesthood—or at least the priests felt it necessary to react to them. It is not possible to date those layers with certainty. Yet, if we assume that the growth of the Levites started with Nehemiah's reform, we may safely locate the Korah redaction in the period after Nehemiah's mission in the mid-fifth century BCE. The layer of the 250 chieftains should be dated before the Korah redaction, which allows a range from the early to mid-Persian period. We will leave further precision to future studies. The two redactions increasingly limit the offering of incense in the sanctuary as the exclusive right of the priesthood, underscoring its more sacred status than animal sacrifice.[85] As a result, the incense rite in the temple emerged as a symbol of priesthood throughout the Hellenistic and Roman periods.[86]

---

85. See further Jeon, "Zadokites," 406–7.

86. See, e.g., T. Levi 10:1; Josephus, *A.J.* 13.282. See further Paul Heger, *The Development of Incense Cult in Israel*, BZAW 245 (Berlin: de Gruyter, 1997), 185–86.

The significance of the incense offering as a symbol of priesthood is also found in Chronicles, particularly in the account of King Uzziah who was punished by leprosy for attempting to offer incense in the temple (2 Chr 26:16–21).[87] The two Zadokite layers in Num 16 can be understood to reflect the initial stage or perhaps even the origin of the special connection between the incense offering and priesthood.

Bibliography

Achenbach, Reinhard. "Die Erzählung von der gescheiterten Landnahme von Kadesch Barnea (Numeri 13–14) als Schlüsseltext der Redaktionsgeschichte des Pentateuchs." *ZABR* 9 (2003): 56–123.

———. *Die Vollendung der Tora: Studien zur Redaktionsgeschichte des Numeribuches im Kontext von Hexateuch und Pentateuch.* BZABR 3. Wiesbaden: Harrassowitz, 2003.

Albertz, Ranier. *Exodus 1–18*. Zürich: TVZ, 2012.

———. *From the Exile to the Maccabees*. Vol. 2 of *A History of Israelite Religion in the Old Testament Period*. Translated by John Bowden. 2 vols. Louisville: Westminster John Knox, 1994.

Artus, Olivier. *Etudes sur le livre des Nombres: Récit, histoire et loi En Nb 13,1–20,13*. OBO 157. Göttingen: Vandenhoeck & Ruprecht, 1997.

Baentsch, Bruno. *Numeri*. HAT 1/2.2. Göttingen: Vandenhoeck & Ruprecht, 1903.

Berquist, Jon L. *Judaism in Persia's Shadow: A Social and Historical*. Minneapolis: Fortress, 1995.

Blenkinsopp, Joseph. *The Pentateuch: An Introduction to the First Five Books of the Bible*. AYBRL. New Haven: Yale University Press, 1992.

Budd, Philip J. *Numbers*. WBC 5. Waco, TX: Word, 1984.

Cataldo, Jeremiah W. *A Theocratic Yehud? Issues of Government in a Persian Province*. LHBOTS 498. New York: T&T Clark, 2009.

Cook, John M. *The Persian Empire*. London: Dent, 1983.

Crüsemann, Frank. "Israel in der Perserzeit: Eine Skizze in Auseinandersetzung mit Max Weber." Pages 205–32 in *Max Webers Sicht des*

---

87. The real purpose of this unrealistic account that the priest tries to banish the king from his royal sanctuary is obviously presented in the words of Azariah. He says that to make incense offering is "for the priests the descendants of Aaron, who are consecrated to make offering" (v. 18).

antiken Christentums: Interpretation und Kritik. Edited by Wolfgang Schluchter. Frankfurt am Main: Suhrkamp, 1985.

Dillmann, August. *Die Bücher Numeri, Deuteronomium und Josua.* 2nd ed. Leipzig: Hirzel, 1886.

Edenburg, Cynthia. *Dismembering the Whole: Composition and Purpose in Judges 19–21.* AIL 24. Atlanta: Scholars Press, 2017.

Frankel, David. *The Murmuring Stories of the Priestly School: A Retrieval of Ancient Sacerdotal Lore.* VTSup 89. Leiden: Brill, 2002.

Frevel, Christian. "The Book of Numbers—Formation, Composition, and Interpretation of a Late Part of the Torah: Some Introductory Remarks." Pages 1–37 in *Torah and the Book of Numbers.* Edited by Christian Frevel, Thomas Pola, and Aaron Schart. FAT 2/62. Tübingen: Mohr Siebeck, 2013.

———. *Mit dem Blick auf das Land die Schöpfung erinnern: Zum Ende der Priestergrundschrift.* HBS 23. Freiburg: Herder, 2000.

Fried, Lisbeth S. *The Priest and the Great King: Temple-Palace Relations in the Persian Empire.* Biblical and Judaic Studies 10. Winona Lake, IN: Eisenbrauns, 2004.

———. "You Shall Appoint Judges: Ezra's Mission and the Rescript of Artaxerxes." Pages 63–89 in *Persia and Torah: The Theory of Imperial Authorization of the Pentateuch.* Edited by James W. Watts. Atlanta: Scholars Press, 2001.

Gerstenberger, Erhard S. *Israel in the Persian Period.* Atlanta: Society of Biblical Literature, 2011.

Gese, Hartmut. *Der Verfassungsentwurf des Ezechiel (Kap. 40–48): Traditionsgeschichtlich untersucht.* BHT 25. Tübingen: Mohr Siebeck, 1957.

Gillingham, S. E. "The Levites and the Editorial Composition of the Psalms." Pages 201–13 in *The Oxford Handbook of the Psalms.* Edited by William P. Brown. New York: Oxford University Press, 2014.

Grabbe, Lester L. *Yehud: A History of the Persian Province of Judah.* Vol. 1 of *A History of the Jews and Judaism in the Second Temple Period.* LSTS 47. London: T&T Clark, 2004.

Gray, George Buchanan. *A Critical and Exegetical Commentary on Numbers.* ICC. Edinburgh: T&T Clark, 1903.

Gunneweg, Antonius H. J. *Leviten und Priester: Hauptlinien der Traditionsbildung und Geschichte des Israelitisch-Jüdischen Kultpersonals.* FRLANT 89. Göttingen: Vandenhoeck & Ruprecht, 1965.

Hanson, Paul D. *The Dawn of Apocalyptic: The Historical and Sociologi-*

cal Roots of Jewish Apocalyptic Eschatology. Rev. ed. Philadelphia: Fortress, 1983.

Haran, Menahem. *Temples and Temple-Service in Ancient Israel: An Inquiry into the Character of Cult Phenomena and the Historical Setting of the Priestly School.* Oxford: Clarendon, 1978.

Heger, Paul. *The Development of Incense Cult in Israel.* BZAW 245. Berlin: de Gruyter, 1997.

Holzinger, Heinrich. *Numeri.* KHCAT 4. Tübingen: Mohr, 1903.

Jeon, Jaeyoung. *From the Reed Sea to Kadesh: Formation of the Pentateuchal Wilderness Narrative.* FAT. Tübingen: Mohr Siebeck (forthcoming).

———. "The Levites (OT/Hebrew Bible)." *EBR* 16:337–46.

———. "Seeking the Hegemony: Scribal Rivalry between the Zadokites and Levites." Pages 97–110 in *Scripture as Social Discourse: Social-Scientific Perspectives on Early Jewish and Christian Writings.* Edited by Todd Klutz at al. London: Bloomsbury T & T Clark, 2018.

———. "The Zadokites in the Wilderness: The Rebellion of Korach (Num 16) and the Zadokite Redaction." *ZAW* 127 (2015): 381–411.

Knohl, Israel. *The Sanctuary of Silence: The Priestly Torah and the Holiness School.* Minneapolis: Fortress, 1995.

Knoppers, Gary N. *Jews and Samaritans: The Origins and History of Their Early Relations.* Oxford: Oxford University Press, 2013.

Kratz, Reinhard Gregor. *The Composition of the Narrative Books of the Old Testament.* Translated by John Bowden. London: T&T Clark, 2000.

Kuenen, Abraham. "Bijdragen tot de critiek van Pentateuch en Jozua: IV. De opstand van Korach, Dathan en Abiram." *ThT* 12 (1878): 139–62.

Levine, Baruch A. *Numbers 1–20: A New Translation with Introduction and Commentary.* AB 4. New York: Doubleday, 1993.

Liver, Jacob. *Studies in Bible and Judean Desert Scrolls* [Hebrew]. Jerusalem: Bialik, 1971.

Loewenstamm, S. E. "Korach, Sons of Korach, Korachites" [Hebrew]. *Encyclopedia Miqrait* 7:261–63.

MacDonald, Nathan. *Priestly Rule: Polemic and Biblical Interpretation in Ezekiel 44.* BZAW 476. Berlin: de Gruyter, 2015.

Magen, Yitzakh. "The Dating of the First Phase of the Samaritan Temple on Mt. Gerizim in Light of Archaeological Evidence." Pages 157–211 in *Judah and the Judeans in the Fourth Century BCE.* Edited by Oded Lipschitz, Gary N. Knoppers, and Rainer Albertz. Winona Lake, IN: Eisenbrauns, 2007.

Magen, Yitzhak, Haggai Misgav, and Levana Tsfania. *The Aramaic, Hebrew and Samaritan Inscriptions*. Vol. 1 of *Mount Gerizim Excavations*. Jerusalem: Staff Officer of Archaeology, 2004.
Milgrom, Jacob. *Numbers*. JPS Torah Commentary. Philadelphia: Jewish Publication Society, 1990.
Min, Kyung-Jin. *The Levitical Authorship of Ezra-Nehemiah*. JSOTSup 409. New York: T&T Clark, 2004.
Nihan, Christophe. *From Priestly Torah to Pentateuch: A Study in the Composition of the Pentateuch*. FAT 2/25. Tübingen: Mohr Siebeck, 2007.
Noth, Martin. *Exodus: A Commentary*. Translated by John Stephen Bowden. Philadelphia: Westminster, 1974.
———. *A History of Pentateuchal Traditions*. Translated by Bernhard W. Anderson. Englewood Cliffs, NJ: Prentice-Hall, 1972.
———. *Numbers: A Commentary*. Translated by James D. Martin. OTL. Louisville: Westminster John Knox, 1968.
Otto, Eckart. *Das Deuteronomium im Pentateuch and Hexateuch: Studien zur Literaturgeschichte von Pentateuch und Hexateuch im Lichte des Deuteronomiumrahmens*. FAT 30. Tübingen: Mohr Siebeck, 2000.
———. "Forschungen zur Priesterschrift." *TRu* 62 (1997): 1–50.
Pakkala, Juha. *Ezra the Scribe: The Development of Ezra 7–10 and Nehemia 8*. BZAW 347. Berlin: de Gruyter, 2004.
Plöger, Otto. *Theokratie und Eschatologie*. WMANT 2. Neukirchen-Vluyn: Neukirchner Verlag, 1959.
Pola, Thomas. *Die ursprüngliche Priesterschrift: Beobachtungen zur Literarkritik und Traditionsgeschichte von Pg*. WMANT 70. Neukirchen-Vluyn: Neukirchener Verlag, 1995.
Römer, Thomas. "De la périphérie au centre: Les livres du Lévitique et des Nombres dans le débat actuel sur le Pentateuque." Pages 3–34 in *The Books of Leviticus and Numbers*. Edited by Thomas Römer. BETL 215. Leuven: Peeters, 2008.
Rooke, Deborah W. *Zadok's Heirs: The Role and Development of the High Priesthood in Ancient Israel*. Oxford: Clarendon, 2000.
Rosenberg, Stephen G. "The Jewish Temple at Elephantine." *NEA* 67 (2004): 4–13.
Rudolph, Wilhelm. *Der "Elohist" von Exodus bis Josua*. BZAW 68. Berlin: Töpelmann, 1938.
Schaper, Joachim. "Rereading the Law: Inner-Biblical Exegesis of Divine Oracles in Ezekiel 44 and Isaiah 56." Pages 125–44 in *Recht und Ethik im Alten Testament: Beiträge des Symposiums "Das Alte Testament und*

die Kultur der Moderne" anlässlich des 100. Geburtstags Gerhard von Rads (1901–1971), Heidelberg, 18.–21. Oktober 2001. Edited by Bernard M. Levinson and Eckart Otto. Altes Testament und Moderne 13. Münster: Lit, 2004.

Schaper, Joachim. *Priester und Leviten im achamenidischen Juda: Studien Zur Kult- und Sozialgeschichte Israels in Persischer Zeit.* FAT 31. Tübingen: Mohr Siebeck, 2000.

Seebass, Horst. *Numeri 10,1–22,1.* BKAT 4.2. Neukirchen-Vluyn: Neukirchener Verlag, 2003.

Smith, Morton. *Palestinian Parties and Politics That Shaped the Old Testament.* 2nd ed. London: SCM, 1987.

Strack, Hermann. *Die Bücher Genesis, Exodus, Leviticus und Numeri.* Munich: Beck'she Verlagsbuchlanung, 1984.

Vanderkam, James C. *From Joshua to Caiaphas: High Priests after the Exile.* Minneapolis: Fortress; Assen: Van Gorcum, 2004.

Vogelstein, Hermann. *Der Kampf zwischen Priestern und Leviten seit den Tagen Ezechiels—Eine historischkritische Untersuchung.* Stettin: Nagel, 1889.

Weimar, Peter. *Studien zur Priesterschrift.* FAT 56. Tübingen: Mohr Siebeck, 2008.

Weinberg, Joel. *The Citizen-Temple Community.* Translated by Daniel L. Smith-Christopher. JSOTSup 151. Sheffield: JSOT Press, 1992.

Wellhausen, Julius. *Die Composition des Hexateuchs und der historischen Bücher des Alten .* Berlin: Reimer, 1885.

———. *Prolegomena zur Geschichte Israels.* Berlin: Reimer, 1883.

Williamson, Hugh G. M. *Studies in Persian Period History and Historiography.* Tübingen: Mohr Siebeck, 2004.

Zenger, Erich. *Einleitung in das Alte Testament.* Stuttgart: Kohlhammer, 1995.

In Between Sources, Fragments, and Redactions: Numbers 16–17 as a Test Case for Reconstructing the Literary History of the Pentateuch

Katharina Pyschny

Pentateuchal research, once a shining star of historical-critical Hebrew Bible study, is currently one of its most controversial and challenging areas.[1] Recent pentateuchal criticism is without doubt characterized by a new complexity that includes a variety of insular models and diverse premises, methods, and terminologies, and not least a significant regional fragmentation.[2] The somehow deadlocked situation "suffers

---

I would like to thank Thomas Römer and Jaeyoung Jeon for the invitation to contribute to the present volume and all their editorial efforts. This essay is based on the analysis of Num 16–17 in Katharina Pyschny, *Verhandelte Führung: Eine Analyse von Num 16–17 im Kontext der neueren Pentateuchforschung*, HBS 88 (Freiburg: Herder, 2017); Pyschny, "Debated Leadership: Conflicts of Authority and Leadership in Num 16–17," in *Debating Authority: Concepts of Leadership in the Pentateuch and the Former Prophets*, ed. Katharina Pyschny and Sarah Schulz, BZAW 507 (Berlin: de Gruyter, 2018), 115–31. Thanks are due to Christian Frevel and Kirsten M. Schäfers for countless fruitful discussions on the book of Numbers at the Ruhr-University Bochum, which have deeply influenced my research on Numbers and the present paper in particular. Furthermore, I am deeply indebted to the École biblique et archéologique française de Jérusalem for granting me a scholarship for the academic year 2018–2019. If not otherwise indicated, translations of the biblical texts are taken from the New King James Version.

1. "Theorien über die Entstehung des Pentateuch im Wandel der Forschung," in *Einleitung in das Alte Testament*, ed. Christian Frevel, 9th ed., Kohlhammer Studienbücher Theologie 1.1 (Stuttgart: Kohlhammer, 2016), 115: "Die Pentateuchforschung, einst Glanzstück der Bibelwissenschaft, ist ihr derzeit wohl schwierigstes und kontroversestes Feld."

2. Christian Frevel, "'Und Mose hörte (es), und es war gut in seinen Augen' (Lev 10,20): Zum Verhältnis von Literargeschichte, Theologiegeschichte und innerbiblischer

from overspecialization and overcompartmentalization," and a viable general consensus does not seem to be on the horizon.³ Yet the latest developments within pentateuchal research attest to a renewed dialogue and a certain desire to overcome the aporias of the current debate. As a consequence, biblical scholars more and more acknowledge the relevance of the book of Numbers, "since most if not all desiderata [of recent pentateuchal research] lead into the wilderness."⁴

The narrative about the rebellion of Korah, Dathan, and Abiram in Num 16–17 in particular can be considered an almost paradigmatic text in Numbers, linked as it is to several problems and questions in current pentateuchal criticism. First, several recent diachronic analyses of Num 16–17 clearly reflect the current dissent in biblical scholarship with regard to the basic explanatory models for the literary growth of the Pentateuch. This text has recently been used to argue in favor of both a documentary hypothesis (e.g., Joel Baden, Ludwig Schmidt) and a fragmentary or supplementary model (e.g., Erhard Blum, Reinhard Achenbach, Christoph Berner, Harald Samuel) with a clear quantitative predominance of the latter. Numbers 16–17, once a shining example for source criticism, becomes more and more the sign of its demise. It is not by chance, however, that Num 16–17 is referred to as an example of how to apply models of textual development by both camps of pentateuchal scholars. Its specific textual and narrative profile, whose literary growth can hardly be reconstructed or explained with one model alone, poses significant challenges to every hypothesis. Numbers 16 clearly includes non-Priestly (Dathan and Abiram plot) and Priestly (250 men and Korah plot) materials, each with its own profile with regard to protagonists, location, themes, terminology, and style. In fact, the non-Priestly and Priestly materials can be

---

Auslegung am Beispiel von Lev 10," in *Gottes Name(n): Zum Gedenken an Erich Zenger*, ed. Ludger Schwienhorst-Schönberger, Ruth Scoralick, and Ilse Müllner, HBS 71 (Freiburg: Herder, 2012), 107; Konrad Schmid, "Der Pentateuch und seine Theologiegeschichte," *ZTK* 111 (2014): 239.

3. Louis Jonker, "Within Hearing Distance? Recent Developments in Pentateuch and Chronicles Research," *OTE* 27 (2014): 123. On the deadlocked situation, see the statement by Reinhard G. Kratz, "The Analysis of the Pentateuch: An Attempt to Overcome Barriers of Thinking," *ZAW* 128 (2016): 529.

4. Christian Frevel, "The Book of Numbers—Formation, Composition, and Interpretation of a Late Part of the Torah: Some Introductory Remarks," in *Torah and the Book of Numbers*, ed. Christian Frevel, Thomas Pola, and Aaron Schart, FAT 2/62 (Tübingen: Mohr Siebeck, 2013), 6.

discerned rather easily using the conventional criteria of literary criticism. Furthermore, the non-Priestly and Priestly threads of action do not refer to each other, and each has a quite autonomous literary character. At the same time, they seem to presuppose various non-Priestly and Priestly traditions as far as their contents and concepts are concerned. Except for the fact that both narrative threads present leadership-related conflicts initiated by exemplary protagonists that are resolved by divine ordeal, they seem to lack significant thematic and structural parallels. This observation inevitably raises the question of the rationale or intention behind the redactional process in which the non-Priestly and Priestly strands were combined. While the strong inner coherence of both threads in Num 16 and the lack of explicit interconnections seem to support a documentary hypothesis, the tables significantly turn as soon as one includes the Priestly material of Num 17. In contrast to the preceding chapter, Num 17 consists of three Priestly episodes that clearly presuppose some events of Num 16 and explicitly refer to them to one extent or another. This hints at a complex growth of the Priestly material itself, which is rather difficult to reconcile with the traditional notion of a Priestly source (P^g) and its secondary extension (P^s). At the same time, it becomes apparent that the relationship between non-Priestly and Priestly material in Num 16–17 is crucial for reconstructing the late stages of the Pentateuch's formation.

Second, recent pentateuchal scholarship is very much engaged in the question of dating the first narrative thread spanning from the primeval history to the conquest of the land. It comes as no surprise that this issue is a highly disputed one. While the Münster model opts for a (late) preexilic hexateuchal narrative thread (*Jerusalemer Geschichtswerk*), a significant number of scholars argue—in different ways—against the existence of a pre-Priestly narrative thread that goes beyond Sinai or Kadesh (e.g., Blum, Eckart Otto, Achenbach, Reinhard G. Kratz, Jan Christian Gertz, Thomas Römer). The question at hand is closely connected to the wilderness narratives in the book of Numbers because this complex of texts is crucial for deciding whether a pre-Priestly continuation of Exodus is traceable in Numbers. In particular, Num 13–14 and 16–17 are linked to questions of the scope of pre-Priestly traditions or the literary character and date of non-Priestly material. While the non-Priestly Dathan-Abiram layer was almost exclusively characterized as pre-Priestly in former scholarship, recent proposals argue for a post-Priestly date in regard to either its origins or its integration into Num 16–17. The parameters are often set not by the textual analysis of Num 16–17 itself but by the systematic frame, which excludes the possibility or even the question of pre-Priestly material in Num 16–17 as such. From a methodological point of view, such argumentation is in danger of circular reasoning. When refraining from the model perspective, the non-Priestly material within Num 16–17 presents a candidate for a pre-Priestly continuation of Exodus that is worth considering. This holds especially true considering that the most recent proposals assume that the Dathan-Abiram layer is older in substance and that its integration into Num 16–17 was carried out in post-Priestly times.

Third, when looking at the developments within history of research on Num 16–17, it becomes quite clear that this narrative is also connected to another hot spot of current pentateuchal research: the question of the literary growth of the Priestly material. In former research, the Priestly strata of Num 16–17 were unanimously assigned to the Priestly source and its secondary supplements. The situation has since drastically changed, though, not least due to the influential trend to reduce the extent of the Priestly source. But the scope and potential of the Priestly traditions within Num 16–17 go far beyond a possible affiliation with P^g: the text provides us with Priestly traditions that clearly underwent a diachronic development more complex than the traditional notion of a *Grundschrift* and its additions. It is noteworthy that the Priestly traditions within Num 17 do not seem to refer to non-Priestly material at all. Instead, they are closely connected to the Priestly layer of Num 16 and create the impression of an episodic continuation (see Num 17:1–5, 6–15, 16–28). Furthermore, it is quite clear that the Priestly traditions within Num 16–17 draw on Priestly ideology and theology known from rather late Priestly traditions (graded holiness, conception of the Levites, etc.). It is exactly this interaction of several aspects that makes Num 16–17 such a representative test case. The classification of its Priestly material, either as supplements to an independent Priestly source or as additions to a conglomerate of Priestly and non-Priestly texts, is essential for deciding between the documentary or the fragmentary hypothesis.

Finally, it is particularly thanks to Achenbach's *Vollendung der Tora* that recent research has become aware of the important role of Num 16–17 in understanding processes that led to the formation of the Pentateuch as Torah.[5] By drawing on other narrative and legislative

---

5. Reinhard Achenbach, *Die Vollendung der Tora: Studien zur Redaktionsgeschichte des Numeribuches im Kontext von Hexateuch und Pentateuch*, BZABR 3 (Wiesbaden: Harrasowitz, 2003).

pentateuchal traditions and transforming them into a paradigmatic narrative, Num 16–17 attests to a strategy of circular self-referencing that in fact indicates a completion of the Torah. It is a significant characteristic of Num 16–17 that all its late redactional processes deal in one way or the other with questions of leadership and authority. A phenomenon that hints at a considerable need for legitimacy on the part of the tradents. But Num 16–17 does not seem to aim at compromise; it remains polyphonic and preserves several lines of conflict. These debates on leadership, authority, and power are often related to actual collisions of interest traceable in the postexilic cult and social history. The literary genesis and its sociohistorical and sociopolitical contexts can thus provide new insights in regard to the *Trägerkreise* of the late stages in the formation of the Pentateuch.

Because Num 16–17 is implicated in several problems and hot spots of current pentateuchal research, it presents an excellent case study for reconstructing the literary growth of the Pentateuch. Against this background, the following will present the literary genesis of Num 16–17 with special emphasis on the character or nature of the different layers found therein as well as their sociohistorical contexts. It will be shown that the final composition of Num 16–17 is to be considered a literary product of the late Persian period, originating within priestly (scribal) groups at the Jerusalem temple. It reflects very complex and multifaceted sociohistorical processes of negotiation and formation linked to priestly authority, leadership, and power.[6]

---

6. The following presentation is focused on conclusions more than detailed textual analysis, historical context, and engagement with secondary sources; I have laid out these details in Pyschny, *Verhandelte Führung*, esp. 97–142. See also Olivier Artus, *Études sur le livre des Nombres: Récit, histoire et loi en Nb 13,1–20,13*, OBO 157 (Fribourg: Academic Press; Göttingen: Vandenhoeck & Ruprecht, 1997); Achenbach, *Vollendung*; Achenbach, "Satrapie, Medinah und lokale Hierokratie: Zum Einfluss der Statthalter der Achämenidenzeit auf Tempelwirtschaft und Tempelordnungen," *ZABR* 16 (2010): 105–44; Christoph Berner, "Wie Laien zu Leviten wurden: Zum Ort der Korachbearbeitung innerhalb der Redaktionsgeschichte von Num 16–17," *BN* 152 (2012): 3–28; Berner, "Vom Aufstand Datans und Abirams zum Aufbegehren der 250 Männer: Eine redaktionsgeschichtliche Studie zu den Anfängen der literarischen Genese von Num 16–17," *BN* 150 (2011): 9–33; Jaeyoung Jeon, "The Zadokites in the Wilderness: The Rebellion of Korach (Num 16) and the Zadokite Redaction," *ZAW* 127 (2015): 381–411; and Harald Samuel, *Von Priestern zum Patriarchen: Redaktions- und traditionsgeschichtliche Studien zu Levi und den Leviten in der Literatur des*

1. The Beginning of the Redactional Process of Numbers 16–17

There is a long-standing consensus about Num 16–17 within pentateuchal research, namely, that the non-Priestly material (the Dathan-Abiram narrative) is the oldest layer of Num 16–17 and thus stands at the beginning of its literary formation.[7] In the systematic frame of the Documentary Hypothesis, such a relative chronology is self-evident and de facto without alternatives, because all non-Priestly traditions (except maybe the D/Dtr ones) are considered pre-Priestly. It is interesting to note, though, that, even when the Dathan-Abiram narrative is understood as a post-Priestly tradition, as is often done in recent proposals, the relative chronology between non-Priestly and Priestly material is considered the same. When refraining from any kind of systematic restriction and focusing on the text itself, there are quite a few valid reasons to consider the oldest Priestly layer within Num 16–17, the 250-men stratum, as the beginning of its literary growth.

First, there is no positive textual evidence within Num 16–17 that clearly proves the dependence of the 250-men layer on the story of Dathan and Abiram. The narrative threads do not intersect, a fact which emphasizes that the diachronic relationship could in principle be reconstructed in both directions.[8] This insight alone does not prove the 250-men to be the oldest layer within Num 16–17, but at least it means that this possibility cannot be categorically excluded. The fact that Deut 11:6 mentions Dathan and Abiram without referring to the Priestly material of Num 16–17 only proves, if anything, that an independent Dathan-Abiram tradition existed before it was combined with other materials.[9] Whether Deut 11:6 attests

---

Zweiten Tempels, BZAW 448 (Berlin: de Gruyter, 2014). See also the article by Dozeman and Jeon in the present volume.

7. For the few exceptions, see Hans-Christoph Schmitt, "Die Suche nach der Identität des Jahweglaubens im nachexilischen Israel: Bemerkungen zur theologischen Intention der Endredaktion des Pentateuch," in *Pluralismus und Identität*, ed. Joachim Mehlhausen (Gütersloh: Kaiser, 1995), 259–78; Urike Schorn, "Rubeniten als exemplarische Aufrührer in Num. 16f/Deut. 11," in *Rethinking the Foundations: Historiography in the Ancient World and in the Bible*, ed. Steven L. McKenzie and Thomas Römer, BZAW 294 (Berlin: de Gruyter, 2000), 251–68; Schorn, *Ruben und das System der zwölf Stämme Israels: Redaktionsgeschichtliche Untersuchungen zur Bedeutung des Erstgeborenen Jakobs*, BZAW 248 (Berlin: de Gruyter, 1997).

8. The only exceptions in Num 16:1–2, 24, 27 are clearly redactional in nature.

9. Lack of reference to Priestly material does not necessarily mean the scribes did not know these traditions. Thus it cannot be said that Deut 11 knew a form of Num

to an *old* Dathan-Abiram tradition depends on its date. Considering that Deut 11:2–7 is assigned not to proto-Deuteronomy but to a late Deuteronomistic layer whose post-Priestly character is often considered at the very least, then it becomes more and more problematic to use Deut 11:6 as an anchor for the relative chronology of Num 16–17.[10]

Second, even though the exposition of the narrative cannot bear the burden of proof (alone) due to its character as a compilation, it is remarkable that the syntax of Num 16:1–2 allows one to reconstruct a sufficient beginning only for the 250-men narrative. Because Dathan and Abiram are introduced anew with a shorter genealogy in verse 12, the exposition is less likely to include an original beginning of the Dathan-Abiram narrative. This impression is further supported by the rather awkward syntax of verses 1–2. As far as the Dathan-Abiram storyline is concerned, a sufficient beginning—including the names of the rebels, their genealogy, and a note referring to their uproar—is bedeviled by, among other things, the finite verb ויקמו in syntactic postposition.[11] In the case of the 250-men narrative, however, the reconstruction of a sufficient beginning is syntactically burdened exclusively by the *waw copulativum* in ואנשים. Without this letter, the text reads as follows: "And 250 men of the children of Israel rose up before Moses."[12] Considering that the other protagonists are named right in front of the 250 men but cannot be linked to sufficient beginnings within verses 1–2, it seems arguable to assign this *waw* to a redaction that integrates Korah and/or Dathan and Abiram into the exposition. It is not plausible to assume that the combination of traditions or an even more complex process of *Fortschreibung* could have worked without such minor editorial maneuvers. This is at the very least more convincing than the

---

16–17 in which non-Priestly and Priestly traditions are already combined and which refers intentionally to Dathan and Abiram alone due to its interest in the land theme.

10. On the post-Priestly character of Deut 11:2–7, see, e.g., Samuel, *Von Priestern zum Patriarchen*, 229, who states that Deut 11 is hardly old.

11. Such an original reading was proposed by Ludwig Schmidt, *Studien zur Priesterschrift*, BZAW 214 (Berlin: de Gruyter, 1993).

12. In this context, it is important to note that קום לפני in v. 2aα does not constitute a doublet to קהל על in v. 3a*. The different terminologies and semantics of the verbs (as well as the related prepositions) clearly indicate a sequence of actions: a plural subject approaches Moses and raises issues against Moses and Aaron afterward. The expression קום לפני alone does not necessarily transport the notion of rebellion and does not suffice as a "vorwegnehmende Zusammenfassung" (Berner, "Vom Aufstand," 20 n. 38).

assumption that verses 1–2, with their strongly composite character, were created as a whole by a redactor.

Third, following the literary criticism of Num 16–17 provided in my dissertation, the 250-men layer is characterized by a textual scope and degree of coherence similar to the Dathan-Abiram stratum.[13] The storyline begins rather abruptly in both cases; there is no itinerary or elaborated context in either literary or narrative respects. Many scholars have argued that the Dathan-Abiram story offers a far better connection to Num 13–14*.[14] This observation is correct in terms of thematic tendency, but it does not prove the Dathan-Abiram layer to be the older one. Even scholars in favor of a supplementary model would have to admit that the Dathan-Abiram story does not present a natural or logical continuation of Num 13–14* and that its current position and context is due to redactional logic and not necessarily to old age.

Fourth, more weight has to be given to the observation that Num 17 does not refer to the Dathan-Abiram storyline at all, at least not with certainty. The fact that Num 17 does not refer to the non-Priestly material is astonishing, especially when the Dathan-Abiram stratum is said to be the starting point of the redactional process in Num 16–17, and there must therefore have been ample opportunity to include references to the tradition at hand. With regard to the redactional logic, it seems far more plausible to assume a process that developed the other way around. The fact that Num 16–17 starts with the conflict surrounding the 250 men might support this impression. Of course, traditions could have been positioned prior to those at hand, but, in this particular case, it is remarkable that, again, the preceding textual passages do not include any kind of reference to the following.

Finally, it has to be pointed out that the renewed announcement of the incense ritual in Num 16:16–17 can be better explained when the 250-men stratum is considered to be the older one. It is often argued that this new announcement became necessary due to the interlude Num 16:7b–15. But the addition of Num 16:7b–11 to the first announcement in verses 5–7a would then have been responsible for creating the duplication in the first place. The plausibility of such a redactional process is at least questionable.

---

13. Pyschny, *Verhandelte Führung*, 187–213, 223–52.

14. For one prominent example, see Aaron Schart, *Mose und Israel im Konflikt: Eine redaktionsgeschichtliche Studie zu den Wüstenerzählungen*, OBO 98 (Fribourg: Academic Press; Göttingen: Vandenhoeck & Ruprecht, 1990).

As an alternative, the duplication could be understood as a *Wiederaufnahme* giving further weight to the idea that verses 12–15, which contain Dathan and Abiram, are secondary in this context.

When these considerations are taken together, it seems far more plausible on a textual level that the 250-men constituted the starting point of the redactional process. As will be shown in the following discussion, this notion fits the literary genesis of Num 16–17 as a whole.

2. The Literary Genesis of Numbers 16–17 and Its Sociohistorical Contexts

2.1. The 250-Men Layer and the Beginnings of the Redaction of Numbers 16–17

As has been shown, the 250-men layer is the starting point of the redaction history of Num 16–17. This Priestly strand—Num 16:2 [without ו], 3–5a [without ועדתו], אל־קרח ואל־כל־עדתו], 6 [without קרח וכל־עדתו], 7a, 18, 35; 17:1–2aα, 3 [without האלה בנפשתם], את מחתות החטאים], 4–5 [without 5bα], 6–14a, 15—recounts a rebellion of 250 Israelite men (אנשים מבני־ישראל) against Moses and Aaron and elaborates on some follow-up incidents.[15] The narrative structure is quite coherent and develops as follows: 250 men whose exact identity or tribal membership remains unclear and who are introduced only as "leaders of the congregation, representatives of the congregation, men of renown" (נשיאי עדה קראי מועד אנשי־שם) gather together against Israel's leadership duo.[16] As is evident on the basis of the following rebuke, the conflict does not focus on the question of lay participation in the cult but constitutes a discourse about leadership claims.[17] The 250 leaders question the authority of Moses and Aaron by referring to the (communal) holiness of the congregation: "You

---

15. For a detailed analysis of this stratum, see Pyschny, *Verhandelte Führung*, 187–214, 223–53.

16. It is difficult to decide with certainty whether the epithets were originally included in the 250-men layer. Such an asyndetic concatenation of epithets is uncommon but nevertheless accords with the rules of Biblical Hebrew. From a narrative point of view, it does make sense to label the rebels as special (leadership) figures within the Israelite community. Thus there is not enough evidence to simply discard the epithets as secondary.

17. See, e.g., Achenbach, *Vollendung*, 89 who describes it an "Anmaßung kultischer Kompetenz." This interpretation does not fully comply with the text, because

take too much upon yourselves, for all the congregation is holy, every one of them, and the Lord is among them. Why then do you exalt yourselves above the assembly of the Lord?"[18] Debate about the relationship between the communal holiness of the congregation and the special position of political and priestly leaders within the community unfolds in the subsequent text through the example of Aaron. An incense ritual performed by the 250 men and by Aaron is supposed to demonstrate who is holy and who is entitled to approach YHWH (v. 5*, ‫וידע יהוה את־אשר־לו ואת־‬ ‫הקדוש והקריב אליו‬). After bringing their (censer) pans before YHWH, the 250 men are consumed by fire coming out from YHWH.[19] As evidenced by the wording, the scenery has clear parallels to Lev 10:1–3, hinting at either a diachronic relationship of dependence or maybe even the same context of origin:[20]

Lev 10:1*
‫ויקחו בני־אהרן נדב ואביהוא איש מחתתו ויתנו בהן אש וישימו עליה‬
‫קטרת ויקרבו לפני יהוה‬

---

the 250 men are commanded by Moses to perform the incense ritual. From a narrative perspective, it is not a pretension of cultic competence.

18. The formulation in v. 3 combines Deuteronomistic (Deut 4:6a; 14:2a, 21) and Priestly (Exod 29:45–46) traditions in order to articulate the men's (misguided) understanding of communal holiness. For further aspects of interpretation and some remarks on the literary unity of this verse, see Pyschny, *Verhandelte Führung*, 194–98.

19. It is important to note that the death of the 250 men does not falsify or contradict the idea of communal holiness as such. Instead, it opposes an understanding of Israel's holiness which would pit the community against political and priestly leaders and intercessory figures.

20. For Lev 10:1–3, see esp. Christophe Nihan, *From Priestly Torah to Pentateuch: A Study in the Composition of the Pentateuch*, FAT 2/25 (Tübingen: Mohr Siebeck, 2007); James W. Watts, *Leviticus 1–10*, HCOT (Leuven: Peeters, 2013); Watts, *Ritual and Rhetoric in Leviticus: From Sacrifice to Scripture* (Cambridge: Cambridge University Press, 2007); Frevel, "'Und Mose hörte (es),'" 104–36; Thomas Hieke, *Levitikus*, HKAT (Freiburg: Herder Verlag, 2014); Hieke, "Priestly Leadership in the Book of Leviticus: A Hidden Agenda," in Pyschny and Schulz, *Debating Authority*, 68–88, esp. 71–72. A reevaluation of the diachronic relationship between Num 16–17* and Lev 10:1–3 can be found in Katharina Pyschny, "Incense-Burning Rituals in the Traditions of the Hebrew Bible and in the Material Culture of Israel/Palestine," in *Contact and Exchange in Incense Practices of the Southern Levant*, ed. Katharina Pyschny, Orientalische Religionen in der Antike (Tübingen: Mohr Siebeck, forthcoming).

Num 16:6–7*

קחו־לכם מחתות קרח וכל־עדתו: ותנו בהן אש ושימו עליהן קטרת לפני יהוה

Lev 10:2

ותצא אש מלפני יהוה ותאכל אותם וימתו לפני יהוה

Num 16:35

ואש יצאה מאת יהוה ותאכל את החמשים ומאתים איש מקריבי הקטרת

The evident parallels to Lev 10:1–3 and the closeness to Lev 16:12–13, the only other biblical reference attesting the combination of אש, מחתה, and קטרת, make it abundantly clear that the emphasis on incense is not purely coincidental. The scenery implies or presupposes that incense practices are conceptually linked to questions of holiness, divine presence, and priestly authority or power. The text clearly attests an attempt to restrict incense rituals to (Aaronide) priests, a strategy that is developed further in the course of the 250-men layer.

First, the following Eleazar episode (Num 17:1–5*)[21] deals with a follow-up problem resulting from the preceding events. Since the (censer) pans of the 250 men have been presented before YHWH, they are holy and must therefore remain within the holy sphere. In line with his priestly

---

21. In contrast to the dominant view among biblical scholars, which does not assign Num 17:1–5 to the 250-men stratum, I consider it an integral part of that stratum. The text includes several formulations that characterize the episode as a continuation of the 250-men layer from Num 16: (1) The (censer) pans (המחתת, Num 17:2) and the fire have a definite article (האש, Num 17:2). From a narrative point of view, they must be considered as already introduced into the narrative (Num 16:6, 17, 18; Num 16:7, 18, 35). (2) Numbers 17:2 mentions a blaze (השרפה), and v. 4 refers to those who were burned up (השרפים). Neither reference can be understood without knowledge of the incident related to the 250 men. (3) The deictic word האלה in Num 17:3 needs some kind of context, and that is provided only by Num 16. (4) There are also several lexematic connections: the word קדש in Num 17:2–3 refers to the holiness theme of Num 16:3, 5, 7 (קדוש); Num 17:3, 4, 5 take up the lexeme קרב from Num 16:5, 9, 10, 17, 35; and Num 17:5 mentions incense, which is likewise a keyword in Num 16:7, 17, 18, 35. Of course, it cannot be excluded that this episode is a very sophisticated supplement to the 250-men stratum. On the textual level, however, it is at least not *necessary* to consider Num 17:1–5 secondary. The abrupt appearance of Eleazar—the common argument—cannot bear the burden of proof alone, especially not when dealing with traditions that are already post-Priestly in nature.

duties as stated in Num 4:16, Eleazar is charged with making the pans into hammered plates as a bronze covering for the altar of burnt offerings.²² By doing so, he protects Israel (and particularly Aaron, the high priest) from impurity and thus plays a fundamental role in securing a functional cult.²³ The short etiology for the bronze altar cover links it symbolically with the legitimacy of the Aaronide priesthood. The altar cover functions as a *permanent sign* (אות, v. 3), a memorial (זכרון, v. 5), of the priestly right to access and exert responsibility for the cult. These priestly rights are specifically linked to incense rituals before YHWH and are explicitly restricted to Aaronides alone (v. 5*, למען אשר לא־יקרב איש זר אשר לא מזרע אהרן הוא להקטיר קטרת לפני יהוה).

Second, this episode is followed by another rebellion against Moses and Aaron in which the conflict increases significantly. Now, the whole congregation shows sympathy with the 250 men and joins in rebelling against Moses and Aaron. The leadership duo is blamed for "killing the people of YHWH" (Num 17:6) and accused of actively participating in the killing of the 250 men.²⁴ This rebellion by the people of Israel provokes YHWH's wrath and causes a plague to break out among the people (Num 17:13–15*). Again it is a priestly protagonist, the high priest Aaron, who resolves this highly dangerous situation by conducting an incense ritual. With his actions, Aaron successfully atones for the people and stops the plague.²⁵ This paradigmatic case not only confirms the protective function

---

22. For the identification of the altar, see Pyschny, *Verhandelte Führung*, 228 n. 19.

23. The problem of impurity seems to be implied; otherwise it would be impossible to explain why Aaron could not deal with the (censer) pans by himself. The issue of impurity is strengthened by two little additions (Num 17:2aβ, 3aα*) in the course of the redactional process.

24. It is very unlikely that the formulation refers to the conflict surrounding Dathan and Abiram. The accusation is articulated by the congregation, which played a significant role in the argumentation of the 250 men (Num 16:3). The phrase "people of YHWH" implies a closeness to the God of Israel that fits only the 250-men stratum.

25. The episode has obvious terminological, thematic, and conceptual parallels to Num 25, such as the plague and a noncultic act of atonement by a priest; see Pyschny, *Verhandelte Führung*, 246–47; Kristen M. Schäfers, "'[…] and the LORD's Anger Was Kindled against Israel' (Num 25:3)—Who's in Charge and Who's to Blame? Punishment, Intercession, and Leadership-Related Competences in Num 25," in Pyschny and Schulz, *Debating Authority*, 132–58, esp. 146–47. For the Priestly concept of atonement, see esp. Bernd Janowski, *Sühne als Heilsgeschehen: Traditions- und religionsgeschichtliche Studien zur Sühnetheologie der Priesterschrift*, 2nd ed., WMANT 55 (Neukirchen-Vluyn: Neukirchener Verlag, 2000).

of the cultic order and its priestly personnel but also presents a positive counterimage to the incense offerings brought near by the 250 men. In contrast to the rebellious men, Aaron succeeds with his incense ritual and is able to ward off YHWH's wrath and restore a salvific relationship between Israel and God by his intercessory and noncultic act of atonement.[26] The 250-men stratum thus ends on a remarkable high note, strongly emphasizing the indispensability of competent cultic personnel, generally, and the high priest in particular.

As far as the nature of the 250-men layer is concerned, it can be stated that the stratum presents a narrative that functions perfectly as an autonomous literary unit. It does not present a natural continuation of its immediately preceding context and does not explicitly refer to the wilderness period. On this basis, the 250-men stratum can be considered an independent Priestly fragment. But this fragment is not without presuppositions in terms of theme and Priestly ideology and theology. In addition, the layer includes significant parallels to other Priestly texts such as Lev 10:1–3; 16* and Num 25* and seems to be familiar with the typical elements of the Priestly murmuring stories. In both cases, the connections are far more than coincidental. Taking both aspects together, the 250-men layer is probably best described as an originally independent fragment situated in the vicinity of the Priestly traditions—a literary satellite being able to draw on Priestly traditions without yet being incorporated into the broader context of the Priestly writings.

Based on the narrative, conceptual, and linguistic profile of the 250-men layer, this tradition can hardly be considered an integral part of the Priestly source. Its sophisticated Priestly terminology and style and, in particular, its highly advanced theological concepts—such as graded holiness, theology of atonement, כבוד, priestly competence, and leadership—clearly attest to a post-Priestly character.[27] This character is also confirmed by

---

26. Incense does not have an atoning function within the cultic order of Exodus–Numbers. Aaron's intercessory incense ritual is therefore a (more or less) proactive apotropaic initiative rather than a (regular) incense *offering*, which is prescribed in an established sacrificial system.

27. For a detailed description of the concept of graded holiness in Numbers and its connection to purity and impurity, see Christian Frevel, "Purity Conceptions in the Book of Numbers in Context: Some General Remarks and Exemplary Considerations on Num 5:1–4," in *Purity and the Forming of Religious Traditions in the Ancient Mediterranean World and Ancient Judaism*, ed. Christian Frevel and Christophe Nihan, Dynamics in the History of Religions 3 (Leiden: Brill, 2012), 369–411.

its closeness to the aforementioned (rather late) Priestly texts. The 250-men stratum can therefore be most probably situated in a Persian-period context. This sociohistorical contextualization can be supported by two distinctive features of the narrative profile: its specific conflict situation and its focus on incense rituals.

The storyline of the 250-men stratum presents an inner-Israelite conflict over issues of leadership, in particular the relationship between lay and priestly leadership. From a sociohistorical perspective, this layer reflects the gradual increase in the strength of the priesthood, or at least its claim to a priestly prerogative, in ancient Israel/Palestine. In my opinion, the particular problems highlighted by the text can be plausibly situated within Israel's phase of consolidation following the collapse of the monarchy and royal cult in the sixth century BCE, hence around the beginning or the middle of the fifth century BCE. It is difficult to tell whether the stratum reflects *actual and concrete* conflicts between priests and *specific, nameable* lay leaders.[28] Still, there can be no doubt that the text reflects leadership-related processes of negotiation and implies a rather complex sociohistorical and religious-historical situation. Furthermore, the aforementioned time frame fits the text's special interest in incense.[29] There can be no doubt that incense rituals were an integral part of the Second Temple cult.[30] At the same time, there is ample extrabiblical evidence that incense practices became particularly popular during the Persian period. This holds true for both cultic and noncultic contexts, both within and outside of the province of Yehud. Incense practices were certainly not restricted to

---

28. See, e.g., Jeon, "Zadokites," esp. 396–400, who argues that the 250-men stratum reflects a Zadokite struggle for their priestly prerogative at the Jerusalem temple against the council of the elders.

29. For the incense practices which stand behind Num 16–17, with special reference to the identification of the מחתת, see Pyschny, *Verhandelte Führung*, 291–302; Pyschny, "Incense-Burning Rituals."

30. See Menahem Haran, *Temples and Temple Service in Ancient Israel: An Inquiry into Biblical Cult Phenomena and the Historical Setting of the Priestly School* (Oxford: Clarendon, 1977); Kjeld Nielsen, *Incense in Ancient Israel*, VTSup 38 (Leiden: Brill, 1986); Wolfgang Zwickel, *Räucherkult und Räuchergeräte: Exegetische und archäologische Studien zum Räucheropfer im Alten Testament*, OBO 97 (Fribourg: Academic Press; Göttingen: Vandenhoeck & Ruprecht, 1990); Paul Heger, *The Development of Incense Cult in Israel*, BZAW 245 (Berlin: de Gruyter, 1997); Melody D. Knowles, *Centrality Practiced: Jerusalem in the Religious Practice of Yehud and the Diaspora in the Persian Period*, ABS 16 (Atlanta: Society of Biblical Literature, 2006).

priests and other elites, as evidenced by the rather crude style of cuboid incense burners.[31] Furthermore, it is safe to assume that incense rituals were not limited to the YHWH cult. The increasing biblical and extrabiblical attestations of (frank)incense suggest an expansion and intensification of long-distance trade involving various aromatic substances.[32] As a result, (frank)incense and other valuable substances became available and affordable in the provinces of the Persian empire. In contrast to this wide range of actual incense practices, several biblical texts attest to the attempt to incorporate incense more strongly into the YHWH cult, as was previously the case on a textual level (Exod 30:1–10; 34:34–38). This attempt is in line with the endeavor to centralize the (legitimate) use of incense with Aaron or the high priest (Lev 10:1–3; 16). The 250-men stratum is evidently a significant part of this textual strategy. In correlation with the extrabiblical evidence, which reflects a multifaceted incense practice in the Persian period, this strategy has to be considered a rather fictive and ideological claim with obvious economic interests as a background.

The 250-men stratum thus reflects the attempt of priestly (scribal) circles at the Jerusalem temple both to enforce their leadership claims against lay elites and to increase their economic power.

2.2. The Korah-Levites Redaction: A Priestly Interlude

In the next step of the redactional process, the 250-men layer is significantly transformed by the Korah-Levites redaction: Num 16:1a, 5a

---

31. For a detailed analysis of these objects, see Christian Frevel and Katharina Pyschny, "A Religious Revolution Devours Its Children: The Iconography of the Persian Period Cuboid Incense Burners," in *Religion in the Achaemenid Persian Empire: Emerging Judaism and Trends*, ed. Diana Edelman, Anne Fitzpatrick-McKinley, and Philippe Guillaume, Orientalische Religionen in der Antike 17 (Tübingen: Mohr Siebeck, 2016), 91–133; Frevel and Pyschny, "Perserzeitliche Räucherkästchen: Zu einer wenig beachteten Fundgattung im Kontext der Thesen E. Sterns," in *A "Religious Revolution" in Yehûd? The Material Culture of the Persian Period as a Test Case*, ed. Christian Frevel, Katharina Pyschny, and Izak Cornelius, OBO 267 (Fribourg: Academic Press; Göttingen: Vandenhoeck & Ruprecht, 2014), 111–220.

32. For a reevaluation of the incense practices in the southern Levant in biblical, archaeological, and historical perspectives in light of the development of long-distance trade, see Katharina Pyschny, ed., *Contact and Exchange in Incense Practices of the Southern Levant*, Orientalische Religionen in der Antike (Tübingen: Mohr Siebeck, forthcoming).

[only אֶל־קֹרַח וְאֶל־כָּל־עֲדָתוֹ], 6 [only קֹרַח וְכָל־עֲדָתוֹ], 7b–11; 17:5bα, 14b).³³
Korah the Levite is added into the text as the prime rebel, and the 250 men are transformed into his (Levitical) congregation.³⁴ The conflict changes from the above-mentioned debate on holiness into an initiative on the part of Levitical cult officials to explicitly strive for priestly rights and responsibilities. This redactional layer is without doubt rather late. It presupposes not only the Levites' genealogy (Exod 6:16–25 and/or Num 3:14–39*) but also the concept of the Levites evident in almost the entirety of Numbers.³⁵ Numbers 16:8–11 presents the centerpiece of the Korah-Levites redaction and clearly complies with the hierarchical structure of cultic personnel developed in the book of Numbers by promoting the indispensability of *both* Aaronides and Levites for a functional cult.³⁶

---

33. For a detailed analysis of this redaction, see Pyschny, *Verhandelte Führung*, 214–21. It is important to note that not all Korah elements within Num 16–17 are considered a part of this stage. The Korah elements responsible for the combination of Priestly and non-Priestly traditions are attributed to a later phase of redaction (see below 2.4).

34. The Korah-Levites redaction invents the protagonist Korah, who up to this moment was known only in the context of genealogies in the Pentateuch and Chronicles. The insertion of Korah intensifies the situation as follows: first, it is pointed out that the leadership claims come from a highly influential Levitical group, the Kohathites; second, the resistance against the leadership duo is situated within closer familial circles, because Korah is the cousin of Moses and Aaron (Exod 6:16–26; Num 3:14–39).

35. Korah is introduced as a Levite and, more specifically, a Kohathite. This element was invented by Num 16–17*. Because Korah's genealogy is inconsistent in Chronicles, one is referred to Exod 6* or Num 3* as possible sources. Exodus 6:16–26 has a particular interest in highlighting the Aaronide and Kohathite lines within the tribe of Levi and somehow prefigures the problem constellation found in Num 16–17*. A similar, most likely secondary, appreciation of the Kohathites can be found in Num 26:58a, 58b–61; see Till Magnus Steiner, "Die Korachiten," in *Trägerkreise in den Psalmen*, ed. Frank-Lothar Hossfeld, Johannes Bremer, and Till Magnus Steiner, BBB 178 (Göttingen: Vandenhoeck & Ruprecht, 2016), 133–60; Samuel, *Von Priestern zum Patriarchen*, 187, 192.

36. See Christian Frevel, "Ending with the High Priest: The Hierarchy of Priests and Levites in the Book of Numbers," in Frevel, Pola, and Schart, *Torah and the Book of Numbers*, 139–63; Frevel, "Transformationen des Charismas: Überlegungen zum Buch Numeri vor dem Hintergrund von Max Webers Veralltäglichungstheorem," in *Glaube in Gemeinschaft: Autorität und Rezeption in der Kirche*, ed. Markus Knapp and Thomas Söding (Freiburg: Herder, 2014), 261–87; Frevel, "Leadership

Then Moses said to Korah, "Hear now, you sons of Levi: Is it a small thing to you that the God of Israel has separated you from the congregation of Israel, to bring you near to Himself, to do the work of the tabernacle of the Lord, and to stand before the congregation to serve them; and that He has brought you near to Himself, you and all your brethren, the sons of Levi, with you? And are you seeking the priesthood also? Therefore you and all your company are gathered together against the Lord. And what is Aaron that you complain against him?" (Num 16:8–11 [NKJV])

The text formulates the Levites' special position in accordance with Num 3; 8; 18 and follows a strategy of double legitimization: "Priesthood and Levitical ministry are correlated and the Levitical part cannot be withdrawn from the priestly and the other way around."[37] A similar notion of "a collateral understanding of the relationship of Levites and priests" as well as their "complementary responsibilities" can be found in Chronicles—an observation which might attest to a connection (even if rather loose) between the Korah-Levites redaction and the Korah traditions in Chronicles.[38] It could be assumed that the Korah traditions had their starting point within Chronicles and found their way into the Pentateuch in order to incorporate or strengthen Levitical leadership in the Torah. If this assumption holds true, it even strengthens the impression that the Korah-Levites redaction aims not simply to devalue the Levites with respect to the Aaronides but to highlight their cultic importance vis-à-vis the Aaronide priests.

Contextualizing this redactional layer sociohistorically is a difficult task because it depends to a great deal on the historical reconstruction of Levitical service in general and in the Second Temple period in particular. These

---

and Conflict: Modelling the Charisma of Numbers," in Pyschny and Schulz, *Debating Authority*, 89–114.

37. Frevel, "Ending," 150. While it is evident that the Korah-Levites redaction presupposes Num 3 and 8, its diachronic relation to Num 18 is more complex. A few parts of Num 18, especially vv. 1–6*, might be considered a parallel development. For the rest, Num 18 seems to consist of later Priestly additions. For a thorough analysis of the relationship among Num 3, 8, and 18, see Christian Frevel, "'… dann gehören die Leviten mir': Anmerkungen zum Zusammenhang von Num 3; 8; und 18," in *Kulte, Priester, Rituale: Beiträge zu Kult und Kultkritik im Alten Testament und Alten Orient*, ed. Stephanie Ernst and Maria Häusl, Arbeiten zu Text und Sprache im Alten Testament 89 (Saint Ottilien: EOS, 2010), 133–58.

38. Gary N. Knoppers, "Hierodules, Priests, or Janitors? The Levites in Chronicles and the History of the Israelite Priesthood," *JBL* 118 (1999): 71–72.

issues are highly complex and disputed, not least due to the lack of extrabiblical sources and the diverse character of the biblical evidence. In line with one of the most recent studies on the Levites by Mark Leuchter, however, it is safe to assume "that during the fifth through fourth centuries BCE, the Levites were in fact incorporated into the sacerdotal ranks of Jerusalem and privy to the Persian empire's intellectual trends mediated through the temple establishment."[39] This basic statement leaves us with a rather wide time frame for a potential context, which has to be concretized based on the specific profile of the Korah-Levites redaction. Recent proposals tend to situate this redactional layer either in the middle or at the end of this time span. Jaeyoung Jeon dates it to the late fifth and mid-fourth century BCE based on the impression "that the text reflects a situation in which the Levites were growing so strong that the priests felt threatened by them."[40] For Achenbach, on the other hand, the redaction presupposes a strong position or a significant religious-political power of priests and reflects their intense striving for theocracy, which is best situated in the late fourth century BCE.[41] Even though both positions make some valid arguments, they share one problematic basic assumption, namely, that the Korah-Levites redaction reflects a *conflict* between (Aaronide) priests and Levites. As was shown above, however, the textual profile of this redaction is more complicated than this. Especially Num 16:8–11, which appears to present a highly anti-Levitical attitude, is well aware and supportive of the indispensable role of the Levites in a functional cult.[42] Such a twofold perspective—a rather strong or established role of the Levites *and* a priestly need for legitimization—hints in my opinion at the sociohistorical context of the mid-to-late fifth century BCE, when an upward movement of the Levites took place at the Jerusalem temple.[43] The

---

39. Mark Leuchter, *The Levites and the Boundaries of Israelite Identity* (Oxford: Oxford University Press, 2017), 222.

40. Jeon, "Zadokites," 403.

41. Achenbach, *Vollendung*, 66–82.

42. Interestingly enough, this was already noted by Antonius H. J. Gunneweg, *Leviten und Priester: Hauptlinien der Traditionsbildung und Geschichte des israelitisch-jüdischen Kultpersonals*, FRLANT 89 (Göttingen: Vandenhoeck & Ruprecht, 1965), 181, who stated: "Sicher dürfte aber nach allem Obigen sein, daß in Num 16 kein Hinweis zu finden ist auf eine 'allmähliche Degradierung' der Leviten oder von Kämpfen und Auseinandersetzungen, unter welchen sich eine solche 'Entwicklung' vollzog."

43. See Joachim Schaper, *Priester und Leviten im achämenidischen Juda: Studien zur Kult- und Sozialgeschichte Israels in persischer Zeit*, FAT 1/31 (Tübingen: Mohr Siebeck, 2000).

Korah-Levites redaction, which clearly originated within priestly (scribal) circles at the temple, witnesses to the priestly attempt to legitimize an inclusive cultic order in which (Aaronide) priests and Levites are understood as complementary.

2.3. The Ordeal of the Rods: An Origin Legend for the High-Priestly Office

The consolidation of Levites and Aaronides already alluded to in the Korah-Levites redaction is made explicit in the next step of the redactional process, when Num 17:16–28 is integrated into Num 16–17.[44] The motif of election is now embedded into the incense ritual (Num 16:5b, 7aβ). As a consequence, the election of Aaron as a representative of the house of Levi (לבית לוי, v. 23) is constituted as the ordeal's actual focus and aim. Even though the text does not mention the title of the high priest, the whole episode—which can be considered a literary unit—reads as an origin legend for the high-priestly office. It starts with YHWH announcing an ordeal and instructing Moses to take a rod from all the leaders of the tribes and write upon it each of their names. As it is stated later on in verse 20, this divine ordeal aims at electing a leader from the community in order to stop the children of Israel complaining against Moses and Aaron. Interestingly enough, the names of the leaders in question are not specified at all, with one very telling exception: Aaron is specifically declared the head of the Levites. After the rods have been placed in the tabernacle before the testimony (לפני העדות), the storyline culminates in Aaron's rod sprouting, putting forth buds, producing blossoms, and yielding ripe almonds (v. 23). All rods are presented publicly to Israel, and each leader takes back his rod. Again, there is one significant exception: Aaron's rod is put back before the testimony, to be kept as a permanent sign, a warning against rebellion (v. 25) and thus against all kinds of questioning of Aaron, the high priest.

Clearly, the scenery deals symbolically with the question of who may approach YHWH and on whom divine holiness and nearness have a positive and beneficial effect. The episode's answer is plain and simple: only Aaron and the tribe of Levi can benefit from being in YHWH's immediate proximity. Aaron's rod, placed permanently within the tabernacle, not

---

44. For the following, see Pyschny, *Verhandelte Führung*, 253–64.

only represents the sanctity of priestly leadership but also the legitimacy of the cultic order instructed at Sinai, including the complementary relationship between (Aaronide) priest and Levite. The necessity of this kind of personnel is further established in verses 27–28, an integral part of the episode, which presents Israel's reaction to the public presentation of the rods and the divine election. By realizing that the tribes perish when they come too close to the divine presence, Israel finally acknowledges specific taboos and regulations within the cultic sphere. The final question in verse 28—"Shall we all utterly die?"—does not reflect impenitence or lack of understanding but is a rhetorical question to which Num 16–17* provides the answer. Israel is endangered by YHWH's presence but at the same time protected from it by the cultic order installed and legitimized by YHWH at Sinai. Aaronides *and* Levites constitute a much-needed buffer in order to prevent Israel from the dangers of coming into the immediate proximity of God. It is only with the existence and the service of (Aaronide) priests and Levites that Israel is enabled to permanently live in the divine presence of YHWH.

Based on linguistic phenomena such as אהל העדת and conceptual presuppositions such as Israel's social order in the book of Numbers, the episode is late and definitely post-P. It has a distinctly autonomous character and is connected to the Priestly material at hand via the election integrated into Num 16:5 and the murmuring motif. Thus it seems plausible that Num 17:16–28 was created for its current context.

Two characteristics of the narrative profile are crucial for identifying a sociohistorical context, the first being an interest in legitimating Aaron as high priest with both cultic and political authority, and the second a clear emphasis on the interconnection between (Aaronide) priest and Levite.[45] Both aspects suggest that the episode fits well into the sociohistorical context of the fourth century BCE, when the history of priests and Levites entered a stable phase of consolidation.[46] In regard to the cultic

---

45. The political dimension of Aaron's leadership is apparent due to the rod ordeal, which aims at the election of a leader representing Israel as a whole. In this context, it is particularly noteworthy that the episode lacks the term עדה, which is attested in almost all other strata: see the 250-men layer, the Korah-Levites redaction, and the Dathan-Abiram stratum; see the table in Pyschny, *Verhandelte Führung*, 94–95. This supports the impression that Israel is presented not as a cultic assembly or community but as a sociopolitical entity.

46. Schaper, *Priester*.

order, Num 17:16–28 could reflect a method of organizing the cult, which was in the process of being established or had already been stabilized. Its relationship to the formation of a high-priestly office is more complicated, though. Even though the historical reconstruction of the high priesthood in pre-Hellenistic times is a highly complex and disputed issue, there is a quasi-consensus in recent scholarship that the high priest played a significant role within the Jerusalemite Judean community in the fifth century BCE.[47] It is highly disputed, though, whether, when, and to what extend the high priest had not only religious but also political authority and power. Recent proposals include negating any kind of political influence of the high priest, assuming a growing political power that is restricted by the governor alone, or imagining an enormous sociopolitical power that included cultic, political, and even military competences.[48] For the fifth century BCE, there is almost no positive evidence attesting to a high-priestly office that is growing in political power at the expense of the governor. By the end of the Persian period, though, the high priest of Jerusalem clearly obtained minting authority, as attested by a Yehud coin bearing a paleo-Hebrew inscription *ywḥnn hkwhn* ("Johanan, the priest") and dating to the transition between the Persian and Hellenistic periods. At this point, "one could say that the temple was undertaking an administrative role," and, in a Persian-period context, the involvement in administration is directly linked to political authority and power.[49] Yet the political power of the high priest was by no means exclusive. The so-called Hezekiah coins dating to the fourth century BCE prove that the minting authority was not restricted to the Jerusalem temple. The coexistence of

---

47. Achenbach, *Vollendung*, 133; Deborah W. Rooke, *Zadok's Heirs: The Role and Development of the High Priesthood in Ancient Israel* (Oxford: Clarendon, 2000), 125–74; Schaper, *Priester*, 221–45; Lisbeth S. Fried, *The Priest and the Great King: Temple-Palace Relations in the Persian Empire*, BJS 10 (Winona Lake, IN: Eisenbrauns, 2004), 8–107; and Jeremiah W. Cataldo, *A Theocratic Yehud? Issues of Government in a Persian Province*, LHBOTS 498 (New York: T&T Clark, 2009), 33–117.

48. For the first proposal, see Rooke, *Zadok's Heirs*, 125–239. For the second, see Achenbach, *Vollendung*, 133. For the third, see James C. Vanderkam, *From Joshua to Caiaphas: High Priests after the Exile* (Minneapolis: Fortress; Assen: Van Gorcum, 2004), 84.

49. Peter R. Bedford, "Temple Funding and Priestly Authority in Achaemenid Judah," in *Exile and Return: The Babylonian Context*, ed. Jonathan Stökl and Caroline Waerzeggers, BZAW 478 (Berlin: de Gruyter, 2015), 341.

political and priestly minting authority hints at a rather close political and economic relationship between temple aristocracy and government.[50]

When correlating this evidence with the analysis of Num 17:16–28, it can be concluded that this episode does not present an origin legend for an actually existing high-priestly office. It has a certain timely proximity to the gradual formation and institutionalization of the high priesthood, but it does not present a later (literary) legitimation of an already established office with political and religious authority and power. It reflects instead a fictional priestly claim for leadership, which, in fact, prevailed in later times.

2.4. The Dathan-Abiram Layer and the Final Composition of Numbers 16–17

The final step of the redactional process integrates Dathan and Abiram, as well as the Reubenites, into Num 16:1–2 and supplements the text with the non-Priestly Dathan-Abiram narrative: Num 16:12–15, 23, 24 (without קרח), 25–26, 27 (without קרח), 28–31, 32 (without 32bα), 33 (without 33bβ), 34.[51] At this point, the Priestly and non-Priestly material is combined and the remaining Korah-Levites elements are integrated. The latter tie Korah together with Dathan and Abiram (Num 16:1b, 24b [only קרח], 27a [only קרח], 32bα) and include the political conflict in the present text (Num 16:16–17, 19–22). By inserting the Dathan-Abiram plot, Num 16–17 gains a completely new level of conflict. The initial question—how does the communal holiness of Israel relate to the special position of individual leaders?—has been addressed so far only using the example of Aaron's special role as (high) priest, but it is now debated with reference to Mosaic authority and leadership.

The Dathan-Abiram layer unfolds as follows: When Moses calls for the Reubenites, Dathan, and Abiram, the latter refuse his call and accuse him of inappropriate leadership ambitions instead (Num 16:12–14). Their rebellious speech, framed by the repetition of "We will not come up" (לא נעלה), culminates in a drastic rejection of the promised land: "*Is it* a small thing that you have brought us up out of a land flowing with milk and honey, to kill us in the wilderness, that you should keep acting like a prince over us? Moreover, you have not brought us into a

---

50. See Christian Frevel, *Geschichte Israels*, Kohlhammer Studienbücher Theologie 1.2 (Stuttgart: Kohlhammer, 2015), 296–97.

51. For a detailed analysis of this layer, see Pyschny, *Verhandelte Führung*, 144–86.

land flowing with milk and honey, nor given us inheritance of fields and vineyards" (vv. 13–14*). After reacting with anger, Moses asks YHWH to ignore their offering (v. 15a) and maintains his innocence (v. 15b). YHWH immediately takes action and asks Moses to command the congregation to move away from the rebels' tents. Followed by the elders, Moses goes to the tents of Dathan and Abiram, where the congregation follows Moses's order and leaves the immediate area but remains within sight and earshot (vv. 26–27a). When Dathan and Abiram stand with their families at the doors of their tents, Moses announces a divine ordeal that aims at illustrating his role as the messenger of God (Num 16:28–30). In line with Moses's announcement, the earth splits apart under the rebels and their families and swallows them up with all their belongings, so that they go down alive into Sheol (Num 16:31–33*). The stratum thus ends with Moses characterized as a true YHWH prophet and legitimized with regard to his authority and leadership.

In contrast to the 250-men layer, the Dathan-Abiram stratum has quite a strong connection to the wilderness period and the land theme. It is furthermore linked to Num 13–14 by the keyword עלה. Yet this stratum can hardly be considered a natural continuation of the spy story whatever its form. Instead, it presents an originally independent non-Priestly fragment that draws on several traditions at hand.

Almost exclusively characterized as a political conflict, too little attention has been drawn to the fact that the Dathan-Abiram layer has some interesting cultic implications that might turn out to be quite fruitful for understanding its sociohistorical context. First, it is noteworthy that the verb עלה, which is used in the phrase לא נעלה at the beginning and the end of the rebellious speech by Dathan and Abiram, has a wide semantic range.[52] In its present context, the formulation could relate to an appearance in front of a superior (Gen 46:31; see also Hos 8:9), a summons (Deut 17:8; 25:7; Judg 4:5; Jer 26:10), or a pilgrimage. In the context of the wilderness narratives, עלה is first and foremost linked to the occupation of the promised land as evidenced by texts such as Exod 3:8, 17; 17:3; Num 13:17, 21–22, 30, 31; 14:40, 42, 44. In fact, there can be no doubt that the formulation alludes to the land theme and expresses a radical rejection of the promised land. Considering that עלה can also denote an encounter with God or, more precisely, the way up to a sanctuary, another semantic

---

52. For the following, see also Hans F. Fuhs, "עלה," *TDOT* 11:76–95.

nuance becomes evident. The phrase could also mean, or at least include, the refusal to go up to the sanctuary or the tent of meeting. Combining both semantic nuances, one cannot escape the impression that the formulation not only rejects the promised land but, as a consequence, also denotes the refusal to go up to the (central) sanctuary within the land.

This interpretation goes in line with the following rebuke by Moses in Num 16:15, which also mentions a cultic aspect, namely, the offerings of the two rebels. This is the second relevant consideration. The rather unexpected mention of an offering, which does not play any role in the subsequent text, has always puzzled biblical scholars, but it fits quite well to the mentioned understanding of לא נעלה. Independent from the exact understanding of מנחה—either as a general term for offerings or as the specific cereal offering known from the Priestly writings—and even though there is no further mention of an offering given by Dathan and Abiram, the narrative logic clearly implies that the two Reubenites regularly make offerings and that their offerings are being rejected. This rejection is grounded in their refusal to go up to the land and the (central) sanctuary. Interestingly enough, the critique seems to be directed not against the lay status of Dathan and Abiram but against offerings outside the land and away from the central sanctuary.

Third, the conceptualization of the tents of Dathan and Abiram supports the view that the conflict has a cultic connotation. Within the narrative logic of the stratum, the rebel tents present a negative counterimage to the tent of meeting. After Dathan and Abiram refuse to go up to the actual tent of meeting, the scene is situated at the entrance and in front of the tents of the wrongdoers. Their tents are surrounded by the congregation, they bear responsibility for putting Israel in danger due to the nature of sin as a contact phenomenon (Num 16:27), and they are places of a divine ordeal. The structural analogies to the tent of meeting are apparent. Following this line of argumentation, the total and permanent destruction of the tents of Dathan and Abiram, which involves not only the two protagonists but also their families and all their goods, turns out to be a very strong plea against presenting offerings outside the land and away from the central sanctuary.

On the basis of these three considerations, the problem of the Dathan-Abiram layer clearly reflects a sociohistorical situation characterized by a regionally differentiated Judaism and the resulting debates over legitimate cult practices in the diaspora(s). This kind of religious-historical circumstance fits the late Persian period, around the beginning or the middle of the fourth century BCE, as famously evident in the Aramaic papyri from Elephantine, a Judean colony in Egypt, as well as other piece of evidence. The correspondence between the leaders of the community and the governor of Yehud, Bagohi, following the destruction of the Yahô-temple by the priests of Khnum (*TAD* A.4.7:25–26; *TAD* A.4.8:23–25) witnesses to negotiations about the question of what kind of offerings are legitimate outside of Samaria and Yehud. Interestingly enough, the joint response by the governors of Yehud and Samaria (see the memorandum in *TAD* A.4.9:9) explicitly mentions that the altar can be used for cereal offerings and frankincense but does not make any reference to burnt offerings (*TAD* A.4.9:9).[53] Cereal offerings and frankincense were obviously considered legitimate offerings by the governors of Yehud and Samaria, but the same did not hold true for animal sacrifices.

A rather similar discourse is attested in the biblical texts. After the Reubenites and Gadites ask for and are granted inheritance in Transjordan in Num 32, this situation gives rise to conflict over legitimate cultic practices in Transjordan, evident in Josh 22. Not only are the analogies to the Elephantine correspondence apparent, but it is also striking that both texts are connected to the Dathan-Abiram layer by the Reubenites theme. The Dathan-Abiram layer may aim (also) at subtly preparing and negatively evaluating the forthcoming events in Num 32 and Josh 22. Yet the Reubenite origins of Dathan and Abiram presuppose the system of twelve tribes divided into nine and one half/two and one half—an observation that also supports a late Persian period contextualization. As argued by Olivier Artus, this scheme is linked to conflicts between center and periphery during this time: "it appears to be a later one, and deals with another reality of Judaism in the late Persian period: it is no longer a question of the diversity of the origins of the members of the community.... It illustrates the geographical diversity of Judaism in this late Persian period, outside the limits of Samaria and Judea."[54] Following this line of

---

53. See also the petition sent to the satrap Arsames (*TAD* A.4.10), which attests the same outcome for the legitimate offerings. All references to the papyri from Elephantine are based on Bezalel Porten and Ada Yardeni, *Letters, Newly Copied, Edited and Translated into Hebrew and English*, vol. 1 of *Textbook of Aramaic Documents from Ancient Egypt* (Winona Lake, IN: Eisenbrauns, 1986).

54. Olivier Artus, "Numbers 32: The Problem of the Two and a Half Transjordanian Tribes and the Final Composition of the Book of Numbers," in Frevel, Pola, Schart, *Torah and the Book of Numbers*, 380.

argument, Dathan and Abiram could represent groups outside of Yehud (and Samaria) who deny the priestly authority of those officiating at the Jerusalem temple or the one at Gerizim ("We will not come up!"). Their cultic and sacrificial practices are strongly rebuked ("Do not respect their offering!") as illegitimate according to Mosaic authority. It is difficult to tell why this literary rebuke goes far beyond the religious-historical situation attested in the Elephantine papyri and reflected in Josh 22. It may reflect a subtle attempt by the Jerusalemite priesthood to expand the claim on sacrifices. This assumption seems plausible, considering that the מנחה described in the Priestly writing is often linked to frankincense. Control over the מנחה thus equals control over frankincense and involves without doubt significant economic benefits.

Be that as it may, when these considerations are taken together, the Dathan-Abiram layer can be situated in the sociohistorical context of the late Persian period. It becomes evident that even the non-Priestly tradition within Num 16–17 has a (rather hidden) Priestly agenda, which seeks to strengthen the priestly authority and leadership of those associated with the Jerusalem temple. This does not necessarily mean that the Dathan-Abiram originated within priestly (scribal) circles, but it definitely explains why this tradition was integrated into Num 16–17 and the broader context of the wilderness period.

2.5. Interim Conclusions

In conclusion, it can be stated that Num 16–17 as a whole is a literary product of the (late) Persian period (mid-fifth to late fourth centuries BCE). It originated within priestly (scribal) groups situated at the Jerusalem temple and reflects very complex and multifaceted sociohistorical processes of negotiation and formation linked to priestly authority, leadership, and power. It ties together and interrelates cultic and political leadership: cult (Aaron) and Torah (Moses) are correlated and leadership claims derived therefrom are legitimized. But, in the end, the agenda of Num 16–17 is a thoroughly Priestly one: while the Priestly traditions legitimize priestly leadership from a rather inward-looking perspective, the non-Priestly tradition protects priestly leadership claims on a transregional level.

Even though the (extrabiblical) evidence remains problematic, it seems safe to assume that Num 16–17 does not presuppose an established theocracy or hierocracy in terms of political authority and power. Instead, it reflects a *plea* for theocratic or hierocratic leadership structures, which are growing in strength toward the end of the Persian period. This priestly plea is ideologically charged and reflects a claim to leadership which, in its totality and universality, was never implemented during Persian times but will prevail in later times.

3. Implications for the Reconstruction of the Literary History of the Pentateuch

Even though one should not overestimate the results provided by the analysis of a single text, the analysis of Num 16–17 might give new impetus to the core problems of pentateuchal research discussed at the beginning of this essay. Needless to say, these implications are rather limited in their purview and tentative in nature. They must be evaluated in light of additional textual analyses.

First, as far as *dissent with regard to the basic explanatory models for the literary growth of the Pentateuch* is concerned, I have opted for a fragmentary hypothesis, even though not in its pure form or in the strictest sense of the word. Both Priestly and non-Priestly traditions have been characterized as originally independent fragments. Yet these fragments are not without presuppositions in regard to style, content, theme, or concept. They do have similarities and even connections to other texts, but they can neither be converted into a linear diachronic development nor be understood as a (natural) narrative continuation of the text in question. Instead, Num 16–17 turned out to be a distinct *Überlieferungsblock*, in a sense a satellite. The starting point for the literary growth of this satellite is a Priestly tradition, which itself undergoes further supplementation before being combined with the non-Priestly material and inserted into the larger context of the wilderness period. This idea does not accord completely with the understanding of editorial techniques established in recent pentateuchal criticism. Older traditions are often referred to as fragments, while a late tradition is automatically characterized as a *Fortschreibung* of a present text whatever its form. In contrast to that, I have argued that we should consider the possible existence of fragments or independent text clusters in the later stages of the Pentateuch's formation as well. Such a consideration has certainly its own methodological problems and challenges, and it does not reduce the complexity of pentateuchal debates. As far as Num 16–17 is concerned, however, it provides the best explanation for the literary character of both the 250-men layer and the Dathan-Abiram stratum which oscillate between literary independence and context dependence.

Thus the current position of Num 16–17(18) might be determined far more by compositional considerations than previously assumed.

Second, when it comes to the *nature and date of the non-Priestly* material, the present analysis also disengaged from recent scholarly consensuses. The Dathan-Abiram stratum is understood neither as part of a source or a larger narrative thread nor as the post-Priestly *Fortschreibung* of a present text whatever its form. Furthermore, I argued that the non-Priestly material does not stand at the beginning of the redactional process of Num 16–17 but was integrated into the text as the final step of its composition. The stratum was considered of post-Priestly origin, confirming the recent trend in pentateuchal research that non-Priestly materials cannot automatically be characterized as pre-Priestly. While my analysis does not necessarily falsify the hypothesis of a pre-Priestly hexateuchal thread, it does show that this assumption cannot be proven on the basis of Num 16–17 (alone). It cannot be excluded that the cultic or Priestly implications mentioned in the analysis have been added during the course of the redactional process. Ultimately, the course is set in the context of literary criticism (e.g., Num 16:15). Be that as it may, it is remarkable that the Dathan-Abiram stratum indicates a larger narrative context (note, e.g., the conceptual parallels to Eldad and Medad in Num 11, the exodus theme, the wilderness situation, refusal of the land), a phenomenon that must be accounted for in a reconstruction of its literary growth and compositional history. The links between the Dathan-Abiram stratum and Num 11; 13–14 argue against a fragmentary hypothesis in its pure form. If one agrees with the existence of pre-Priestly material in Num 11; 13–14, then the Dathan-Abiram layer remains a candidate for a pre-Priestly hexateuchal thread. This notion is determined not only by the given systematic frame but also by the degree of coherence to be expected from a narrative thread. In my opinion, it is not the question of narrative junctions that poses a crux for the assumption of a narrative thread but the series of quite unconnected murmuring stories. This problem also arises if one follows a supplementary model, insofar one still has to explain why these narratives were not more clearly interconnected in the course of the redactional process. So the question of a pre-Priestly hexateuchal narrative thread remains open. But my analysis confirmed once more that the murmuring stories within Numbers present a decisive complex of texts that is still not adequately evaluated in terms of pentateuchal models and might require thorough consideration of new basic models and editorial techniques.

Third, also in regard to the *nature and literary growth of* the *Priestly material*, I have developed some ideas here that might give new impetus to recent pentateuchal scholarship. In contrast to the quasi-consensus of former and current research, the 250-men layer was identified as the oldest stratum of Num 16–17 and the starting point of its literary genesis. Based on linguistic phenomena and conceptual similarities or analogies to other late Priestly texts, this stratum was considered post-Priestly. Furthermore, it was argued that this layer is neither a secondary addition to an independent Priestly source nor a supplement to a present text whatever its form. Instead, the 250-men layer was characterized as a Priestly fragment that was originally autonomous as a written text but not necessarily as far as the tradition history is concerned. This Priestly text was first supplemented as a separate textual block with other Priestly material. This inner-Priestly process of supplementation includes the Levitization of the 250-men layer by the Korah-Levites redaction, which presupposes the Levites' concepts from Num 3 and 8 and complies with the cultic order of the book of Numbers. This phenomenon shows how Priestly legislation is taken up and transformed or incorporated into a narrative. As evidenced by Num 18*, however, this procedure initiates the production of further legislative materials. And as shown by Num 17:16–28, the Priestly supplementations also include texts that have been created for the present context. All these observations and insights—the independent literary growth of Priestly texts, their creative and productive approach to existing (rather late) Priestly traditions, and the different editorial techniques—are still not adequately dealt with or completely resolved in current pentateuchal models. The idea of Priestly fragments may help dissolve the plurality and complexity of Priestly redactional process—for instance, in the case of the narrative-legislative text clusters in the book of Numbers (Num 11–15; 16–18; 20–25)—from a successive development into a simultaneous one.

Fourth and last, the significance of Num 16–17 for the *formation of the Pentateuch as Torah* has been confirmed, given its status as a product of the (late) Persian period, every single stratum of which, as well as the redactional process as a whole, is connected to complex and manifold processes of negotiation, formation, and institutionalization within the history of early Judaism(s). Numbers 16–17 witnesses to the fact that postexilic hope of restoration focused or relied no longer on royal but on priestly authority and leadership. The redaction history of these chapters shows how theocratic—or, rather, hierocratic—claims of leadership gradually won out and were successively embedded into the text. The processes of legitimization are directed at priestly prerogatives in general and the institutionalization of the high-priestly office in particular. It became evident that the development of the high priesthood can be traced not only on a literary-narrative level but also with regard to the composition history of the Pentateuch. With the concept of a high priest who exerts religious and political power, Num 16–17 preordains an office and specific leadership claims that prevail in early Hellenistic times. I have described the overall agenda of the final composition of Num 16–17 as Priestly through and through, supporting the conclusion that this narrative has to be situated within priestly (scribal) groups at the Jerusalem temple.

Bibliography

Achenbach, Reinhard. *Die Vollendung der Tora: Studien zur Redaktionsgeschichte des Numeribuches im Kontext von Hexateuch und Pentateuch*. BZABR 3. Wiesbaden: Harrasowitz, 2003.

———. "Satrapie, Medinah und lokale Hierokratie: Zum Einfluss der Statthalter der Achämenidenzeit auf Tempelwirtschaft und Tempelordnungen." *ZABR* 16 (2010): 105–44.

Artus, Olivier. *Études sur le livre des Nombres: Récit, histoire et loi en Nb 13,1–20,13*. OBO 157. Fribourg: Academic Press; Göttingen: Vandenhoeck & Ruprecht, 1997.

———. "Numbers 32: The Problem of the Two and a Half Transjordanian Tribes and the Final Composition of the Book of Numbers." Pages 367–82 in *Torah and the Book of Numbers*. Edited by Christian Frevel, Thomas Pola, and Aaron Schart. FAT 2/62. Tübingen: Mohr Siebeck, 2013.

Bedford, Peter R. "Temple Funding and Priestly Authority in Achaemenid Judah." Pages 336–51 in *Exile and Return: The Babylonian Context*. Edited by Jonathan Stökl and Caroline Waerzeggers. BZAW 478. Berlin: de Gruyter, 2015.

Berner, Christoph. "Vom Aufstand Datans und Abirams zum Aufbegehren der 250 Männer: Eine redaktionsgeschichtliche Studie zu den Anfängen der literarischen Genese von Num 16–17." *BN* 150 (2011): 9–33

———. "Wie Laien zu Leviten wurden: Zum Ort der Korachbearbeitung innerhalb der Redaktionsgeschichte von Num 16–17." *BN* 152 (2012): 3–28.

Cataldo, Jeremiah W. *A Theocratic Yehud? Issues of Government in a Persian Province*. LHBOTS 498. New York: T&T Clark, 2009.

Frevel, Christian. "The Book of Numbers—Formation, Composition, and Interpretation of a Late Part of the Torah: Some Introductory Remarks." Pages 1–37 in *Torah and the Book of Numbers*. Edited by Christian Frevel, Thomas Pola, and Aaron Schart. FAT 2/62. Tübingen: Mohr Siebeck, 2013.

———. "'… dann gehören die Leviten mir': Anmerkungen zum Zusammenhang von Num 3; 8; und 18." Pages 133–58 in *Kulte, Priester, Rituale: Beiträge zu Kult und Kultkritik im Alten Testament und Alten Orient*. Edited by Stephanie Ernst and Maria Häusl. Arbeiten zu Text und Sprache im Alten Testament 89. Saint Ottilien: EOS, 2010.

———. "Ending with the High Priest: The Hierarchy of Priests and Levites in the Book of Numbers." Pages 139–63 in *Torah and the Book of Numbers*. Edited by Christian Frevel, Thomas Pola, and Aaron Schart. FAT 2/62. Tübingen: Mohr Siebeck, 2013.

———. *Geschichte Israels*. Kohlhammer Studienbücher Theologie 1.2. Stuttgart: Kohlhammer, 2015.

———. "Leadership and Conflict: Modelling the Charisma of Numbers." Pages 89–114 in *Debating Authority: Concepts of Leadership in the Pentateuch and the Former Prophets*. Edited by Katharina Pyschny and Sarah Schulz. BZAW 507. Berlin: de Gruyter, 2018.

———. "Purity Conceptions in the Book of Numbers in Context: Some General Remarks and Exemplary Considerations on Num 5:1–4." Pages 369–411 in *Purity and the Forming of Religious Traditions in the Ancient Mediterranean World and Ancient Judaism*. Edited by Christian Frevel and Christophe Nihan. Dynamics in the History of Religions 3. Leiden: Brill, 2012.

———. "Transformationen des Charismas: Überlegungen zum Buch Numeri vor dem Hintergrund von Max Webers Veralltäglichungstheorem." Pages 261–87 in *Glaube in Gemeinschaft: Autorität und Rezeption in der Kirche*. Edited by Markus Knapp and Thomas Söding. Freiburg: Herder, 2014.

———. "'Und Mose hörte (es), und es war gut in seinen Augen' (Lev 10,20): Zum Verhältnis von Literargeschichte, Theologiegeschichte und innerbiblischer Auslegung am Beispiel von Lev 10." Pages 104–36 in *Gottes Name(n): Zum Gedenken an Erich Zenger*. Edited by Ludger Schwienhorst-Schönberger, Ruth Scoralick, and Ilse Müllner. HBS 71. Freiburg: Herder, 2012.

Frevel, Christian, and Katharina Pyschny. "Perserzeitliche Räucherkästchen: Zu einer wenig beachteten Fundgattung im Kontext der These E.

Sterns." Pages 111–220 in *A "Religious Revolution" in Yehûd? The Material Culture of the Persian Period as a Test Case.* Edited by Christian Frevel, Katharina Pyschny, and Izak Cornelius. OBO 267. Fribourg: Academic Press; Göttingen: Vandenhoeck & Ruprecht, 2014.

———. "A Religious Revolution Devours Its Children: The Iconography of the Persian Period Cuboid Incense Burners." Pages 91–133 in *Religion in the Achaemenid Persian Empire: Emerging Judaism and Trends.* Edited by Diana Edelman, Anne Fitzpatrick-McKinley, and Philippe Guillaume. Orientalische Religionen in der Antike 17. Tübingen: Mohr Siebeck, 2016.

Fried, Lisbeth S. *The Priest and the Great King: Temple-Palace Relations in the Persian Empire.* BJS 10. Winona Lake, IN: Eisenbrauns, 2004.

Fuhs, Hans F. "עלה." *TDOT* 11:76–95.

Gunneweg, Antonius H. J. *Leviten und Priester: Hauptlinien der Traditionsbildung und Geschichte des israelitisch-jüdischen Kultpersonals.* FRLANT 89. Göttingen: Vandenhoeck & Ruprecht, 1965.

Haran, Menahem. *Temples and Temple Service in Ancient Israel: An Inquiry into Biblical Cult Phenomena and the Historical Setting of the Priestly School.* Oxford: Clarendon, 1977.

Heger, Paul. *The Development of Incense Cult in Israel.* BZAW 245. Berlin: de Gruyter, 1997.

Hieke, Thomas. *Levitikus.* HKAT. Freiburg: Herder Verlag, 2014.

———. "Priestly Leadership in the Book of Leviticus: A Hidden Agenda." Pages 68–88 in *Debating Authority: Concepts of Leadership in the Pentateuch and the Former Prophets.* Edited by Katharina Pyschny and Sarah Schulz. BZAW 507. Berlin: de Gruyter, 2018.

Janowski, Bernd. *Sühne als Heilsgeschehen: Traditions- und religionsgeschichtliche Studien zur Sühnetheologie der Priesterschrift.* 2nd ed. WMANT 55. Neukirchen-Vluyn: Neukirchener Verlag, 2000.

Jeon, Jaeyoung. "The Zadokites in the Wilderness: The Rebellion of Korach (Num 16) and the Zadokite Redaction." *ZAW* 127 (2015): 381–411.

Jonker, Louis. "Within Hearing Distance? Recent Developments in Pentateuch and Chronicles Research." *OTE* 27 (2014): 123–46.

Knoppers, Gary N. "Hierodules, Priests, or Janitors? The Levites in Chronicles and the History of the Israelite Priesthood." *JBL* 118 (1999): 71–72.

Knowles, Melody D. *Centrality Practiced: Jerusalem in the Religious Practice of Yehud and the Diaspora in the Persian Period.* ABS 16. Atlanta: Society of Biblical Literature, 2006.

Kratz, Reinhard G. "The Analysis of the Pentateuch: An Attempt to Overcome Barriers of Thinking." *ZAW* 128 (2016): 529–61.

Leuchter, Mark. *The Levites and the Boundaries of Israelite Identity*. Oxford: Oxford University Press, 2017.

Nielsen, Kjeld. *Incense in Ancient Israel*. VTSup 38. Leiden: Brill, 1986.

Nihan, Christophe. *From Priestly Torah to Pentateuch: A Study in the Composition of the Pentateuch*. FAT 2/25. Tübingen: Mohr Siebeck, 2007.

Porten, Bezalel, and Ada Yardeni. *Letters, Newly Copied, Edited and Translated into Hebrew and English*. Vol. 1 of *Textbook of Aramaic Documents from Ancient Egypt*. Winona Lake, IN: Eisenbrauns, 1986.

Pyschny, Katharina, ed. *Contact and Exchange in Incense Practices of the Southern Levant*. Orientalische Religionen in der Antike. Tübingen: Mohr Siebeck, forthcoming.

———. "Debated Leadership: Conflicts of Authority and Leadership in Num 16–17." Pages 115–31 in *Debating Authority: Concepts of Leadership in the Pentateuch and the Former Prophets*. Edited by Katharina Pyschny and Sarah Schulz. BZAW 507. Berlin: de Gruyter, 2018.

———. "Incense-Burning Rituals in the Traditions of the Hebrew Bible and in the Material Culture of Israel/Palestine." In *Contact and Exchange in Incense Practices of the Southern Levant*. Edited by Katharina Pyschny. Orientalische Religionen in der Antike. Tübingen: Mohr Siebeck, forthcoming.

———. *Verhandelte Führung: Eine Analyse von Num 16–17 im Kontext der neueren Pentateuchforschung*. HBS 88. Freiburg: Herder, 2017.

Rooke, Deborah W. *Zadok's Heirs: The Role and Development of the High Priesthood in Ancient Israel*. Oxford: Clarendon, 2000.

Samuel, Harald. *Von Priestern zum Patriarchen: Redaktions- und traditionsgeschichtliche Studien zu Levi und den Leviten in der Literatur des Zweiten Tempels*. BZAW 448. Berlin: de Gruyter, 2014.

Schäfers, Kristen M. "'[…] and the LORD's Anger Was Kindled against Israel' (Num 25:3)—Who's in Charge and Who's to Blame? Punishment, Intercession, and Leadership-Related Competences in Num 25." Pages 132–58 in *Debating Authority: Concepts of Leadership in the Pentateuch and the Former Prophets*. Edited by Katharina Pyschny and Sarah Schulz. BZAW 507. Berlin: de Gruyter, 2018.

Schaper, Joachim. *Priester und Leviten im achämenidischen Juda: Studien zur Kult- und Sozialgeschichte Israels in persischer Zeit*. FAT 1/31. Tübingen: Mohr Siebeck, 2000.

Schart, Aaron. *Mose und Israel im Konflikt: Eine redaktionsgeschichtliche Studie zu den Wüstenerzählungen.* OBO 98. Fribourg: Academic Press; Göttingen: Vandenhoeck & Ruprecht, 1990.

Schmid, Konrad. "Der Pentateuch und seine Theologiegeschichte." *ZTK* 111 (2014): 239–70.

Schmidt, Ludwig. *Studien zur Priesterschrift.* BZAW 214. Berlin: de Gruyter, 1993.

Schmitt, Hans-Christoph. "Die Suche nach der Identität des Jahweglaubens im nachexilischen Israel: Bemerkungen zur theologischen Intention der Endredaktion des Pentateuch." Pages 259–78 in *Pluralismus und Identität.* Edited by Joachim Mehlhausen. Gütersloh: Kaiser, 1995.

Schorn, Urike. *Ruben und das System der zwölf Stämme Israels: Redaktionsgeschichtliche Untersuchungen zur Bedeutung des Erstgeborenen Jakobs.* BZAW 248. Berlin: de Gruyter, 1997.

———. "Rubeniten als exemplarische Aufrührer in Num. 16f/Deut. 11." Pages 251–68 in *Rethinking the Foundations: Historiography in the Ancient World and in the Bible.* Edited by Steven L. McKenzie and Thomas Römer. BZAW 294. Berlin: de Gruyter, 2000.

Steiner, Till Magnus. "Die Korachiten." Pages 133–60 in *Trägerkreise in den Psalmen.* Edited by Frank-Lothar Hossfeld, Johannes Bremer, and Till Magnus Steiner. BBB 178. Göttingen: Vandenhoeck & Ruprecht, 2016.

Vanderkam, James C. *From Joshua to Caiaphas: High Priests after the Exile.* Minneapolis: Fortress; Assen: Van Gorcum, 2004.

Watts, James W. *Leviticus 1–10.* HCOT. Leuven: Peeters, 2013.

———. *Ritual and Rhetoric in Leviticus: From Sacrifice to Scripture.* Cambridge: Cambridge University Press, 2007.

Zenger, Erich. "Theorien über die Entstehung des Pentateuch im Wandel der Forschung." Pages 87–135 in *Einleitung in das Alte Testament.* Edited by Christian Frevel. 9th ed. Kohlhammer Studienbücher Theologie 1.1. Stuttgart: Kohlhammer, 2015.

Zwickel, Wolfgang. *Räucherkult und Räuchergeräte: Exegetische und archäologische Studien zum Räucheropfer im Alten Testament.* OBO 97. Fribourg: Academic Press; Göttingen: Vandenhoeck & Ruprecht, 1990.

The Formation of the Wilderness Narratives in the Book of Numbers

Ndikho Mtshiselwa

In recent decades, biblical scholars have departed from the traditional view that Moses wrote the five books of the Pentateuch. The classical version of the Documentary Hypothesis proposed by Julius Wellhausen, which dominated pentateuchal studies through most of the twentieth century, claimed that the authors of J, E, D, and P were responsible for the composition of the Pentateuch.[1] Although some scholars subscribe to the Neo-Documentary Hypothesis, recent scholarly efforts to provide a new compositional model that would replace the classical Documentary Hypothesis necessitate a renewed debate on the question of who wrote the Pentateuch.[2] The growing interest in scribal activities in Jerusalem and Samaria, particularly in the postexilic period also gives credence to the investigation of the authorship of the Pentateuch. The interest of this essay lies in the scribal activities of groups in the postexilic period who were not only probably responsible for the formation of the wilderness narratives in the book of Numbers but also contributed to the production of the Pentateuch. Asking who wrote Num 11:1–20:13 necessitates an inquiry into both the dating of pentateuchal scribal activity, especially that associated with the formation of the wilderness narrative in Numbers, and the authorship of such scribal activities. This chapter thus focuses on the date of pentateuchal scribal activity and the question of who wrote some of the selected layers of Num 11:1–20:13. The scribal circles investigated in the

---

1. Julius Wellhausen, *Die Composition des Hexateuchs und der historischen Bücher des Alten Testaments* (Berlin: de Gruyter, 1963).

2. See, e.g., Joel S. Baden, *J, E, and the Redaction of the Pentateuch*, FAT 68 (Tübingen: Mohr Siebeck, 2009).

present essay include the Zadokite priests, the Levites, the Samaritans, and the Transjordanians.

1. Dating Pentateuchal Scribal Activity

Based on the *terminus a quo* argument, Baruch Spinoza submitted that the books from Genesis to Kings "were written by a single historian, who wished to relate the antiquities of the Jews from their first beginning down to the first destruction of the city."[3] Spinoza had Ezra in mind. Making a similar point, Ranier Albertz notes that "Ezra was ordered to prepare, publish, and implement a document that can be inferred from the Artaxerxes re-script (Ezra 7:14, 25–26). This document, called 'the law of God of heaven' (v. 21), probably consists of the entire Pentateuch."[4] Spinoza's claim that a single historian, Ezra, was responsible for the Enneateuch was abandoned following Wilhelm Martin Leberecht de Wette's observation of stylistic and theological contradictions in the literature.[5] De Wette's contribution became the basis for the idea of a seventh-century BCE origin for the first edition of Deuteronomy, the dating of the older sources in the books of Genesis–Numbers (J/E) between the tenth and eighth centuries, and the claim that the Priestly laws had been inserted into the Hexateuch only in the Persian period.[6] These ideas fit within the framework of the Documentary Hypothesis espoused by Abraham Kuenen and

---

3. Baruch de Spinoza, *A Theologico-political Treatise and a Political Treatise*, trans. R. H. M. Elwes (New York: Dover, 2004), 128.

4. Rainer Albertz, "The Controversy about Judean versus Israelite Identity and the Persian Government: A New Interpretation of the Bagoses Story (Jewish Antiquities XI.297–301)," in *Judah and the Judeans in the Achaemenid Period: Negotiating Identity in an International Context*, ed. Oded Lipschits, Gary N. Knoppers, and Manfred Oeming (Winona Lake, IN: Eisenbrauns, 2011), 483–504.

5. Wilhelm Martin Leberecht de Wette, *Opuscula Theologica* (Berlin: Reimer, 1830), 149–68.

6. Wilhelm Martin Leberecht de Wette, *Beiträge zur Einleitung in das Alte Testament*, 2 vols. (Halle: Schimmelpfennig, 1806), 1:170; Karl Heinrich Graf, "Die sogenannte Grundschrift des Pentateuch," *Archiv für die wissenschaftliche Erforschung des Alten Testaments* 1 (1869): 466–77; Thomas Römer, "'Higher Criticism': The Historical and Literary-Critical Approach—with Special Reference to the Pentateuch," in *The Nineteenth Century: A Century of Modernism and Historicism*, vol 3.1 of *Hebrew Bible/Old Testament*, ed. Magne Sæbø (Göttingen: Vandenhoeck & Ruprecht, 2013), 415–16; Thomas Römer, "How to Date Pentateuchal Texts: Some Case Studies," in *The Formation of the Pentateuch: Bridging the Academic Cultures of Europe, Israel, and*

Julius Wellhausen, among others.⁷ Like some European biblical scholars, African Pentateuch commentators have bid farewell to the Documentary Hypothesis.⁸ As will be shown below, the idea that the book of Numbers was probably produced by various authors makes it difficult to hold on to this model. Departure from the classical Documentary Hypothesis necessitates renewed debate on the question of who wrote the Pentateuch. In addition, the growing interest in scribal activity in Jerusalem and Samaria also gives credence to the need to investigate the authorship of the Pentateuch. The question of who wrote the Pentateuch is linked to renewed debate about the dating of pentateuchal texts. Before I address the issue of who wrote the Pentateuch—and, more important, the wilderness narrative in the book of Numbers—some remarks on the dating of the Pentateuch are in order.

The criteria for dating the pentateuchal text by external and internal comparisons seems to be a step in the right direction.⁹ The first version of the book of Deuteronomy is parallel to Neo-Assyrian texts, particularly loyalty oaths. The similarities between the loyalty oath (*adê*) of Esarhaddon discovered in the temple of Tayinat and Deut 28 suggest that the authors of the first version of Deuteronomy used these Neo-Assyrian texts, which can be "dated quite precisely to 672" BCE.¹⁰ Although the preceding parallel hints at a seventh-century date for the core of the book of Deuteronomy,

---

North America, ed. Jan Christian Gertz, Bernard M. Levinson, Dalit Rom-Shiloni, and Konrad Schmid, FAT 111 (Tübingen: Mohr Siebeck, 2016), 359.

7. Abraham Kuenen, *A Historical-Critical Inquiry into the Origin and Composition of the Hexateuch* (London: Macmillan, 1886); Wellhausen, *Die Composition*.

8. Esias E. Meyer, *The Jubilee in Leviticus 25: A Theological Ethical Interpretation from a South African Perspective* (Münster: LIT, 2005); Meyer, "Dating the Priestly Text in the Pre-exilic Period: Some Remarks about Anachronistic Slips and Other Obstacles," *Verbum et Ecclesia* 31 (2010): 1–6; Vincent N. N. Mtshiselwa, "Re-reading the Israelite Jubilee in Leviticus 25:8–55 in the Context of Land Redistribution and Socio-Economic Justice in South Africa: An African Liberationist Perspective" (PhD diss., University of South Africa, 2015).

9. Römer, "How to Date," 367–70.

10. Römer, "How to Date," 368; see also Hans Ulrich Steymans, *Deuteronomium 28 und die adê zur Thronfolgeregelung Asarhaddons: Segen und Fluch im Alten Orient und in Israel*, OBO 145 (Göttingen: Vandenhoeck & Ruprecht, 1995); Steymans, "Die neuassyrische Vertragsrhetorik der 'Vassal Treaties of Esarhaddon' und das Deuteronomium," in *Das Deuteronomium*, ed. Georg Braulik, ÖBS 23 (Frankfurt am Main: Lang, 2003), 89–152; Eckart Otto, *Das Deuteronomium: Politische Theologie und Rechtsreform in Juda und Assyrien*, BZAW 284 (Berlin: de Gruyter, 1999); and Jacob

sixth- and fifth-century dates for the edition and revision of the book remain plausible.¹¹ Based on the consensus that the book of Numbers is the latest in the Pentateuch, it makes sense to date Numbers after both the core of the book of Deuteronomy and its revision. The idea that the book of Numbers is more recent than the book of Deuteronomy and that it was created as a late bridge between a Priestly Triteuch and the book of Deuteronomy supports a postexilic date for Numbers.¹² The formation of Numbers as a separate book is also more recent than Genesis, Exodus, and Leviticus.¹³ A postexilic date for the production of Numbers is plausible especially if the "most secure date for the existence of pentateuchal texts is the Persian period."¹⁴ The point that the first and the last parts of Numbers contain features noticeable in Exodus, Leviticus, and Deuteronomy indicates that the scroll of Numbers was created at the very end of the process of the canonization of the Torah.¹⁵ Albertz notes that the earliest parts of the book of Numbers came into being for the first time within the post-Priestly D-composition in the middle of the fifth century BCE.¹⁶ The idea of a counterbalance of Deuteronomistic

---

Lauinger, "Esarhaddon's Succession Treaty at Tell Tayinat: Text and Commentary," *JCS* 64 (2012): 87–123.

11. Römer, "How to Date," 369; see also F. García López, "Le Roi d'Israël: Dt 17,14–20," in *Das Deuteronomium: Entstehung, Gestalt und Botschaft*, ed. Norbert Lohfink, BETL 68 (Leuven: Peeters, 1985), 277–97; Bernard M. Levinson, "The Reconceptualization of Kingship in Deuteronomy and the Deuteronomistic History's Transformation of the Torah," *VT* 51 (2001): 511–34; Ernest W. Nicholson, "'Do Not Dare to Set a Foreigner over You': The King in Deuteronomy and 'The Great King,'" *ZAW* 118 (2006): 46–61; Rainer Albertz, "A Possible *Terminus ad Quem* for the Deuteronomic Legislation? A Fresh Look at Deut. 17:16," in *Homeland and Exile: Biblical and Ancient Near Eastern Studies in Honour of Bustenay Oded*, ed. Gershon Galil, Markham Geller, and A. Millard, VTSup 130 (Leiden: Brill, 2009), 271–96.

12. Thomas Römer, "Israel's Sojourn in the Wilderness and the Construction of the Book of Numbers," in *Reflection and Refraction: Studies in Biblical Historiography in Honour of A. Graeme Auld*, ed. Robert Rezetko, Timothy H. Lim, and W. Brian Aucker, VTSup 113 (Leiden: Brill, 2007), 419–45.

13. Römer, "Israel's Sojourn," 427.

14. Römer, "How to Date," 370.

15. Römer, "Israel's Sojourn," 444.

16. Christian Frevel, "The Book of Numbers—Formation, Composition, and Interpretation of a Late Part of the Torah: Some Introductory Remarks," in *Torah and the Book of Numbers*, ed. Christian Frevel, Thomas Pola, and Aaron Schart (Tübingen: Mohr Siebeck, 2013), 13; Rainer Albertz, "Das Buch Numeri jenseits der Quellentheorie. Eine Redaktionsgeschichte, von Num 20–24 (Teil I und II)," *ZAW* 123 (2011): 336–37; Eckart Otto, "The Books of Deuteronomy and Numbers in One Torah: The

with Priestly traditions makes sense because Num 11–20 contains instances where the authors draw on Deuteronomistic and Priestly texts in order to retell the story of the wilderness wanderings. For instance, a late Deuteronomistic layer is noticeable in Num 10:29–36; 11:14–17, 24b–30; 12:1–10; 13–14; 21:1–3, 4–20.[17] In recent European discussion of the Pentateuch, it has begun to be accepted that the authors of the wilderness narrative added Num 13–14; 16–18; 20:1–13 to a P-composition (P1) extending from Gen 1 to Lev 16, which was later extended by the Holiness School (P2).[18] The pentateuchal redaction (P4 and P5), Num 25–36, which is related to Deut 34, was succeeded by a final redactor in the early fourth century BCE. I concur with Christian Frevel that Num 25–36 is ascribed to one or two very late and almost end-compositional Priestly strata, the pentateuchal redactors (P4 and P5), which are later than Josh 13–21. At this level, one observes an evolution of the Pentateuch and its relationship to the Hexateuch and the Enneateuch that involves a redactor integrating former publications on the exodus narrative, the late D-composition, and links between the books of Numbers and Joshua.[19]

The point that the Priestly texts in the book of Numbers are later than P1 and P2 in Exodus and Leviticus becomes significant in dating Numbers. It is increasingly accepted in biblical scholarship that "there is no trace of P in Numbers 13–14 or, for that matter, in the book of Numbers as a whole, so that P was said to end in the Sinai-pericope."[20] Yet redactional activities, which illustrate the use of P1 and P2, are evident in the book of Numbers. Frevel has correctly noted that the text of Num 13–14; 16–17; 20 "has linguistic and conceptual peculiarities if it is read against the background of a Priestly source in Exodus, but that is related to the

---

Book of Numbers Read in the Horizon of the Postexilic *Fortschreibung* in the Book of Deuteronomy; New Horizons in the Interpretation of the Pentateuch," in ed. Frevel, Pola, and Schart *Torah and the Book of Numbers*, 384.

17. Albertz, "Das Buch Numeri," 336–37.
18. Frevel, "Book of Numbers," 13.
19. Frevel, "Book of Numbers," 12–13.
20. Eckart Otto, "The Integration of the Post-exilic Book of Deuteronomy into the Post-Priestly Pentateuch," in *The Post-Priestly Pentateuch: New Perspectives on Its Redactional Development and Theological Profiles*, ed. Federico Giuntoli and Konrad Schmid (Tübingen: Mohr Siebeck, 2015), 336–37; see also Christophe Nihan, *From Priestly Torah to Pentateuch: A Study in the Composition of the Pentateuch*, FAT 2/25 (Tübingen: Mohr Siebeck, 2007); Frevel, "Book of Numbers," 11.

plot of the Sinai narrative or at least sorted into the wilderness."[21] Even on a geographical level, Num 11–20 shifts from the allusions to Sinai in Num 10 to the wilderness. Numbers 11–20 no doubt embraces the Sinai pericope.[22] On a linguistic level, Num 13–14 may be ascribed to a later supplement. Christophe Nihan notes that the phraseology of H (P2) is significantly more diffuse in Numbers than in Exodus and Leviticus.[23] But he also argues explicitly against significant redactional traces of H in the book of Numbers. For Nihan, "the so-called 'Priestly' legislation in Numbers is hardly comparable to the few limited HS interpolations detected elsewhere in Exodus and Leviticus."[24] Although Israel Knohl argues that the Holiness School (HS) is represented in almost the entire Pentateuch and is ultimately responsible for the final composition of the Pentateuch, the idea of a redactional layer of P2 remains inconclusive.[25] Because Lev 17–26 was a post-Priestly supplement and never literarily independent, it is fitting to correlate the formation of Lev 17–26 with a post-Priestly redaction of the Pentateuch.[26] Again, because the Priestly texts in the book of Numbers are later than the P-composition (P1) and Holiness School (P2), the finalization of the production of Numbers may fit within the scribal activity of the pentateuchal redactor. If P2 is presumably dated to the second half of the sixth century BCE, as scholars such Esias Meyer have argued, some earliest parts of Numbers are probably traceable to the fifth century BCE.[27]

The relationship between the book of Numbers and the prophetic books also point to a postexilic date for Numbers. Hosea 9:10, a text that contains the oldest allusion to the wilderness tradition, states that YHWH found Israel in the wilderness, while Hos 2:16–17 alludes to the restoration

---

21. Frevel, "Book of Numbers," 18.

22. Thomas Römer, "Egypt Nostalgia in Exodus 14–Numbers 21," in Frevel, Pola, and Schart *Torah and the Book of Numbers*, 68.

23. Nihan, *From Priestly Torah to Pentateuch*, 571.

24. Nihan, *From Priestly Torah to Pentateuch*, 571–72.

25. Israel Knohl, *The Sanctuary of Silence: The Priestly Torah and the Holiness School* (Minneapolis, MN: Fortress, 1995), 101–6; see also Knohl, "Who Edited the Pentateuch?," in *The Pentateuch: International Perspectives on Current Research*, ed. Thomas B. Dozeman, Konrad Schmid, and Baruch J. Schwartz; FAT 78 (Tübingen: Mohr Siebeck, 2011), 359–67; Frevel, "Book of Numbers," 16.

26. Otto, "Integration," 338; see Karl Elliger, *Leviticus*, HAT 1/4 (Tübingen: Mohr Siebeck, 1966); Alfred Cholewiński, *Heiligkeitsgesetz und Deuteronomium: Eine vergleichende Studie*, AnBib 66 (Rome: Biblical Institute, 1976).

27. Meyer, *Jubilee*, 223.

of the Israelites in the desert that symbolizes Israel's election by YHWH.[28] Prophetic texts such as Amos 2:10; 5:25; and Jer 7:22 indicate that the original tradition of Israel's sojourn in the desert was a positive tradition (Hos 2:16–17; 9:10).[29] In addition, Jer 2–6 presents the wilderness as period characterized by the experience of love (Jer 2:2). One wonders whether the authors of Jeremiah and Hosea drew on Num 11–20 or the opposite. As Thomas Römer has observed, contrary to the view that the books of Jeremiah and Hosea allude to Exodus and Numbers, "the wilderness stories in Exodus and especially in Numbers should be understood as reinterpretations of a former positive tradition."[30] The presentation of the wilderness story in a negative light, especially at a later stage, rather than its initial positive light suggests that there was agreement as well as disagreement between the authors of Num 11:1–20:13 and the authors of Hos 9, Amos 5, and Jer 7. Although the authors of the wilderness narratives in Numbers drew on the books of Hosea, Amos, and Jeremiah, they disagreed in their presentation of the narrative(s) (Hos 9:10; Amos 5:25; Jer 7:22). Perhaps at a later stage in the Persian period some events led the authors of Numbers to narrate the stories of rebellion in Num 11:1–20:13. Interestingly, Num 11:4–35 also picks up both the unpleasant situation and the restoration of the Judeans found in Ezek 37, a possible late, Persian-period addition to the nook of Ezekiel.[31] The statement, "our life is

---

28. Römer, "Israel's Sojourn," 430. Hosea 9, particularly v. 3, stems from a Deuteronomistic redaction of the book; see Gale A. Yee, *Composition and Tradition in the Book of Hosea: A Redaction Critical Investigation*, SBLDS 102 (Atlanta: Scholars Press, 1987), 196, 209, 221.

29. Römer, "Israel's Sojourn," 430–31.

30. Römer, "Israel's Sojourn," 431; see also Thomas B. Dozeman, "Hosea and the Wilderness Wandering Tradition," in *Rethinking the Foundations: Historiography in the Ancient World and in the Bible, Essays in Honour of John Van Seters*, ed. Steven L. McKenzie and Thomas Römer, BZAW 294 (Berlin: de Gruyter, 2000), 55–70.

31. Christophe Nihan, "The Memory of Ezekiel in Postmonarchic Yehud," in *Remembering Biblical Figures in the Late Persian and Early Hellenistic Periods: Social Memory and Imagination*, ed. Diana V. Edelman and Ehud Ben Zvi (Oxford: Oxford University Press, 2013), 416 has already noted postexilic additions to the book of Ezekiel such as the oracles against Gog in chapters 38–39. In the same vein, Römer, "Israel's Sojourn," 437 identifies Ezek 36:37; 37:1–5; and 39:29 as postexilic additions to the book of Ezekiel. Moreover, Ezekiel's vision of the dried bones in chapter 37 is likely a postexilic prophecy that captured the exilic experience of the Israelites. Because it makes sense to locate the reference to the restoration of Israel shortly after its occurrence, it is reasonable to date the latter vision to the postexilic period.

dried up," recalls a complaint which is quoted in Ezekiel's vision of dry bones: "They say: our bones are dried up" (Ezek 37:11). The links between the book of Numbers and the postexilic prophetic books not only indicate agreement between the authors of Num 11:4–35 and authors of postexilic prophecy but also suggest that Numbers is later than Amos (eighth century), Jeremiah (sixth–fifth centuries), and Hosea (sixth century).[32]

Internal comparison of the narratives in Num 11–20 reveals various stages in the production of the wilderness narrative. Support for the idea of a successive redaction of pentateuchal texts seems to be growing among scholars. As in the formation of Num 27–36, the theory of successive supplementation may also apply in part to Num 11–20. According to Römer, the growth of the wilderness narrative can be outlined as follows:

> (1) Numbers 13–14; (2) Num 11:4–35 and 20:1–13. Here we encounter for the first time the idea of a wilderness time characterised by rebellions of Israel and its leaders. This stage possibly coincides with the transformation of Exodus 15–17 into rebellion accounts; (3) Num 12:2–9 and 12:1, 10–15. Perhaps the author of these stories also created Num 11:1–3 as an introduction, which like Numbers 12 but against 11:4–35, insists on Moses' intercession. The same author might perhaps also be detected in Num 21:4–9 (the story of the snake plague): here again Moses and YHWH are almost presented as a "couple" (see esp. Num 21:5, 7: "the people came to Moses and said, 'We have sinned by speaking against YHWH and against you…'") and again all depends on Moses' intercession; (4) Numbers 16–17, in several stages and probably together with Numbers 15 and 18–19.[33]

Importantly, the scribal activities in Römer's proposal fit into the postexilic period. The second narrative in Num 11:4–23 and the third story in Num 12 display an interesting redactional activity, because the points that

---

32. Römer, "Israel's Sojourn," 437. On the date of Amos, see Aren M. Maeir, "The Historical Background and Dating of Amos VI 2: An Archaeological Perspective from Tell eṣ-Ṣâfi/Gath," *VT* (2004): 327. On the date of Hosea, see Craig Davis, *Dating the Old Testament* (New York: RJ Communications, 2007), 271. And on the date of Jeremiah, see Jacob Milgrom, "The Date of Jeremiah, Chapter 2," *JNES* 14.2 (1955): 69; Marvin A. Sweeney, "Dating Prophetic Texts," *HS* 48 (2007): 66.

33. Römer, "Israel's Sojourn," 442. For a detailed argument that Num 21:4–9 belongs to the very last layers of the Pentateuch, see Erik Aurelius, *Der Fürbitter Israels: Eine Studie zum Mosebild im Alten Testament*, ConBOT 27 (Stockholm: Almqvist & Wiksell, 1988), 187–202.

Num 11 and 12 are related and that the author of Num 12 corrects ideas expressed in Num 11 suggest different redactional levels. For instance, Num 12:6–8 makes a point that Moses is incomparable to other human beings, as he is the only person who sees the תמונה ("form") of YHWH.³⁴ This point is not made in Num 11. In addition, unlike Num 11:11–15, Num 12:3 presents Moses's humility. In Num 11:11–55, Moses is portrayed as arrogant and bad-tempered in the way he speaks to YHWH.³⁵ At a later stage, still in the postexilic period, the author of Num 12, although drawing on Num 11, equally departed from the views articulated in Num 11. In Num 11:4–34, the people are punished and Moses is vindicated after their complaint against YHWH, while, in Num 12, Moses's authoritative status is validated after its denial by Miriam and Aaron. This instance also reveals a conflict of theological and ideological position between the authors of Num 11 and 12. In these texts, Miriam, a figure who represents the prophets, and Aaron, a character who represents the priests, rebel against Moses. However, unlike Num 11, Num 12 restores the exclusive authority of Moses with the idea that no human being is comparable to him. Departing from both Num 11:24–30 and Exod 24:9–11, Num 12 moves closer to Deut 4:12, 15 and Deut 34:10–12. Deuteronomy 4:12 and 15 claim that no human has seen the face of YHWH, while Deut 34:10–12 states that "never since has there arisen a prophet in Israel like Moses, whom YHWH knew face to face." Because Deut 34:10–12 belongs to the last redactional layer of the Pentateuch, Num 12 may also be ascribed to a final pentateuchal redactor who contested the idea of Exod 24:9–11 and Num 11:24–30.

In Num 13–14, the people refute the whole divine project of the exodus.³⁶ One therefore wonders why the redactor of the wilderness narratives in the book of Numbers presents the rejection of the divine exodus project in the postexilic period. A closer look at Num 11:4–35 is thus in order. As already noted by Römer, as well as Frank Crüsemann, the author of Num 11:4–35 provides a revised reading of Exod 16, 18, and 24 as well as Deut 1:9–18 and 18:9–18 from the perspective of postexilic prophecy.³⁷ The point that Num 11 alludes to the combination of manna and quails in Exod

---

34. See also Römer, "Israel's Sojourn," 439.
35. Römer, "Israel's Sojourn," 440.
36. Römer, "Israel's Sojourn," 435.
37. Römer, "Israel's Sojourn," 437; see also Frank Crüsemann, "Le Pentateuque, une Tora: Prolégomènes à l'interprétation de sa Forme Finale," in *Le Pentateuque en question: Les origines et la composition des cinq premiers livres de la Bible à la lumière*

16, a text that forms part of the pentateuchal redaction suggests that Num 11 is later than Exod 16 as well as Exod 14:11–12, a text on which Exod 16 is based.[38] Thus, Num 11 cannot be ascribed to a literary stage earlier than Exod 14 and 16, and ascribing Num 11:18–20 to a pentateuchal redaction is reasonable. It may therefore be safe to view Num 13–14—most importantly, Num 14—as a postexilic text that is "based on the latest redaction of Exodus 14, which turned Moses' plea for fearlessness into a response to the Egypt nostalgia uttered by the people."[39] Numbers 13–14 presents the rebellion against the exodus. The rejection of the divine exodus project that is nuanced in the theme of the return to Egypt is also mentioned in Neh 9:17. There is no reason to refute the view that Neh 9:17 juxtaposes Exod 14:12 and Num 14:4.[40] Exodus 14:12 shows the reluctance of Judeans to leave Egypt, while Num 14:4 reveals their aspiration to select a leader and return to Egypt. The point that Num 14:4 is used by the author of Neh 9 suggests that Numbers is partly older than Nehemiah.

In the accounts of establishing the judicial system of Israel in both Exod 18:13–27 and Deut 1:9–18, Moses's leadership role devolves to other figures. In Exod 24:9–11, Moses transfers the authority to lead the Israelites to Aaron, Nadab, Abihu, and seventy of the elders of Israel (Exod 24:9; 14). Taking their cue from Exod 24:9–10, a post-Priestly layer in the multilayered text of Exod 24, as well as from Exod 18:13–27 and Deut 1:9–18, the authors of Num 11 present Moses's complaint (vv. 11–15), which subsequently "provokes the gift" of Moses's spirit to seventy representatives

---

des recherches récentes, ed. Albert de Pury and Thomas Römer, MdB 19 (Geneva: Labor et Fides, 2002), 357.

38. Eckart Otto, *Das Deuteronomium im Pentateuch und Hexateuch: Studien zur Literaturgeschte von Pentateuch und Hexateuch im Litchte des Deuteronomiumsrahmen*, FAT 30 (Tübingen: Mohr Siebeck, 2000), 36–45; Jan Christian Gertz, *Tradition und Redaktion in der Exoduserzählung: Untersuchungen zur Endredaktion des Pentateuch*, FRLANT 186 (Göttingen: Vandenhoeck & Ruprecht, 1999), 202; Römer, "Egypt Nostalgia," 74, 76. The point that Exod 16:4a, 5, 21, 27–30 are far from being Priestly texts, while Exod 16:2, 9–10, 14–15a, 31–35 are typical Priestly texts suggests that the chapter as a whole is a work of a redactor who combined the works of other sources. See also Römer, "Egypt Nostalgia," 74–75. It therefore makes sense to view Exod 16 as a work of a pentateuchal redactor who also consulted a Priestly text tradition.

39. Römer, "Egypt Nostalgia," 78.

40. Römer, "Egypt Nostalgia," 72; see also George W. Coats, *Rebellion in the Wilderness: The Murmuring Motif in the Wilderness Tradition in the Old Testament* (Nashville: Abingdon, 1986), 246.

of the people who then become "prophets like Moses."⁴¹ Because Moses has no more privilege than the seventy elders in Num 11:17, 25, he partly ceases to be the sole incomparable prophet. The prophesying of the seventy elders is a consequence of the people's complaint about the manna and Moses's complaint against YHWH. It becomes clear that the authors of Numbers drew on the work of the post-Priestly authors. In addition, a post-Priestly redactor transformed the original stories in Exod 15:22–24 and Exod 16, which did not include reference to a complaint. This was done by inserting, first, a cry to YHWH in Exod 15:24–25a, second, an allusion to the giving of the "commandments," and, third, a refusal to keep the "commandments" and the law in Exod 16:28.⁴² Also, unlike the post-Priestly redactor of Exod 15–17, the author of Num 11:1–3 inserted divine punishment as YHWH's response to the people's complaint, which is abated by Moses's intervention. What this means is that the author of Num 11:1–3 may be later than that of Exod 15–17.

In sum, a date for Numbers that is navigated within the framework of the Documentary Hypothesis is inconclusive. That is, dating the books of Genesis to Numbers to the tenth and eighth centuries would be unreasonable. The idea of dating the pentateuchal text using external and internal comparisons sheds some helpful light on the possible date of Numbers. The relationship of Numbers to the revision of the legal core of Deuteronomy points to a late fifth- or fourth-century BCE date for the production of Numbers, especially when sixth- and fifth-century dates are considered for the edition and revision of Deuteronomy. The composition of Numbers could be dated to the time of the post-Priestly D-composition, that is, the middle of the fifth century BCE and later. Furthermore, it is reasonable to date Numbers later than P1 and P2 if a secure date for P2 is the second half of the sixth century BCE. The relationships between Numbers and the prophetic books of Amos, Hosea, and Jeremiah imply a date that is later than the eighth century, the sixth century, and the first half of the fifth century BCE (with the exception of the book of Jeremiah, which may be dated in the sixth century BCE with some layer that may be afforded a

---

41. Römer, "Israel's Sojourn," 438.
42. Römer, "Israel's Sojourn," 432–33; William Johnstone, "The Use of Reminiscences in Deuteronomy in Recovering the Two Main Literary Phases in the Production of the Pentateuch," in *Abschied vom Jahwisten: die Komposition des Hexateuch in der jüngsten Diskussion*, ed. Jan Christian Gertz, Konrad Schmid, and Markus Witte; BZAW 315 (Berlin: de Gruyter, 2002), 245–63.

fifth century date).⁴³ There is thus a compelling argument for dating Numbers—and, more importantly, the wilderness narrative within it—to the fifth and fourth centuries BCE or probably slightly later. As mentioned before, the earliest parts of Numbers may be afforded a fifth century BCE date, while later additions may be dated in the fourth century BCE or even later. Based on this date for Numbers, we can try to determine who wrote the book, and the wilderness narrative in particular.

2. Who Wrote the Wilderness Stories in Numbers?

Numbers 11–20 hints at the presence of various groups that probably coproduced the book of Numbers. The groups include the Zadokite priests, the Levites, the elders (lay leaders),⁴⁴ and to a certain extent, the Samaritans and Transjordanians.

2.1. The Zadokite Priests

The contribution of the Zadokite priests is discernible in the production of Numbers. As mentioned above, although there is no P1 (P) and P2 (H) in Numbers, redactional activities that indicate the use of P1 and P2 are noticeable in the book. For instance, Num 15 presupposes Lev 24:10–23.⁴⁵ Although P2 is often associated with the last stages of the composition of the Torah, the fact that P2 is used in Numbers suggests not only that that H was not the last voice in the formation of the Pentateuch but also that the Zadokite priests produced the latest layers in the fourth century BCE.⁴⁶ For Reinhard Achenbach, the last redactional touches in Numbers are a product of theocracy-minded Zadokite priests. The Zadokites who not only legitimized the office of Eleazar in the narrative of Aaron's death

---

43. For a fifth-century date of texts such as Jer 33:23–26, see C. Lombaard, "The Strange Case of the Patriarchs in Jeremiah 33:26," *AcT* 35.2 (2015): 43.

44. Limited by the scope of the present essay, I refer to the detailed discussion of lay scribal activity in Jaeyoung Jeon, "The Zadokites in the Wilderness: The Rebellion of Korach (Num 16) and the Zadokite Redaction," *ZABR* 127 (2015): 381–411.

45. Frevel, "Book of Numbers," 24.

46. For P2 and the last stages of composition, see Knohl, *Sanctuary*, 101–6; Knohl, "Who Edited," 78; and Frevel, "Book of Numbers," 16. For the role of the Zadokites, see Reinhard Achenbach, "Das Heiligkeitsgesetz und die sakralen Ordnungen des Numeribuches im Horizont der Pentateuchredaktion," in *The Books of Leviticus and Numbers*, ed. Thomas Römer (Leuven: Peeters, 2008), 175.

(Num 20:22–29) but also authored the postexilic *Fortschreibung* in Deut 10:6–7; 11:2 are connected with the postexilic *Fortschreibungen* in the book of Numbers.[47] The legitimization of Eleazar's succession of Aaron as well as the covenant of eternal priesthood for Phinehas at Baal Peor (Num 25:6–15) presents a "strong argument for the exclusivity of the Zadokite priesthood."[48] At issue in the Chronicler's report of the appointment of Ithamar's descendants and the Zadokites as priests in the Jerusalem temple was the exclusive priestly rights of the Zadokites. The Chronicler shows that David appointed Ithamar's descendants, along with the Zadokites, as priests in the Jerusalem temple (1 Chr 24:1–6) As Jaeyoung Jeon has observed, "still in the Persian period the exclusive priesthood of the Zadokites was not yet commonly admitted by other socio-religious groups in Jerusalem."[49] For instance, 1 Chr 6:35–38 reveals the contests over the exclusive rights of the Zadokite priests, as the "exclusive priesthood of the Zadokites was not yet commonly admitted by other socio-religious groups in Jerusalem."[50] The text of Num 16 shows Aaron's rights and how the Zadokites benefitted from them. The discernible layers in Num 16 point to "stages of the Zadokites' struggle for their exclusive, priestly prerogatives" with the elders of the community and the Levites at the later stage, particularly in the late fifth and early fourth centuries BCE.[51] Because of the aforementioned possible date for Numbers, I am skeptical of Achenbach's dating of the redaction of Num 16 to the late fourth century BCE when the Zadokites were strong enough to pursue a theocracy.[52] In the late fifth and early fourth centuries BCE, the Zadokites were already contending for exclusive priestly rights.

It is noteworthy that, like Num 11, the text of Num 16–17 contrasts with Num 12.[53] Numbers 16–17 may be understood in part as a later

---

47. Otto, "Books of Deuteronomy and Numbers," 394.
48. Jeon, "Zadokites," 405–6.
49. Jeon, "Zadokites," 406 n. 90; see also Rainer Albertz, *A History of Israelite Religion in the Old Testament Period*, 2 vols. (Louisville: Westminster John Knox, 1994), 1:486; Paul Heger, *The Development of Incense Cult in Israel*, BZAW 245 (Berlin: de Gruyter, 1997), 231; Nihan, *From Priestly Torah to Pentateuch*, 607.
50. Jeon, "Zadokites," 406 n. 90.
51. Jeon, "Zadokites," 403.
52. Reinhard Achenbach, *Die Vollendung der Tora: Studien zur Redaktionsgeschichte des Numeribuches im Kontext von Hexateuch und Pentateuch*, BZABR 3 (Wiesbaden: Harrassowitz, 2003), 66.
53. Römer, "Israel's Sojourn," 441–42.

redactional response to Num 12 that seeks to enhance the status of the Aaronide priesthood.[54] Like Lev 10, Num 17 emphasizes the holiness of the Aaronide priesthood. At a later redactional level, Num 15 and 18–19 pick up the idea of the restoration of Moses's authority in Num 12, which, in turn, contrasts with Num 11.

Also worthy of note is the cultic practice of incense offering that is explicitly assigned to the Aaronide priests. Numbers 16:8–11 refutes the Levites' interest in duties of the priesthood, particularly the burning of incense. Although verses 8–11 belong to the layer of Korah and the Levites—"vv. 1a, 5, 6bβ, 7b, 8–11, 16–17, 19–24, 26 (וידבר אל העדה לאמר only) 27a, 32b," as Jeon correctly notes—the objection to the Levites' interest in priestly duties reveals the interest of the Zadokite priests.[55] In addition, the contrast between Korah's censer that caused a plague among the people (Num 17:11) and Aaron's legitimate censer that stopped the plague (Num 17:13) points to the interest of the Zadokite circles. Moses's instruction to Aaron to use the incense is also consistent with how incense is offered on the Day of Atonement (Lev 16:12).[56] This link further reinforces the holiness motif that may be attributed to P2, which is now picked up by the Zadokite priests to argue for exclusive rights to priestly practices. That the Zadokite priests participated in the process of the formation of Numbers is indisputable, especially if they sought to protect their cultic rights. But it is also important to consider the contributions of the Levites to the production of Numbers and, more importantly, to the wilderness narrative in the book.

2.2. The Levitical Priests?

Jeon and Achenbach assign the composition of Num 16 to the Zadokite priests. For Jeon, "the rebellion story in Num 16 was formed in a single-phase redaction from two independent stories of the Reubenites and the 250 chieftains of the congregation."[57] Also, "this redaction added the passages of Korach and the Levites to the two independent stories and consequently converted the whole periscope into a rebellion led by Korach."[58]

---

54. Römer, "Israel's Sojourn," 422.
55. Jeon, "Zadokites," 386.
56. Heger, *Development*, 57; Jeon, "Zadokites," 387 n. 21.
57. Jeon, "Zadokites," 410.
58. Jeon, "Zadokites," 410.

Achenbach also argues that the redaction of Num 16 was carried out by the Zadokite priests.[59] According to Jeon, though, the aim of this redaction was for the Zadokite priests to establish and defend the priestly prerogatives through their struggle with the elders of the community and later with the Levites in Persian Yehud.[60] As Jeon has discerned the possibility that the elders, the Levites, and the Zadokite priests coexisted during the period of the Persian rule, could it be that the Levites exercised their scribal abilities and contributed to the composition of Num 16?[61]

Deuteronomy and Deuteronomistic literature distinguish between two different notions of Levites, namely, the Levitical priests and the Levites in local towns who were not priests because they were deprived of priesthood by the Zadokites.[62] As will be shown shortly, the Levitical priests had judicial authority (Deut 17:9; 21:5), were responsible for preserving and teaching the law (Deut 17:18), and were linked to the centralized temple (Deut 18:1). Suffice it to note that the Deuteronomic concept of Levitical priests is controversial, as its preexilic origin is contested. This controversy is, however, beyond the scope of the present study.[63]

Although the redaction of Num 16 originated in Zadokite circles, as scholars such as Achenbach and Eckart Otto have decisively argued, one wonders whether the Levitical priests were in the position to write and participate in the process of producing Numbers. Kyung-Jin Min argues that the support offered by the Persian authorities ranged from priests (538–520 BCE) to elders (520–515 BCE) and later to the Levites (433 BCE onward).[64] A cardinal question, therefore, is: ` the Levitical priests in the position (especially of power and influence) to contribute to the composition of biblical texts, especially Num 16? The texts of Neh 6:17–7:3; 13:4–5, 10–13, 28 reveal that, around 433 BCE, there was a growing alliance between the priests, Nehemiah, Judean aristocrats, and influential

---

59. Achenbach, *Vollendung*, 66.
60. Jeon, "Zadokites," 403, 410.
61. Jeon, "Zadokites," 403.
62. Jaeyoung Jeon, "The Levites," *EBR* 16:336–46.
63. For details of the controversy around the concept of the Levitical priests and who the Levites were, see Jeon, "Levites," 1–9; Knohl, *Sanctuary*, 71–85, 210–11; Nadav Na'aman, "Sojourners and Levites in the Kingdom of Judah in the Seventh Century," *ZABR* 14 (2008): 237–79; Mark Leuchter, "'The Levite in Your Gates': The Deuteronomic Redefinition of Levitical Authority Author(s)," *JBL* 126 (2007): 417–36.
64. Kyung-Jin Min, *The Levitical Authorship of Ezra-Nehemiah*, JSOTSup 409 (New York: T&T Clark, 2004), 116–37; Jeon, "Zadokites," 403.

foreigners such as Tobiah and Sanballat. This alliance caused Nehemiah to "not solely rely on the priests for his nationalistic reform."[65] Clearly, the alliance came at a cost for the Levites and singers, as they were abused by the Judean aristocrats during Nehemiah's absence (Neh 13:10). The Judean aristocrats and priestly authorities did not support the so-called Levitical reform (Neh 13:10), which confirms the gradual growth of the power and influence of the temple personnel around 433 BCE.[66] Interestingly, "the Levites, singers, and the gatekeepers, who were originally separated groups until the times of the composition of Ezra-Nehemiah, seem to have been united in the course of time and eventually appear in Chronicles as branches of the Levite family with well-established genealogies" (1 Chr 9:17–21).[67] The Chronicler projects the Levites as influential, especially in the Davidic kingdom as they occupy positions such as administrators (1 Chr 23:4; 26:29–32; 2 Chr 19:11), judges (1 Chr 23:4; 26:29; 2 Chr 19:8), warriors (1 Chr 26:6, 9, 30, 32), scribes (1 Chr 24:6), teachers (2 Chr 17:7–9), and even prophets (1 Chr 25:5).[68] Importantly, 1 Chr 24:6 confirms the Levites' scribal abilities. Since the possibility of Levitical authorship for Chronicles (or passages that are pro-Levitical) may not be completely ruled out, the idea of a Levitical scribal contribution outside the books of Chronicles may be entertained.

Mark A. Christian assumes that "already in the eighth and certainly during the seventh century, and as part of the general increase in literacy at that time, many Levites acquired the requisite scribal ability and historical and theological knowledge" that was required of scribes who participated in the preliminary production of layers of the Hebrew Bible.[69] The interest of this article, however, lies in the second half of the fifth century as well as the first half of the fourth century BCE (Neh 8), which witnessed an increase in cultic activity.[70] In Jerusalem, the Levitical priests had the

---

65. Jeon, "Zadokites," 402; cf. Joachim Schaper, *Priester und Leviten im Achämenidischen Juda: Studien zur Kultund Sozialgeschichte Israels in Persischer Zeit*, FAT 31 (Tübingen: Mohr Siebeck, 1999), 230–31.

66. Schaper, *Priester und Leviten*, 237, 290; Jeon, "Zadokites," 402.

67. Jeon, "Zadokites," 402.

68. Leuchter, "Levite," 417–36. Importantly, Leuchter also focuses on the functions of the local Levites in the late monarchic period.

69. Mark A. Christian, "Priestly Power that Empowers: Michel Foucault, Middletier Levites, and the Sociology of 'Popular Religious Groups' in Israel," *JHS* 9 (2009): 6.

70. Reinhard Achenbach, "Die Tora und die Propheten im 5. und 4. Jh. v. Chr.," in *Tora in der Hebräischen Bibel: Studien zur Redaktionsgeschichte und synchronen Logik*

opportunity to participate in official administrative matters on a higher level as well as in major cultic events and in the composition of sacred literature alongside Zadokite Levites and Aaronide Levites.[71] Nehemiah 13:13 confirms this observation.[72]

Mark Leuchter entertains the idea that, for instance, the Levitical priests in Jerusalem wrote Ur-Deuteronomy around the seventh century BCE.[73] This scribal activity resulted in the provision of regulations for the special care of the marginalized fellow local Levites (Deut 14:29; 16:11; 18:68).[74] It also seems that the Levitical priests contributed to scribal activities with the view of protecting their own privileged status as priests (Deut 17:8–13; 18:1, 3–4; 24:8). The text of Deut 17 affirms the power and influential status held by the Levitical priests. Besides cultic authority, the judicial authority of the Levitical priests is also discernible (Deut 17:8–9). Importantly, Levitical priests who had experienced a significant increase in religiopolitical status later had the wherewithal to influence so-called official religion.[75] As mentioned above, Deut 17:18 not only shows that the law of the priest precedes the law of the king but also confirms both the collaborative participation of the Levitical priests in the production of the Torah and the Levitical authoritative oversight of the Torah. It is therefore hardly accidental that Deut 17:18 places the Torah at a level of importance before the Levitical priests, as they were active participants in the production of some of the texts in the Pentateuch.

In Deut 17:18, there seems to be a link between the king, the law, and the priest (cf. Ezra 7:12, 21; 2 Kgs 17:27). The close association between the Levites and the Torah and the role of authoritative oversight of the Torah suggest the scribal activity of the Levitical priests. Nehemiah 8:7–9 also confirms that the "authority of the Levites extends even to the supervision of the copying of the law."[76] Christian argues that, while "it remains

---

diachroner Transformationen, ed. Reinhard Achenbach, Martin Arneth, and Eckart Otto (Wiesbaden: Harrassowitz, 2007), 33–34.

71. Christian, "Priestly Power," 5.

72. Nehemiah 13:13 reads: "And I appointed as treasurers over the storehouses the priest Shelemiah, the scribe Zadok, and Pedaiah of the Levites, and as their assistant Hanan son of Zaccur son of Mattaniah, for they were considered faithful; and their duty was to distribute to their associates."

73. Leuchter, "Levite," 417–36.

74. Leuchter, "Levite," 417–36.

75. Christian, "Priestly Power," 55.

76. Christian, "Priestly Power," 53.

true that the priests do not receive a specific command to write or copy the code—a circumstance that would assure them influence in an official publication—this should not surprise us."[77] He further attempts to resolve the problem raised in the preceding argument by stating that the "Levitical priests may have struck a compromise with pro-monarchic elements within the governing class that the law—which stood to benefit both priestly and non-priestly royal scribes—would be included as law without mentioning their hands-on involvement in its formulation."[78] Although Christian's argument is speculative, the close association of the Levitical priests with the king and the law allows one to imagine their involvement in the production of the Torah. A close look at the stories of Dathan and Abiram, of the 250 chieftains, and of Korah and the Levites in Num 16 is in order.

Jeon's reconstruction of the Num 16 narratives, which is not far from the consensus among biblical scholars, seems convincing.[79] For him, the story of Dathan and Abiram is identified as follows: verses 1, 2 (only ויקמו לפני משה), 12–15, 25, 26 (without וידבר אל העדה לאמר), 27, 28–31, 32 (without אשר לקרח ואת כל הרכוש), 33–34.[80] The story of the 250 chieftains comprises verses 2 (excluding ויקמו לפני משה), 3–4, 6 (with the exception of קרח וכל עדתו), 7 (without רב לכם בני לוי), 18, 35.[81] Verses 1a, 5, 6bβ, 7b, 8–11, 16–17, 19–24, 26 (excluding וידבר אל העדה לאמר), 27 a, 32b constitute the story of Korah and Levites.[82] My interest in the debate about the layers of Num 16 is focused on their authorship, particularly the contribution, if any, of the Levitical priest. As mentioned above, there is no clear indication that there is any authorship other than the Zadokite priests. Yet how do we account for the clear criticism of the Levites and the apparent contestation of their privileged status and influence? The clear criticism of the Levites in the story of Korah and Levites confirms the scribal activity of the Zadokite priests who opposed the Levitical priests. We can discern neither the authorship nor the redaction of the Levitical priests in the latter story. Yet the abrupt insertion of the Levites in the story of Dathan and Abiram as well as the apparently inserted mention of Korah and the Levites at the editorial stage of the story of the 250 chieftains is intriguing.

---

77. Christian, "Priestly Power," 51.
78. Christian, "Priestly Power," 51.
79. Jeon, "Zadokites," 381–411.
80. Jeon, "Zadokites," 383.
81. Jeon, "Zadokites," 385.
82. Jeon, "Zadokites," 386.

It is likely, then, that the Levitical priests contributed to the production of Num 16.

The recognition of the roles of the Levites and the priests extends from the fifth century BCE well into the Hellenistic period.[83] The inscriptions found at Mount Gerizim from the early Hellenistic period that contain Levitical and especially Zadokite names such as Amram, Eliezer, Pinchas (Phinehas?), and Levi with the title "priest" presuppose the influence of either the Zadokite priests or the Levitical priests from the fifth century to the Hellenistic period.[84] That influence may be imagined in the scribal activities of that time. The mention and the role of the Levites in Deut 27:14, a text that is related to Josh 8:30–35, "connects them to the venerated site; the cultic interest in Mounts Ebal and Gerizim," and the Samaritans.[85] Besides the Levitical priests in Jerusalem, one wonders whether there were local Levites or Levitical priests in Samaria who were venerated enough to be mentioned alongside Amram, Eliezer, and Pinchas in the inscriptions associated with Mount Gerizim. Otherwise, is this juxtaposition meant to allude to the influential and authoritative priestly circles, extending to Samaria and the diaspora, who participated in the scribal activities that produced the Pentateuch?

2.3. Samaritans and Transjordanians?

The view by Römer and Israel Finkelstein that "the emphasis on northern traditions, *particularly in Numbers*, could tentatively be understood as 'Samaritan input,'" that "the compilation of the Torah cannot be understood as an exclusively Judahite phenomenon," and that the integration of the northern traditions in Numbers "can be understood as a concession to the Samaritans or as a claim by the Samaritans in postexilic times"

---

83. Jeon, "Zadokites," 56; see also Reinhard Achenbach, "Der Pentateuch, Seine Theokratischen Bearbeitungen und Josua–2 Könige," in *Les dernières rédactions du Pentateuque, de l'Hexateuch et de l'Ennéateuque*, ed. Thomas Römer and Konrad Schmid, BETL 203 (Leuven: Peeters, 2007), 226–27; Gary N. Knoppers, *Jews and Samaritans: The Origins and Early History of Their Relations* (Oxford: Oxford University Press, 2013), 128.

84. Jeon, "Zadokites," 406; Knoppers, *Jews and Samaritans*, 128.

85. Christian, "Priestly Power," 37. See also Eckart Otto, "Pentateuch und Hexateuch jenseits von Jerusalem und Juda? Die 'Endredaktion' von Pentateuch und Hexateuch in Samaria und Diaspora: Zu einem Buch von Dany R. Nocquet," *ZABR* 23 (2017): 14.

necessitates an inquiry into the presence of literary contributions by the Samaritans and the diaspora in Numbers.[86] The point made above that the earliest parts of Numbers may be afforded a fifth-century BCE date, while later additions may be dated to the fourth century BCE or even later hints at the presence of a literary contribution from the diaspora in Numbers.[87] In addition, the point that the city of Jerusalem is central in many parts of the Hebrew Bible but not in the Pentateuch, and the connection between Num 14 and Num 26, as well as Num 32 allow one to imagine the presence of the diaspora in the book of Numbers.[88]

While acts of rebellion feature in the wilderness narrative in the form of rebellious acts on the part of the spies and the heads of the community (Num 13:26–33), the community (Num 14:1–4, 10a, 44), the Levites (Num 16: 1a, 5, 6b, 7b, 8–11, 16–17, 19–24, 26 [excluding וידבר אל העדה], 27a, 32b), and Moses and Aaron (Num 20:1–13), Caleb and Joshua are cast in a positive light as faithful figures. Because Caleb belongs to Judah and Joshua to Ephraim, their positive depiction implies that "any Israelite, from the north or from the south, can identify himself with these exemplary characters within the narrative."[89] Importantly, the characters of Caleb and Joshua symbolize Samaritan and Judean Judaism, respectively.[90] It is thus reasonable to deduce that Jews were found in the promised land and in the diaspora, as reflected in Num 13–14. Numbers 13:4–15 recalls Deut 27:12–13, a text that is related to Josh 8:30–35.[91] Similar to

---

86. Israel Finkelstein and Thomas Römer, "Early North Israelite 'Memories' of Moab," in *The Formation of the Pentateuch: Bridging the Academic Cultures of Europe, Israel, and North America*, ed. Jan Christian Gertz, Bernard M. Levinson, Dalit Rom-Shiloni, and Konrad Schmid (Tübingen: Mohr Siebeck, 2016), 726, emphasis added.

87. Otto, "Pentateuch und Hexateuch," 1.

88. Jean-Louis Ska, "Why Does the Pentateuch Speak so Much of Torah and so Little of Jerusalem?," in *The Fall of Jerusalem and the Rise of the Torah*, ed. Peter Dubovský, Dominik Markl, and Jean-Pierre Sonnet, FAT 107 (Tübingen: Mohr Siebeck, 2016), 113.

89. Olivier Artus, "Numbers 32: The Problem of the Two and a Half Transjordanian Tribes and the Final Composition of the Book of Numbers," in Frevel, Pola, and Schart, *Torah and the Book of Numbers*, 373.

90. Artus, "Numbers 32," 380.

91. Otto, "Pentateuch und Hexateuch," 4. The list of the scouts in Num 13:4–15 includes Shammua son of Zakkur, Shaphat son of Hori, Caleb son of Jephunneh, Igal son of Joseph, Hoshea son of Nun, Palti son of Raphu, Gaddiel son of Sodi, Gaddi son of Susi, Ammiel son of Gemalli, Sethur son of Michael, Nahbi son of Vophsi, and Geuel son of Maki.

Deut 27:12–13, Num 13:4–15 later mentions the tribes of Reuben, Simeon, Judah, Issachar, Ephraim (not mentioned in Deut 27:12–13), Benjamin, Zebulun, Manasseh (a tribe of Joseph), Dan, Asher, Naphtali, and Gad, with the exception of Levi. The tribes of Simeon, Levi, Judah, Issachar, Joseph, and Benjamin are linked to Mount Gerizim (Deut 27:12), while the tribes of Reuben, Gad, Asher, Zebulun, Dan, and Naphtali are associated with Mount Ebal (Deut 27:13). The fact that Deut 27:12–13 omits the tribe of Ephraim, while Num 13:4–15 omits the tribe of Levi is beside the point. The argument here is that Num 13:4–15 and Deut 27:12–13 presuppose the worship of YHWH in Samaritan circles, which, in turn, may point in the direction of the production of Numbers.

The presence of the tribes of Ephraim and Manasseh, as well as priestly cultic activity, on Mount Gerizim opens a window of inquiry into the activities of the priests in Samaritan circles.[92] The Samaritans viewed the constructed altar (sanctuary) on Mount Gerizim (probably after the resettlement of Shechem ca. 480–475 BCE) as the site of worship.[93] In contrast to Deut 12:13–18, a text which shows that the chosen place for YHWH's worship was usually Jerusalem, Deut 27:5–10 envisions Ebal as the other place of worship. Like Deut 27, Josh 8:30–35 confirms that Moses authorized that the altar where YHWH should be worshiped should be located at Mount Ebal.[94] The consideration of cultic places other than Jerusalem, such as Bethel or Samaria,[95] and most importantly Mount Gerizim and

---

92. Knoppers, *Jews and Samaritans*, 128; see also Reinhard Pummer, *The Samaritans: A Profile* (Grand Rapids: Eerdmans, 2015).

93. Yitzakh Magen, "The Dating of the First Phase of the Samaritan Temple on Mt. Gerizim in Light of Archaeological Evidence," in *Judah and the Judeans in the Fourth Century B.C.E.*, ed. Oded Lipschitz, Gary N. Knoppers, and Rainer Albertz (Winona Lake, IN: Eisenbrauns, 2007), 176; Dany R. Nocquet, *La Samarie, la diaspora et l'achèvement de la Torah*, OBO 284 (Fribourg: Academic Press; Göttingen: Vandenhoeck & Ruprecht, 2017), 113. On the significance of Shechem in both Deut 27 and Josh 24 and the redactional analysis of Deut 27 (including parallels between Deut 26:16–18 and Deut 27:9–10), see Christophe L. Nihan, "The Torah between Samaria and Judah: Shechem and Gerizim in Deuteronomy and Joshua," in *The Pentateuch as Torah: New Models for Understanding Its Promulgation and Acceptance*, ed. Gary N. Knoppers and Bernard M. Levinson (Winona Lake, IN: Eisenbrauns, 2007), 193, 206–23.

94. Otto, "Pentateuch und Hexateuch," 5.

95. Thomas Römer, "Cult Centralization in Deuteronomy 12: Between Deuteronomistic History and Pentateuch," in *Das Deuteronomium zwischen Pentateuch und*

Transjordan (as I will shortly show), indicates that priestly duties were also performed outside of Jerusalem. That is, in the postexilic period, the priesthood operated both in the temple and in sanctuaries simultaneously. If that is the case, as I am inclined to believe, the idea that the Samaritans contributed to the composition of the Pentateuch, specifically to the book of Numbers, may not be ruled out. The circle of priests from Samaria probably coproduced Num 12:1–16 with other authors, as will be argued shortly.

The connection between the wilderness narrative in Num 11:1–20:13 and Num 32 points in the direction of Judaism in the diaspora. As Olivier Artus rightly states, Num 32 deals with the structural organization of Judaism in the diaspora that is "depicted through the fiction of the Transjordanian tribes."[96] Importantly, Num 32 highlights the authority of the high priest "over the sanctuary, the Levites and the community" as already mentioned in Num 16–18.[97] The presence of Eleazar underscores the authority of the priests in the government of diaspora Jews. Worthy of note is that the Transjordanian tribes receive instructions from Moses (Num 32:28) when they approach Moses, Eleazar the priest, and the leaders of the congregation (Num 32:2). Although, in the narrative, the Transjordanian tribes and Moses's group reached an agreement, Num 32 insinuates that rules were imposed upon the Jews in the diaspora.[98] The agreement included the settlement in Transjordan and the building of the cities (Num 32:34–38). According to Josh 22:10–34, the Transjordanian tribes built a massive altar by the Jordan. In Josh 22:16, Phinehas the son of Eleazar, the priest who may be considered an ancestor of the Zadokites, and ten rulers—one ruler from the chief house of every tribe of Israel (Josh 22:13–14)—interpreted the construction of the altar as a rebellion against YHWH.[99] In Josh 22:19, they do not regard the altar as the משכן (dwelling place) of YHWH. In response to the accusation, the Transjordanian tribes link the altar to YHWH (Josh 22:22). Joshua 22:28 states that the altar was

---

Deuteronomistiscem Geschichitswerk, ed. Eckart Otto and Reinhard Achenbach (Göttingen: Vandenhoeck & Ruprecht, 2004), 178.

96. Artus, "Numbers 32," 375. The Transjordanian tribes were Reuben and Gad, as well as the half tribe of Manasseh.

97. Artus, "Numbers 32," 375.

98. Artus, "Numbers 32," 375.

99. On Phinehas as ancestor of the Zadokites, see Otto, "Books of Deuteronomy and Numbers," 389.

תבנית, a "copy" or "replica," of the altar of YHWH. Also, part of the reason for constructing the altar was to enable future generations to narrate the story of the Transjordanian tribes to the rest of the Judean tribes (Josh 22:24). The altar built by the Transjordanian tribes was no doubt accepted by the Judeans in the promised land as an altar for the worship of YHWH (Josh 22:30). Otto's suggestion that the link between Josh 22 and Num 32 reveals the legitimization of the YHWH cults and the communities in Transjordan is therefore on point.[100]

In addition to the texts of Num 13–14; 32; Deut 27; Josh 8; 22, the texts of Num 12, Deut 7, and Ezra 9 are worthy of note. In Num 12, legitimization of Moses's privileged status, which is a response to Num 11, is curiously paired with legitimization of the marriages with foreign women. YHWH's punishment of Miriam because of her complaint against Moses's marriage to a Cushite woman as well as his defense of Moses's privileged status necessitates an intertextual reading of Num 12, Deut 7:3–6, and Ezra 9:1–3.[101] In a period in which Israel's identity was contested, it appears that the author of Num 12 was familiar with the Deuteronomistic ideology behind Deut 7 and Ezra 9. Miriam must have represented a Deuteronomistic group that, in the Persian period, did not approve of the idea of Judean men marrying foreign women (Deut 7:3). Miriam's punishment shows that the late Deuteronomistic theology and ideology expressed in Deut 7:3–6 as well as in Ezra 9:1–3 was contested.[102] Reading Num 12 in light of Deut 7 and Ezra 9 has led to the view that "the author of Numbers 12 may represent the ideology of a 'liberal' Diaspora Judaism" that did not place emphasis on the distortion of the Jewish identity through marriage to a foreigner but that elevated the Torah.[103] Furthermore, in the case of Num 12, where the identity of the scribe is less certain, it is possible to detect influence from the diaspora. One may further ask: Was the author of Num 12 familiar with aspects of Deut 7?

Deuteronomy 7:1–6 presents a memory that served to caution the postexilic community about the consequences of allowing foreign nationals to contest and distort their identity. Distortion of identity is often intertwined with apostasy in the book of Deuteronomy (Deut 9:16, 21;

---

100. Otto, "Pentateuch und Hexateuch," 2.
101. Deuteronomy 7:3–6 prohibits intermarriage with foreign women. Ezra 9:1–3 presents a negative reception of the idea of intermarriages with foreign women.
102. Römer, "Israel's Sojourn," 440.
103. Römer, "Israel's Sojourn," 440.

11:28; 13:6; 31:9). The distortion of identity resulted in neglect and renunciation of the established religious faith in YHWH or abandonment of previous loyalty to YHWH. Interestingly, Deut 7:4 shows that apostasy would kindle YHWH's anger and lead to Israel's annihilation and, invariably, the destruction of Jerusalem, an observation already made by Otto in the case of Deut 12.[104] It is noteworthy that Israel's apostasy, which led to the destruction of the cultic silent objects and symbols, is associated with relationships with foreign nationals (12:1–5). The concern about kindling YHWH's anger based on the people's close association with foreign nations may therefore explain Miriam's actions, which are problematized by the authors of Num 12. Problematizing Miriam's actions in Num 12:1–16 elevates Moses's privileged status rather than affirming the rejection of relationships with foreign nations. We may therefore imagine "the author of Numbers 12 as representing the ideology of a 'liberal' Diaspora Judaism."

There is scholarly consensus that the second half of the Persian period saw the birth of the Torah and of Judaism as a Torah-related religion.[105] For Judeans living in the diaspora, the idea that Jewish identity was linked to a prohibition on marrying foreign women was not convincing. In the diaspora, the revelation of the Torah was fundamental to the identity of the Judeans.[106] They preferred the idea that Israel was constituted by the Torah. As mentioned above with regard to the development of the wilderness narrative, Römer has correctly placed the laws and regulations of Num 15 and 18–19 after the rest of the wilderness narratives.[107] Numbers 15 and 18–19 therefore affirm the legitimization of Moses's privileged status in Num 12 but further make reference to the Torah.[108]

---

104. Eckart Otto, "Born out of Ruins: The Catastrophe of Jerusalem as *Accoucheur* to the Pentateuch in the Book of Deuteronomy," in Dubovsky, Markl, and Sonnet, *Fall of Jerusalem and the Rise of the Torah*, 159 does not relate Deut 12 to Deut 7, although YHWH's anger is mentioned in both texts.

105. Römer, "Israel's Sojourn," 420.

106. Römer, "Israel's Sojourn," 443.

107. Römer, "Israel's Sojourn," 442.

108. Numbers 15:22–24, 36, 40 show how the instructions given to the people by YHWH through Moses are followed. The instructions to the Levites in Num 18:25–32 and commands about the water of cleansing that are given to the people through Moses and Aaron (Num 19:1) confirms Moses's authoritative status. Moses is not criticized in these texts but affirmed. In that case, his privileged status is affirmed.

Frevel notes that the term *tôrâ* in Num 15:16 and 29 alludes to law and instructions. However, in Num 19:14 the preceding term "introduces a subset of the law of handling death and contact with corpses."[109] In Exod 12:49, especially in the collective sense of *tôrâ* meaning "law" or "instructions," the term in our present inquiry is used with regard to the Pesah (Passover); it is stated that the same law applies to the resident and the stranger.[110] Although located in a different status, all people were obliged to the laws of the Torah. The point that this equalization follows the treatment of resident aliens in the Holiness Code (P2) implies that foreigners had to comply with some but not all the laws of the Torah and that they could be assimilated under one and the same law.[111] The idea that foreigners were assimilated under the Priestly Torah—that is, Priestly rules—explains the punishment of Miriam as well as the rejection of ideas held by the group represented by Miriam in the Persian period. This is mainly because the elevation and subsequent legitimization of Moses was, in fact, regarded as the legitimization of the law.[112] Based on the consensus that the law was given to Moses by YHWH, the law is legitimized in the Pentateuch and given authoritative status because Moses is elevated. Because Miriam represents the prophets, it is necessary to briefly consider the idea of the existence or absence of a prophet like Moses in the context of the elevation of the Torah, which was embraced by the diaspora community. As mentioned above, the legitimization of Moses that presupposes the elevation of the Torah likely legitimized Torah in many a community. Although it should still be proven that the Torah was accepted by diaspora communities already in the Persian period, "there is a general agreement that the second half of the Persian period saw the birth of the Torah and of Judaism as a Torah-related religion."[113] Also, because the revelation of the Torah was fundamental to the identity of

---

109. Frevel, "Book of Numbers," 23

110. Frevel, "Book of Numbers," 23; see also Reinhard Achenbach, "Gêr–Nåkhrî–Tôshav–Zâr: Legal and Sacral Distinctions Regarding Foreigners in the Pentateuch," in *The Foreigner and the Law: Perspectives from the Hebrew Bible and the Ancient Near East*, ed. Reinhard Achenbach, Rainer Albertz, and Jakob Wöhrle, BZABR 16 (Wiesbaden: Harrassowitz, 2011), 29, 40–42. See the slightly different terminology used in Lev 19:34; 24:22 and Num 9:14.

111. Frevel, "Book of Numbers," 23.

112. Jeffrey Stackert, *A Prophet Like Moses: Prophecy, Law and Israelite Religion* (Oxford: Oxford University Press, 2014), 34.

113. Römer, "Israel's Sojourn," 420.

the Judeans in the diaspora and because they preferred the idea that Israel was constituted by the Torah, we may imagine the point that the Torah was embraced by the diaspora community.[114]

Stephen L. Cook argues that a figure from prophetic literature, Jeremiah, is a prophet like Moses.[115] Yet he does not convincingly explain the contradiction between Deut 18:15, which states that "the LORD your God will raise up for you a prophet like me from among your own brothers. You must listen to him," and Deut 34:10 which states that, "since then, no prophet has risen in Israel like Moses, whom the LORD knew face to face." Konrad Schmid explains the discrepancy between Deut 34:10 and Deut 18:15 as follows:

> The reason is most likely to be found in the need to break apart the chain of prophetic succession starting with Moses. Whereas Deut 18:15 envisions such a succession between Moses as arch-prophet and his successors, Deut 34:10 wants to separate Moses from all other prophets. The reason for this separation between 'Moses' and the 'prophets' is most easily found in the formation of Torah: Moses has to be separated from the prophets as soon as the Torah is seen as superior to the Prophets (i.e. the prophetic books Joshua—Malachi as section of the canon referred to as 'Prophets').[116]

The reference to the law in Num 15:16 partly explains the view that Moses was incomparable to other prophets including Jeremiah. If the Pentateuch was meant to receive any prominence, the person who is most related to both the Priestly Torah and the Pentateuch—Moses—would justifiably be placed above other prophets. Moses is above all other prophets because the figure Moses is distinct from Mosaic law. YHWH's direct communication with Moses in Num 12 confirms the distinctness of Moses. If Moses the lawgiver "was the last Israelite prophet, after which the law he mediated became normative," it makes sense to give attention to the elevation

---

114. On the role of the Torah for Judean identity in diaspora, see Römer, "Israel's Sojourn," 443.

115. Stephen L. Cook, "Those Stubborn Levites: Overcoming Levitical Disenfranchisement," in *Levites and Priests in History and Tradition*, ed. Mark A. Leuchter and Jeremy M. Hutton (Atlanta: Society of Biblical Literature, 2011), 161.

116. Konrad Schmid, "The Late Persian Formation of the Torah: Observations on Deuteronomy 34," in Lipschits, Knoppers, and Albertz, *Judah and the Judeans in the Fourth Century B.C.E.*, 248.

of the Torah.[117] The debate over the legitimization of Moses, the elevation of the Torah, and the Torah's accommodation of foreigners permits one to imagine the diaspora community as a contributor to the production of the Pentateuch and most importantly the book of Numbers. The Samaritans and the Transjordanians may thus be imagined as contributors to the production of Num 15:1–16, especially given that this text is sympathetic to the idea of relations with people outside of Jerusalem.

3. Conclusion

The wilderness story in Numbers is a complex piece of literature in the Hebrew Bible. The present article has sought to investigate the scribal activities of various groups in the postexilic period who not only contributed to the production of the wilderness narratives in the book of Numbers but also played a role in the overall production of the Pentateuch. The chapter shows that an inquiry into the authorship of the Pentateuch partially clarifies the authorship of Num 11:1–20:13. The book of Numbers was the last project in the production of the Pentateuch. This study shows that, to establish the authorship of the book of Numbers and of the wilderness narrative, it is necessary first to revisit debate about the date of Numbers. Pentateuchal texts and scholarship point to a date around the fifth and the fourth centuries BCE for the production of Numbers and for the various stages of the wilderness narrative.

The Zadokite priests, Levitical priests, and probably the Samaritans and Transjordanians, as well as the elders (or lay leaders, who are not part of the focus of this essay) participated in the production of Numbers. While Spinoza proposed that Numbers was written in the mid-fifth and the first half of the fourth centuries BCE, it was these scribal groups, not Ezra who participated in the production of Numbers and subsequently the formulation of the Pentateuch. I would not situate the production of Numbers in the late Persian or Hellenistic periods, as suggested by Achenbach. In the period suggested by this essay, the producers of Numbers, particularly of the wilderness narrative, included the elders (lay leaders), the Levitical priests, possibly the Samaritan and Transjordanian (priestly and lay leadership) circles, and the Zadokite priests who could have sought the redaction of the wilderness narration (and of Numbers).

---

117. Stackert, *Prophet*, 34.

Bibliography

Achenbach, Reinhard. "Gêr-Nåkhrî-Tôshav-Zâr: Legal and Sacral Distinctions Regarding Foreigners in the Pentateuch." Pages 29–51 in *The Foreigner and the Law: Perspectives from the Hebrew Bible and the Ancient Near East*. Edited by Reinhard Achenbach, Rainer Albertz, and Jakob Wöhrle. BZABR 16 Wiesbaden: Harrassowitz, 2011.

———. "Das Heiligkeitzgesetz und die sakralen Ordnungen des Numeribuches im Horizont der Pentateuchredaktion." Pages 145–76 in *The Books of Leviticus and Numbers*. Edited by Thomas Römer. Leuven: Peeters, 2008.

———. "Der Pentateuch, Seine Theokratischen Bearbeitungen und Josua–2 Könige." Pages 225–53 in *Les dernières rédactions du Pentateuque, de l'Hexateuch et de l'Ennéateuque*. Edited by Thomas Römer and Konrad Schmid. BETL 203. Leuven: Peeters, 2007.

———. "Die Tora und die Propheten im 5. und 4. Jh. v. Chr." Pages 26–71 in *Tora in der Hebräischen Bibel: Studien zur Redaktionsgeschichte und synchronen Logik diachroner Transformationen*. Edited by Reinhard Achenbach, Martin Arneth, and Eckart Otto. Wiesbaden: Harrassowitz, 2007.

———. *Die Vollendung der Tora: Studien zur Redaktionsgeschichte des Numeribuches im Kontext von Hexateuch und Pentateuch*. BZABR 3. Wiesbaden: Harrassowitz, 2003.

Albertz, Rainer. "Das Buch Numeri jenseits der Quellentheorie: Eine Redaktionsgeschichte, von Num 20–24 (Teil I und II)." ZAW 123 (2011): 171–83, 336–47.

———. "The Controversy about Judean versus Israelite Identity and the Persian Government: A New Interpretation of the Bagoses Story (Jewish Antiquities XI.297–301)." Pages 483–504 in *Judah and the Judeans in the Achaemenid Period: Negotiating Identity in an International Context*. Edited by Oded Lipschits, Gary N. Knoppers, and Manfred Oeming. Winona Lake, IN: Eisenbrauns, 2011.

———. *A History of Israelite Religion in the Old Testament Period*. 2 vols. Louisville: Westminster John Knox, 1994.

———. "A Possible *Terminus ad Quem* for the Deuteronomic Legislation? A Fresh Look at Deut. 17:16." Pages 271–96 in *Homeland and Exile: Biblical and Ancient Near Eastern Studies in Honour of Bustenay Oded*. Edited by Gershon Galil, Markham Geller, and A. Millard. VTSup 130. Leiden: Brill, 2009.

Artus, Olivier. "Numbers 32: The Problem of the Two and a Half Transjordanian Tribes and the Final Composition of the Book of Numbers." Pages 367–82 in *Torah and the Book of Numbers*. Edited by Christian Frevel, Thomas Pola, and Aaron Schart. Tübingen: Mohr Siebeck, 2013.

Aurelius, Erik. *Der Fürbitter Israels: Eine Studie zum Mosebild im Alten Testament*. ConBOT 27. Stockholm: Almqvist & Wiksell, 1988.

Baden, Joel S. *J, E, and the Redaction of the Pentateuch*. FAT 68. Tübingen: Mohr Siebeck, 2009.

Cholewiński, Alfred. *Heiligkeitsgesetz und Deuteronomium: Eine vergleichende Studie*. AnBib 66. Rome: Biblical Institute, 1976.

Christian, Mark A. "Priestly Power that Empowers: Michel Foucault, Middle-tier Levites, and the Sociology of 'Popular Religious Groups' in Israel." *JHS* 9 (2009): 2–81.

Coats, George W. *Rebellion in the Wilderness: The Murmuring Motif in the Wilderness Tradition in the Old Testament*. Nashville: Abingdon, 1986.

Cook, Stephen L. "Those Stubborn Levites: Overcoming Levitical Disenfranchisement." Pages 155–70 in *Levites and Priests in History and Tradition*. Edited by Mark A. Leuchter and Jeremy M. Hutton. Atlanta: Society of Biblical Literature, 2011.

Crüsemann, Frank. "Le Pentateuque, une Tora: Prolégomènes à l'interprétation de sa Forme Finale." Pages 339–60 in *Le Pentateuque en question: Les origines et la composition des cinq premiers livres de la Bible à la lumière des recherches récentes*. Edited by Albert de Pury and Thomas Römer. MdB 19. Geneva: Labor et Fides, 2002.

Davis, Craig. *Dating the Old Testament*. New York: RJ Communications, 2007.

Dozeman, Thomas B. "Hosea and the Wilderness Wandering Tradition." Pages 55–70 in *Rethinking the Foundations: Historiography in the Ancient World and in the Bible, Essays in Honour of John Van Seters*. Edited by Steven L. McKenzie and Thomas Römer. BZAW 294. Berlin: de Gruyter, 2000.

Elliger, Karl. *Leviticus*. HAT 1/4. Tübingen: Mohr Siebeck, 1966.

Finkelstein, Israel, and Thomas Römer. "Early North Israelite 'Memories' of Moab." Pages 711–28 in *The Formation of the Pentateuch: Bridging the Academic Cultures of Europe, Israel, and North America*. Edited by Jan Christian Gertz, Bernard M. Levinson, Dalit Rom-Shiloni, and Konrad Schmid. Tübingen: Mohr Siebeck, 2016.

Frevel, Christian. "The Book of Numbers—Formation, Composition, and Interpretation of a Late Part of the Torah: Some Introductory Remarks." Pages 1–37 in *Torah and the Book of Numbers*. Edited by Christian Frevel, Thomas Pola, and Aaron Schart. Tübingen: Mohr Siebeck, 2013.

García López, F. "Le Roi d'Israël: Dt 17,14–20." Pages 277–97 in *Das Deuteronomium: Entstehung, Gestalt und Botschaft*. Edited by Norbert Lohfink. BETL 68. Leuven: Peeters, 1985.

Gertz, Jan Christian. *Tradition und Redaktion in der Exoduserzählung: Untersuchungen zur Endredaktion des Pentateuch*. FRLANT 186. Göttingen: Vandenhoeck & Ruprecht, 1999.

Graf, Karl Heinrich. "Die sogenannte Grundschrift des Pentateuch." *Archiv für die wissenschaftliche Erforschung des Alten Testaments* 1 (1869): 466–77.

Heger, Paul. *The Development of Incense Cult in Israel*. BZAW 245. Berlin: de Gruyter, 1997.

Jeon, Jaeyoung. "The Levites." *EBR* 16:336–46.

———. "The Zadokites in the Wilderness: The Rebellion of Korach (Num 16) and the Zadokite Redaction." *ZABR* 127 (2015): 381–411.

Johnstone, William. "The Use of Reminiscences in Deuteronomy in Recovering the Two Main Literary Phases in the Production of the Pentateuch." Pages 245–63 in *Abschied vom Jahwisten: die Komposition des Hexateuch in der jüngsten Diskussion*. Edited by Jan Christian Gertz, Konrad Schmid, and Markus Witte. BZAW 315. Berlin: de Gruyter, 2002.

Knohl, Israel. *The Sanctuary of Silence: The Priestly Torah and the Holiness School*. Minneapolis, MN: Fortress, 1995.

———. "Who Edited the Pentateuch?" Pages 359–67 in *The Pentateuch: International Perspectives on Current Research*. Edited by Thomas B. Dozeman, Konrad Schmid, and Baruch J. Schwartz. FAT 78. Tübingen: Mohr Siebeck, 2011.

Knoppers, Gary N. *Jews and Samaritans: The Origins and Early History of Their Relations*. Oxford: Oxford University Press, 2013.

Kuenen, Abraham. *A Historical-Critical Inquiry into the Origin and Composition of the Hexateuch*. London: Macmillan, 1886.

Lauinger, Jacob. "Esarhaddon's Succession Treaty at Tell Tayinat: Text and Commentary." *JCS* 64 (2012): 87–123.

Leuchter, Mark. "'The Levite in Your Gates': The Deuteronomic Redefinition of Levitical Authority Author(s)." *JBL* 126 (2007): 417–36.

Levinson, Bernard M. "The Reconceptualization of Kingship in Deuteronomy and the Deuteronomistic History's Transformation of the Torah." *VT* 51 (2001): 511–34.

Lombaard, C. "The Strange Case of the Patriarchs in Jeremiah 33:26." *AcT* 35.2 (2015): 36–49.

Maeir, Aren M. "The Historical Background and Dating of Amos VI 2: An Archaeological Perspective from Tell eṣ-Ṣâfi/Gath." *VT* (2004): 327.

Magen, Yitzakh. "The Dating of the First Phase of the Samaritan Temple on Mt. Gerizim in Light of Archaeological Evidence." Pages 157–211 in *Judah and the Judeans in the Fourth Century B.C.E.* Edited by Oded Lipschitz, Gary N. Knoppers, and Rainer Albertz. Winona Lake, IN: Eisenbrauns, 2007.

Meyer, Esias E. "Dating the Priestly Text in the Pre-exilic Period: Some Remarks about Anachronistic Slips and Other Obstacles." *Verbum et Ecclesia* 31 (2010): 1–6.

———. *The Jubilee in Leviticus 25: A Theological Ethical Interpretation from a South African Perspective.* Münster: LIT, 2005.

Milgrom, Jacob. "The Date of Jeremiah, Chapter 2." *JNES* 14.2 (1955): 65–69.

Min, Kyung-Jin. *The Levitical Authorship of Ezra-Nehemiah.* JSOTSup 409. New York: T&T Clark, 2004.

Mtshiselwa, Vincent N. N. "Re-reading the Israelite Jubilee in Leviticus 25:8–55 in the Context of Land Redistribution and Socio-Economic Justice in South Africa: An African Liberationist Perspective." PhD diss., University of South Africa, 2015.

Na'aman, Nadav. "Sojourners and Levites in the Kingdom of Judah in the Seventh Century." *ZABR* 14 (2008): 237–79.

Nicholson, Ernest W. "'Do Not Dare to Set a Foreigner over You': The King in Deuteronomy and 'The Great King.'" *ZAW* 118 (2006): 46–61.

Nihan, Christophe. *From Priestly Torah to Pentateuch: A Study in the Composition of the Pentateuch.* FAT 2/25. Tübingen: Mohr Siebeck, 2007.

———. "The Memory of Ezekiel in Postmonarchic Yehud." Pages 415–48 in *Remembering Biblical Figures in the Late Persian and Early Hellenistic Periods: Social Memory and Imagination.* Edited by Diana V. Edelman and Ehud Ben Zvi. Oxford: Oxford University Press, 2013.

———. "The Torah between Samaria and Judah: Shechem and Gerizim in Deuteronomy and Joshua." Pages 187–223 in *The Pentateuch as Torah: New Models for Understanding Its Promulgation and Acceptance.*

Edited by Gary N. Knoppers and Bernard M. Levinson. Winona Lake, IN: Eisenbrauns, 2007.

Nocquet, Dany R. *La Samarie, la diaspora et l'achèvement de la Torah*. OBO 284. Fribourg: Academic Press; Göttingen: Vandenhoeck & Ruprecht, 2017.

Otto, Eckart. "The Books of Deuteronomy and Numbers in One Torah: The Book of Numbers Read in the Horizon of the Postexilic *Fortschreibung* in the Book of Deuteronomy; New Horizons in the Interpretation of the Pentateuch." Pages 383–97 in *Torah and the Book of Numbers*. Edited by Christian Frevel, Thomas Pola, and Aaron Schart. Tübingen: Mohr Siebeck, 2013.

———. "Born out of Ruins: The Catastrophe of Jerusalem as *Accoucheur* to the Pentateuch in the Book of Deuteronomy." Pages 155–68 in *The Fall of Jerusalem and the Rise of the Torah*. Edited by Peter Dubovský, Dominik Markl, and Jean-Pierre Sonnet. FAT 107. Tübingen: Mohr Siebeck, 2016.

———. *Das Deuteronomium: Politische Theologie und Rechtsreform in Juda und Assyrien*. BZAW 284. Berlin: de Gruyter, 1999

———. *Das Deuteronomium im Pentateuch und Hexateuch: Studien zur Literaturgeschte von Pentateuch und Hexateuch im Litchte des Deuteronomiumsrahmen*. FAT 30. Tübingen: Mohr Siebeck, 2000.

———. "The Integration of the Post-exilic Book of Deuteronomy into the Post-Priestly Pentateuch." Pages 331–41 in *The Post-Priestly Pentateuch: New Perspectives on Its Redactional Development and Theological Profiles*. Edited by Federico Giuntoli and Konrad Schmid. Tübingen: Mohr Siebeck, 2015.

———. "Pentateuch und Hexateuch jenseits von Jerusalem und Juda? Die 'Endredaktion' von Pentateuch und Hexateuch in Samaria und Diaspora. Zu einem Buch von Dany R. Nocquet." *ZABR* 23 (2017): 303–9.

Pummer, Reinhard. *The Samaritans: A Profile*. Grand Rapids: Eerdmans, 2015.

Römer, Thomas. "Cult Centralization in Deuteronomy 12: Between Deuteronomistic History and Pentateuch." Pages 166–80 in *Das Deuteronomium zwischen Pentateuch und Deuteronomistiscem Geschichitswerk*. Edited by Eckart Otto and Reinhard Achenbach. Göttingen: Vandenhoeck & Ruprecht, 2004.

———. "Egypt Nostalgia in Exodus 14–Numbers 21." Pages 66–86 in *Torah and the Book of Numbers*. Edited by Christian Frevel, Thomas Pola, and Aaron Schart. Tübingen: Mohr Siebeck, 2013.

———. "'Higher Criticism': The Historical and Literary-Critical Approach—with Special Reference to the Pentateuch." Pages 393–423 in *The Nineteenth Century: A Century of Modernism and Historicism*. Vol 3.1 of *Hebrew Bible/Old Testament*. Magne Sæbø. Göttingen: Vandenhoeck & Ruprecht, 2013.

———. "How to Date Pentateuchal Texts: Some Case Studies." Pages 357–70 in *The Formation of the Pentateuch: Bridging the Academic Cultures of Europe, Israel, and North America*. Edited by Jan Christian Gertz, Bernard M. Levinson, Dalit Rom-Shiloni, and Konrad Schmid. FAT 111. Tübingen: Mohr Siebeck, 2016.

———. "Israel's Sojourn in the Wilderness and the Construction of the Book of Numbers." Pages 419–45 in *Reflection and Refraction: Studies in Biblical Historiography in Honour of A. Graeme Auld*. Edited by Robert Rezetko, Timothy H. Lim, and W. Brian Aucker. VTSup 113. Leiden: Brill, 2007.

Schaper, Joachim. *Priester und Leviten im Achämenidischen Juda: Studien zur Kult und Sozialgeschichte Israels in Persischer Zeit*. FAT 31. Tübingen: Mohr Siebeck, 1999.

Schmid, Konrad. "The Late Persian Formation of the Torah: Observations on Deuteronomy 34." Pages 237–51 Pages in *Judah and the Judeans in the Fourth Century B.C.E.* Edited by Oded Lipschitz, Gary N. Knoppers, and Rainer Albertz. Winona Lake, IN: Eisenbrauns, 2007.

Ska, Jean-Louis. "Why Does the Pentateuch Speak so Much of Torah and so Little of Jerusalem?" Pages 113–28 in *The Fall of Jerusalem and the Rise of the Torah*. Edited by Peter Dubovský, Dominik Markl, and Jean-Pierre Sonnet. FAT 107. Tübingen: Mohr Siebeck, 2016.

Spinoza, Baruch de. *A Theologico-political Treatise and a Political Treatise*. Translated by R. H. M. Elwes. New York: Dover, 2004.

Stackert, Jeffrey. *A Prophet Like Moses: Prophecy, Law and Israelite Religion*. Oxford: Oxford University Press, 2014.

Steymans, Hans Ulrich. *Deuteronomium 28 und die adê zur Thronfolgeregelung Asarhaddons: Segen und Fluch im Alten Orient und in Israel*. OBO 145. Göttingen: Vandenhoeck & Ruprecht, 1995.

———. "Die neuassyrische Vertragsrhetorik der 'Vassal Treaties of Esarhaddon' und das Deuteronomium." Pages 89–152 in *Das Deuteronomium*. Edited by Georg Braulik. ÖBS 23. Frankfurt am Main: Lang, 2003.

Sweeney, Marvin A. "Dating Prophetic Texts." *HS* 48 (2007): 55–73.

Wellhausen, Julius. *Die Composition des Hexateuchs und der historischen Bücher des Alten Testaments.* Berlin: de Gruyter, 1963.
Wette, Wilhelm Martin Leberecht de. *Beiträge zur Einleitung in das Alte Testament.* 2 vols. Halle: Schimmelpfennig, 1806.
———. *Opuscula Theologica.* Berlin: Reimer, 1830.
Yee, Gale A. *Composition and Tradition in the Book of Hosea: A Redaction Critical Investigation.* SBLDS 102. Atlanta: Scholars Press, 1987.

Perspectives of the Diaspora and
Samaritan Communities

Transjordan in the Book of Numbers

Olivier Artus

The last chapters of the book of Numbers have often been considered supplements to the book, written by late post-Priestly redactors without any evident unity. Martin Noth wrote about Num 26–36: "No proper sequence is maintained in this whole complex of later additions. We shall have to reckon with the fact that the individual units were simply added one after the other in the order in which they appeared."[1] As Rainer Albertz has written, many recent commentaries of these texts have difficulty identifying their authors more precisely.[2] Horst Seebass speaks here of a "Numerikomposition" written at the end of the fourth century BCE.[3] Ulrich Fistill ascribes Num 21:21–36:13 to a post-Priestly redactor using and unifying different older materials.[4] But identifying these last chapters of the book of Numbers as a post-Priestly or as an independent late composition does not answer the question about the function of these chapters in the context of the book of Numbers and, beyond this book, in the context of the Pentateuch or the Hexateuch. Chapters 26–36 deal with the second generation of the sons of Israel who left Egypt. According to Num 26, Moses and Eleazar take a census of this generation (Num 26:3–4a) at the command of YHWH, before YHWH confirms the perspective of a

---

1. Martin Noth, *Numbers: A Commentary*, OTL (Philadelphia: Westminster, 1968), 10.
2. Rainer Albertz, "A Pentateuchal Redaction in the Book of Numbers? The Late Priestly Layers of Num 25–36," *ZAW* 125 (2013): 220–33.
3. Horst Seebass, *Numeri*, vol. 3, BKAT 4.3 (Neukirchen-Vluyn: Neukirchener Verlag, 2007).
4. Ulrich Fistill, *Israel und das Ostjordanland: Untersuchungen zur Komposition von Num 21,21–36,13 im Hinblick auf die Entstehung des Buches Numeri*, ÖBS 30 (Frankfurt-am-Main: Lang, 2007), 108–9.

settlement in the land, as well as of the sharing of the land between the tribes (Num 26:52–56).[5]

In this context, Num 32 is amazing. After the victory against Sihon and Og and the conquest of Gilead and Bashan, related by Num 21:21–35, two and a half tribes—Gad, Reuben, and half Manasseh—ask to settle in Transjordan. This demand, leading to a debate, is finally agreed to by Moses.

Beginning with Num 13, the narratives dealing with the perspective of the settlement reference only Canaan. An initial reading of Num 32 might therefore give the impression that this narrative contradicts in some way the global perspective of the book of Numbers. From both military and legal points of view, the book of Numbers deals with the preparation for the settlement of the tribes in Canaan. The borders of Canaan are precisely described in Num 34:1–11 and exclude the territory of the two and a half tribes in Transjordan. On the other hand, some legal texts in Num 27–36 presuppose the settlement of these two and a half tribes: the law about the inheritance of the patrimony (נחלה) of the daughters of Zelophehad (Num 27:1–11 and 36:1–12) and the laws about the Levitical cities and cities of refuge for murderers (Num 35).

The interpretation of the story of the settlement of two and a half tribes in Transjordan is therefore challenging from an exegetical point of view as well as from a sociohistorical point of view. This article will try to offer an interpretation that fits within a relevant interpretation of the book of Numbers in the context of the Pentateuch.

1. A Review of Some Recent Hypotheses

Exegetical analysis of the stories about the conquest of Transjordan and of the settlement of two and half tribes in these territories requires us to consider the close parallels that are found between the historiography of Deut 1–3 and many narratives of Numbers.

The work of Eckart Otto constitutes a new step in understanding of Deut 1–3. He reconstructs in these chapters two main layers: a Moab redaction and a hexateuchal redaction.[6] According to Otto, the purpose of the Moab redaction is to substitute a covenant in Moab for the covenant at Horeb. The Moab covenant is linked with the writing of the book of the

---

5. Numbers 26:3–4a contradicts Num 26:4b: ובני ישראל היצאים מארץ מצרים.
6. Eckart Otto, "Die Literaturgeschichte von Deuteronomium 1–3," *ZABR* 14 (2008): 86–236.

Torah by Moses (Deut 31:9, 24). After crossing the Jordan, the gift of the law is complete, and the Torah now has the function of accompanying the life of the people. This explains the narrative of the death of Moses at the end of the book of Deuteronomy, which also fits with Deut 1:37-38 and 3:23-28: once Moses writes the law for the people, his presence is no longer needed for the survival of Israel. When compared with Num 20:12, this Dtr presentation of the motives of the death of Moses is totally different from Num 20:12, where Moses's death is the consequence of his disobedience.

According to Otto, a hexateuchal redaction of Deut 1-3 comes later than the Moab redaction and is designed to integrate Deuteronomy into the Hexateuch, connecting Priestly and Deuteronomistic traditions. This hexateuchal redaction homogenizes the narratives of Numbers and Deuteronomy that deal with disobedience at Kadesh (Num 13-14; Deut 1:19-46) and with the conquest of Transjordan (Num 21:10-35; 32; Deut 2:2-3:22).

Reinhard Achenbach proposes an analysis of the book of Numbers that fits Otto's hypothesis: the hexateuchal redaction of Numbers integrates older narratives at the same time it builds a compromise between the P and Dtr traditions.[7] This redaction is also responsible for a rewriting of Deut 1-3 that integrates it into the larger context of the Hexateuch.[8]

The conclusions of Albertz, in his analysis of Num 20-24, do not differ much from the scheme proposed by Achenbach. The oldest layer corresponds to the bridge built between a P Tetrateuch and D; according to Albertz, it is similar to what Erhard Blum called the "D-Komposition" (KD).[9] Most of the later material is ascribed to a hexateuchal composition that differs from the former narratives of Deut 1-3. Indeed, Num 20:14-21 and the stories about Balaam have a negative view of Edom and Moab.[10] According to Albertz, Num 24 is the former conclusion to the

---

7. Reinhard Achenbach, *Die Vollendung der Tora: Studien zur Redaktionsgeschichte des Numeribuches im Kontext von Hexateuch und Pentateuch*, BZABR 3 (Wiesbaden: Harrassowitz, 2003), 335-44, 352-88.

8. Achenbach, *Die Vollendung*, 335-88.

9. This idea was highlighted particularly by Thomas Römer, "Das Buch Numeri und das Ende des Jahwisten: Anfragen zur 'Quellenscheidung' im vierten Buch des Pentateuch," in *Abschied vom Jahwisten: Die Komposition des Hexateuch in der jügsten Diskussion*, ed. Jan Christian Gertz, Konrad Schmid, and Markus Witte, BZAW 315 (Berlin: de Gruyter, 2002), 215-31, 220-31. See Erhard Blum, *Studien zur Komposition des Pentateuch*, BZAW 189 (Berlin: de Gruyter, 1990).

10. Rainer Albertz, "Das Buch Numeri jenseits der Quellentheorie: Eine Redaktionsgeschichte von Num 20-24," *ZAW* 123 (2011): 171-83.

book of Numbers, an initial ending to the narrative of the conquest of Transjordan. Numbers 25–36 might have been added later to the book, including the story of the settlement of two and half tribes. According to Albertz, these chapters are substitutes for the conquest and settlement narratives in the book of Joshua. They can be understood only in the context of a pentateuchal redaction.[11] Albertz considers that Num 25–36 (rather than 26–36) correspond to this post-Priestly pentateuchal redaction, as the subunits of Num 25–36 are closely linked by a network of identical or similar words and phrases; I will return to this topic later.[12]

Let us finally quote Reinhard Kratz, who offers another interpretation of the relationship between Deut 1–3 and Numbers: according to Kratz, Deut 1–3 creates a connection between the textual material of Exodus–Numbers and the rest of the book of Deuteronomy in a very late composition.[13]

This short review of the research leads to the conclusion that Num 25–36 or 26–36 were added to the book in the latest phases of its composition. But there is no unanimity about the specific function of these chapters. Do they constitute a collection of late supplements, gathered without order? An initial reading of Num 26–36 leads to the conclusion that the text deals with many different topics without any evident thematic or theological link. Let us now consider the characteristics of the narratives of Numbers dealing with Transjordan.

2. Narrative Presentation of Transjordan in the Book of Numbers

2.1. The Theological Logic of the Succession of Two Generations in Deuteronomy 1–3 and in the Book of Numbers

The main topic of Deut 1 is the disobedience of the first generation, resulting in the modification of Israel's itinerary and the death of this first generation (Deut 2:14–16) after a peaceful crossing of the territories of

---

11. Albertz, "Pentateuchal Redaction," 220–33.
12. Albertz, "Pentateuchal Redaction," 237.
13. Reinard Gregor Kratz, "Der literarische Ort des Deuteronomiums," in *Liebe und Gebot: Studien zum Deuteronomium*, ed. Reinard Gregor Kratz and Hermann Spieckermann, FRLANT 190 (Göttingen: Vandenhoeck & Ruprecht, 2000), 101–20; Kratz, "The Pentateuch in Current Research: Consensus and Debate," in *The Pentateuch*, ed. Thomas B. Dozeman, Konrad Schmid, and Baruch J. Schwartz, FAT 78 (Tübingen: Mohr Siebeck, 2011), 39–45.

Edom and Moab (Deut 2:2–12). Then come narratives about the victories against the Amorites (Deut 2:17–37) and Og, king of Bashan (3:1–7), as well as the story of the settlement of two and a half tribes in Transjordan (Deut 3:12b–20). The stories of the battles against the Amorites—their defeat in Deut 1:41–44 and their victory in Deut 2:17–37—frame the description of the peaceful crossing through Edom and Moab.

As we know, the unbroken narrative of Deut 1–3 has parallels in Numbers, but these parallels are scattered throughout the book: Judges are appointed in Deut 1:9–18, parallel to the story of the elders in Num 11:24–30. The first generation disobeys in Deut 1:19–28, parallel to Num 14:1–4. The generation that will not enter the land (apart from Caleb) is punished in Deut 1:34–35, parallel to Num 14:21–24. They are defeated by the Amorites in Deut 1:41–45, parallel to Num 14:39–45. The Israelites peacefully cross the territory of Edom and Moab in Deut 2:1–13, 18–23, parallel to Num 20:14–21 and 21:10–20. They defeat Sihon and Og in Deut 2:24–3:12a, parallel to Num 21:21–35. And the two and half tribes settle in Transjordan in Deut 3:12b–22, parallel to Num 32. According to Deut 1–3, the punishment following the revolt of the people does not cancel the promise of the land (Deut 1:8). In the latest phases of the composition of the text, the story of Deut 1:19–46 has been harmonized with its parallels in the book of Numbers, as shown by the introduction of specific topics from Numbers, such as reference to Caleb in Deut 1:36 and to the genealogy of Caleb and Joshua in Deut 1:36, 38, as well as the expression וטפכם אשר אמרתם לבז in Deut 1:39a, parallel to Num 14:3, 31.[14]

With regard to Moses, the story of Deut 1–3 exposes a specific issue that has no parallel in Numbers. According to Deut 1:37; 3:23–27, the punishment of the first generation implies the death of Moses. Thus Deut 1:37 proposes an explanation of Moses's death that differs from both Num 20:12 and Deut 34:7. Numbers 20:12 links the fate of Moses to the sin that he committed: Moses (like Aaron) failed to reveal the holiness of YHWH in front of the people. On the other hand, Deut 34:7 links Moses's death to the common fate of the humans (Gen 6:3). The destiny of Moses as described by Deut 1:37; 3:23–27 could seem to contradict his faithfulness to YHWH, particularly underlined by Deut 1:29–31. Indeed, according to Deut 1:29–31, Moses's discourse responds to the disobedience of the

---

14. Reinhard Achenbach, "Die Erzählung von der der gescheiterten Landnahme von Kadesch Barnea (Numeri 13–14) als Schlüsseltext der Redaktionsgeschichte des Pentateuchs," *ZABR* 9 (2003): 71.

people, who refuse to enter the land, quite differently from the parallel story of Numbers, in which Caleb and Joshua—not Moses—encourage the conquest of the land by the first generation (Num 13:30; 14:6–9). So, according to Deut 1–3, Moses's death is not the consequence of his unfaithfulness. It is needed by the theological project of Deuteronomy. As Otto shows, the Moab covenant is related to the writing of the book of the Torah by Moses (Deut 31:9).[15] The gift of the law will replace the presence of Moses among the people, who will get a new leader—Joshua—but no more laws.

Finally, according to Deut 1–3, YHWH himself leads the people through all these events. His orders are sometimes challenged by the opposition of the people or by Moses himself, who asks to accompany the people into the land. But the narrative of Deut 1–3 highlights the authority of YHWH over history. According to this perspective, the settlement of two and half tribes in Transjordan is part of this historical divine project.

2.2. Victory before the Amorites and Settlement in Transjordan in Deuteronomy 1–3 and in the Book of Numbers

2.2.1. Numbers 21 and Deuteronomy 2:1–3, 12a

According to Deut 2:1–3, 12a, the victory against the Amorites is given a theological meaning; as Fistill notes, the fiction of the Amorites underlines the theological dimension of the text. Through the fiction of the victory against these people, the biblical narrative reasserts the faithfulness of YHWH to his promises.[16] On the contrary, the parallel text of Num 21:21–33 is totally secularized, integrating former war traditions.[17] On the other hand, there is a close parallel between the story of the victory over Og of Bashan in Deut 3:2–7 and Num 21:33–35. The parallelism between Num 21:34 and Deut 3:2 reflects the process of integrating older narratives from the book of Numbers into the larger context of a Hexateuch:

Num 21:34

ויאמר יהוה אל־משה אל־תירא אתו כי בידך נתתי אתו ואת־כל־עמו ואת־ארצו

---

15. Otto, "Die Literaturgeschichte," 86–236.
16. Fistill, *Israel*, 201–2.
17. Albertz, "Das Buch Numeri," 179–80.

Deut 3:2

ויאמר יהוה אלי אל־תירא אתו כי בידך נתתי אתו ואת־כל־עמו ואת־ארצו

2.2.2. Numbers 32 and Deuteronomy 3:12b–22

As we saw, the story of Num 32 is parallel to Deut 3:12b–22. Two main differences characterize these narratives. First, even if two and a half tribes are finally allowed to settle in Transjordan, this territory stays outside the borders of the land given to Israel according to their description in Num 34:1–12. So settling in Transjordan is presented as a choice that means withdrawing from YHWH's historical project for Israel.

Second, the behavior of the two and a half tribes is criminalized by the narrative of Num 32. Numbers 32 insists on the initiative of the two and a half tribes themselves in this settlement, which is a major difference from the narrative of Deut 3:12b–22. This initiative leads to a sharp discussion with Moses. Numbers 32:6–15, a later supplement to the narrative, appraises the behavior of these tribes as even worse than the initial narrative did.[18] They are now compared to the first generation, whose members were condemned to death because of their apostasy. But, according to the narrative of Deut 3:12b–22, the settlement of the tribes is legitimate and follows the order transmitted by Moses.

---

18. The parenetic discourse of Num 32:6–15 presupposes chapters 13 and 14 of Numbers in their final compositional form as Achenbach, *Die Vollendung*, 383–88 described it: v. 9 quotes the toponym אשכל, which belongs to the earliest textual layer of Num 13, while v. 13 presupposes the punishment narrated in Num 14:28–35, which belongs to the latest layer of the narrative. Verse 12 is quite interesting because it links the expressions Caleb ben Jephunneh and Joshua bin Nun (found in Num 14:30 and, in the opposite order, in Num 14:6, 38), and at the same time refers to Caleb as a Kenizzite, just as in Josh 14:6, 14; 15:17; Judg 3:9, 11. Furthermore, it should be noted that the parenetic discourse of vv. 6–15 uses the rare root נ.ו.א, *hiphil*, found in vv. 7 and 9, and also four times in chapter 30 (vv. 6, 6, 9, 12). Finally, vv. 6–15 appear to be late, presupposing different traditions about Caleb. This speech is an original composition, written for parenetic purposes and integrating some post-Deuteronomistic material such as the toponym Kadesh-Barnea in v. 8, which is also used in Deut 1:19; 9:23. Let us also notice the break at v. 33, in the last part of the narrative of Num 32, which for the first time in this chapter refers to the half tribe of Manasseh. From v. 1, the narrative mentions only the sons of Gad and the sons of Ruben, Moreover, v. 33 refers to the narrative of Num 21, describing the victory over Sihon and Og. So v. 33 can be considered a late supplement in Num 32, along with vv. 34–38, which can be considered a gloss.

2.3. Conclusions

The narrative in Num 21 does not offer any theological evaluation of the conquest of the territories of Sihon and Og. The story of the victory against Og in Num 21:33-35 is a close parallel to Deut 3:1-4 and constitutes a later addition to an ancient tradition about Sihon that was integrated into a larger composition when the old narratives of Numbers were connected with Deuteronomy. Unlike Num 21, the narrative of Num 32 is highly theological. Numbers 32 echoes a debate about the possibility of living out Judaism far from Canaan, namely, far from the temple and from its priestly authorities—in Numbers 32, Eleazar.

3. Numbers 32 in Context: Questions about Delimitation and Specificity in the Third Part of the Book of Numbers.

3.1. The Structure of Numbers 27-36

According to geographical criteria, Numbers 22-36 are unified through common reference to Moab. Let us first notice a difference between Num 22:1 and the other occurrences.[19] The expression לירדן מעבר is specific to Num 22:1. In in the majority of the occurrences in Num 26-36, the preposition על precedes the word ירדן. Albertz explains this difference by identifying two redactors, one in Num 22-24 and a second in Num 25-36.[20] Anyway, it is clear that chapters 22-24 deal with specific narrative and theological themes—stories about Balaam the relationship between Israel and foreigners—and that their ties with chapters 25-36 are not evident. Moreover, the unity of chapters 25-36 is also quite difficult to demonstrate. The narrative links between the story of the apostasy of Peor (Num 25:2-3, 6, 16-18) and the war against the Midianites (Num 31:2-3, 16) are evident. But Num 31 is integrated in a literary structure that excludes Num 25: the census of Num 26 introduces the story of the second generation, and chapters 27-36 have a palindromic structure. Even if they are not part of the same stage of the composition, the laws about

---

19. Num 22:1: בערבת מואב מעבר לירדן; Num 26:3, 63: בערבת מואב מעבר על־ירדן; Num 33:48; 36:13: אל ערבת מואב אשר על ירחו ירדן; Num 31:12: ירחו בערבת מואב מעבר; Num 33:49, 50; 35:1: בערבת מואב; על ירדן ירחו.

20. Albertz, "Pentateuchal Redaction," 228.

the daughters of Zelophehad frame chapters 27–36.[21] Chapters 28–30 and chapter 35 go together, as they all deal with cultic regulations and with the topic of land, as the cult requires vegetal and animal offerings to YHWH that are linked with the work of the land.[22] At the center of the structure, chapters 31–34 deal with the themes of war and conquest. So, beyond the diversity of themes in Num 27–36, the structure of the text seems to reflect a global composition, leading me to consider this last part of the book of Numbers as a whole.

3.2. Specificity of Vocabulary and Topics in the Last Part of the Book of Numbers

The preceding conclusion is reinforced by the specificity of vocabulary in the last part of the book of Numbers. Use of the vocabulary of patrimony and inheritance is concentrated in chapters 26–36, particularly אחזה, "property" (Num 27:4, 7; 32:5, 22, 29, 32; 35:2, 8, 28) and נחלה, "patrimony" (Num 16:14; 18:20–21, 23, 24 [2x], 26; 26:53, 54 [2x], 56, 62; 27:7 [2x], 8–11; 32:18–19, 32; 33:54; 34:2, 14–15; 35:2, 8; 36:2 [2x], 3 [3x], 4 [4x], 7 [2x], 8 [2x], 9 [2x], 12). As Albertz shows, Num 27–36 is the only place in the Pentateuch where the two words are combined in the expression אחזת נחלה: Num 27:7; 32:32; 35:2.[23] In the same way, the topic of drawing lots (גורל) for tribal territories is found only in chapters 27–36: Num 26:55–56; 33:54; 34:13; 36:2–3. And the majority of the occurrences of the word מחנה, "camp," are found in the story of the first generation of the people: apart from Num 31:12–13, 19, 24, the occurrences are concentrated in Num 1–19.

If we combine these observations, we can conclude that new topics characterize the last part of the book of Numbers: אחזה "property," גורל "lot," and נחלה "patrimony," as well as בנה "building/rebuilding" (Num 32:16, 24, 34, 37, 38). Israel is no longer an army on the move, as it was in Num 2 or Num 10. It has become a community of farmers settling in the land, sharing the territory, and preparing the worship of YHWH by offering the products of the soil. So a question rises about the specificity of chapters 26:36. Are they only a later supplement that has to be considered

---

21. Achenbach, *Die Vollendung*, 567–73 and Itamar Kislev, "Numbers 36,1–12: Innovation and Interpretation," *ZAW* 122 (201): 249–59.
22. With Albertz, "Pentateuchal Redaction," 225.
23. Albertz, "Pentateuchal Redaction," 228.

and interpreted independently from the rest of the book of Numbers? Or do they have connections with the rest of the book, in the context of which they can be interpreted?

3.3. Connections between Numbers 26–36 and 1–25

There is a network of relationships between Num 26–36 and the previous parts of the book of Numbers. As Itamar Kislev has shown, the census of Num 26 was reworked to be inserted in its current literary context, explicitly referring to Num 1 (Num 26:63–64), as well as preparing for both the story of the daughters of Zelophehad (Num 26:33) and the story of the sharing of the land (Num 26:52–56).[24] As Dennis T. Olson has demonstrated, the two censuses in Num 1 and Num 26 are essential in the global structure of the book.[25] Numbers 1–25 deal with the first generation of the people who left Egypt, and Num 26–36 deal with the second generation, presented as a paradigm for all future generations.

There is also an evident connection between Num 1, Num 13, and Num 34. According to these three chapters, the heads of the people—called ראש in Num 1:16; 13:3 and נשיא in Num 1:16; 13:2; 34:18—one delegate for each tribe, are given three missions: to take a census of the community (Num 1), to appoint scouts (Num 13), and to share the land (Num 34).

Numbers 26 and 32 refer to the story of disobedience and sin at Kadesh. The conclusion of the census of Num 26 (Num 26:64–65) underlines the death of the whole of the first generation, apart from Caleb and Joshua (Num 14). And the story of the settlement of two and a half tribes in Transjordan compares these tribes with the sinners of Num 14 (Num 32:6–15).

Finally, the census of the Levites recalls the law of Num 18: the Levites will not receive any patrimony (נחלה, Num 18:24), so the census of the Levites takes place apart from the census of the twelve other tribes (Num 26:57–62, particularly v. 62).

We can reach the conclusion that there is network of connections between Num 1–25 and Num 26–36 that invite us to interpret chapters 26–36 in the larger context of the whole composition of the book of Numbers.

---

24. Itamar Kislev, "The Census of the Israelites in the Plains of Moab (Numbers 26): Sources and Redaction," *VT* 63 (2013): 236–60; Kislev, "The Numbers of Numbers: The Census Account in the Book of Numbers," *ZAW* 128 (2016): 189–204.

25. Dennis T. Olson, *The Death of the Old and the Birth of the New: The Framework of the Book of Numbers and the Pentateuch* (Chico, CA: Scholars Press, 1985).

3.4. Numbers 26–36 in the Context of the Book of Numbers

Numbers 1–25 relate the story of the first generation of people who left Egypt. Two main parts can be delimited in this story: the organization of the community (Num 1–10) and the disobedience of the members of the community, which leads to their death (Num 11–20, with stories of disobedience and punishment in Num 11; 13–14; 16; 20:1–13). Indeed, chapters 11–20 describe the rebellion of all the members of the community: spies who are the heads of the tribes (Num 13), the assembly of the people (Num 14), the Levites (Num 16), and finally Moses and Aaron themselves (Num 20:1–13).

Only two characters remain faithful, Caleb and Joshua, who are related to the two largest tribes in the south and the north: Caleb belongs to Judah, Joshua to Ephraim. This means that any Israelite, from the north or from the south, can identify with these exemplary characters within the narrative. The last part of the book, Num 26:64–65 and the speech in Num 32:6–15, quote the narrative of Num 14, evoking the paradigmatic example offered by Caleb and Joshua.

Two categories of rebellion are described in Num 11–20. The first consists of rebellions related to the historical or military project of YHWH. The spies sent to Canaan bring discredit on the land (Num 13), and the community refuses to conquer Canaan (Num 14). The hypothesis that these chapters are polemical seems promising: Num 13–14 could be intended to criticize the Jews of the diaspora for remaining outside Canaan. This would fit with the perspective of the discourse of Moses in Num 32, who criticizes the two and a half tribes of Transjordan. They are authorized to dwell beyond the Jordan, but this choice is met with hard criticism and suspicion from the leaders of the community. The second category of rebellion involves those related to the religious project of YHWH. Korah and his Levitical supporters protest the hierarchy of holiness according to which the community is organized (Num 16:1–3, 8–11). The consequences of this rebellion are the same as in Num 14: exclusion from the community and condemnation to death.

The rebellions thus affect both the cultic organization of the community and the military project of the conquest of the land. These two topics are already connected in Num 1–10. On the one hand, chapters 1–10 are organized according to a hierarchy of holiness, dealing first with the community (Num 1–2) and then with the Levites (Num 3–4), the priests (Num 5–6), and finally the sanctuary (Num 7–8). On the other hand, the community itself is structured and presented as a group of armies (צבא) surrounding the tent of the meeting (Num 2 [21x]; 10:11–28 [17x]). The preparation of the conquest of Canaan thus requires both military organization of the community and cultic organization according to which the community is invited to offer to God a proper cult.[26]

In this context, the attempt of two and a half tribes to dwell in Transjordan not only has military consequences, but also constitutes an attempt to live out an alternative Judaism far from the authority of the priests, especially the high priest. The two and a half tribes of Transjordan challenge the authority of the high priest and so challenge the hierocratic organization of the community described in the post-Priestly composition of the book of Numbers: their will to dwell in Transjordan breaks the unity of the camp, described by Num 2:10–12 and Num 10:18–20, which stipulate that the tribes of Reuben and Gad belong to the southern part of the camp.[27] Staying on their own in Transjordan, the two and half tribes remove themselves from a structure, the center of which is the tent of the meeting worshiped by the priests. The contrast with Deut 3:12–17 is remarkable, as there the settlement of tribes in Transjordan fits with YHWH's historical project.

4. Transjordan in the Book of Numbers: Attempt at an Interpretation

Beyond gathering of many different literary materials, the book of Numbers has been unified by a late post-Priestly redaction. The topographic data and the succession of the two censuses are used by the redactors to give the book a global structure describing the destiny of two first generations who left Egypt. The story of the first generation is described in the first part of the book. Their organization according to a logic of holiness

---

26. See the analysis of Achenbach, *Die Vollendung der Tora*, 483–88: Num 2 deals with the organization of the community, described according to both a "military geography" and a cultic logic. The tribes are arranged in the perspective of the march but also gathered around the tent of the meeting, which is coherent with a hierocratic and theocratic ideology.

27. The first two parts of the book of Numbers (Num 1–10 and 11–21), the composition of which has been attributed to post-Priestly authors, describe a community organized according to a hierarchy of holiness. The priests, helped by the Levites, serve the sanctuary, which is situated at the center of the community. Dwelling in Transjordan, the two and a half tribes challenge this centralized organization and set up a geographical distance between themselves and the central authority of the high priest.

in the desert of Sinai (Num 1–10) is followed by stories of sin, principally at Kadesh (Num 13:1–20, 21), that lead to the death of this first generation (Num 1–25). The second generation inherits the promise of land, as well as the cultic organization that the first generation was given through Moses and Aaron. A new high priest, and a new lay leader, Joshua, are established by YHWH.

In this context, the project of a settlement in Transjordan is sharply criticized, as it does not fit with the hierocratic organization of the community and with the military project of conquering Canaan. The two and a half tribes are finally authorized to stay in Transjordan, but the alternative they represent seems to challenge the theological project that the book of Numbers highlights. How could this alternative be interpreted? Two solutions can be suggested: First, the two and half tribes could symbolize the possibility that Judeans can live outside Canaan and stay in diaspora. In this hypothesis, Num 32 certainly represents a sharp criticism of this choice. Second, the results of archeological digs attest the existence of new settlements in Moab during the Persian period, and the scenario of two and half tribes dwelling in Transjordan could correspond to this historical reality.[28] Numbers 32 could allude to the settlement of Jewish groups beyond the Jordan and require their subordination to the authorities of the community, particularly to the priestly authorities.

The hypothesis that the last chapters of the book of Numbers are a part of a pentateuchal redaction therefore does not really fit with this theology, as these chapters are theologically coherent with the rest of the book of Numbers. Indeed, chapters 26–36 describe an organization of the community that highlights the specific responsibilities of the priests. But, at the same time, this hierocratic organization seems to be challenged by an alternative, presented by the narrative as life in Transjordan. The fiction of the two and a half tribes echoes the possibility of living outside of Canaan in the diaspora, as well as in Transjordan itself. This possibility is already mentioned in Deut 3, but the parallel story of Num 32 now criticizes this possibility from a hierocratic perspective. This hierocratic perspective corresponds to the main issues highlighted

---

28. Cf. Russell Hobson, "Were Persian-Period 'Israelites' Bound by Ethnicity of Religious Affiliation? The Case of the Southern Transjordan," in *Religion in the Achaemenid Persian Empire*, ed. Diana Edelman, Anne Fitzpatrick-McKinley, and Phillippe Guillaume, Orientalische Religionen in der Antike 17 (Tübingen: Mohr Siebeck, 2016), 36–56.

by the post-Priestly redaction of the book of Numbers, which is unified by a network of key words and expressions and therefore unified from a theological point a view.[29] According to the post-Priestly composition of the book, the vocation of Israel consists in living in the land of Canaan under the authority of the high priests and inside the borders described by Num 34:1–11.

Bibliography

Achenbach, Reinhard. "Die Erzählung von der der gescheiterten Landnahme von Kadesch Barnea (Numeri 13–14) als Schlüsseltext der Redaktionsgeschichte des Pentateuchs." *ZABR* 9 (2003): 56–123.
Achenbach, Reinhard. *Die Vollendung der Tora, Studien zur Redaktiongeschichte des Numeribuches im Kontext vom Hexateuch und Pentateuch.* Wiesbaden: Harrassowitz, 2003.
Albertz, Rainer. "Das Buch Numeri jenseits der Quellentheorie: Eine Redaktionsgeschichte von Num 20–24." *ZAW* 123 (2011): 171–83.
———. "A Pentateuchal Redaction in the Book of Numbers? The Late Priestly Layers of Num 25–36." *ZAW* 125 (2013): 220–33.
Blum, Erhard. *Studien zur Komposition des Pentateuch.* BZAW 189. Berlin: de Gruyter, 1990.
Fistill, Ulrich. *Israel und das Ostjordanland: Untersuchungen zur Komposition von Num 21,21–36,13 im Hinblick auf die Entstehung des Buches Numeri.* ÖBS 30. Frankfurt-am-Main: Lang, 2007.
Hobson, Russell. "Were Persian-Period 'Israelites' Bound by Ethnicity of Religious Affiliation? The Case of the Southern Transjordan." Pages 36–56 in *Religion in the Achaemenid Persian Empire.* Edited by Diana Edelman, Anne Fitzpatrick-McKinley, and Phillippe Guillaume. Orientalische Religionen in der Antike 17. Tübingen: Mohr Siebeck, 2016.
Kislev, Itamar. "The Census of the Israelites in the Plains of Moab (Numbers 26): Sources and Redaction." *VT* 63 (2013): 236–60.
———. "Numbers 36,1–12: Innovation and Interpretation." *ZAW* 122 (201): 249–59.
———. "The Numbers of Numbers: The Census Account in the Book of Numbers." *ZAW* 128 (2016): 189–204.

---

29. The main critique of the behavior of the Transjordan tribes is found in Num 32:6–15: Moses's discourse alludes to the post-Priestly narrative of the rebellion in Kadesh (Num 14:1a, 2–3, 5–10, 26–28).

Kratz, Reinard Gregor. "Der literarische Ort des Deuteronomiums." Pages 101–20 in *Liebe und Gebot: Studien zum Deuteronomium*. Edited by Reinard Gregor Kratz and Hermann Spieckermann. FRLANT 190. Göttingen: Vandenhoeck & Ruprecht, 2000.

———. "The Pentateuch in Current Research: Consensus and Debate." Pages 31–61 in *The Pentateuch*. Edited by Thomas B. Dozeman, Konrad Schmid, and Baruch J. Schwartz. FAT 78. Tübingen: Mohr Siebeck, 2011.

Noth, Martin. *Numbers: A Commentary*. OTL. Philadelphia: Westminster, 1968.

Olson, Dennis T. *The Death of the Old and the Birth of the New: The Framework of the Book of Numbers and the Pentateuch*. Chico, CA: Scholars Press, 1985.

Otto, Eckart. "Die Literaturgeschichte von Deuteronomium 1–3." *ZABR* 14 (2008): 86–236.

Römer, Thomas. "Das Buch Numeri und das Ende des Jahwisten: Anfragen zur 'Quellenscheidung' im vierten Buch des Pentateuch." Pages 215–31 in *Abschied vom Jahwisten: Die Komposition des Hexateuch in der jüngsten Diskussion*. Edited by Jan Christian Gertz, Konrad Schmid, and Markus Witte. BZAW 315. Berlin: de Gruyter, 2002.

Seebass, Horst. *Numeri*. Vol. 3. BKAT 4.3. Neukirchen-Vluyn: Neukirchener Verlag, 2007.

What Is the Contribution of the Samaritans to the Pentateuch?

Innocent Himbaza

The history and the text of the Samaritans have become a trend in biblical studies. On the one hand, Samaritans claim to keep the true and holy Torah of Moses. On the other hand, their Pentateuch seems to have the same origin as the one read by Jews and Christians. It is therefore most appropriate to clarify what would have been the contribution of Samaritans to the first and common edition of the Pentateuch. If the Pentateuch was first published as a compromise document, how and what do we know about the factions who contributed to its text? Can one identify the contribution of the Samaritans to that common Pentateuch? This article suggests some answers to such difficult questions.

1. Historical Challenge

Many aspects of the historical context of the Pentateuch production continue to elude us. Indeed, the historical context of the fifth and the beginning of the fourth centuries BCE between Gerizim and Jerusalem is still fiercely debated. Notwithstanding, different sources refer to some attested names of that period. Nehemiah refers to the kings of Persia: Artaxerxes I (465–425) and Darius II (425–405). Nehemiah 2:10, 4:2; *TAD* A.4.9, and *WD* 22 refer to Sanballat as the governor of Samaria, while *TAD* A.4.9 and Josephus (*A.J.* 11.297–303) refer to his son Delayah in the same role.[1] Nehemiah, *TAD* A.4.9, and Josephus (*A.J.* 11.297–303)

---

1. Étienne Nodet, "Sânballaṭ de Samarie," *RB* 122 (2015): 340–54. The name *Sanballat* occurs sometimes in the papyri of Wadi Daliyeh, and many scholars have asserted that there was a Sanballatide dynasty. For discussion, see Frank M. Cross, "The Papyri and Their Historical Implications," in *Discoveries in the Wâdī ed-Dâliyeh*,

mention Nehemiah and Bagohi as governors of Yehud. The high priests in Jerusalem at this time are Elyashib (according to Neh 13:28), Yoyada, and Yohanan (according to Neh 12:11, 22, 23; TAD A.4.9; Josephus, *A.J.* 11.297). Even though these names are attested by independent witnesses, it is difficult to know exactly how they interacted with each other. On the one hand, many details are given by Josephus. On the other hand, it has become common in scholarship to question his version. Not only that, Josephus may not only have confused the dates of some historical events, but also have reflected an ideological tendency against the Samaritans.[2]

On the historical level, new challenge comes from scholars who consider that the community of Gerizim and the community of Jerusalem interaction with one another for a long time, such that one cannot assert that there were tensions between them until the end of the third century BCE. One of the recent publications dealing with this point of view is *Juda und Samaria*, by Benedikt Hensel. Hensel points out two main subjects to be discussed. The first concerns the relationship between Judah

---

ed. Paul W. Lapp and Nancy L. Lapp, AASOR 41 (Cambridge: American Schools of Oriental Research, 1974), 17–29, esp. 21–22; Cross, *From Epic to Canon: History and Literature in Ancient Israel* (Baltimore: Johns Hopkins University Press, 2000), 151–72, esp. 156; Natan Schur, *History of the Samaritans*, 2nd ed., BEATAJ 18 (Frankfurt am Main: Lang, 1992), 27–29; Jürgen Zangenberg, ΣAMAPEIA: Antike Quellen zur Geschichte und Kultur der Samaritaner in deutscher Übersetsung, Texte und Arbeiten zum neutestamentlichen Zeitalter 15 (Tübingen: Franke, 1994), 297–99; Alan D. Crown, "Another Look at Samaritan Origin," in *Essays in Honour of G. D. Sexdenier: New Samaritan Studies of the Société d'Etudes Samaritaines*, vols. 3–4 of *Proceedings of the Congress of Oxford 1990, Yarnton Manor and Paris 1992, Collège de France, with Lectures Given at Hong Kong 1993 as Participation in the ICANAS Congress*, ed. Alan D. Crown and Lucy A. Davey (Sydney: Mandelbaum, 1995), 133–55; Mary Joan W. Leith, *Wadi Daliyeh I: The Wadi Daliyeh Seal Impressions*, DJD 24 (Oxford: Clarendon, 1997), 10; and Douglas M. Gropp, "Sanballat," in *Encyclopedia of the Dead Sea Scrolls*, ed. Lawrence H. Schiffman and James C. Vanderkam, 2 vols. (Oxford: Oxford University Press, 2000), 2:823–25.

2. Menahem Mor, "The Persian, Hellenistic and Hasmonaean Period," in *The Samaritans*, ed. Alan D. Crown (Tübingen: Mohr Siebeck, 1989), 1–18; Étienne Nodet, *Flavius Josèphe, Les Antiquités Juives, Livres X et XI, Introduction et texte, Traduction et notes* (Paris: Cerf, 2010), 155 n. 2; Rainer Albertz, "The History of Judah and Samaria in the Late Persian and Hellenistic Periods as a Possible Background of the Late Editions of the Book of the Twelve," in *Perspectives on the Foundation of the Book of the Twelve: Methodological Foundations, Redactional Processes, Historical Insights*, ed. Rainer Albertz, James D. Nogalski, and Jakob Wöhrle, BZAW 433 (Berlin: de Gruyter, 2012), 303–18.

and Samaria from the sixth to the second centuries BCE.[3] According to Hensel, there was "no rivalry between the provinces of Yehud and Samaria or between the YHWH-worshippers in the South and the North to be dated *before* the 3rd century BCE."[4] During the Persian period, there were two groups of YHWH worshipers living in two independent provinces, and there were contacts and interactions between them. The tangible cooperation between both denominations is the common Pentateuch, as a compromise document of the cultic communities of Mount Gerizim and Mount Zion. The relationship between Judah and Samaria may have deteriorated in the third century but more likely around 200 BCE. Rivalries arose from the fact that Judah and Samaria were now united in one large province, and Yahwists experienced two official sanctuaries. Hensel concludes that, on the historical level, the Jewish polemic against the Gerizim community is attested during the second century BCE.

The second main subject Hensel deals with is the date of 2 Kgs 17:24–41.[5] This question has been discussed many times in scholarship.[6] The value of the study of this chapter for the edition of the Pentateuch is obvious. Hensel draws attention to the probable peaceful context in which the Pentateuch was produced. In that case, 2 Kgs 17 cannot reflect the situation of the fifth century, because there were regular contacts between Samaria and Judah between the sixth and the second centuries BCE.

Hensel asserts that, on the biblical level, the anti-Samaritan polemic found in Ezra–Nehemiah as well as in 2 Kgs 17:24–41 cannot be dated long before the Ptolemaic period as attested by extrabiblical sources.[7] To reinforce his argument, he observes that the syntax of 2 Kgs 17:24–41 is late and reflects the influence of Aramaic. He especially points out the frequent use of participles with a finite verb such as היה or participles used as predicates with pronouns or negations.[8]

Hensel thus concludes that the rivalry, the anti-Samaritan polemic, and the separation between the communities of Gerizim and Zion occurred at

---

3. Benedikt Hensel, *Juda und Samaria: Zum Verhältnis zweier nach-exilischer Jahwismen*, FAT 110 (Tübingen: Mohr Siebeck, 2016), 195–230.

4. Hensel, *Juda und Samaria*, 474.

5. Hensel, *Juda und Samaria*, 367–90.

6. For a recent *status questionis*, see Magner Kartveit, "The Date of II Reg 17,24–41," *ZAW* 126 (2014): 31–44.

7. Hensel, *Juda und Samaria*, 384–86.

8. Hensel, *Juda und Samaria*, 379–80.

the beginning of the Hasmonean period during the second century BCE.[9] His point is summarized in German and in English in thirteen theses at the end of his book.[10]

To respond to Hensel's assertions, I would like to point out that there is no rivalry between the two communities in the late Persian/early Hellenistic period, because only Jerusalem rejected Gerizim. Indeed, Samaritans always claimed to belong to the same people and to themselves be YHWH worshipers, and it seems that they were.[11] Thus one cannot explain the problem between Jews and Samaritans in terms of rivalry. Like Hensel and other scholars, I see the true rivalry during the second century BCE, when both Jews and Samaritans rejected each other.[12]

In the Persian period, the community of YHWH worshipers deals especially with the problem of identity. The question is to what extent some people may have been thought to belong to the same group as those who were allowed to reorganize Yahwism or rebuild the temple of Jerusalem. This context is reflected in some biblical texts such as the book of Ezra-Nehemiah, on the one hand, and by the book of Ruth, on the other. The first opts for exclusion, while the second opts for inclusion.[13] As many

---

9. Hensel, *Juda und Samaria*, 207–8.

10. Hensel, *Juda und Samaria*, 413–15, 473–75; Benedikt Hensel, "Cult Centralization in the Persian Period: Biblical and Historical Perspectives," *Sem* 60 (2018): 221–72.

11. Reinhard Pummer, "Samaritanism: A Jewish Sect of an Independent Form of Yahwism?," in *Samaritans: Past and Present—Current Studies*, ed. Menachem Mor and Friedrich V. Reiterer, SJ 53, Studia Samaritana 5 (Berlin: de Gruyter, 2010), 1–24.

12. Stefan Schorch, "The Construction of Samari(t)an Identity from the Inside and from the Outside," in *Between Cooperation and Hostility: Multiple Identities in Ancient Judaism and the Interaction with Foreign Powers*, ed. Rainer Albertz and Jakob Wöhrle; JAJSup 11 (Göttingen: Vandenhoeck & Ruprecht, 2013), 135–49; and Innocent Himbaza, "Les Samaritains: Leur temple, leur clergé et leur texte de reference; Une approche historique," in preparation.

13. Irmtraud Fischer, *Rut: Übersetzt und ausgelegt*, HThKAT (Freiburg: Herder, 2001), 86–94; André Lacoque, *Le livre de Ruth*, CAT 17 (Geneva: Labor et Fides, 2004), 26–38, translated by K. C. Hanson as *Ruth: A Continental Commentary* (Minneapolis: Fortress, 2004), 18–32; Peter H. W. Lau, *Identity and Ethics in the Book of Ruth: A Social Identity Approach*, BZAW 416 (Berlin: de Gruyter, 2011), 90–119; Robert L. Cohn, "Overcoming Otherness in the Book of Ruth," in *Imagining the Other and Constructing Israelite Identity in the Early Second Temple Period*, ed. Ehud Ben Zvi and Diana Edelman, LHBOTS 591 (London: Bloomsbury T&T Clark, 2014), 163–81; Hugh G. M. Williamson, *Ezra Nehemiah*, WBC 16 (Waco, TX: Word, 1985), 139–62,

scholars have convincingly shown, both tendencies are reflected in the Pentateuch.[14] For instance, the land of Moab, which is the homeland of Ruth, is evaluated both negatively (Num 25:1–5; Deut 23:4–7) and positively (Deut 2:9–12; 28:69) in the Pentateuch. It is most probable, then, that such an attempt of legitimation and delegitimation occurred during the Persian period.[15]

From the linguistic perspective, and more precisely the frequency of the use of היה followed by a participle, one should accept that 2 Kgs 17:24–41 is a special case as one of the witnesses of late Biblical Hebrew.[16] One should also observe, however, that this syntagm occurs elsewhere in all the parts of the Hebrew Bible. The syntax of a participle used as predicate with a pronoun, such as עשים הם in 2 Kgs 17:34, 40,41, is also found in Ezek 8:6, 9, 13. Thus, since late Biblical Hebrew is situated in the postexilic period between the sixth and second centuries BCE, one should not restrict 2 Kgs 17 to the latest part of this long period.[17]

391–402; Joseph Blenkinsopp, *Ezra-Nehemiah: A Commentary*, OTL (Philadelphia: Westminster, 1988), 185–201, 352–66; Titus Reinmuth, *Der Bericht Nehemias: Zur literarischen Eigenart, traditionsgeschichtlichen Prägung und innerbiblischen Rezeption des Ich-Berichts Nehemias*, OBO 183 (Fribourg: Universitätsverlag; Göttingen: Vandenhoeck & Ruprecht, 2002), 305–24; Klaus-Dietrich Schunck, *Nehemia*, BKAT 23.2 (Neukirchen-Vluyn: Neukirchener Verlag, 2009), 377–400; Cian Power, "Constructions of Exile in the Persian Period," in *Myths of Exile: History and Metaphor in the Hebrew Bible*, ed. Anne Katrine Gudme and Ingrid Hjelm (London: Routledge, 2015), 65–78; Kristin Weingart, "What Makes an Israelite an Israelite? Judean Perspectives on the Samaritans in the Persian Period," *JSOT* 42 (2017): 155–75.

14. Bernard S. Jackson, "Ruth, the Pentateuch and the Nature of Biblical Law: In Conversation with Jean Louis Ska," in *The Post-Priestly Pentateuch: New Perspectives on Its Redactional Development and Theological Profiles*, ed. Federico Giuntoli and Konrad Schmid, FAT 101 (Tübingen: Mohr Siebeck, 2015), 75–111; Federico Giuntoli, "Ephraim, Manasseh, and Post-exilic Israel: A Study of the Redactional Expansions in Gen 48 Regarding Joseph's Sons," in Giuntoli and Schmid, *Post-Priestly Pentateuch*, 203–32; Richard J. Bautch, "Holy Seed: Ezra 9–10 and the Formation of the Pentateuch," in *The Formation of the Pentateuch: Bridging the Academic Cultures of Europe, Israel, and North America*, ed. Jan C. Gertz et al., FAT 111 (Tübingen: Mohr Siebeck, 2016), 525–42.

15. Tamara Cohn Eskenazi, "Imagining the Other in the Construction of Judahite Identity in Ezra-Nehemia," in Ben Zvi and Edelman, *Imagining the Other*, 230–56.

16. Jan Joosten, *The Verbal System of Biblical Hebrew: A New Synthesis Elaborated on the Basis of Classical Prose*, JBS 10 (Jerusalem: Simor, 2012), 390–96.

17. Jan Joosten, "The Distinction between Classical and Late Biblical Hebrew as Reflected in Syntax," *HS* 46 (2005): 327–39; Joosten, *Verbal System*, 377.

According to Magnar Kartveit, who observes the same linguistic traits in 2 Kgs 17:24–41, the two units of this passage (2 Kgs 17:24–34a, 41 and 17:34b–40) are both from the Persian period, and they are anti-Samaritan polemics.[18] I tend to sympathize with Kartveit on the period to which these verses are assigned. Although some verses of 2 Kgs 17 are surely late, the rejection of Samaritans as full members of the community of YHWH worshipers was reflected in this chapter earlier than the second century BCE.

2. Fifth-Century BCE Edition of the Pentateuch

The second half of the fifth century BCE constitutes the historical context for the Gerizim community, with its temple, clergy, and sacrificial activities. It is now accepted that there was no temple on Mount Gerizim before that time.[19] At the same period, two other centers of YHWH worshipers existed in Jerusalem and Elephantine in Egypt.

The Elephantine papyri assert that the temple of the Jewish community was already there when the Persian king Cambyses gained control over the country in 525 BCE (*TAD* A.4.7). When this temple was destroyed, however, only the political authorities of Yehud and Samaria stood up for its rebuilding (*TAD* A.4.9). Yohanan (Yehohanan according to the papyrus), who was the high priest of Jerusalem, did not answer

---

18. Kartveit, "Date," 34–37, 41–44.

19. *Contra* the Samaritan Chronicle; see John Macdonald, *The Samaritan Chronicle No. II (or Sepher Ha-Yamim), From Joshua to Nebuchadnezzar*, BZAW 107 (Berlin: de Gruyter, 1969), 92–93. See also Yitzhak Magen, "The Dating of the First Phase of the Samaritan Temple on Mount Gerizim in Light of the Archaeological Evidence," in *Judah and the Judeans in the Fourth Century BCE*, ed. Oded Lipschits, Gary N. Knoppers, and Rainer Albertz (Winona Lake, IN: Eisenbrauns, 2007), 157–211; Magen, *A Temple City*, vol. 2 of *Mount Gerizim Excavations* (Jerusalem: Israel Antiquities Authority, 2008), 167, 175; Jan Dušek, *Aramaic and Hebrew Inscriptions from Mt. Gerizim and Samaria between Antiochus III and Antiochus IV Epiphanes*, CHANE 54 (Leiden: Brill, 2012), 3; Reinhard Pummer, "Was There an Altar or a Temple in the Sacred Precint on Mt. Garizim?," *JSJ* 47 (2016): 1–21. According to Benyamim Tsedaka, "Reevaluation of Samaritan Studies Due to the New Discoveries in Excavations and Research," in *Die Samaritaner und die Bibel: The Samaritans and the Bible*, ed. Jörg Frey, Ursula Schattner-Rieser, and Konrad Schmid, SJ 70, Studia Samaritana 7 (Berlin: de Gruyter, 2012), 419–25, Mount Gerizim itself was considered the temple until the fifth century BCE.

the request of 410 BCE from the Elephantine community to support the rebuilding of their temple (*TAD* A.4.7). Can his silence be interpreted as a sign that Jerusalem was against a different Jewish temple in Egypt? If this is the case, religious authorities in Jerusalem may also have looked unfavorably upon the temple of Gerizim. But they had no power to prevent its building, because the Persian political authority was in favor of it. In any case, it is likely that the second temple in Jerusalem preceded that of Mount Gerizim.[20]

Even though reasons for building the temple on Mount Gerizim are discussed, I consider its raising a signal of tensions among YHWH worshipers. The books of Ezra and Neh 13 reflect a context of strained relationships resulting from the questions of identity and who are the true representatives of Israel. At first, purists in Jerusalem may have expressed distrust toward those who were not considered true members of the people. In a second step, they may have excluded them.[21] Yet one should recognize that such a tension-ridden context is not favorable to the production of a compromise document, such as the Pentateuch, that would be accepted by all.

We have, then, three possible solutions to this problem. First, the Pentateuch as a compromise document was produced in a different context, that is, before the time when a part of the people was not yet rejected. Second, the Pentateuch was produced at that time, but there were no tensions. Different tendencies collaborated to reach a peaceful compromise. Third, the Pentateuch was produced in the context of tensions, but a strong external authority guaranteed that representatives of the north and of the south would be somehow satisfied and that different tendencies would be taken into account.

I prefer a combination of the first and the third possibilities. In my opinion, the project of writing the history (of the faith) of Israel with its laws may have begun before tensions appeared among members of the same people. Among other reasons, the problem of the identity and

---

20. According to the majority of scholars, the second temple of Jerusalem was rebuilt in 515 BCE under Darius I. But some voices claim that it was rebuilt in the first half of the fifth century under Artaxerxes I. See Diana V. Edelman, *The Origins of the 'Second' Temple: Persian Imperial Policy and the Rebuilding of Jerusalem*, Bible Word (London: Equinox, 2005).

21. Josephus, *A.J.* 11.298–301, reflects the same conflicts to be dated to the same period of the fifth century BCE.

heritage of Israel arose and led to the growing tensions and ultimately rejection of those who were not considered the true Israel. Yet it seems that the common literary project was not yet accomplished when tensions began. It is likely that one of explanation for those tensions is the existence of a dispute about the proper place of adoration of YHWH.[22] If this is the case, the Persian authorities of both provinces, Yehud and Samaria, may have avoided the marginalization of the northern Yahwists. It should be remembered that the involvement of the political authorities in religious affairs is well attested in this period. Indeed, governors Bagohi of Yehud and Delayah of Samaria together approved the rebuilding of the Jewish temple at Elephantine and defined the accepted sacrifices to be offered there. The same kind of joint venture concerning the production of a literary work is then highly probable.[23] The book of Nehemiah also reflects political involvement in religious affairs concerning the Sabbath or the use of the chambers of the house of God (Neh 13). One should add that the interests of Persian authorities may have changed over time. Thus they may have influenced religious life differently in Judah and in Samaria.[24]

The Pentateuch was thus published as the lowest common denominator among the different tendencies. At the same time problems such as the inheritance of the promised land and the place of adoration of YHWH were left unsolved. In addition to the question of identity, members of the

---

22. Innocent Himbaza, "Accomplissement en Josué de Deutéronome 27,2–8 et 11,29–30 dans la perspective de l'Hexateuque et du Pentateuque," *Transeu* 50 (2018): 105–23.

23. Although the theory of the Persian imperial authorization raised many questions and was questioned by many scholars, one should not exclude any implication of the Persian authorities; see Peter Frei and Klaus Koch, *Reichsidee un Reichsorganisation im Perserreich: Zweite, bearbeitte un stark erweiterte Auflage*, OBO 55 (Fribourg: Universitätsverlag; Göttingen: Vandenhoeck & Ruprecht, 1996). For further discussion on the Persian imperial authorization, see James W. Watts, ed., *Persia and Torah: The Theory of Imperial Authorization of the Pentateuch*, SymS 17 (Atlanta: Society of Biblical Literature, 2001); Konrad Schmid, "The Persian Imperial Authorization as a Historical Problem and as a Biblical Construct: A Plea for Distinctions in the Current Debate," in *The Pentateuch as Torah, New Models for Understanding Its Promulgation and Acceptance*, ed. Gary N. Knoppers and Bernard M. Levinson (Winona Lake, IN: Eisenbrauns, 2007), 23–38; and Kyong-Jin Lee, *The Authority and Authorization of Torah in the Persian Period*, CBET 64 (Leuven: Peeters, 2011).

24. Albertz, "History," 309–14.

diaspora may have rejected the idea of living exclusively in the promised land.[25] The Pentateuch reflects many other points of compromise such that one can think of a compilation of the diverse components of the heritage of Israel.[26] The prominent figure of Moses was seemingly the catalyst for the compromise, because he is recognized by all sides as their legislator.

3. Second-Century BCE Corrections

Jews and Samaritans may have read the same texts of the Pentateuch for a long time, maybe until the second century BCE when they rejected each other. It is assumed here that a schism occurred at that time and both sides corrected the text in order to match their respective worship sites. One of the interesting observations is that the main corrections introduced (by both sides) in the Pentateuch concern the place where YHWH is to be worshiped.[27] Contrary to what was asserted for a long time, the Dead Sea Scrolls show that Samaritans were not responsible for harmonizations. They may have chosen the harmonized text in order to use a perfect Torah without textual and literary discrepancies. Moreover, scholars have observed that Samaritans stopped harmonizing their text, contrary to many harmonizing texts known from Qumran.[28]

---

25. Some scholars point out a supplementary argument that Persian authorities may have been against the aggressive conquest of the same land under Joshua; see Rainer Albertz, "The Formative Impact of the Hexateuch Redaction: An Interim Result," in Giuntoli and Konrad Schmid, *Post-Priestly Pentateuch*, 73–74; Thomas Römer, "The Problem of the Hexateuch," in Gertz et al., *Formation of the Pentateuch*, 813–27.

26. Innocent Himbaza, "Le Pentateuque a-t-il été compilé et édité en hate?," *Sem* 60 (2018): 159–81.

27. Innocent Himbaza, "'Le lieu que le Seigneur aura choisi': Une perspective narrative, historique et philologique," *Sem* 58 (2016): 115–34.

28. Ester Eshel and Hanan Eshel, "Dating the Samaritan Pentateuch's Compilation in Light of the Qumran Biblical Scrolls," in *Emanuel: Studies in Hebrew Bible, Septuagint and Dead Sea Scrolls in Honor of Emanuel Tov*, ed. Shalom M. Paul and Eva Ben-David, VTSup 94 (Leiden: Brill, 2003), 215–40; Sidnie White Crawford, *Rewriting Scripture in Second Temple Times* (Grand Rapids: Eerdmans, 2008), 146–49; Molly M. Zahn, "The Samaritan Pentateuch and the Scribal Culture of Second Temple Judaism," *JSJ* 46 (2015): 285–313, esp. 310. According to Emanuel Tov, "From Popular Jewish LXX-SP Texts to Separate Sectarian Texts: Insights from the Dead Sea Scrolls," in *The Samaritan Pentateuch and the Dead Sea Scrolls*, ed. Michael Langlois, Contributions to

While the Pentateuch was published as a compromise document during the Persian period, its later corrections reflect the schism between Jews and Samaritans. Such literary additions and/or corrections were introduced in the Samaritan Pentateuch as well as in the pre-Masoretic text later in the second century BCE, during the Hasmonean period.[29] The most famous text considered to be a Samaritanism is the particular Samaritan tenth commandment introduced in both Exod 20 and Deut 5.[30] It urges people to build an altar on Mount Gerizim and to offer sacrifices there. This text was, however, not created at that time. It was only compiled from Deut 11:29–30 and 27:2–7.

4. The Pentateuch as a Compromise Document and the Contribution of the Samaritans

The compromise in the Pentateuch mostly concerns the priestly and lay circles of Jerusalem, while some concessions may have been granted to the diaspora and the Yahwists of Samaria.[31] Such assertions show that our understanding of compromise applied to the Pentateuch should take into account the complexity of the unknown details in this case.

Samaritans recognize only the Pentateuch and reject the rest of the Prophets and Writings. This point can be explained historically, because only the Pentateuch was promulgated as a compromise document and accepted by different groups of YHWH worshipers.

Although the edition of the Pentateuch is still debated, the majority of scholars date it at the end of the fifth and the beginning of the fourth centuries BCE. According to Sara Japhet, the book of Ezra–Nehemiah (dated

---

Biblical Exegesis and Theology (Leuven: Peeters, 2019), 19–40, the harmonizing texts on which the Samaritan Pentateuch is based circulated as majority texts.

29. Eugene Ulrich, *The Dead Sea Scrolls and Developmental Composition of the Bible*, VTSup 169 (Leiden: Brill, 2015), 215–27.

30. According to Schorch, the so-called Samaritan tenth commandment is a pre-Samaritan text as well. See Stefan Schorch, "The So-Called Gerizim Commandment in the Samaritan Pentateuch," in *The Samaritan Pentateuch and the Dead Sea Scrolls*, ed. Michael Langlois, CBET 94 (Leuven: Peeters, 2019), 77–97; Schorch, "Die prä-samaritanischen Fortschreibungen," in *Schriftgelehrte Fortschreibungs- und Auslegungsprozesse: Textarbeit im Pentateuch, in Qumran, Ägypten und Mesopotamien*, ed. Walter Bührer, FAT 2/108 (Tübingen: Mohr Siebeck, 2019), 113–32.

31. Diana V. Edelman et al., *Opening the Books of Moses*, Bible World (Sheffield: Equinox, 2012), 104–10.

toward 350 BCE) reflects the Pentateuch in its final form.³² Yet this date does not pertain to the composition of all the texts. On the one hand, linguistics demonstrate that many texts of the Pentateuch were composed much earlier.³³ On the other hand, many late literary redactions are also well attested.³⁴

In recent years, scholars have pointed out that some passages of Genesis, such as the Joseph story (Gen 37–50) and some passages of Deuteronomy, such as Deut 11 and 27, come from the Samaritan contribution to the Pentateuch or at least from the northern scribes.³⁵ One of the main points demonstrating the contribution of the Samaritans as northern YHWH worshipers results from the treatment accorded significant northern places such as the region of Shechem. Indeed, the region of Shechem is depicted positively from Genesis to Joshua.³⁶ Moreover, on the narrative

---

32. Sara Japhet, "What May Be Learned from Ezra-Nehemiah about the Composition of the Pentateuch?," in Gertz et al., *Formation of the Pentateuch*, 543–60.

33. William M. Schniedewind, "Linguistic Dating, Writing Systems, and the Pentateuchal Sources," in Gertz et al., *Formation of the Pentateuch*, 345–56; Thomas Römer, "How to Date Pentateuchal Texts: Some Cases Studies," in Gertz et al., *Formation of the Pentateuch*, 357–70; Jakob Wöhrle, "There's No Master Key! The Literary Character of the Priestly Stratum and the Formation of the Pentateuch," in Gertz et al., *Formation of the Pentateuch*, 391–403.

34. Konrad Schmid, "Post-Priestly Additions in the Pentateuch: A Survey of Scholarship," in Gertz et al., *Formation of the Pentateuch*, 589–604.

35. Genesis 37–50 was often understood to originate in the Egyptian diaspora; see Thomas Römer, "The Joseph Story in the Book of Genesis," in Giuntoli and Schmid, *Post-Priestly Pentateuch*, 185–201. Some recent publications consider these chapters as coming from Samaritans; see Hensel, *Juda und Samaria*, 183–87; Thomas Römer in this volume. For an earlier northern origin, see Erhard Blum and Kristin Weingart, "The Joseph Story: Diaspora Novella or North Israelite Narrative?," *ZAW* 129 (2017): 501–21. Matthew C. Genung, *The Composition of Genesis 37*, FAT 2/95 (Tübingen: Mohr Siebeck, 2017), 204–12 dates the composition of Joseph story in the north after P but before LXX. For the book of Deuteronomy, see Stefan Schorch, "The Samaritan Version of Deuteronomy and the Origin of Deuteronomy," in *Samaria, Samarians, Samaritans: Studies on Bible, History and Linguistics*, ed. József Zsengellér, SJ 66; Studia Samaritana 6 (Berlin: de Gruyter, 2011), 23–37.

36. Gary N. Knoppers, "Mt. Gerizim and Mt. Zion: A Study in the Early History of the Samaritans and Jews," *SR* 34 (2005): 309–38; Himbaza, "Accomplissement"; Dany R. Nocquet, *La Samarie, la Diaspora et l'achèvement de la Torah: Territorialiés et internationalités dans l'Hexateuque*, OBO 284 (Fribourg: Academic Press; Göttingen: Vandenhoeck & Ruprecht, 2017), 39–114, 313–14, 318–21, also recognizes the posi-

and literary level, many promises encountered in Genesis to Deuteronomy are accomplished in Joshua. It is therefore likely that there was at least a common project to write the history of Israel from the beginning to the inheritance of the promised land, in the form of the Hexateuch. The northern Samaritan side was obviously active as one of the contributors to this project during the fifth century BCE.[37]

Yet we do not know how YHWH worshipers proceeded to come to a compromise text. The Pentateuch looks like a compilation of different material with different tendencies. Global redactions may have tried to put them in order.[38] The compromise may therefore be understood as the acceptance (even if compelled) of the diverse literary heritage of members of the same people. Beyond their role in the literary documents, the extent of which we do not know, the major contribution of the Samaritans to the Pentateuch is probably the positive view of places and etiological nar-

---

tive image of Shechem from Genesis to Joshua. He explains it as the contribution of the Samaritan pole of Yahwism against the Judean Deuteronomistic historiography, which contests the legitimacy of Samaria. Because Nocquet sees the tensions between the two poles, he explains the final state of the Pentateuch as a result of the prominent contribution of Samaria and the diaspora, while the Judean community is weakened during the fifth century. My point is that the Pentateuch is a compromise document in which the Judean pole also plays a major role. The growing weight of the Judean pole may be seen in the rejection of the Hexateuch, because the Pentateuch no longer shows the inheritance of the promised land, where Shechem may have played its prominent role as the chosen place.

37. Albertz, "Formative Impact," 53–74. It seems to me that the date of the Samaritan contribution to the Pentateuch as a compromise document cannot be the second century as asserted by Paul Carbonaro, "Les Samaritains et la naissance du Pentateuque," *RB* 120 (2013): 42–71, esp. 51, 68–69. He considers Samaritans as the fathers of the Pentateuch in the Alexandrine context of the second century BCE. At that time, they may have added Deuteronomy 27 and 29–34. My point is that, in the period when Jews and Samaritans clearly rejected each other, Jews would simply have refused the addition of chapters coming from Samaritans. Thus, because Deut 27 and 29–34 are recognized by the Jews, Deuteronomy was completed and accepted by all sides long before the second century BCE. Furthermore, the LXX, as the translation of the Pentateuch in Greek that contains Deut 27 and 29–34, antedates the period proposed by Carbonaro.

38. Albert de Pury and Thomas Römer, eds., *Le Pentateuque en question: Les origines et la composition des cinq premiers livres de la Bible à la lumière des recherches récentes*, 3rd ed., MdB 19 (Geneva: Labor et Fides, 2002); Knoppers and Levinson, *The Pentateuch as Torah*; Thomas B. Dozeman, Konrad Schmid, and Baruch J. Schwartz, eds., *The Pentateuch: International Perspectives on Current Research*, FAT 78 (Tübingen: Mohr Siebeck, 2011).

ratives in the northern part of the country. Redactors of the Pentateuch obviously took this aspect into account.

5. The Pentateuch against the Hexateuch and the Beginning of Irreconcilable Divergences

Three main hypotheses have been offered to explain why the Pentateuch was chosen and the Hexateuch was rejected.[39] The first is the singularity of Moses as the legislator whose work ends in the book of Deuteronomy. The second is the position of the diaspora that not all the members of the people should necessarily live in the promised land. Third is the possible position of the Judean intellectuals or the Persian authorities who would not accept the violent conquest of the same land. I think the problem of the place where YHWH is to be worshiped also contributed to rejecting the Hexateuch. As has been observed, the region of Shechem, with the two mountains surrounding it, Ebal and Gerizim, is consecrated by the Hexateuch as the place chosen by God to put God's name. Indeed, the book of Deuteronomy (11:29–30; 27:2–8) calls on the people to congregate, to pronounce benedictions and curses, to build an altar, and to offer sacrifices there, and the book of Joshua contains the accomplishment of those prescriptions. In Joshua (8:30–35; 24) Shechem is the place where the whole people is gathered to offer sacrifices, to read the Torah, and to renew the covenant with God.

On the literary level, if the book of Joshua is separated from the Pentateuch and read within the rest of the Prophets, the place of Shechem becomes one of the many other places to worship. In that case, the Prophets can assert that Jerusalem is the ultimate chosen place. It is thus possible to correlate the rejection of the Hexateuch—or, more precisely, the restriction of the compromise to the Pentateuch—with the beginning of irreconcilable

---

39. For an overview of the theories and discussions on the Pentateuch and Hexateuch, see Thomas Römer, "La construction du Pentateuque, de l'Hexateuque et de l'Ennéateuque: Investigations préliminaires sur la formation des grands ensembles littéraires de la Bible hébraïque," in *Les dernières rédactions du Pentateuque, de l'Hexateuque et de l'Ennéateuque*, ed. Thomas Römer and Konrad Schmid; BETL 203 (Leuven: Peeters, 2007), 9–34, esp. 19–22; Christophe Nihan and Thomas Römer, "Le débat actuel sur la formation du Pentateuque," in *Introduction à l'Ancien Testament*, ed. Thomas Römer, Jean-Daniel Macchi, and Christophe Nihan; MdB 49 (Geneva: Labor et Fides, 2009), 158–84, esp. 178–80; Thomas Römer, "Conflicting Models of Identity and the Publication of the Torah in the Persian Period," in Albertz and Wöhrle, *Between Cooperation and Hostility*, 33–51, esp. 46–47.

divergences, if not the rejection of Samaritans by Jews. This is the beginning of the future schism between communities of YHWH worshipers. Tensions are observable both in the building of a temple on Mount Gerizim and in the development of a literary historiography (the Prophets) that did not take into account the opinions in the northern community. The rejection of the Hexateuch thus reflects the end of the peaceful period and the beginning of difficult relationships among YHWH worshipers.

6. Lack of Compromise in the Prophets and Writings and the Rejection of the Samaritans

Comparison between the Hexateuch and the rest of the Prophets shows an important difference in how northern places and narratives are presented. Indeed, Shechem has a positive image in the Hexateuch, while it is portrayed negatively in the Prophets, particularly the book of Judges, as a place of division, apostasy, and crime (Judg 9; 1 Kgs 12; Jer 41:4–7; Hos 6–9). It is therefore likely that the earlier project was reduced and the compromise document was limited to the Pentateuch. As a consequence, the question of the inheritance of the promised land was not resolved in the Pentateuch. The rejection of the Hexateuch and the adoption of the Pentateuch may then reflect the beginning of tensions which led to the rejection of the Yahwists of Samaria.

The main difference between the Pentateuch (or the Hexateuch) and the rest of the Prophets and Writings, especially the Former Prophets, is that the north is portrayed negatively on the whole. Other scholars, such as Ingrid Hjelm, have pointed out this phenomenon.[40] Kings of the Northern Kingdom are illegitimate and violent, their reigns are often too short, and they act against YHWH. And, even though not all the kings of the Southern Kingdom act faithfully toward YHWH, they perpetuate the Davidic monarchy, they reign in the chosen place of Jerusalem (1 Kgs 8:16, 44; 11:13, 36; 1 Kgs 14:21; 21:7; 23:27), and the succession is often peaceful. Since the division of the kingdom, many northern places such as Shechem, Bethel, Tirzah, and Samaria reflect the division, conspiracy, apostasy, and crime. Thus 2 Kgs 17, about the deportation of Israel and its replacement with a mixture of people, is not the only negative appreciation of the north. The Prophets and the Writings lead to the conclusion that their redac-

---

40. Ingrid Hjelm, "Samaria, Samaritans and the Composition of the Hebrew Bible," in Mor and Reiterer, *Samaritans*, 91–103.

tors remained distant from the Samaritans.[41] The distance between them is tangible during the fourth and third centuries BCE. Zechariah 11:14 may refer to such a distance.[42] Yet this observation may not exclude connections between the two communities in some circumstances.[43]

Because the majority of the compilation and redaction dealing with the history of Israel and Judah occurred during the Persian period, it is also likely that the case of Samaria and Jerusalem remained a matter of concern. Further, because the Pentateuch reflects a positive appreciation of the north, it is likely that the Prophets and the Writings, which reflect a negative appreciation of the same region, are marked by the rejection of Samaritans. The Gerizim community did not participate in the (final) redaction of the Prophets and the Writings, or it may have balanced the historiography concerning the north.[44] The result may have been different, as is the case for the Pentateuch. Indeed, Jews and Samaritans read and shared the same text of the Pentateuch for a long time.[45]

---

41. It seems that there is no conflict between the exiled (גלה) and nonexiled (people of the land) during the ancient Persian period; see Jacques Vermeylen, "Les anciens déportés et les habitants du pays: La crise occultée du début de l'époque perse," *Transeu* 39 (2010): 175–206; Jean-Daniel Macchi and Christophe Nihan, "Le prétendu conflit entre exilés et non-exilés dans la province de Yehud à l'époque achéménide: Plaidoyer pour une approche différenciée," *Transeu* 42 (2012): 19–47. But it seems also likely that such a conflict existed during the second half of the fifth century BCE.

42. Hinkley G. Mitchell, J. M. Powis Smith, and Julius August Bewer, *A Critical and Exegetical Commentary on Haggai, Zechariah, Malachi and Jonah*, ICC (Edinburgh: T&T Clark, 1912), 310–11; Ina Willi-Plein, *Haggai, Sacharja, Maleachi*, ZBK 24.4 (Zürich: TVZ, 2007), 188–89; Jackob Wöhrle, *Der Abschluss des Zwölfprophetenbuches: Buchübergreifende Redaktionsprozesse in den späten Sammlungen*, BZAW 389 (Berlin: de Gruyter, 2008), 91–92 n. 86; Albertz, "History," 304–5.

43. Christophe Nihan, "The Torah between Samaria and Judah: Shechem and Gerizim in Deuteronomy and Joshua," in Knoppers and Levinson, *Pentateuch as Torah*, 187–223, esp. 190–91.

44. Samaritan writings reflect a knowledge of the Prophets in a different version; see Macdonald, *Samaritan Chronicle*; Jean-Daniel Macchi, *Les Samaritains: Histoire d'une légende, Israël et la province de Samarie*, MdB 30 (Geneva: Labor et Fides, 1994), 22–33; Ingrid Hjelm, *The Samaritans and Early Judaism: A Literary Analysis*, JSOTSup 303 (Sheffield: Sheffield Academic, 2000), 254–72; Robert T. Anderson and Terry Gilles, *The Keepers: An Introduction to the History and Culture of the Samaritans* (Peabody, MA: Hendrickson, 2002), 10–13.

45. Gary N. Knoppers, "Parallel Torahs and Inner-Scriptural Interpretation: The Jewish and Samaritan Pentateuchs in Historical Perspective," in Dozeman, Schmid, and Schwartz, *Pentateuch*, 507–31.

It is thus obvious that the difference between the treatment of the north in the Pentateuch, on the one hand, and in the Prophets, on the other hand, reflects a lack of compromise that can be explained by the rejection of the northern part by the southern one. Tensions between Gerizim and Jerusalem are observable at the end of the fifth century BCE. The collaboration in reconstructing their common historiography was no longer possible. From that time on, the southern part considered itself the only representative of the people of God. This reflection is older than the third and second centuries BCE, even though it was accentuated in that period.[46]

7. Conclusion

The Pentateuch looks like a compilation of documents from diverse origins. Some of them probably come from the north and maybe from the Samaritans. Yet the contribution of the Samaritans to the Pentateuch is not known, because all the documents thought to come from the north cannot be labelled "Samaritan." The book of Deuteronomy, whose provenance in the north or the south is still discussed, contains chapters in favor of the Samaritans' positions, especially those dealing with Shechem in general and Mount Gerizim in particular (Deut 11 and 27).[47] One can therefore not exclude the possibility that such chapters are part of the contribution of the Samaritans. It has been observed that some recent publications also tentatively explain the Joseph story (Gen 37–50) as coming from the Samaritans.[48]

More than the presumed documents from the Samaritan side, the major contribution of the Samaritans is probably the positive attitude of

---

46. My point on the historical aspect of the rejection of the Samaritans (not the rivalry between Jews and Samaritans) is given in Himbaza, "Les Samaritains."

47. It should be remembered that the Samaritan tenth commandment is made up of verses coming from those chapters. On the provenance of Deuteronomy, see Cynthia Edenburg and Reinhard Müller, "A Northern Provenance for Deuteronomy? A Critical Review," *HBAI* 4.2 (2015): 148–61; Gary N. Knoppers, "The Northern Context of the Law-Code in Deuteronomy," *HBAI* 4.2 (2015): 162–83; Ingrid Hjelm, "Northern Perspectives in Deuteronomy and Its Relation to the Samaritan Pentateuch," *HBAI* 4.2 (2015): 184–204; Magnar Kartveit, "The Place That the Lord Your God Will Choose," *HBAI* 4.2 (2015): 205–18; Adrian Schenker, "Der Ort, und dem Jhwhs Name wohnt. Eine oder mehrer Stätten?" *HBAI* 4.2 (2015): 219–29.

48. See note 36.

the Pentateuch toward places and events of the northern part of the country. This positive attitude, disseminated in pentateuchal narratives, may have been guaranteed under their influence. Contrary to this, the Prophets reflect an overall negative appreciation of the northern places. This evaluation would demonstrate that some changes intervened between the edition of the Pentateuch and that of the Prophets. Those changes were most probably related to the rejection of the Samaritans, who no longer participated in the effort to elaborate a common historiography.

Bibliography

Albertz, Rainer. "The Formative Impact of the Hexateuch Redaction: An Interim Result." Pages 53–74 in *The Post-Priestly Pentateuch: New Perspectives on Its Redactional Development and Theological Profiles*. Edited by Federico Giuntoli and Konrad Schmid. FAT 101. Tübingen: Mohr Siebeck, 2015.

———. "The History of Judah and Samaria in the Late Persian and Hellenistic Periods as a Possible Background of the Late Editions of the Book of the Twelve." Pages 303–18 in *Perspectives on the Foundation of the Book of the Twelve: Methodological Foundations, Redactional Processes, Historical Insights*. Edited by Rainer Albertz, James D. Nogalski, and Jakob Wöhrle. BZAW 433. Berlin: de Gruyter, 2012.

Anderson, Robert T., and Terry Gilles. *The Keepers: An Introduction to the History and Culture of the Samaritans*. Peabody, MA: Hendrickson, 2002.

Bautch, Richard J. "Holy Seed: Ezra 9–10 and the Formation of the Pentateuch." Pages 525–42 in *The Formation of the Pentateuch: Bridging the Academic Cultures of Europe, Israel, and North America*. Edited by Jan Christian Gertz, Bernard M. Levinson, Dalit Rom-Shiloni, and Konrad Schmid. FAT 111. Tübingen: Mohr Siebeck, 2016.

Blenkinsopp, Joseph. *Ezra-Nehemia: A Commentary*. OTL. Philadelphia: Westminster, 1988.

Blum, Erhard, and Kristin Weingart. "The Joseph Story: Diaspora Novella or North Israelite Narrative?" *ZAW* 129 (2017): 501–21.

Carbonaro, Paul. "Les Samaritains et la naissance du Pentateuque." *RB* 120 (2013): 42–71.

Cohn, Robert L. "Overcoming Otherness in the Book of Ruth." Pages 163–81 in *Imagining the Other and Constructing Israelite Identity in the Early Second Temple Period*. Edited by Ehud Ben Zvi and Diana Edelman. LHBOTS 591. London: Bloomsbury T&T Clark, 2014.

Crawford, Sidnie White. *Rewriting Scripture in Second Temple Times*. Grand Rapids: Eerdmans, 2008.

Cross, Frank M. "The Papyri and Their Historical Implications." Pages 17–29 in *Discoveries in the Wâdî ed-Dâliyeh*. Edited by Paul W. Lapp and Nancy L. Lapp. AASOR 41. Cambridge: American Schools of Oriental Research, 1974.

Cross, Frank M. *From Epic to Canon: History and Literature in Ancient Israel*. Baltimore: Johns Hopkins University Press, 2000.

Crown, Alan D. "Another Look at Samaritan Origin." Pages 133–55 in *Essays in Honour of G. D. Sexdenier: New Samaritan Studies of the Société d'Etudes Samaritaines*. Vols. 3–4 of *Proceedings of the Congress of Oxford 1990, Yarnton Manor and Paris 1992, Collège de France, with Lectures Given at Hong Kong 1993 as Participation in the ICANAS Congress*. Edited by Alan D. Crown and Lucy A. Davey. Sydney: Mandelbaum, 1995).

De Pury, Albert, and Thomas Römer, eds. *Le Pentateuque en question: Les origines et la composition des cinq premiers livres de la Bible à la lumière des recherches récentes*. 3rd ed. MdB 19. Geneva: Labor et Fides, 2002.

Dozeman, Thomas B., Konrad Schmid, and Baruch J. Schwartz, eds. *The Pentateuch: International Perspectives on Current Research*. FAT 78. Tübingen: Mohr Siebeck, 2011.

Dušek, Jan. *Aramaic and Hebrew Inscriptions from Mt. Gerizim and Samaria between Antiochus III and Antiochus IV Epiphanes*. CHANE 54. Leiden: Brill, 2012.

Edelman, Diana V. *The Origins of the 'Second' Temple: Persian Imperial Policy and the Rebuilding of Jerusalem*. Bible Word. London: Equinox, 2005.

Edelman, Diana V., Philip R Davies, Christophe Nihan, and Thomas Römer. *Opening the Books of Moses*. Bible World. Sheffield: Equinox, 2012.

Edenburg, Cynthia, and Reinhard Müller. "A Northern Provenance for Deuteronomy? A Critical Review." *HBAI* 4.2 (2015): 148–61.

Eshel, Ester, and Hanan Eshel. "Dating the Samaritan Pentateuch's Compilation in Light of the Qumran Biblical Scrolls." Pages 215–40 in *Emanuel: Studies in Hebrew Bible, Septuagint and Dead Sea Scrolls in Honor of Emanuel Tov*. Edited by Shalom M. Paul and Eva Ben-David. VTSup 94. Leiden: Brill, 2003.

Eskenazi, Tamara Cohn. "Imagining the Other in the Construction of Judahite Identity in Ezra-Nehemia." Pages 230–56 in *Imagining the Other and Constructing Israelite Identity in the Early Second Temple Period*. Edited by Ehud Ben Zvi and Diana Edelman. LHBOTS 591. London: Bloomsbury T&T Clark, 2014.

Fischer, Irmtraud. *Rut: Übersetzt und ausgelegt*. HThKAT. Freiburg: Herder, 2001.

Frei, Peter, and Klaus Koch. *Reichsidee un Reichsorganisation im Perserreich: Zweite, bearbeitte un stark erweiterte Auflage*. OBO 55. Fribourg: Universitätsverlag; Göttingen: Vandenhoeck & Ruprecht, 1996.

Genung, Matthew C. *The Composition of Genesis 37*. FAT 2/95. Tübingen: Mohr Siebeck, 2017.

Giuntoli, Federico. "Ephraim, Manasseh, and Post-exilic Israel: A Study of the Redactional Expansions in Gen 48 Regarding Joseph's Sons." Pages 203–32 in *The Post-Priestly Pentateuch: New Perspectives on Its Redactional Development and Theological Profiles*. Edited by Federico Giuntoli and Konrad Schmid. FAT 101. Tübingen: Mohr Siebeck, 2015.

Gropp, Douglas M. "Sanballat." Pages 823–25 in vol. 2 of *Encyclopedia of the Dead Sea Scrolls*. Edited by Lawrence H. Schiffman and James C. Vanderkam. 2 vols. Oxford: Oxford University Press, 2000.

Hensel, Benedikt. "Cult Centralization in the Persian Period: Biblical and Historical Perspectives." *Sem* 60 (2018): 221–72.

Hensel, Benedikt. *Juda und Samaria: Zum Verhältnis zweier nach-exilischer Jahwismen*. FAT 110. Tübingen: Mohr Siebeck, 2016.

Himbaza, Innocent. "Accomplissement en Josué de Deutéronome 27,2–8 et 11,29–30 dans la perspective de l'Hexateuque et du Pentateuque." *Transeu* 50 (2018): 105–23.

———. "'Le lieu que le Seigneur aura choisi': Une perspective narrative, historique et philologique." *Sem* 58 (2016): 115–34.

———. "Le Pentateuque a-t-il été compilé et édité en hate?" *Sem* 60 (2018): 159–81.

———. "Les Samaritains: Leur temple, leur clergé et leur texte de reference; Une approche historique." In preparation.

Hjelm, Ingrid. "Northern Perspectives in Deuteronomy and Its Relation to the Samaritan Pentateuch." *HBAI* 4.2 (2015): 184–204.

———. "Samaria, Samaritans and the Composition of the Hebrew Bible." Pages 91–103 in *Samaritans: Past and Present—Current Studies*. Edited by Menachem Mor and Friedrich V. Reiterer. SJ 53. Studia Samaritana 5. Berlin: de Gruyter, 2010.

———. *The Samaritans and Early Judaism: A Literary Analysis*. JSOTSup 303. Sheffield: Sheffield Academic, 2000.
Jackson, Bernard S. "Ruth, the Pentateuch and the Nature of Biblical Law: In Conversation with Jean Louis Ska." Pages 75–111 in *The Post-Priestly Pentateuch: New Perspectives on Its Redactional Development and Theological Profiles*. Edited by Federico Giuntoli and Konrad Schmid. FAT 101. Tübingen: Mohr Siebeck, 2015.
Japhet, Sara. "What May Be Learned from Ezra-Nehemiah about the Composition of the Pentateuch?" Pages 543–60 in *The Formation of the Pentateuch: Bridging the Academic Cultures of Europe, Israel, and North America*. Edited by Jan Christian Gertz, Bernard M. Levinson, Dalit Rom-Shiloni, and Konrad Schmid. FAT 111. Tübingen: Mohr Siebeck, 2016.
Joosten, Jan. "The Distinction between Classical and Late Biblical Hebrew as Reflected in Syntax." *HS* 46 (2005): 327–39.
———. *The Verbal System of Biblical Hebrew: A New Synthesis Elaborated on the Basis of Classical Prose*. JBS 10. Jerusalem: Simor, 2012.
Kartveit, Magner. "The Date of II Reg 17,24–41." *ZAW* 126 (2014): 31–44.
———. "The Place That the Lord Your God Will Choose." *HBAI* 4.2 (2015): 205–18.
Knoppers, Gary N. "Mt. Gerizim and Mt. Zion: A Study in the Early History of the Samaritans and Jews." *SR* 34 (2005): 309–38.
———. "The Northern Context of the Law-Code in Deuteronomy." *HBAI* 4.2 (2015): 162–83.
———. "Parallel Torahs and Inner-Scriptural Interpretation: The Jewish and Samaritan Pentateuchs in Historical Perspective." Pages 507–31 in *The Pentateuch: International Perspectives on Current Research*. Edited by Thomas B. Dozeman, Konrad Schmid, and Baruch J. Schwartz. FAT 78. Tübingen: Mohr Siebeck, 2011.
Lacoque, André. *Le livre de Ruth*. CAT 17. Geneva: Labor et Fides, 2004.
———. *Ruth: A Continental Commentary*. Translated by K. C. Hanson. Minneapolis: Fortress, 2004.
Lau, Peter H. W. *Identity and Ethics in the Book of Ruth: A Social Identity Approach*. BZAW 416. Berlin: de Gruyter, 2011.
Lee, Kyong-Jin. *The Authority and Authorization of Torah in the Persian Period*. CBET 64. Leuven: Peeters, 2011.
Leith, Mary Joan W. *Wadi Daliyeh I: The Wadi Daliyeh Seal Impressions*. DJD 24. Oxford: Clarendon, 1997.

Macchi, Jean-Daniel, and Christophe Nihan. "Le prétendu conflit entre exilés et non-exilés dans la province de Yehud à l'époque achéménide: Plaidoyer pour une approche différenciée." *Transeu* 42 (2012): 19–47.

Macchi, Jean-Daniel. *Les Samaritains: Histoire d'une légende, Israël et la province de Samarie*. MdB 30. Geneva: Labor et Fides, 1994.

Macdonald, John. *The Samaritan Chronicle No. II (or Sepher Ha-Yamim), From Joshua to Nebuchadnezzar*. BZAW 107. Berlin: de Gruyter, 1969.

Magen, Yitzhak. "The Dating of the First Phase of the Samaritan Temple on Mount Gerizim in Light of the Archaeological Evidence." Pages 157–211 in *Judah and the Judeans in the Fourth Century BCE*. Edited by Oded Lipschits, Gary N. Knoppers, and Rainer Albertz. Winona Lake, IN: Eisenbrauns, 2007.

Magen, Yitzhak. *A Temple City*. Vol. 2 of *Mount Gerizim Excavations*. Jerusalem: Israel Antiquities Authority, 2008.

Mitchell, Hinkley G., J. M. Powis Smith, and Julius August Bewer. *A Critical and Exegetical Commentary on Haggai, Zechariah, Malachi and Jonah*. ICC. Edinburgh: T&T Clark, 1912.

Mor, Menahem. "The Persian, Hellenistic and Hasmonaean Period." Pages 1–18 in *The Samaritans*. Edited by Alan D. Crown. Tübingen: Mohr Siebeck, 1989.

Nihan, Christophe. "The Torah between Samaria and Judah: Shechem and Gerizim in Deuteronomy and Joshua." Pages 187–223 in *The Pentateuch as Torah, New Models for Understanding Its Promulgation and Acceptance*. Edited by Gary N. Knoppers and Bernard M. Levinson. Winona Lake, IN: Eisenbrauns, 2007.

Nihan, Christophe, and Thomas Römer. "Le débat actuel sur la formation du Pentateuque." Pages 158–84 in *Introduction à l'Ancien Testament*. Edited by Thomas Römer, Jean-Daniel Macchi, and Christophe Nihan. MdB 49. Geneva: Labor et Fides, 2009.

Nocquet, Dany R. *La Samarie, la Diaspora et l'achèvement de la Torah: Territorialiés et internationalités dans l'Hexateuque*. OBO 284. Fribourg: Academic Press. Göttingen: Vandenhoeck & Ruprecht, 2017.

Nodet, Étienne. *Flavius Josèphe, Les Antiquités Juives, Livres X et XI, Introduction et texte, Traduction et notes*. Paris: Cerf, 2010.

———. "Sânballaṭ de Samarie." *RB* 122 (2015): 340–54.

Power, Cian. "Constructions of Exile in the Persian Period." Pages 65–78 in *Myths of Exile: History and Metaphor in the Hebrew Bible*. Edited by Anne Katrine Gudme and Ingrid Hjelm. London: Routledge, 2015.

Pummer, Reinhard. "Samaritanism: A Jewish Sect of an Independent Form of Yahwism?" Pages 1–24 in *Samaritans: Past and Present—Current Studies*. Edited by Menachem Mor and Friedrich V. Reiterer. SJ 53. Studia Samaritana 5. Berlin: de Gruyter, 2010.

———. "Was There an Altar or a Temple in the Sacred Precint on Mt. Garizim?" *JSJ* 47 (2016): 1–21.

Reinmuth, Titus. *Der Bericht Nehemias: Zur literarischen Eigenart, traditionsgeschichtlichen Prägung und innerbiblischen Rezeption des Ich-Berichts Nehemias*. OBO 183. Fribourg: Universitätsverlag; Göttingen: Vandenhoeck & Ruprecht, 2002.

Römer, Thomas. "Conflicting Models of Identity and the Publication of the Torah in the Persian Period." Pages 33–51 in *Between Cooperation and Hostility: Multiple Identities in Ancient Judaism and the Interaction with Foreign Powers*. Edited by Rainer Albertz and Jakob Wöhrle. JAJSup 11. Göttingen: Vandenhoeck & Ruprecht, 2013.

———. "How to Date Pentateuchal Texts: Some Cases Studies." Pages 357–70 in *The Formation of the Pentateuch: Bridging the Academic Cultures of Europe, Israel, and North America*. Edited by Jan Christian Gertz, Bernard M. Levinson, Dalit Rom-Shiloni, and Konrad Schmid. FAT 111. Tübingen: Mohr Siebeck, 2016.

———. "The Joseph Story in the Book of Genesis." Pages 185–201 in *The Post-Priestly Pentateuch: New Perspectives on Its Redactional Development and Theological Profiles*. Edited by Federico Giuntoli and Konrad Schmid. FAT 101. Tübingen: Mohr Siebeck, 2015.

———. "La construction du Pentateuque, de l'Hexateuque et de l'Ennéateuque: Investigations préliminaires sur la formation des grands ensembles littéraires de la Bible hébraïque." Pages 9–34 in *Les dernières rédactions du Pentateuque, de l'Hexateuque et de l'Ennéateuque*. Edited by Thomas Römer and Konrad Schmid. BETL 203. Leuven: Peeters, 2007.

———. "The Problem of the Hexateuch." Pages 813–27 in *The Formation of the Pentateuch: Bridging the Academic Cultures of Europe, Israel, and North America*. Edited by Jan Christian Gertz, Bernard M. Levinson, Dalit Rom-Shiloni, and Konrad Schmid. FAT 111. Tübingen: Mohr Siebeck, 2016.

Schenker, Adrian. "Der Ort, und dem Jhwhs Name wohnt. Eine oder mehrer Stätten?" *HBAI* 4.2 (2015): 219–29.

Schmid, Konrad. "The Persian Imperial Authorization as a Historical Problem and as a Biblical Construct: A Plea for Distinctions in the

Current Debate." Pages 23–38 in *The Pentateuch as Torah, New Models for Understanding Its Promulgation and Acceptance.* Edited by Gary N. Knoppers and Bernard M. Levinson. Winona Lake, IN: Eisenbrauns, 2007.

———. "Post-Priestly Additions in the Pentateuch: A Survey of Scholarship." Pages 589–604 in *The Formation of the Pentateuch: Bridging the Academic Cultures of Europe, Israel, and North America.* Edited by Jan Christian Gertz, Bernard M. Levinson, Dalit Rom-Shiloni, and Konrad Schmid. FAT 111. Tübingen: Mohr Siebeck, 2016.

Schniedewind, William M. "Linguistic Dating, Writing Systems, and the Pentateuchal Sources." Pages 345–56 in *The Formation of the Pentateuch: Bridging the Academic Cultures of Europe, Israel, and North America.* Edited by Jan Christian Gertz, Bernard M. Levinson, Dalit Rom-Shiloni, and Konrad Schmid. FAT 111. Tübingen: Mohr Siebeck, 2016.

Schorch, Stefan. "The Construction of Samari(t)an Identity from the Inside and from the Outside." Pages 135–49 in *Between Cooperation and Hostility: Multiple Identities in Ancient Judaism and the Interaction with Foreign Powers.* Edited by Rainer Albertz and Jakob Wöhrle. JAJSup 11. Göttingen: Vandenhoeck & Ruprecht, 2013.

———. "Die prä-samaritanischen Fortschreibungen." Pages 113–32 in *Schriftgelehrte Fortschreibungs- und Auslegungsprozesse: Textarbeit im Pentateuch, in Qumran, Ägypten und Mesopotamien.* Edited by Walter Bührer. FAT 2/108. Tübingen: Mohr Siebeck, 2019.

———. "The Samaritan Version of Deuteronomy and the Origin of Deuteronomy." Pages 23–37 in *Samaria, Samarians, Samaritans: Studies on Bible, History and Linguistics.* Edited by József Zsengellér. SJ 66. Studia Samaritana 6. Berlin: de Gruyter, 2011.

———. "The So-Called Gerizim Commandment in the Samaritan Pentateuch." Pages 77–97 in *The Samaritan Pentateuch and the Dead Sea Scrolls.* Edited by Michael Langlois. CBET 94. Leuven: Peeters, 2019.

Schunck, Klaus-Dietrich. *Nehemia.* BKAT 23.2. Neukirchen-Vluyn: Neukirchener Verlag, 2009.

Schur, Natan. *History of the Samaritans.* 2nd ed. BEATAJ 18. Frankfurt am Main: Lang, 1992.

Tov, Emanuel. "From Popular Jewish LXX-SP Texts to Separate Sectarian Texts: Insights from the Dead Sea Scrolls." Pages 19–40 in *The Samaritan Pentateuch and the Dead Sea Scrolls.* Edited by Michael Langlois. Contributions to Biblical Exegesis and Theology. Leuven: Peeters, 2019.

Tsedaka, Benyamim. "Reevaluation of Samaritan Studies Due to the New Discoveries in Excavations and Research." Pages 419–25 in *Die Samaritaner und die Bibel: The Samaritans and the Bible*. Edited by Jörg Frey, Ursula Schattner-Rieser, and Konrad Schmid. SJ 70. Studia Samaritana 7. Berlin: de Gruyter, 2012.

Ulrich, Eugene. *The Dead Sea Scrolls and Developmental Composition of the Bible*. VTSup 169. Leiden: Brill, 2015.

Vermeylen, Jacques. "Les anciens déportés et les habitants du pays: La crise occultée du début de l'époque perse." *Transeu* 39 (2010): 175–206

Watts, James W., ed. *Persia and Torah: The Theory of Imperial Authorization of the Pentateuch*. SymS 17. Atlanta: Society of Biblical Literature, 2001.

Weingart, Kristin. "What Makes an Israelite an Israelite? Judean Perspectives on the Samaritans in the Persian Period." *JSOT* 42 (2017): 155–75.

Willi-Plein, Ina. *Haggai, Sacharja, Maleachi*. ZBK 24.4. Zürich: TVZ, 2007.

Williamson, Hugh G. M. *Ezra Nehemiah*. WBC 16. Waco, TX: Word, 1985.

Wöhrle, Jackob. *Der Abschluss des Zwölfprophetenbuches: Buchübergreifende Redaktionsprozesse in den späten Sammlungen*. BZAW 389. Berlin: de Gruyter, 2008.

Wöhrle, Jakob. "There's No Master Key! The Literary Character of the Priestly Stratum and the Formation of the Pentateuch." Pages 391–403 in *The Formation of the Pentateuch: Bridging the Academic Cultures of Europe, Israel, and North America*. Edited by Jan Christian Gertz, Bernard M. Levinson, Dalit Rom-Shiloni, and Konrad Schmid. FAT 111. Tübingen: Mohr Siebeck, 2016.

Zahn, Molly M. "The Samaritan Pentateuch and the Scribal Culture of Second Temple Judaism." *JSJ* 46 (2015): 285–313.

Zangenberg, Jürgen. ΣΑΜΑΡΕΙΑ: Antike Quellen zur Geschichte und Kultur der Samaritaner in deutscher Übersetzung. Texte und Arbeiten zum neutestamentlichen Zeitalter 15. Tübingen: Franke, 1994.

Shechem and Bethel in the Patriarchal Narratives: A Samaritan Rereading of Gen 12:1–9* and 35:2–4?

Dany Nocquet

In the biblical tradition, Shechem is an important city. With Abram traveling to Canaan in Gen 12:6, Shechem is the first stop mentioned in the promised land. During the entry into Canaan in the book of Joshua, Shechem is the place where Israel is unified and the last city named in Josh 24. This site is already known in Judg 9 as a Canaanite sanctuary dedicated to Baal worship and is also well attested as the first royal city of Israel under Jeroboam I, after the separation of the two kingdoms of Israel and Judah, in 1 Kgs 12:28.[1] Shechem was the first capital of the Northern Kingdom, and Samaria was succeeded by Shechem under the new Omride dynasty, according to 1 Kgs 16:24.[2]

The archeological evidence has demonstrated the great antiquity of the site from the Middle Bronze Age up to Iron II.[3] Shechem was a significant tax collection center under the monarchy of the Northern Kingdom, even

---

I am very thankful to John Pickering and Jan Albert Roetman for their remarks on my contribution and for the improvements to the English text of this article.

1. Volkmar Fritz, "Abimelech und Sichem in Jdc I nX [Ri 9]," in *Studien zur Literatur und Geschichte des alten Israel*, SBAB 22 (Stuttgart: Katholisches Bibelwerk, 1997), 187–203; Dany Nocquet, *Le livret noir de Baal: La polémique contre Baal dans la Bible Hébraïque et l'ancien Israël*, Actes et Recherche (Geneva: Labor et Fides, 2004), 75–87.

2. Pierre Gibert, "Sichem et Béthel, sanctuaires d'Israël (Genèse 35,1–5)," in *Jacob: Commentaire à plusieurs voix de—Ein mehrstimmiger Kommentar zu—A Plural Commentary of Gen 25–36; Mélanges offerts à Albert de Pury*, ed. Jean-Daniel Macchi and Thomas Römer, MdB 44 (Geneva: Labor et Fides, 2001), 248–56.

3. Mario Liverani, *La Bible et l'invention de l'histoire: Histoire ancienne d'Israël* (Paris: Gallimard, 2010), 125–28; LaMoine F. DeVries, *Cities of the Biblical World* (Peabody, MA: Hendrickson, 1997), 231–37; Edward F. Campbell, "Shechem," NEAEHL 4:1345–54.

after the foundation of Samaria, alongside the regional sanctuaries of Dan and Bethel. Destroyed by the Assyrians during their military campaign in 722 BCE, Shechem was partially reoccupied but then deserted during the sixth and the beginning of the fifth centuries. A new period of prosperity is attested at the end of the Persian period to the end of the second century BCE, before its collapse during the Hasmonean domination at the beginning of the first century BCE. A sign of Shechem's renewal in the Persian period is attested by the recent discovery of a Yahwistic temple on Mount Gerizim, built in the middle of the fifth century.[4]

References to Shechem are studied together with references to Bethel as an Israelite sanctuary.[5] The old sanctuary of Bethel was also very significant according to Amos 7:10–17;[6] the worship of YHWH was celebrated in the old royal sanctuary of Bethel until the exile. Rebuilt by the Assyrians in 724, Bethel was a cultic center where the Assyrians allowed the "God of the country," YHWH, to return to his worshipers, according to 2 Kgs 17:24–27.[7] In 2 Kgs 23:15, we are told how Josiah then destroyed the cultic center at Bethel, which was still in use. Whatever may be the historicity of this account, the tradition of the conquest of Bethel testifies to the new situation under Josiah against a background of diminishing Assyrian power and to the beginning of his cultic reform aimed at centralizing YHWH worship in Jerusalem. In fact, Bethel was not destroyed during

---

4. Yitzhak Magen, "The Dating of the First Phase of the Samaritan Temple on Mount Garizim in Light of the Archeological Evidence," in *Judah and the Judeans in the Fourth Century BCE*, ed. Oded Lipschits, Gary N. Knoppers, and Rainer Albertz (Winona Lake, IN: Eisenbrauns, 2007), 157–211; Magen, "Mt. Gerizim Sanctuary, Its History and Enigma of Origin," *HBAI* 3.1 (2014): 111–33.

5. This essay deals mainly with the place of Shechem in the patriarchal narratives. For a full study of the mentions of Bethel, see Dany Nocquet, *La Samarie et la diaspora et l'achèvement de la Torah: Territorialités et internationalités dans l'Hexateuque*, OBO 281 (Fribourg: Academic Press; Göttingen: Vandenhoeck & Ruprecht, 2017), 41–91.

6. See first the Jacob cycle and Gen 28. On the history of Bethel, see Joseph Blenkinsopp, "Bethel in the Neo-Babylonian Period," in *Judah and the Judeans in the Neo-Babylonian Period*, ed. Oded Lipschits and Joseph Blenkinsopp (Winona Lake, IN: Eisenbrauns, 2003), 93–105; Ernst Axel Knauf, "Bethel: The Israelite Impact on Judean Language and Literature," in *Data and Debates: Essays in the History and Culture of Israel and Its Neighbors in Antiquity*, AOAT 407 (Münster: Ugarit-Verlag, 2013), 277–328; and Jean-Marie Van Cangh, "Béthel: archéologie et histoire," in *Quelle maison pour Dieu?*, ed. Camille Focant, LD Hors série (Paris, Cerf, 2003), 39–48.

7. Van Cangh, "Béthel," 44–45; Barbara Leicht, "Bet-El: Das Tor des Himmels," *Welt und Umwelt der Bibel* 16.4 (2011): 38–39.

the Babylonian campaign against Judah, and its cultic activity continued there during the exilic period, while Mizpah was the administrative center for Babylonian rule. This cultic role explains why Bethel was considered a threat to the centrality of Jerusalem by the community of people who returned from exile and why Bethel is depicted in a very critical way, as it is in 1 Kgs 12–13.[8] On the contrary, Shechem and Bethel are often positively mentioned from Genesis to Joshua (Gen 12; 28; 35:1–8; Josh 24). This essay tries to highlight the literary significance of Shechem and Bethel in the patriarchal narratives of Gen 12:6–9 and 35:2–4.

2. Shechem and Bethel in Gen 12:6–9

The first mention of Shechem, Gen 12:6, occurs in the first story of Abram, at the end of the primeval history and the beginning of the patriarchal narratives, where the story of Israel is introduced. In this text, Shechem is the first place where Abram arrived as a sojourner in Canaan after leaving Haran, following the divine promise. Genesis 11:27–12:9 contains three parts:[9] (1) A difficult situation for a group of migrants is described in Gen 11:27–32, where Sarah is barren and Lot is an orphan, yet they went forth into Canaan. (2) Genesis 12:1–6 is YHWH's speech in Haran revealing their future, followed by Abram's obedience and arrival in the land of Canaan at Shechem. (3) YHWH's revelation in the land of Canaan comes in Gen 12:7–9, where Abram moves and worships YHWH at Bethel.

Genesis 11:27–32 introduces the main topics in the narrative of Abram and tells of a double uprooting, genealogical and territorial, for

---

8. No archeological evidence confirms the destruction of Bethel by Josiah. Verse 15 of 2 Kgs 23 would be an exilic addition when Bethel competed with Jerusalem; see Knauf, "Bethel," 277–328; Blenkinsopp, "Bethel," 93–105; Diana V. Edelman et al., eds., *Clés pour le Pentateuque: Etat de la recherche et thèmes fondamentaux*, trans. Françoise Smyth and Corrine Lanoir, MdB 65 (Geneva: Labor et Fides, 2013), 79–80; Victor A. Hurowitz, "Babylon in Bethel: New Light on Jacob's Dream," in *Orientalism, Assyriology and the Bible*, ed. Steven Winford Halloway, Hebrew Bible Monographs 10 (Sheffield: Sheffield Phoenix, 2006), 436–48. For further discussion of the critical depiction of Bethel, see Dany Nocquet, "L'unité prophétique d'Israël et de Juda (1R 13,1–34)," in *Le roi Salomon, un héritage en question: Hommage à Jacques Vermeylen*, ed. Claude Lichtert and Dany Nocquet, Le livre et le rouleau 33 (Brussels: Lessius, 2008), 300–322.

9. YHWH's speech at the moment of Abram's departure from Haran and his arrival in Canaan structures the story in three parts.

Terah's family. Genesis 12:1–4, in the middle of this difficult family situation, relates an unexpected speech by YHWH opening a new future and new possibilities only for Abram's family.[10] The divine order to Abram to set out from "his country, his kindred, and his father's house" involves separation from his family in order to enter his own future.[11] This breakup with his family and his past is immediately followed by a promise, in Gen 11:31, in which YHWH successfully completes the plan left unfinished by Terah to enter the land of Canaan.[12] In Gen 11:30, God gives Abram not only an assurance about his continuity despite Sarah's barrenness but also a great name and new fame in spite of the weakness of his family.[13] As a new established figure and sign of the divine blessing, Abram also becomes a figure for divine judgement: from now on each group or person is judged according to their positive or negative attitude toward him.[14] This determines the relationship to YHWH to be either a blessing or a curse.[15] In addition to the new role of Abram, the divine words conclude with an universal promise: "and in you shall all families of the earth be blessed."[16] With these promises, the call of Abram establishes a founda-

---

10. André Wenin, "Abraham: Élection et salut, réflexions exégétiques et théologiques sur Genèse 12 dans son contexte narratif," *RTL* 27 (1996): 20–42.

11. The same expression is used here as in Gen 22:2, which indicates that the two texts belong to a similar redactional layer. See also Wis 2:10–13. Jean-Louis Ska, "The Call of Abraham and Israel's Birth-Certificate (Gen 12:1–4a)," in *The Exegesis of the Pentateuch, Exegetical Studies and Basic Questions*, FAT 66 (Tübingen: Mohr Siebeck, 2009), 46–66 argues that the divine speech of Gen 12:1–4a is a late addition to P narrative and presupposes P and D layers of composition.

12. The expression "a land that I will show you" is also used in the case of Moses in Deut 34:4. This connection is highlighted by Eckart Otto, "Deuteronomium und Pentateuch," in *Die Tora: Studien zum Pentateuch, Gesammelte Aufsätze*, BZABR 9 (Wiesbaden: Harrassowitz, 2009), 202–11. A post-P redaction in Deut 34:4 sums up the original appearance of YHWH in Gen 12 by using the same expressions to confirm the achievement of the promise: Gen 12:7 and Deut 34:4; Gen 50:24; Exod 33:3 and Deut 34:4; Gen 27:1 and Deut 34:7.

13. Ishmael and Moses are subjects of a similar promise in Gen 21:13 and Exod 32:10. The promise of a "great name" is similar to God's promise to David in 2 Sam 7:9.

14. The name of Abram as blessing can be compared to Isa 19:24 and Zech 8:13. Abram has the same function as a king in mediating or symbolizing the divine blessing of the people.

15. It is noteworthy that, in this verse, Abram has the same role as the law in Deut 28.

16. The root ברך is used in a reflexive way (*niphal*). Abram is a model of the

tional character with a royal function, a person of universal significance for all humankind.[17]

3. Shechem in Gen 12:1–9

Arriving from Haran in Gen 12:6, Shechem is the first place named in the land of Canaan where Abram settled.[18] It is noticeable that Shechem is designated as מקום שכם. This term is not commonly used to designate a place name, but it can point toward Deut 12, where the term מקום is the chosen place of worship for YHWH.[19] This first qualification is significant for the use of Shechem later on in the Pentateuch—Gen 33–35; Deut 11; 27 (Mount Gerizim near Shechem)—as well as in Josh 24, where Shechem is the symbol of Israel's unity.[20]

Thus Shechem is not only the first town to be named in the Hebrew Bible, but the site is also the location for the first appearance of YHWH in the land of Canaan, when he announces for the second time the promise of the land for Abram and his seed. Shechem is the birthplace of the history of Israel in Canaan and also the birthplace of YHWH worship, as the following verses confirm with the building of an altar marking the appearance of YHWH at Shechem in the land of Canaan. The area of Shechem is associated with the "oak tree of Moreh," which plays an important role in Gen 35:2–4.[21] With the arrival of Abram at Shechem, Gen 12:6–9 ensures

---

divine blessing rather than its deliverer. As the example for this new relationship with YHWH, all families can hope for the same good relationship to YHWH. The universalism of Gen 12 is repeated in Gen 18:18 and 22:18, where the words "nation and people" replace the word "family."

17. Ska, "Call," 46–66. For the royal function of spreading the divine blessing, M. Arnaud Sérandour, "Religions du Proche-Orient ouest-sémitique ancien: Aspects de l'idéologie royale dans la Bible hébraïque," *Annuaire de l'École Pratique des Hautes Études. Sciences religieuses* 107 (1998): 199–205.

18. LXX adds this lesson: "he passed through the land 'in its length' to the place of Shechem, to the oak tree 'of the high place.'"

19. The law of the cultic centralization in Deut 12 uses the phrase, "the place which the LORD your God shall choose" as a chorus.

20. On Mount Gerizim near Shechem, see Christophe Nihan, "L'autel sur le mont Garizim: Deutéronome 27 et la rédaction de la torah entre Samaritains et Judéens à l'époque achéménide," *Transeu* 36 (2008): 97–124.

21. The significance of Shechem finds a continuity in Deut 11:28–30 during the entry into the land of Canaan where the mountains of Gerizim and Ebal (near Shechem) play an important role. Concerning the link between Gen 12:6–9 and

that the history of Israel begins in its northern region, at a site associated with the Jacob tradition. Genesis 12:6–9 enhances and legitimates Shechem as the oldest center for the worship of YHWH in Israel. This aim is confirmed in the following narrative by the fact that Shechem is closely linked with Bethel, another northern Israelite city. Together, the two cities delimit the north of Israel as the first territory in which YHWH's presence was made known through a theophany and marked with the building of altars.[22] These topographical and religious indices demonstrate a continuity in Gen 13:1–4, after the wife-sister narrative in Egypt, in Gen 12:10–20. A resumptive repetition, or *Wiederaufnahme*, is at the work between Gen 12:9 and 13:1, evident in the expressions "to the Negev" and "Bethel and Ai."

> Abram passed through the land as far as the site of Shechem, to the oak of Moreh. Now the Canaanite was then in the land. The LORD appeared to Abram and said, "To your descendants I will give this land. So he built an altar there to the LORD who had appeared to him. Then he proceeded from there to the mountain on the east of Bethel, and pitched his tent, with Bethel on the west and Ai on the east; and there he built an altar to the LORD and called upon the name of the LORD. Abram journeyed on, continuing toward the Negev. (Gen 12:6–9 KJV)

> So Abram went up from Egypt to the Negev, he and his wife and all that belonged to him, and Lot with him. Now Abram was very rich in livestock, in silver and in gold. He went on his journeys from the Negev as far as Bethel, to the place where his tent had been at the beginning, between Bethel and Ai, to the place of the altar which he had made there formerly; and there Abram called on the name of the LORD. (Gen 13:1–4 KJV)

The topography of Gen 13:1–3 confirms the importance of the area of Bethel as a cultic place for YHWH between Shechem and the Negev.[23]

Deut 11:30, see Detlef Jericke, "Der Berg Garizim im Deuteronomium," *ZAW* 124 (2012): 213–28. Three sites play a major role as original centers of Yahwism: Gerizim, Shechem, Gilgal.

22. Abram settled between Bethel and Ai. Bethel belongs to a Judean province in the Babylonian and Persian periods; see Detlef Jericke, *Abraham in Mamre: Historische und exegetische Studien zur Region von Hebron und zu Genesis 11,27–19,38*, CHANE 17 (Leiden: Brill, 2003), 100–105.

23. Such a position will be enhanced in the story of Gen 28 and the Jacob cycle; see Wolfgang Zwickel, "Der Altarbau Abrahams zwischen Bethel und Aï (Gen 12f.)," *BZ* 36 (1992): 207–19.

In the promise of the land in Shechem (Gen 12:7), as in Gen 13:14-16, YHWH is identifying the territory from north to south without describing borders. In the texts, the promised land and the religious geography are described as territories without mentioning Judah.[24] The surprising absence of the land of Judah at the very beginning of the Abraham narrative may be a reason why Gen 14 was added, with its meeting between Abram and Melchizedeq, king of Salem (Jerusalem).[25]

4. A Historical Reading of Genesis 12:1-9*

Scholars have distinguished different redactional levels in Gen 12:1-9 from the beginning of scholarship.[26] An exegetical tradition tried to see in Gen 12 an old narrative written to legitimate David's dynasty by creating links with Hebron and literary proximity between Gen 12:3 and 2 Sam 7:9. The literary connection between the two passages has been discussed only recently,[27] and the discussion has shown that how the divine speech of YHWH, as in the references to Shechem and Bethel, are the work of a post-P and post-D scribal hand. Genesis 12:1-9, as the inaugural narrative of the Abraham cycle, belongs to the final stage of pentateuchal redaction.[28]

---

24. Jericke, *Abraham*, 289-90, considers the absence of Jerusalem provocative.

25. It is a way to reintroduce a mention of the central participation of Judah in the history of Israel. Gen 12-13 was originally a narrative with a geography of redemption without Jerusalem and Judah; see David M. Carr, *Reading the Fractures of Genesis: Historical and Literary Approaches* (Louisville, KY: Westminster John Knox, 1996), 163-66.

26. For a survey of the research, see Matthieu Collin, "Une tradition ancienne dans le cycle d'Abraham? Don de la terre et promesse en Gen 12-13," in *Le Pentateuque*, ed. Pierre Haudebert, LD 151 (Paris, Cerf, 1992), 209-28; Lothar Ruppert, "'Zieh fort ... in das Land, das ich dir zeigen werde' (Gn 12,1): Der wegweisende und erscheinende Gott in Gn 12 und 13," in *Ce Dieu qui vient: Mélanges offerts à Bernard Renaud*, ed. Raymond Kuntzmann (Paris: Cerf, 1995), 69-94. Joel S. Baden, "The Morpho-Syntax of Genesis 12:1-3: Translation and Interpretation," *CBQ* 72 (2010): 223-37 tries to give a new impetus to the old Documentary Hypothesis of Julius Wellhausen. He reads the story as belonging to the J document. See also Ska, "Call," 46-66.

27. Olivier Artus, "La question de l'interprétation de la figure d'Abraham comme 'figure royale,'" in Lichtert and Nocquet, *Le roi Salomon, un héritage en question*, 149-64.

28. Among the arguments, the mention of Ur of the Chaldeans presupposes the Babylonian period, when this designation is typically used; see Erhard Blum, *Die Komposition der Vatergeschichte*, WMANT 57 (Neukirchen-Vluyn: Neukirchener Verlag,

This redactional position is based on vocabulary and topical repetitions, as well as on the observation that Shechem and Bethel do not play any role in the rest of the Abraham narrative.[29]

In the postexilic context, Abram's journey from Ur of the Chaldeans to Canaan is often compared to the return of the Judeans to the province of Yehud from their exile in Babylon. The call of Abram to leave his homeland should be read as a call to return for the Babylonian גלה. Abraham would then be the model for a returnee coming back to Jerusalem.[30] Such a reading has to take into account the following question: How can Abraham be interpreted as the figure of a returnee to Judah when the story of his coming into Canaan and journey through the land does not even hint at Jerusalem and Judah? Such a global reading of Abram's cycle raises additional questions. On a literary level, according to the main scholarly trend, Gen 11:27–32 and 12:4b–5 belong to the P document. The other part of the text, Gen 12:1–9* is ascribed to a non-P redaction. This analysis is based on the tension between the P text of Exod 6:2–7 (esp. v. 3), where Abraham does not know the name of YHWH, and Gen 12:9, where he

---

1984), 190; Carr, *Reading*, 172–76; Jericke, *Abraham*, 267–68; Jean-Louis Ska, "L'appel d'Abraham," in *Deuteronomy and Deuteronomic Literature: Festschrift C.H.W. Brekelmans*, ed. Marc Vervenne and Johan Lust, BETL 133 (Leuven: Peeters, 1997), 367–89; Thomas Römer, "Abraham Traditions in the Hebrew Bible outside the Book of Genesis," in *The Book of Genesis: Composition, Reception, and Interpretation*, ed. Craig A. Evans, Joel N. Lohr, and David L. Petersen, VTSup 152 (Leiden: Brill, 2012), 159–80.

29. Genesis 13:2–3, 14–17 are also additions to a primary narrative; see the following note.

30. Carr, *Reading*, 172–74 situates the promises in the exilic period or at the beginning of the postexilic period, as does Liverani, *La Bible*, 354, 357, to whom the Abrahamic traditions are reflecting the return from exile. Likewise, Israel Finkelstein and Neil Asher Silberman, *La Bible dévoilée: Les nouvelles révélations de l'archéologie* (Paris: Bayard, 2001), 58–61 think that the Abraham cycle is focusing on Judah on the basis of the Hebron tradition and the cave of Machpelah. See also Jean-Louis Ska, *Les énigmes du passé: Histoire d'Israël et récit biblique*, Le livre et le rouleau 14 (Brussels: Lessius, 2001), 42: "Le but de ce passage est de présenter Abraham comme l'ancêtre de la communauté qui est revenue de Babylone pour reconstruire Jérusalem et son temple.... Le message est clair: la bénédiction promise à Abraham vaut également pour tous ceux qui sont revenus de la Mésopotamie après l'Exil pour s'établir dans le terre de Canaan"; and Thomas Römer, "Abraham and Moses, a (Not So) Friendly Competition," in *And God Saw That It Was Good (Gen 1:12): The Concept of Quality in Archeology, Philology and Theology*, ed. Filip Čapek and Petr Sláma, Beiträge zum Verstehen der Bibel 42 (Vienna: LIT Verlag, 2020), 100–101.

calls upon the name of YHWH. This tension allows us to understand the text of Gen 12:1–9* as the work of a post-P and post-D redactor.[31] But the question remains: If the journey of Abram can be an allusion to the multiple phases of return from Babylonia in the late sixth and fifth centuries, why does Gen 12:1–9 avoid naming the area of Jerusalem and Judah? The omission of Jerusalem remains surprising if the purpose of the narrative is to call for a return to Judah![32]

As noted above, Shechem and Bethel are the first steps of Abram's journey into Canaan at the very beginning of Israel's history, as well as the founding places of YHWH worship before his settlement in Hebron in Gen 13:18.[33] Abram is arriving not only from Ur of the Chaldeans but also from Haran, neither of which is among the Mesopotamian sites known to have been settlements of deportees, according to Ezra 3:15; Esd 2:59; 8:17; and Neh 7:61.[34] The name of Haran occurs in the speech of the official spokesman of King Sennacherib during the siege of Jerusalem in 701 BCE: "Did the gods of those nations which my fathers have destroyed deliver them, even Gozan and Haran and Rezeph and the sons of Eden who were in Telassar?" (Isa 37:12 NASB; see also 2 Kgs 19:12).[35] The three cities in the verse are known to have been situated in the north of Syria in upper Mesopotamia. Haran is mentioned beside Gozan, an area or tributary of

---

31. See note 30.

32. Similar remarks can be found in Jericke, *Abraham*, 289.

33. On Gen 13:18, see Jericke, *Abraham*, 236–96. Hebron does not belong to Yehud in the Persian period, according to Jericke, *Abraham*, 16–34 and 93–96. According to Oded Lipschits, *The Fall and Rise of Jerusalem: The History of Judah under the Babylonian Rule* (Winona Lake, IN: Eisenbrauns, 2005), 149, "the Negev, the Hebron Mountains, and the southern and central Shephelah were separated from the province of Judah. These areas became the center for another national territorial unit: Idumea." On the debate about the borderline of Yehud, see John W. Wright, "Remapping Yehud: The Borders of Yehud and the Genealogies of Chronicles," in *Judah and the Judeans in the Persian Period*, ed. Oded Lipschits and Manfred Oeming (Winona Lake, IN: Eisenbrauns, 2006), 67–89.

34. These sites are placed in the vicinity of Babylon by Liverani, *La Bible*, 295–97. On Ur of the Chaldeans and Haran, see Pierre Villard, "Les séjours d'Abraham à Harran," in *Les routes du Proche-Orient ancien: Des séjours d'Abraham aux routes de l'encens*, ed. André Lemaire (Paris: Desclée, 2000), 41–50; and Leicht, "Bet-El."

35. This propaganda speech shows how the seizure of towns in antiquity was due less to the powerlessness of the divinity of the captured city than to the divine acceptance of the leadership of Assur.

the Euphrates.[36] Gozan and the surrounding area is the place to which some of the Israelite deportees were exiled after the conquest of Samaria: "In the ninth year of Hoshea, the king of Assyria captured Samaria and carried Israel away into exile to Assyria, and settled them in Halah and Habor, on the river of Gozan, and in the cities of the Medes" (2 Kgs 17:6; see also 2 Kgs 18,11; 19:12; 1 Chr 5:26).[37] The places mentioned in the verse have not been precisely identified, so there is some uncertainty about where the northern Israelites were taken during the exile. However, the city of Haran belongs to this area of upper Mesopotamia, and the city is also associated with the Jacob cycle in Gen 27:43; 28:10, and 29:4, a tradition of northern Israel.[38] Furthermore, the journey of Abram from Haran to Shechem anticipates and prepares the way for Jacob to flee from Canaan (more specifically Bethel, Gen 28:10-22) to Haran and return to Canaan (more specifically Shechem, Gen 33:18-20). Through this similarity, there is an alignment of the two founding figures of Abraham and Jacob. The fact that Jacob's family settled in Haran indicates that a part of the original identity of Israel belongs to ancient Syria.[39]

These few remarks allow the story of Gen 12:1-9* to be read as more than just a memory of the Judean exile. If the references to Ur of the Chal-

---

36. Steven W. Holloway, "Harran: Cultic Geography in the Neo-Assyrian Empire and Its Implications for Sennacherib's 'Letter to Hezekiah' in 2 Kings," in *The Pitcher Is Broken: Memorial Essays for Gösta W. Ahlström*, ed. Steven W. Holloway and Lowell K. Handy, JSOTSup 190 (Sheffield: Sheffield Academic, 1995), 276-314.

37. Liverani, *La Bible*, 205-8.

38. On the location of Haran, see E. Lipinski, "Aramaic-Akkadian Archives from the Gozan-Harran Area," in *Biblical Archaeology Today: Proceedings of the International Congress on Biblical Archaeology, Jerusalem, April 1984*, ed. Janet Amitai (Jerusalem: Israel Exploration Society, 1985), 340-48, who regards the area of Haran-Gozan as a geographical unity. On the link with the Jacob cycle, see Albert de Pury, "Le cycle de Jacob comme légende autonome des origines d'Israël" (93-108) and "Situer le cycle de Jacob: Quelques réflexions, vingt-cinq ans plus tard" (119-46) in *Die Patriarchen und die Priesterschrift: Les Patriarches et le document sacerdotal, Gesammelte Studien zu seinem 70. Geburtstag, recueil d'articles, à l'occasion de son 70e anniversaire*, ed. Jean-Daniel Macchi, Thomas Römer, and Konrad Schmid, ATANT 99 (Zürich: TVZ, 2010); de Pury, "La tradition patriarcale en Genèse 12-35," in *Le Pentateuque en question*, ed. Albert de Pury, MdB 19 (Geneva: Labor et Fides, 1989), 259-70.

39. Daniel E. Fleming, "Emar: On the Road from Harran to Hebron," in *Mesopotamia and the Bible: Comparative Explorations*, ed. Mark W. Chavalas and K. Lawson Younger Jr., JSOTSup 341 (London: Sheffield Academic, 2002), 222-50 enhances the Aramean origins of Israel.

deans can refer to the Judean exile, the divine words and the story of the arrival at Shechem in Gen 12:1–4a, 6–9 are a literary contribution from the fifth-century BCE Samaritan community. Genesis 12:1–9* is a Samaritan reformulation of the Abraham tradition originally belonging to the area of Hebron in the south.[40]

Abram, the figure of the Babylonian deportee, becomes the patriarch who legitimates the Yahwistic orthodoxy of the Samaritan community in the Persian period. The construction of Shechem as the location where YHWH first appears in Gen 12:1–9*, and thus the original center of Yahwism in Canaan, questions the cultic centrality and unity of Jerusalem.[41]

In the Pentateuch, Gen 12:6–9, with Shechem and Bethel, and Deut 27:4 with Mount Gerizim as the cultic place of the Samaritan community, confirm the plurality of Yahwistic centers in the Persian period.[42] Genesis 12:1–9, which recalls the birth of YHWH worship in Shechem and Bethel, could be interpreted as a response to the critical assertions about Samaria in the historical books. In 2 Kgs 17:24–41, we find a negative image of Samaria and its inhabitants as a mixed population practicing religious syncretism. The book of Nehemiah tells how the Judean community has to be separated from the Samaritan Sanballat (Neh 2:19–20; 3:33–35; 4:1–4).[43] The interpretation of Gen 12:1–9* as a particularly *Samaritan*

---

40. Israel Finkelstein and Thomas Römer, "Comments on the Historical Background of the Abraham Narrative. Between 'Realia' and 'Exegetica,'" *HBAI* 3 (2014): 9–10: "Summing up, there was an old Judahite tradition relating Abraham to a sanctuary and his grave, but this tradition was drastically transformed already in the Persian period."

41. Joshua 24:1–3 interprets Abraham's departure from Haran as a religious separation. Haran and Ur are known as cultic places for Sin, the moon god. The name Terah in Hebrew can be related to the moon; see René Labat et al., *Les religions du Proche-Orient: Textes et traditions sacrés babyloniens-ougaritiques-hittites* (*Le trésor spirituel de l'humanité*) (Paris: Fayard–Denoël, 1970), 280–86; Tamara M. Green, *The City of the Moon God: Religious Traditions of Harran*, RGRW 114 (Leiden: Brill, 1992). Jericke, *Abraham*, 289–90 reads this passage as a challenge to the unity of Jerusalem: "Gen 12,6–9; 13,18 hält dagegen: legitime Kultorte gibt es auch außerhalb von Jerusalem. Die erzählerische Spitze ist allein schon dem Itinerar von Gn 12,6–9; 13,8 zu entnehmen. Der Weg von Bet-El nach Hebron im Altertum wie heute, führte selbstverständlich durch Jerusalem. Die Nichterwähnung der Stadt erscheint provokativ."

42. Nocquet, *La Samarie*, 318–22.

43. Gary N. Knoppers, *Jews and Samaritans: The Origins and History of Their Early Relations* (New York: Oxford University Press, 2013), 159–60. In my judgment, the struggles depicted in Ezra-Nehemiah testify to internal Judean debates about iden-

reformulation and interpretation of the Abraham cycle takes into account the significance of a Samaritan community around its Yahwistic sanctuary on Mount Gerizim during the second half of the fifth century.

5. Shechem in Genesis 35:2-4

Shechem appears again in the Jacob cycle, in Gen 35:2-4, in a short story about the removal of foreign gods. One of the questions raised by Gen 35:1-4 is whether or not it is a continuation of Gen 12:1-9*. Genesis 35:1-4 tells how Jacob asks the Israelites to put away foreign gods, and they gave him their earrings.[44] The story takes place after the arrival at Shechem, where he has bought a field and built an altar to "El, God of Israel" (Gen 33:18-20). After the arrival of Jacob's family at Shechem, Gen 34 relates the slaughter of the Shechemites. In Gen 35:1, the divine order to leave Shechem for Bethel again recalls the journey of Abram from Shechem to Bethel in Gen 12:7-9. Genesis 35:1-4 refers to the theophany of YHWH during Jacob's dream in Gen 28:10-22. This story identifies Elohim and YHWH, an identification that continues through Gen 35. In the Jacob cycle, Gen 35:2-4 has to be read both as a response to the divine revelation at Bethel (Gen 28:10-22) and as the realization of the order to leave Laban's family (Gen 31:11-13). Genesis 35:2-4 belongs to a chapter that leads Jacob to Bethel, in which Jacob and his family flee the area of Shechem and the inhabitants of the land under the protection of "the Terror of God" (Gen 35:5).[45] The notice of Gen 35:2-5 is followed by events that again highlight the greatness of Bethel as a cultic place for El in Gen 35:6-15.[46]

---

tity, ethnicity, nationality. The very definition of "Israel" becomes a contested topic in a world in which a number of communities, whether more narrowly or more broadly defined, claim to continue the legacy of the descendants of Jacob.

44. At the end of v. 4 and the removal of the gods, the LXX adds "and he destroyed them until today."

45. Uwe Becker, "Jakob in Bet-El und Sichem," in *Die Erzväter in der biblischen Tradition: Festschrift für Matthias Köckert*, ed. Anselm C. Hagedorn and Henrik Pfeiffer (Berlin: de Gruyter, 2009), 159-85; Gibert, "Sichem et Béthel," 248-56; Victor A. Hurowitz, "Who Lost an Earring? Genesis 35:4 Reconsidered," *CBQ* 62 (2000): 28-32; Martin Rose, "L'itinérance du jacobus Pentateuchus: Réflexions sur Genèse 35,1-15," in *Lectio difficilior probabilior, l'exégèse comme expérience de décloisonnement: Mélanges offerts à Françoise Smyth-Florentin*, ed. Thomas Römer, DBAT 12 (Heidelberg: Dielheim, Selbstverlag der Autoren, 1991), 113-26.

46. Genesis 35 relates the building of an altar in Bethel and its naming as "El

Just as Shechem was the first Yahwistic cult place named at the beginning of the Abraham cycle, it also plays an important role against the foreign gods in the last chapter of the Jacob cycle. It is especially noteworthy that the place is also identified as the "tree of Shechem," "oak tree" (אלון, Gen 12:6), and "oak" (אלה, Gen 35:4).[47] Furthermore, Gen 35:2–4 is a bridge that links Gen 12:1–9* and Josh 24:23–24 with the mention of foreign gods:

Abram passed through the land as far as **the site of Shechem**, to **the oak of Moreh**. Now the Canaanite was then in the land. (Gen 12:6 KJV)

"Now therefore, put away the **strange gods** which are in your midst, and incline your hearts to the LORD, the God of Israel." The people said to Joshua, "We will serve the LORD our God and we will obey His voice." (Josh 24:23 KJV)

So Jacob said to his household and to all who were with him, "Put away the **strange gods** which are among you, and purify yourselves and change your garments; and let us arise and go up to Bethel, and I will make an altar there to God, who answered me in the day of my distress and has been with me wherever * I have gone." So they gave to Jacob all the **strange gods** which they had the rings which were in their ears, and Jacob hid them under the **oak which was near Shechem**. (Gen 35:2–4 KJV)

The trees of Gen 12:6 and 35:4 seem to be the same type of tree under two different names. Whatever it could be, Gen 12:6, as cultic center for YHWH, is first realized in Gen 35:4. In this text, Shechem becomes the cultic center for YHWH alone, as a grave for the foreign gods, אלהי הנכר. The iconoclastic tendency initiated by Jacob in Gen 35 is similarly repeated in Jos 24:23–26, where a carved stone plays a comparable role with that of the oak tree.[48] There is therefore a continuity between the beginning of the history of Israel and its achievement in Canaan. In Gen 35:5 and Josh

---

Bethel" (v.7). Gen 35:9–12 describes a new appearance of El Shaddai with a divine speech in which the name of Jacob is changed to Israel (cf. Gen 32:29–30). Gen 35:13–15 recalls YHWH's revelation in Gen 28:10–22.

47. The identification of these trees remains a question.
48. In Josh 24:26, a carved stone is erected in the sanctuary, under the oak tree, to witness the covenant made between Israel and YHWH. The phrase "foreign gods" is used in DtrH in Judg 10:16 and 1 Sam 7:3 and belongs to the theology of YHWH alone. In using the same expression, the other late occurrences in Josh 24:23 and Gen 35:2, 4 develop another purpose: the enhancement of the cultic orthodoxy of Shechem.

24:23–26, Shechem is the first cultic center (Gen 12:6) where Israel gives up and turns away from (סור) the worship of foreign gods. Some scholars, however, interpret the burying of the foreign gods as a controversial polemic against Shechem. This reading is based on the link with Exod 32:2–6, as well as the opposition to Josh 24, where Shechem is the place of covenant and unity.[49] Jacob's demand would be an act of defiling the sanctuary at Shechem.[50] The interpretive difficulty in Gen 35:2–4 is how to understand Jacob's action in hiding or burying the earrings under the tree of Shechem. The verb טמן is ordinarily used for the concealment of daily objects or misdeeds (Exod 2:12).[51] There is no example of burying statues as an act of defiling a sanctuary in the Hebrew Bible.[52] The gesture made by Jacob has to be understood as the continuation of Rachel's action in Gen 31:34–35. In Gen 31:19, Rachel has stolen the teraphim in order not to adopt the gods of her father. On the contrary, when Laban is searching for his teraphim in Gen 31:33–35, she put them in the camel's furniture and sat upon them, claiming that she was menstruating.[53] Just as Rachel defiled the gods of her father and demonstrated the inanity of the teraphim, Jacob shows the futility and uselessness of the foreign gods in Israel by burying them at Shechem.[54] Thus, by preserving the sanctuary and the worship of the God of Jacob from

---

49. On the link with Exod 32, see Becker, "Jakob," 171: "eine kaum verhüllte Polemik gegen Sichem." On Josh 24, see Nadav Na'aman, "The Law of the Altar in Deuteronomy and the Cultic Site Near Shechem," in *Rethinking the Foundations: Historiography in the Ancient World and in the Bible; Essays in Honour of John Van Seters*, ed. Thomas Römer and Steven L. McKenzie, BZAW 294 (Berlin: de Gruyter, 2000), 141–61; Christophe Nihan, "The Torah between Samaria and Judah: Shechem and Gerizim in Deuteronomy and Joshua," in *The Pentateuch as Torah: New Models for Understanding Its Promulgation and Acceptance*, ed. Gary N. Knoppers and Bernard M. Levinson (Winona Lake, IN: Eisenbrauns, 2007), 199 n. 35.

50. Shechem is defiled not only to profane a place for a while but also to desecrate Shechem and prevent any further possibility of worshiping God there.

51. Hurowitz, "Who Lost an Earring?," 28–32 understands earrings not as Israelite jewelry but as earrings worn by the statues of gods. With his demand, Jacob avoids the use of gold and silver for idolatry.

52. The desecration of a sanctuary is accomplished through the destruction of the altar or by the defilement of a grave; see 2 Kgs 23:17.

53. In Gen 31:35, she said: "I cannot rise up before thee; for the custom of women is upon me." She has defiled the gods of her father.

54. Victor P. Hamilton, *The Book of Genesis: Chapters 18–50*, NICOT (Grand Rapids: Eerdmans, 1995), 374–76 also brings together the deeds of Rachel and Jacob. The act of burying the teraphim is an act of rejecting the gods of Laban.

defilement by foreign gods, the orthodoxy of Israel's worship is maintained at Shechem. Even if Gen 12:6 and 35:4 use different Hebrew words for "tree," there is a continuity.[55] The tree near the sanctuary serves as reminder of the worship of YHWH there and the elimination of foreign gods in Canaan. In Josh 24:23, the erected stone under the oak tree has a similar function as a reminder of the covenant and the rejection of foreign gods.[56]

Interpreting Gen 35:2–4 as a criticism of Shechem seems difficult to justify. Furthermore, Deuteronomistic theology finds a legacy in the sanctuary of Shechem: the expression "put away the foreign gods" in Gen 35:2 is known from DtrH in Judg 10:16; 1 Sam 7:3 and also appears in 2 Chr 33:15.[57] Genesis 35:2–4 also anticipates Josh 24 (see v. 23), and Jacob is in a sense the forerunner of Joshua.[58] If Gen 35:2–4 can be interpreted positively, Shechem becomes an authentic Israelite cultic center where no other gods are celebrated.[59] The following verbs support this interpretation. The first verb, טהר, in the purification order of Gen 35:2b is the only occurrence in Genesis. The use of this command means that the people of the house of Jacob are aware of the defilement linked to the worship of other gods. The need to fulfill this requirement before being able to enter into worship of the only God (YHWH) presupposes the Levitical laws of purity. Leviticus 14:17–19; 15:13; 16:19, 30 allow the integration of a leper into the congregation of Israel. The next order in Gen 35:2b, "to change their garments" (חלף), also occurs in Gen 41:14 when Joseph enters into the service of Pharaoh and benefits from a radical change in social status.[60] It is a positive way to indicate a change of situation.

---

55. Gibert, "Sichem et Béthel," 254.

56. The new function for the oak tree in Gen 35:2–4 is an interesting way of transforming the image of the tree, so often a symbol of unfaithfulness to YHWH: Deut 12:2; 1 Kgs 14:23; 2 Kgs 16:4; 17:10; Isa 57:5; Jer 2:20; 3:6, 13; Ezra 6:13.

57. DtrH often illustrates the lack of fidelity to YHWH as in 1 Kgs 11:1–6.

58. On the link between Gen 35 and Josh 24, see Gibert, "Sichem et Béthel," 252–53. According to Josh 24:23, the rejection of the foreign gods is described as a part of a solemn public act that engages Israel to serve only YHWH in the context of the renewal of the covenant at Shechem. On Jacob as a forerunner of Joshua, note that Gen 35:2–4 and Deut 31:16, as the only references to foreign gods in the Pentateuch, use a typical phrase from DtrH.

59. If Gen 35 is a polemic against Shechem, it would be necessary to make the same polemical reading of Josh 24, but such a reading of Josh 24 does not seem possible.

60. The other use is in 2 Sam 12:20: when David learns about the death of his first son, he changes his clothes to return to a normal life.

Far from expressing criticism of Shechem, the iconoclastic act should be interpreted instead as a founding act that authorizes the journey to Bethel and the building of an altar and establishment of worship there. Developing the continuity and between Shechem and Bethel as in Gen 12:6–9, the story of Gen 35:2–6 enhances the two northern sanctuaries as the original places of YHWH worship.[61] Shechem and Bethel are the places where YHWH appears first to Abram (Gen 12:7) and to Jacob (Gen 28:12–15), and where Abram and Jacob build the first altars for YHWH (Gen 12:8; 35:7). Genesis 35:2–6 constructs the event of Shechem as an original act of iconoclastic worship of YHWH.[62] Therefore, Shechem also plays a significant role in the promotion of Bethel.[63]

6. A Historical Reading of Genesis 35:2–4

Recent research on the redactional history of Gen 35 has found that the verses generally attributed to P are the earliest layer: Gen 35:6a, 9, 13, 15, 22b–28. The P document had its continuation in Esau's genealogy in Gen 36:1–14. Genesis 35:1–5, 6b, 7, 8, 14, 16 was traditionally considered E.[64] Recent research identifies the final stage of a Bethel redaction in Gen 35:1, 6b, 7, 8, 14, 16. The Bethel redaction illustrates the important position of Bethel during the exilic period in the sixth century and the beginning of the fifth century, also reflecting its rivalry with Jerusalem.[65] In this research, Gen 35:2–5 is interpreted as a later addition to the Bethel redaction.[66] Therefore, Uwe Becker reads Gen 35:2–5 as a polemic against Shechem to enhance Bethel as the only true cultic center for YHWH. According

---

61. A similar reading can be found in Gibert, "Sichem et Béthel," 255, but, for him, Gen 35:2–6 belongs to a monarchical period and legtimates the northern sanctuaries.

62. Gibert, "Sichem et Béthel," 255–56.

63. Gen 35:2–4 is correcting the ambiguity of DtrH in 2 Kgs 17:24–41.

64. For a study of the entire text of Gen 35, see Becker, "Jakob," 171–76. The identification of Bethel with Luz is not certain, and a late redactor is responsible for this identification, as well as for the coming of Jacob to Bethel in Gen 28:11. The *Bet-El-Bearbeitung* in Gen 35:1, 6aβ, 7, 8, 16a raises a question: Why is P relating the encounter with God twice?

65. Knauf, "Bethel," 277–328.

66. According to Erhard Blum, "The Jacob Tradition," in Evans, Lohr, and Petersen, *Book of Genesis*, 181–211, esp. 193–95. Genesis 35:2–5 belongs to a post-P redaction because of the link with Josh 24:2.

to him, this passage would be a criticism of the temple at Mount Gerizim in the middle of the fifth century and against the Samaritan community.[67]

In my opinion, the thesis of a rivalry between Shechem and Bethel does not take into account the literary proximity between Gen 35:2–4, Gen 12:6–9, and Josh 24:23–24 noted above. It is not necessary to see Gen 35:2–4 as a later addition to the final stage of Gen 35. Genesis 35:2–4, where Shechem is a high place for the Israelite orthodoxy, can belong to the same level of redaction that strengthens the position of Bethel. Such an apology for Shechem and Bethel in Gen 35 should be understood as a late literary rewriting which comes from the Samaritan community at the end of the fifth century.[68]

7. Conclusion

This short article focused on Gen 12:6–9 and 35:2–4 has shown how the patriarchal narratives of Abraham and Jacob enhance and legitimate the cities of Shechem and Bethel as cultic centers in northern Israel. The strategic position of these stories in the narratives of Abraham and Jacob, as well as a shared vocabulary and a common theological intention, demonstrate the cultic orthodoxy of these two Israelite sanctuaries. The continuity between Gen 12:1–9* and Gen 35:2–4 (as well as Josh 24:23–26) supports the proposal that they belong to the same late stage of redaction, a post-P and post-D layer at the end of the fifth century. The repeated mention of Shechem and Bethel reflects the strength of the Samaritan community around its sanctuary on Mount Gerizim. In the context of Hebrew Bible research, such an enhancement of Shechem and Bethel should be interpreted as a part of the Samaritan contribution to the literary formation of the Pentateuch.[69]

---

67. On Gen 35:9–15, see Blum, "Jacob Tradition," 193–95. Gen 35 recalls Gen 32:29; Gen 28:18 and Gen 28:19 are a late revision that presupposes P. See also Becker, "Jakob," 178: "Aber weder an Sichem noch an Bet-El scheint P eines eignes theologisches Interesse zu haben; die Orte kommen in der Grundschrift (sonst) nicht vor."

68. A last mention of Shechem is in Gen 37:12–14. It does not play any important role in the Joseph story except for the transport of his bones in Gen 50:35, which ends in Shechem in Josh 24:32.

69. Reinhard Pummer, "The Samaritans and Their Pentateuch," in Knoppers and Levinson, *Pentateuch as Torah*, 237–69; Knauf, "Bethel," 277–328; and Nocquet, *La Samarie*, 318–22. Nihan, "Garizim et Ebal dans le Pentateuque," 203 concludes his study by saying that the formation of the Pentateuch is the result of a compromise

Bibliography

Artus, Olivier. "La question de l'interprétation de la figure d'Abraham comme 'figure royale.'" Pages 149–64 in *Le roi Salomon, un héritage en question: Hommage à Jacques Vermeylen*. Edited by Claude Lichtert and Dany Nocquet. Le livre et le rouleau 33. Brussels: Lessius, 2008.

Baden, Joel S. "The Morpho-Syntax of Genesis 12:1–3: Translation and Interpretation." *CBQ* 72 (2010): 223–37.

Becker, Uwe. "Jakob in Bet-El und Sichem." Pages 159–85 in *Die Erzväter in der biblischen Tradition: Festschrift für Matthias Köckert*. Edited by Anselm C. Hagedorn and Henrik Pfeiffer. Berlin: de Gruyter, 2009.

Blenkinsopp, Joseph. "Bethel in the Neo-Babylonian Period." Pages 93–107 in *Judah and the Judeans in the Neo-Babylonian Period*. Edited by Oded Lipschits and Joseph Blenkinsopp. Winona Lake, IN: Eisenbrauns, 2003.

Blum, Erhard. *Die Komposition der Vatergeschichte*. WMANT 57. Neukirchen-Vluyn: Neukirchener Verlag, 1984.

———. "The Jacob Tradition." Pages 181–211 in *The Book of Genesis: Composition, Reception, and Interpretation*. Edited by Craig A. Evans, Joel N. Lohr, and David L. Petersen. VTSup 152. Leiden: Brill, 2012.

Campbell, Edward F. "Shechem." *NEAEHL* 4:1345–54.

Carr, David M. *Reading the Fractures of Genesis: Historical and Literary Approaches*. Louisville, KY: Westminster John Knox, 1996.

Collin, Matthieu. "Une tradition ancienne dans le cycle d'Abraham? Don de la terre et promesse en Gen 12–13." Pages 209–28 in *Le Pentateuque*. Edited by Pierre Haudebert. LD 151. Paris, Cerf, 1992.

DeVries, LaMoine F. *Cities of the Biblical World*. Peabody, MA: Hendrickson, 1997.

Edelman, Diana V., et al., eds. *Clés pour le Pentateuque: Etat de la recherche et thèmes fondamentaux*. Translated by Françoise Smyth and Corrine Lanoir. MdB 65. Geneva: Labor et Fides, 2013.

Finkelstein, Israel, and Neil Asher Silberman. *La Bible dévoilée: Les nouvelles révélations de l'archéologie*. Paris: Bayard, 2001.

---

in the fourth century BCE: "La compilation et la publication du Pentateuque dans le courant du IVe siècle apparaissent désormais comme le résultat d'un compromis entre les élites de Judée et de Samarie."

Finkelstein, Israel, and Thomas Römer. "Comments on the Historical Background of the Abraham Narrative. Between 'Realia' and 'Exegetica.'" *HBAI* 3 (2014): 3–23.
Fleming, Daniel E. "Emar: On the Road from Harran to Hebron." Pages 222–50 in *Mesopotamia and the Bible: Comparative Explorations*. Edited by Mark W. Chavalas and K. Lawson Younger Jr. JSOTSup 341 London: Sheffield Academic, 2002.
Fritz, Volkmar. "Abimelech und Sichem in Jdc I nX [Ri 9]." Pages 187–203 in *Studien zur Literatur und Geschichte des alten Israel*. SBAB 22. Stuttgart: Katholisches Bibelwerk, 1997.
Gibert, Pierre. "Sichem et Béthel, sanctuaires d'Israël (Genèse 35,1–5)." Pages 248–56 in *Jacob: Commentaire à plusieurs voix de—Ein mehrstimmiger Kommentar zu—A Plural Commentary of Gen 25–36; Mélanges offerts à Albert de Pury*. Edited by Jean-Daniel Macchi and Thomas Römer. MdB 44. Geneva: Labor et Fides, 2001.
Green, Tamara M. *The City of the Moon God: Religious Traditions of Harran*. RGRW 114. Leiden: Brill, 1992.
Hamilton, Victor P. *The Book of Genesis: Chapters 18–50*. NICOT. Grand Rapids: Eerdmans, 1995.
Holloway, Steven W. "Harran: Cultic Geography in the Neo-Assyrian Empire and Its Implications for Sennacherib's 'Letter to Hezekiah' in 2 Kings." Pages 276–314 in *The Pitcher Is Broken: Memorial Essays for Gösta W. Ahlström*. Edited by Steven W. Holloway and Lowell K. Handy. JSOTSup 190. Sheffield: Sheffield Academic, 1995.
Hurowitz, Victor A. "Babylon in Bethel: New Light on Jacob's Dream." Pages 436–48 in *Orientalism, Assyriology and the Bible*. Edited by Steven Winford Halloway. Hebrew Bible Monographs 10. Sheffield: Sheffield Phoenix, 2006.
———. "Who Lost an Earring? Genesis 35:4 Reconsidered." *CBQ* 62 (2000): 28–32.
Jericke, Detlef. *Abraham in Mamre: Historische und exegetische Studien zur Region von Hebron und zu Genesis 11,27–19,38*. CHANE 17. Leiden: Brill, 2003.
———. "Der Berg Garizim im Deuteronomium." *ZAW* 124 (2012): 213–28.
Knauf, Ernst Axel. "Bethel: The Israelite Impact on Judean Language and Literature." Pages 277–328 in *Data and Debates: Essays in the History and Culture of Israel and Its Neighbors in Antiquity*. AOAT 407. Münster: Ugarit-Verlag, 2013.

Knoppers, Gary N. *Jews and Samaritans: The Origins and History of Their Early Relations*. New York: Oxford University Press, 2013.

Labat, René, et al. *Les religions du Proche-Orient: Textes et traditions sacrés babyloniens-ougaritiques-hittites (Le trésor spirituel de l'humanité)*. Paris: Fayard–Denoël, 1970.

Leicht, Barbara. "Bet-El: Das Tor des Himmels." *Welt und Umwelt der Bibel* 16.4 (2011): 38–39.

Lipinski, E. "Aramaic-Akkadian Archives from the Gozan-Harran Area." Pages 340–48 in *Biblical Archaeology Today: Proceedings of the International Congress on Biblical Archaeology, Jerusalem, April 1984*. Edited by Janet Amitai. Jerusalem: Israel Exploration Society, 1985.

Lipschits, Oded. *The Fall and Rise of Jerusalem: The History of Judah under the Babylonian Rule*. Winona Lake, IN: Eisenbrauns, 2005.

Liverani, Mario. *La Bible et l'invention de l'histoire: Histoire ancienne d'Israël*. Paris: Gallimard, 2010.

Magen, Yitzhak. "The Dating of the First Phase of the Samaritan Temple on Mount Garizim in Light of the Archeological Evidence." Pages 157–211 in *Judah and the Judeans in the Fourth Century BCE*. Edited by Oded Lipschits, Gary N. Knoppers, and Rainer Albertz. Winona Lake, IN: Eisenbrauns, 2007.

———. "Mt. Gerizim Sanctuary, Its History and Enigma of Origin." *HBAI* 3.1 (2014): 111–33.

Na'aman, Nadav. "The Law of the Altar in Deuteronomy and the Cultic Site Near Shechem." Pages 141–61 in *Rethinking the Foundations: Historiography in the Ancient World and in the Bible; Essays in Honour of John Van Seters*. Edited by Thomas Römer and Steven L. McKenzie. BZAW 294. Berlin: de Gruyter, 2000.

Nihan, Christophe. "L'autel sur le mont Garizim: Deutéronome 27 et la rédaction de la torah entre Samaritains et Judéens à l'époque achéménide." *Transeu* 36 (2008): 97–124.

———. "The Torah between Samaria and Judah: Shechem and Gerizim in Deuteronomy and Joshua." Pages 187–223 in *The Pentateuch as Torah: New Models for Understanding Its Promulgation and Acceptance*. Edited by Gary N. Knoppers and Bernard M. Levinson. Winona Lake, IN: Eisenbrauns, 2007.

Nocquet, Dany. *Le livret noir de Baal: La polémique contre Baal dans la Bible Hébraïque et l'ancien Israël*. Actes et Recherche. Geneva: Labor et Fides, 2004.

———. *La Samarie et la diaspora et l'achèvement de la Torah: Territorialités et internationalités dans l'Hexateuque.* OBO 281. Fribourg: Academic Press; Göttingen: Vandenhoeck & Ruprecht, 2017.

———. "L'unité prophétique d'Israël et de Juda (1R 13,1–34)." Pages 300–322 in *Le roi Salomon, un héritage en question: Hommage à Jacques Vermeylen.* Edited by Claude Lichtert and Dany Nocquet. Le livre et le rouleau 33. Brussels: Lessius, 2008.

Otto, Eckart. "Deuteronomium und Pentateuch." Pages 168–28 in *Die Tora: Studien zum Pentateuch, Gesammelte Aufsätze.* BZABR 9. Wiesbaden: Harrassowitz, 2009.

Pummer, Reinhard. "The Samaritans and Their Pentateuch." Pages 237–69 in *The Pentateuch as Torah: New Models for Understanding Its Promulgation and Acceptance.* Edited by Gary N. Knoppers and Bernard M. Levinson. Winona Lake, IN: Eisenbrauns, 2007.

Pury, Albert de. "Le cycle de Jacob comme légende autonome des origines d'Israël." Pages 93–108 in *Die Patriarchen und die Priesterschrift: Les Patriarches et le document sacerdotal, Gesammelte Studien zu seinem 70. Geburtstag, recueil d'articles, à l'occasion de son 70e anniversaire.* Edited by Jean-Daniel Macchi, Thomas Römer, and Konrad Schmid. ATANT 99. Zürich: TVZ, 2010.

———. "Situer le cycle de Jacob: Quelques réflexions, vingt-cinq ans plus tard." Pages 119–46 in *Die Patriarchen und die Priesterschrift: Les Patriarches et le document sacerdotal, Gesammelte Studien zu seinem 70. Geburtstag, recueil d'articles, à l'occasion de son 70e anniversaire.* Edited by Jean-Daniel Macchi, Thomas Römer, and Konrad Schmid. ATANT 99. Zürich: TVZ, 2010.

———. "La tradition patriarcale en Genèse 12–35." Pages 259–70 in *Le Pentateuque en question.* Edited by Albert de Pury. MdB 19. Geneva: Labor et Fides, 1989.

Römer, Thomas. "Abraham and Moses, a (Not So) Friendly Competition." Pages 99–109 in *And God Saw That It Was Good (Gen 1:12): The Concept of Quality in Archeology, Philology and Theology.* Edited by Filip Čapek and Petr Sláma. Beiträge zum Verstehen der Bibel 42. Vienna: LIT Verlag, 2020.

———. "Abraham Traditions in the Hebrew Bible outside the Book of Genesis." Pages 159–80 in *The Book of Genesis: Composition, Reception, and Interpretation.* Edited by Craig A. Evans, Joel N. Lohr, and David L. Petersen. VTSup 152. Leiden: Brill, 2012.

Rose, Martin. "L'itinérance du jacobus Pentateuchus: Réflexions sur Genèse 35,1–15." Pages 113–26 in *Lectio difficilior probabilior, l'exégèse comme expérience de décloisonnement: Mélanges offerts à Françoise Smyth-Florentin*. Edited by Thomas Römer. DBAT 12. Heidelberg: Dielheim, Selbstverlag der Autoren, 1991.

Ruppert, Lothar. "'Zieh fort … in das Land, das ich dir zeigen werde' (Gn 12,1): Der wegweisende und erscheinende Gott in Gn 12 und 13." Pages 69–94 in *Ce Dieu qui vient: Mélanges offerts à Bernard Renaud*. Edited by Raymond Kuntzmann. Paris: Cerf, 1995.

Sérandour, M. Arnaud "Religions du Proche-Orient ouest-sémitique ancien: Aspects de l'idéologie royale dans la Bible hébraïque." *Annuaire de l'École Pratique des Hautes Études. Sciences religieuses* 107 (1998): 199–205.

Ska, Jean-Louis. "L'appel d'Abraham." Pages 367–89 in *Deuteronomy and Deuteronomic Literature: Festschrift C.H.W. Brekelmans*. Edited by Marc Vervenne and Johan Lust. BETL 133. Leuven: Peeters, 1997.

———. "The Call of Abraham and Israel's Birth-Certificate (Gen 12:1–4a)." Pages 46–66 in *The Exegesis of the Pentateuch, Exegetical Studies and Basic Questions*. FAT 66. Tübingen: Mohr Siebeck, 2009.

———. *Les énigmes du passé: Histoire d'Israël et récit biblique*. Le livre et le rouleau 14. Brussels: Lessius, 2001.

Van Cangh, Jean-Marie. "Béthel: archéologie et histoire." Pages 39–48 in *Quelle maison pour Dieu?* Edited by Camille Focant. LD Hors série. Paris, Cerf, 2003.

Villard, Pierre. "Les séjours d'Abraham à Harran." Pages 41–50 in *Les routes du Proche-Orient ancien: Des séjours d'Abraham aux routes de l'encens*. Edited by André Lemaire. Paris: Desclée, 2000.

Wenin, André. "Abraham: Élection et salut, réflexions exégétiques et théologiques sur Genèse 12 dans son contexte narratif." *RTL* 27 (1996): 20–42.

Wright, John W. "Remapping Yehud: The Borders of Yehud and the Genealogies of Chronicles." Pages 67–89 in *Judah and the Judeans in the Persian Period*. Edited by Oded Lipschits and Manfred Oeming. Winona Lake, IN: Eisenbrauns, 2006.

Zwickel, Wolfgang. "Der Altarbau Abrahams zwischen Bethel und Aï (Gen 12f.)." *BZ* 36 (1992): 207–19.

Ancient Sources Index

Hebrew Bible/Old Testament

Genesis
Reference	Page(s)
2–3	107–8
2:5	102
3:13–19	102, 111
3:23–24	100–102
4:16	101
6:3	277
9:4	137
10	42–43, 105–7
11:1–9	104, 107
11:2	103–4
11:27–25:10	113–14
12:1–3	107, 110
12:1–9	313, 317–23
12:3	129
12:6	313
12:6–9	315–18
12:7	319
13:1–4	318
17:10–14	129
25:6	103
35:2–4	324–29
46:31	225

Exodus
Reference	Page(s)
2:12	326
3:8	225
4	55, 66
4:1–17	67
4:2	67
4:13–17	15, 66
4:17	67
6	15, 64, 194
6:2–7	320, 326
6:14–26	14, 62, 190, 194, 218
6:26	14
7:1	66
12:15	142
12:19	142–43
12:25–27	145
12:48–49	127–29, 140, 145–46, 153–54
12:49	125, 261
14	56
14:11–12	246
15	247
16	246
17:8–16	81
17:14	29
18:13–27	246
19:6	193
20	298
22:20	143–44
24:4	29, 246
24:9–11	92–93, 245–46
24:11	93
24:13–14	80–81
25:22	86
29	7, 174
29:4–6	164
29:14	85
29:45–56	212
30:1–10	217
32	15, 64–65
32:17–18	82
32:21	64
33:7–11	73, 76–77, 80, 182
33:9	76, 82

Ancient Sources Index

Exodus (cont.)
33:11	79–81, 98, 183
34:28	29
34:34–48	217
35–40	37–38
40	8, 174

Leviticus
1–16	125
4:12	85
9	8, 179, 182
9:23	83
9:26	164
10:1	212
10:1–3	212–13, 215, 217
10:2	213
10:8	96
11	156
11:1	86
13;1	86
13:46	85
15:1	86
16	8, 130, 179, 215, 217
16:12–13	213, 250
16:29	125, 130, 132, 155
17	134, 136, 138
17:3	152
17:10–12	137
18	153
19:18	144
19:33–34	143–44
20	153
20:2	142
22:18	142
23:48	145
24:10–23	151, 248
24:22	125, 140, 154
25:14	144
25:47	123

Numbers
4:1–20	83
4:16	214
5:5–6:20	168
6:24–26	32, 167
7:8	170
9:1–14	170
9:9–14	128
9:14	125, 128, 145–46, 153
10:29–32	175
10:33	83
11	79, 82, 84, 86–88, 93, 244–47, 250
11:1–3	244
11:1–20:13	237–63
11:16–17	73, 77–78, 182
11:24b–30	73, 77, 82, 182
11:25	86–87, 91
11:26–29	81
12	79, 84–86, 90–91, 245, 250, 258–60
12:1	78, 85
12:2	78
12:4–10	73
12:6–8	67, 78, 86
12:13–15	78
13–14	182, 225, 245, 256
13:4–16	92, 257
14	256
14:4	246
14:6–9	92
14:10	83
14:11–12	246
14:21–24	277
14:30–32	92
14:39–45	277
14:44	83
15	248, 250, 260–63
15:14	123, 153
15:15–16	125, 140, 146
15:22–31	134, 138, 154
15:25–26	139, 142
15:35	85
16–17	62, 63, 203–32
16	64–65, 91, 164–66, 169–73, 177–96, 249–54
16:1–2	170–71, 177, 209
16:3	172, 179, 188, 193
16:5–7	210, 222
16:6–7	213
16:8–10	64, 172, 179, 182, 190, 210

16:8–11	219–20	28:16–15	145
16:12–15	178, 224	32	227, 256, 258, 277, 285
16:15	226	33:2	29
16:17	179, 210	34:1–11	274, 286
16:18	179, 188	35	274
16:19	83	35:13–15	133
16:26	178	35:15	133, 142
16:27	226	36:1–12	274
16:28–30	225		
16:31–33	225	Deuteronomy	
16:35	172, 179, 213	1–3	274–77
17	250	1:9–18	84, 245–46
17:1–5	179, 188–89, 213	1:13–14	84
17:6	214	1:19–46	275
17:7	83	1:29–31	277
17:11	250	1:36	277
17:13–15	214, 250	1:37–38	275, 277
17:16–27	63, 67, 221–24	1:39	111, 115
18:1–24	63	1:41–44	277
19:10	131	2:1–3	278
20:1–13	244, 256	2:2–12	277,
20:6	83	2:9–12	293
20:12	275	2:12	278
20:22–29	249	2:14–16	276–77
21:4–29	244, 275	3:1–4	280
21:21–35	277–78	3:2	278–79
21:33–35	278	3:2–7	278
21:34	278–79	3:12–22	277, 279
22–24	37, 108	4	115
23:7	108	4:12	245
24	275	5	298
24:14–24	39	6	31
25	215	7	259
25(26)–36	273, 276	7:3	259
25:1–5	293	7:4	260
25:6–15	194, 249	7:6	193, 259
26	256	9	65
26(27)–36	280–84	10:6–7	249
26:3–4	273	10:8–9	83
26:9–11	190	10:14–22	115
27:1–11	274	10:19	143–44
27:3	190	11	299, 317
27:11	132	11:2	249
27:12–23	169	11:2–7	209
27:19–21	92	11:6	170, 177, 208–9

Ancient Sources Index

Deuteronomy (cont.)		20:9	133, 157
11:29–30	298	21	92
12	260, 317	22	227–28, 258–59
14:2	193	24	313, 315, 317
14:29	253	24:23–24	325–29
17:8	225, 253		
17:8–13	253	Judges	
17:9	251	1:1	100
17:18	251	3:9	279
18	67	3:11	279
18:1	251	4:5	225
18:15	262	9	21, 302, 313
21:5	251	10:16	325
23:4–7	293	13:25	87
25:7	225	18:12	81
26:19	193		
27	257, 259, 299	1 Samuel	
27:4	32, 59, 323	2:17	81
27:12–13	256–57	7:3	325, 327
27:14	255	10:5–13	86
28	239	11:6	86
28:9	193	16:13–14	87
28:43–44	123		
28:69	293	2 Samuel	
29:10	126	1:5	81
31:9	29, 83	2:14	81
31:9–13	60	7:9	319
31:12	126	12:20	327
31:14–15	73, 82–83, 91	14:17	115
31:22	29		
31:23	73, 82, 91	1 Kings	
33:10	61	7:39	101
34	55, 58–59, 84, 163, 168, 241	5:10	104
34:4	316	8:16	302
34:10–12	79–80, 245, 262	8:44	302
		8:62–63	188
Joshua		11:13	302
8:30–35	255–57	11:36	302
8:33	157	12	64
8:35	126–27	12:28	313
13–21	241	14:21	302
14:1–5	92	16:24	313
18–19	163–64	21:7	302
19:51	92	23:27	302
20:1–9	134		

2 Kings		Hosea	
2:14–15	87	9	243
17:6	322	9:10	242
17:24–41	291, 293–94, 314, 323		
17:27	253	Joel	
18:11	322	4:18	101
19:12	321–22		
23:15	314	Amos	
		5	243
Isaiah		5:25	243
11	87		
19:24	316	Job	
37:12	321	5:12	115
56	154	37:17	105
Jeremiah		Ruth	
6:20	188	1:1	100
7:22	243		
26:10	225	Daniel	
29:1	90	1:4	115
36:10	34	1:17	115
38:1	34	9:13	115
41:4–7	21, 302	9:22	115
		9:25	115
Ezekiel		11:33	115
1:16	91	11:35	115
7:26	90	12:3	115
8	88, 188	12:10	115
8:2	91		
8:7–13	90, 293	Ezra	
10:1	91	2:68	186
14:7	147	3	190
17:2	91	3:15	321
27	106	5	186
37	243	7:12	253
37:11	244	7:21	253
39:28–29	82	7:14	238
44	194–95	7:25–26	238
45:1	150	8	190
47:1	101	8:17	195
47:13–48	149–50	9	259
47:22–23	148	10:8	187
48	149–50		
		Nehemiah	
		2:19–20	323

Ancient Sources Index

Nehemiah (cont.)
3:33–35	323
4:1–4	323
7	190, 251
7:1	191
7:61	321
8	252
8:13	60, 186
9:17	246
10:39	63
11:13	186
12:11	290
12:22–23	290
13	295
13:10–13	191, 196, 251–52
13:28	195, 290

1 Chronicles
6:1–15	194
6:35–38	249
6:49–53	194
9:14–44	191
9:19–20	194
15:16	151
17:7	252
19:9	190
19:31	190
22:2	155
23:33	252
24:1–6	249, 252
25:5	252
26:1	190
26:29	252

2 Chronicles
2:16	155
20:19	190
20:25	155
26:16–21	19, 197
33:15	327

Ancient Near Eastern Texts

Elephantine (*TAD*)
A4.1	184
A4.7	294
A4.7:18–19	93
A4.7:25–26	227
A4.8:17–18	93
A4.8:23–25	227
A4.9	295, 277, 289–90, 294–95
A4.9–10	184, 189, 277

Wadi Daliyeh (*WD*)
22	289

Deuterocanonical Books

Judith
4:6–8	89
11:14	89
15:8	89

Sirach
45:17	61

1 Maccabees
12:5–6	89

2 Maccabees
1:10	89
4:43–50	89
11:27	89

3 Maccabees
1:6–8	89

Dead Sea Scrolls

4QGen^b	31
11QT 56:2–6	61

Ancient Jewish Writers

Josephus, *Antiquitates judaicae*
11.297–303	289–90, 295
11.335	195
12.138–46	89, 187
13.62–73	195

13.282	196
14.91	89
14.163–184	89

Josephus, *Bellum judaicum*

1.170	89
2.331	89
2.336	89

Josephus, *Contra Apionem*

2.165	183

New Testament

Matthew

5:22	89
26:59	89

Mark

15:42–43	89

Luke

22:66	89
23:50–51	89

John

11:47	89

Acts

4–5	89

Mishnah

Sanhedrin

11:2	88

Modern Authors Index

Achenbach, Reinhard 6–9, 18, 74, 84, 126, 166, 173–92, 204–7, 220, 248–51, 275
Albertz, Rainer 6, 9, 11–12, 62, 74, 76, 83–85, 126, 187, 193, 238, 240, 273, 275–76, 280–81, 300
Artus, Olivier 13, 20, 77, 82, 85, 207, 227, 319
Auld, Graeme 8
Baden, Joel S. 5, 30, 40, 237, 319
Berquist Jon L. 12, 183, 187
Blenkinsopp, Joseph 58, 109, 112, 114, 116, 293, 315
Blum, Ehrhard 4, 6, 22, 33, 36–37, 74, 76, 80, 83, 113, 193, 205, 275
Budd, Philip J. 77, 185
Carr, David M. 4–5, 33, 116, 139, 320
Carter, Charles E. 12
Cataldo, Jeremiah W. 183–84, 223
Coats, George W. 78, 246
Crüsemann, Frank 11, 39, 57, 109, 187, 245
Davies, Philip R. 12
Dahmen, Ulrich 63
Dietrich, Walter 8–9, 29, 293
Dozeman, Thomas B. 4, 13, 18, 65, 74, 88, 208, 243
Dušek, Jan 59, 294
Edenburg, Cynthia 114, 177, 304
Eissfeldt, Otto 73, 77
Elliger, Karl 101, 136, 144, 242
Finkelstein, Israel 7, 34, 58, 225, 256, 323
Fohrer, Georg 74, 77
Frevel, Christian 5, 7, 157, 163, 203, 215–19, 240–42, 261
Frei, Peter 56–57, 296
Fried Lisbeth S. 148, 183, 223,
Fritz, Volkmar 74, 77–78, 82, 313
Galling, Kurt 269
García López, Félix 39, 240
Gerstenberger, Erhard S. 12, 187
Gertz, Jan C. 6, 15, 67, 76, 80, 84, 101–2, 112, 205
Gottwald, Norman K. 12
Grabbe, Lester L. 32, 89, 186
Graf, Karl H. 238
Gray, George B. 18, 74, 77, 139, 165–81, 185, 196
Greenberg, Moshe 148, 150
Gressmann, Hugo 74, 77
Gunneweg, Antonius H. J. 74, 82, 87, 90, 194, 290
Hanson, Paul D. 11, 194
Haran, Menahem 5, 73, 188, 216
Hendel, Ronald 40
Hensel, Benedikt 290–92
Himbaza, Innocent 13, 20–21, 292, 296–97, 299,
Holzinger, Heinrich 73, 77, 129, 132, 146, 185
Hutzli, Jürg 13, 15–16, 109, 113,
Japhet, Sara 128, 155, 298
Jeon, Jaeyoung 62, 64–65, 91, 166, 186, 190–94, 220, 249–50
Johnstone, William 247
Jonker, Louis C. 204
Keel, Othmar 34, 37
Kislev, Itamar 13, 18, 133–34, 154, 281–82
Knauf, Ernst A. 42, 57, 134, 135, 328
Knierim, Rolf P. 55

Modern Authors Index

Knohl, Israel 73, 105, 125–26, 133, 155–56, 185, 242, 248, 251
Knoppers, Gary N. 219, 255, 257, 299, 304, 323
Koch, Klaus 43, 57, 296
Köckert, Matthias 8, 76, 81, 324
Kratz, Reinhard G. 5, 7, 41, 58, 103, 111–16, 204–5, 276
Kuenen, Abraham 8, 73, 77, 173, 184–85, 238
Lange, Armin 30–31
Levin, Christoph 4, 102, 108, 110,
Levine, Baruch A. 93, 136, 145, 185
Leuchter, Mark 220, 235, 251–53
Lipiński, Edward 322
Lohfink, Norbert 8
Macdonald, John 294, 303
MacDonald, Nathan 41–42, 194–95
Magen, Yitzhak 59, 195, 257, 294, 314
McCarter, Kyle P. 33–34, 36
Meyer, Rudolf 63
Milgrom, Jacob 73, 96, 125, 131–32, 137, 144, 152–53, 156, 185, 244
Müller, Reinhard 304
Nicholson, Ernest W. 155, 240
Nihan, Christophe 5, 8, 42, 59, 61, 105, 123–28, 131, 144, 152, 156, 164, 182, 212, 241–43, 301, 317, 326, 329
Nocquet, Dany R. 257, 299–300, 323
Noth, Martin 8, 74, 77–78, 82, 86, 88, 132, 137, 163, 165, 174, 182, 273
Otto, Eckart 6–7, 9, 41, 57–59, 74, 76, 83, 164, 173, 181–82, 205, 239–42, 246, 249, 251, 253, 257, 259–60, 274–75, 278, 316
Pakkala, Juha 42, 191
Perlitt, Lothar 8
Plöger, Otto 11, 187
Pola, Thomas 7–8, 164
Popper, Julius 30–31
Pummer, Reinhard 257, 292, 294, 329
Pury, Albert de 6, 107, 109, 113, 322
Rad, Gerhard von 10, 106, 108, 116,
Rendtorff, Rolf 4, 109
Richelle, Mattheiu 33–34, 36

Rollston, Christopher 33–34, 36
Rooke, Deborah W. 183–84, 193, 223
Römer, Thomas 5–9, 13–15, 29, 32, 41–42, 56, 59, 66–67, 85, 102, 105, 107, 111, 113–15, 157, 163, 205, 208, 238–50, 255–62, 275, 297, 299–301, 313, 320, 322–24, 326
Rudolph, Wilhelm 74, 77, 185
Rose, Martin 4, 108, 324
Samuel, Harald 35, 63, 204, 207
Schart, Aaron 78, 157, 163, 203, 210,
Schmid, Hans H 3
Schmid, Konrad 6, 13–14, 39–40, 44, 81, 84, 111–16, 262, 296, 299
Schmid, Ludwig 63, 204, 209
Schmidt, Werner H. 56
Schmitt, Hans-Christoph 39, 80, 208
Schmitt, Rüdiger 37
Schaper, Joachim 183, 191, 194, 220, 222–23, 252
Seebass, Horst 77, 82, 139, 166, 273
Stackert, Jeffrey 261, 263
Steck, Odil H. 11, 35, 39
Schwartz, Baruch J. 5, 75, 135–38, 144
Ska, Jean-Louis 8, 57, 92, 157, 256, 293, 316–17, 319–20
Smith, Morton 11, 124, 187, 193
Tov, Emanuel 30–32, 297
Ulrich, Eugene 31, 298
Van Seters, John 3–4, 74, 108, 114
VanderKam, James C. 183, 193, 290
Vermeylen, Jacques 42, 303
Watts, James W. 212, 296
Weber, Max 11, 75, 187
Weinberg, Joel 12, 60, 186
Weinfeld, Moshe 125, 154
Wellhausen, Julius 8, 74, 77, 144, 155, 183–85, 237, 239
Wenham, Gordon J. 102, 105, 144
Wette, W. M. L. de 238
Williamson, Hugh G. M. 186, 292
Wright, John W. 321
Zenger, Erich 5, 8, 76, 164, 204
Zimmerli, Walther 82, 88, 149
Zwickel, Wolfgang 216, 318

Subject Index

Abraham story, formation. *See* formation of the Abraham story
diaspora communities
  of Babylonia, 22, 58, 114, 180, 193, 320–23
  of Egypt (Elephantine), 59, 60–61, 188–89, 195, 227, 294–95
  of Transjordan, 227–28, 284–56, 258–60, 284–86
formation of the Abraham story, 113–14, 315–24
formation of the Pentateuch
  and ancient Near East, 40–44, 60
  and literacy, 33–40
  new models of, 6–7, 10–12, 173–84, 203–11, 238–48, 273–76
  and Qumran texts, 31–32
  traditional model of, 3–6, 10, 116–73, 184–85, 237, 239–40
formation of the primeval story, 107–13
genealogy, 14–15, 62, 190, 193–94, 209, 218, 328
Joshua (figure of), 80–83, 91–93, 256–57, 227–28, 282–85
  and elders, 81–82
leadership struggle. *See* power struggle and scribal debates
Moses as prophet, 78–80, 247, 261–62. *See also* power struggle and scribal debates: Moses and Aaron
non-Priestly text
  context of, 317–19, 324–28
  dating of, 319–24, 328–29
  post-Priestly text/layer, 6–7, 83–85, 113–14, 224–29

  pre-Priestly text/layer, 114–17
Numbers 26–36
  distinct vocabulary, 281, 282,
  lateness, 282–84
Pentateuch, formation. *See* formation of the Pentateuch
power struggle and scribal debates
  Moses and Aaron, 61–63, 66–67, 78–79, 221,
  priests and elders (lay leaders), 66–67, 85–87, 90–93, 186–89, 216–17
  priests (Aaronides and/or Zadokites) and Levites, 64–66, 189–92, 192–96, 219–21, 223–24
  prophets and elders, 86–87
Priestly text/source
  end of P, 7–10
  late Priestly texts/layers, 9–10, 127–34, 141–51, 211–15, 217–19
primeval story, formation. *See* formation of the primeval story
Samaritans
  and Mount Gerizim, 59, 257,
  pentateuchal contributions of, 255–57, 298–301, 315–29
  Samaritan schism, 291, 295–97, 301–4
  and their community, 289–94
settlement/conquest, 20, 227–28, 274, 276–80, 282, 285, 321
social context
  monarchic period, 33–38, 40–42, 243–45, 252–54
  Persian period, 10–12, 38–39, 42–44, 60, 254–55, 294–97, 319–24
  Hellenistic period, 39–40, 297–98

social groups
- elders group, 86–87, 88–90, 90–93, 186–89
- Levitical group, 189–92, 250–55
- priestly group, 90–93, 192–96, 222–24, 248–50
- prophetic group, 75, 79–82, 86, 262

staff (rod)
- of Aaron, 63, 68, 221–22,
- of Moses, 66–68

Table of Nations (Gen 10), 42–44, 104–7

tent of meeting
- Priestly (tabernacle), 38, 85–86, 168, 182
- non-Priestly, 73–75, 76–80, 85

torah
- promulgation of, 56–61, 260–62

www.ingramcontent.com/pod-product-compliance
Lightning Source LLC
Chambersburg PA
CBHW021932290426
44108CB00012B/810